# TROUBLED
# INDUSTRIES
# IN THE
# UNITED STATES
# AND JAPAN

# TROUBLED INDUSTRIES IN THE UNITED STATES AND JAPAN

**HONG W. TAN AND HARUO SHIMADA**
**Editors**

**A RAND Study**
**St. Martin's Press**
**New York**

Scholarly & Reference Division,
St. Martin's Press, 175 Fifth Avenue,
New York, N.Y. 10010

First published in the United States of America in 1994
Printed in the United States of America
Designed by Acme Art, Inc

ISBN 0-312-10249-6

RAND research is available on a wide variety of topics. To receive more
information on RAND publications, contact RAND Distribution Services,
1700 Main Street, Santa Monica, CA 90407-2138, (310) 451-7002,
Fax: (310) 451-6971, Internet: order@rand.org

**Library of Congress Cataloging-in-Publication Data**

Troubled industries in the United States and Japan / edited by Hong W. Tan
    and Haruo Shimada.
        p.   cm.
    ISBN 0-312-10249-6
    1. United States—Industries. 2. Japan—Industries. 3. Industry
and state—United States. 4. Industry and state—Japan.
    5. Structural adjustment (Economic policy)—United States.
    6. Structural adjustment (Economic policy)—Japan. I. Tan, Hong
    W., 1949- . II. Shimada, Haruo, 1943- . III. Rand Corporation.
HC103.T7  1994
338.0952—dc20                                          93-27920
                                                            CIP

# CONTENTS

## FOREWORD

In 1987, RAND received a three-year grant from the U.S.-Japan Foundation to study "Policies and Mechanisms Used in the U.S. and Japan to Deal with Declining or Non-Competitive Industries." Under the leadership of Hong W. Tan, a core group of scholars and businessmen was formed to study selected declining industries common to both countries, to identify the reasons why some industries are offered adjustment assistance, and why some policies are more effective than others. At the same time, the Japan Center for Economic Research received a grant from the Japan Industrial Policy Research Institute to conduct a parallel study with similar objectives. Professor Haruo Shimada took the initiative to organize a group including scholars and both business and union leaders. Given the coincidence of interests, it was natural for both groups to organize joint conferences and to exchange views on their research findings. Quite frankly, there existed at the outset some debate over the term "declining industry," but repeated discussions enabled us to bring about a very satisfactory outcome.

Now, some seven years later, the United States is recovering from an extended recession, and Japan's financial institutions are facing stock market losses. Some industries damaged seriously by the recession are trying eagerly to restructure themselves. It is noteworthy that the activities of these industries are not limited to their domestic markets but rather have extended their sphere worldwide. What was readily apparent in the 1980s has become a reality in the 1990s—that domestic policies in each country have a direct and significant effect on the economic well-being of the other. Public policy decisions on the following questions are crucial to the industrial performances in both countries in the years to come. What industries are critical to each nation, and should they be "saved"? What role should recession and designated cartels, tariffs and quotas, antitrust, or antidumping laws play in public policies toward troubled industries? Or should the market be allowed to have its way and only modest public intervention be offered in the form of job training and relocation assistance to displaced workers?

Whatever the choices made, this timely volume gives us a comprehensive picture of the behavior and incentives that have characterized policy decision-making toward industries in each country in the past two decades.

The findings reported in this collection are the product of an unusual level of collaboration between researchers, advisors, and institutions in both countries. The collaborations include the co-editors, Drs. Tan (RAND and the World Bank) and Shimada (Keio University); leading business and labor leaders from both countries, sharing their experiences and reviewing and discussing the authors' findings; chapters from authors in both countries; institutional cooperation between the Japan Center for Economic Research (JCER) and RAND; and funding variously from the Japan Industrial Policy Research Institute, JCER, the U.S.-Japan Foundation, RAND, and the RAND Center for U.S.-Japan Relations.

The views expressed in the chapters within do not necessarily reflect the opinions or policies of the collaborating institutions or the sponsors of this project.

*David W. Lyon*
Vice President
RAND
Santa Monica, California

*Yutaka Kosai*
President
JCER
Tokyo

## PREFACE

For both the United States and Japan, the changing circumstances of the world economy since the 1970s have brought into sharp focus the need for each country to restructure industry and to transfer human and capital resources from noncompetitive sectors to more productive uses. Because adjustment costs fall disproportionately on specific industries, groups of workers, and communities, these groups and their political representatives often form potent lobbies for protectionist legislation unless effective policies and adjustment mechanisms are developed. In both countries, then, the problem is to formulate policies that facilitate broad, economy-wide gains from resource reallocation, while minimizing the adjustment costs imposed on particular groups and industries.

*Troubled Industries in the United States and Japan* is the outgrowth of a program of joint research by RAND Corporation and the Japan Center for Economic Research (JCER) to study the issues of troubled industries. Our focus on the United States and Japan was motivated by the perception, first, that domestic adjustment policies cannot be evaluated in isolation, given the high degree of economic interdependence between the two countries; and second, that important insights can be gained from comparing each country's approach to the problems of troubled and restructuring industries. With this perspective, RAND and JCER initiated a three-year collaborative project involving key business and labor leaders, policymakers, and researchers from the United States and Japan. This book contains papers presented and discussed at two conferences, in Tokyo in March 1989, and in Santa Monica, California, in April 1990.

The book is divided into five sections. Part I provides a broad overview and summaries of papers, their main findings and some policy implications. Part II reviews the theoretical literature and discusses an analytic framework for evaluating alternative public policies toward troubled industries. Part III provides overviews and analyses of U.S. and Japanese policies toward troubled industries. Part IV compares workforce adjustments, the responsiveness of factor proportions to changing price signals, and the organization of research and development (R&D) in the two countries. Part V includes case studies of several troubled industries—machine tools (U.S.), industrial fasteners (U.S.), and cement (U.S. and Japan). These case studies focus on the relationships between the restructuring efforts of firms in specific industries and government policies.

We believe that this book will be of value to policymakers dealing with issues of industrial restructuring and trade policy, to business leaders, and to an informed audience with interests in U.S.-Japan relations. It is the first comprehensive study in English to compare the industrial adjustment experiences of distressed manufacturing industries in the United States and Japan. It is also distinctive in the breadth and depth of issues studied. It includes contributions by economic theorists, specialists on industrial organization and technology, and labor economists. A variety of analytic tools are used by authors: some chapters are descriptive; others rely on mathematical models and simulations to derive policy implications; still others use econometric methods to empirically test hypotheses on real data. By bringing a broad array of disciplinary and analytic methods to bear on the subject, the contributors provide many new insights into the policy and adjustment issues facing troubled industries in the United States and Japan.

Our greatest debt is to our U.S. and Japanese colleagues whose research made this book possible. Their chapters benefited greatly from the constructive comments and insights provided by their fellow researchers and advisors. We acknowledge the participation of Timothy Dunne, Mark Roberts, and Toshihiro Horiuchi, who also presented papers at these conferences. We owe a special debt to our Japanese and U.S. advisors, who took time out of busy schedules to share their insights as former members of government, leaders of industry and organized labor, policymakers, and specialists on U.S.-Japan relations. We acknowledge the invaluable contributions of Shinji Fukukawa, Iwao Fujiwara, Kensuke Koga, Yutaka Kosai, Yoshitaro Magoku, and Nobuichi Tsuruoka from Japan, and William Niskanen, William Klopman, Malcolm Lovell, David Lyon, Hugh Patrick, Lynn Williams, Charles Wolf, and Ron Aqua from the United States.

In the organization of this joint project, I received a great deal of help and encouragement from several colleagues. Both Katusaki Terasawa and Hiromichi Mutoh played key roles in assembling the U.S. and Japanese research teams and in organizing conferences. Malcolm Lovell was instrumental in bringing on board many of the other U.S. advisors and in providing a sounding board for the RAND project. I owe a special debt to Valeria Wright, who helped administer the RAND project, organized conferences, and typed and corrected innumerable drafts of each paper with energy and good cheer; to RAND editor, Malcolm Palmatier, who contributed to the Introduction and edited and proofread the entire manuscript for style and lucidity; and to Cynthia Kumagawa, RAND Books, who worked tirelessly with the editors, contributors, and publishers to bring this volume to press. Finally, to my wife, Michal Arnett, whose unflagging support and encouragement made this research possible, I dedicate this book.

The book would not have been possible without the generous support of the U.S.-Japan Foundation of New York for the RAND project, funding from the Industrial Policy Institute of Japan for the Japan Center for Economic Research, and supplementary resources provided by both research institutions. Editing of the final manuscript was completed with support from the RAND Center for U.S.-Japan relations.

*Hong W. Tan*

# CONTRIBUTORS AND CONFERENCE PARTICIPANTS

## Contributors

| | |
|---|---|
| ARTHUR J. ALEXANDER | RAND and Japan Economic Institute, USA |
| WILLIAM R. GATES | Naval Postgraduate School, USA |
| ELIZABETH LEWIS | RAND, USA |
| FRANK LICHTENBERG | Columbia University, USA |
| JOHN MCMILLAN | University of California in San Diego, USA |
| HIROMICHI MUTOH | Japan Center for Economic Research, Japan |
| MALCOLM PALMATIER | RAND, USA |
| ATSUSHI SEIKE | RAND and Keio University, Japan |
| SUEO SEKIGUCHI | Seikei University, Japan |
| HARUO SHIMADA | Keio University, Japan |
| HONG W. TAN | RAND and World Bank, USA |
| KATSUAKI L. TERASAWA | RAND and Naval Postgraduate School, USA |
| RYUHEI WAKASUGI | Yokohama National University, Japan |
| YOSHIE YONEZAWA | Aoyama Gakuin University, Japan |

## Conference Participants

| | |
|---|---|
| RON AQUA | U.S.-Japan Foundation of New York, USA |
| TIMOTHY DUNNE | Center for Economic Studies, Census Bureau, USA |
| IWAO FUJIWARA | Japan Metal Industrial Workers Union, Japan |
| SHINJI FUKUKAWA | Former Administrative Vice-Minister, MITI, Japan |
| TOSHIHIRO HORIUCHI | Japan Center for Economic Research, Japan |
| WILLIAM KLOPMAN | Former CEO, Burlington Industries, USA |
| KENSUKE KOGA | Nippon Steel Corporation, Japan |
| YUTAKA KOSAI | Japan Center for Economic Research, Japan |
| MALCOLM LOVELL | National Planning Association, USA |
| DAVID LYON | RAND, USA |
| YOSHITARO MAGOKU | DuPont-Toray Company, Japan |
| WILLIAM NISKANEN | Cato Institute, USA |
| HUGH PATRICK | Columbia University, USA |
| MARK ROBERTS | Pennsylvania State University, USA |
| NOBUICHI TSURUOKA | Mitsubishi Heavy Industries, Japan |
| LYNN WILLIAMS | United Steel Workers of America, USA |
| CHARLES WOLF | RAND, USA |

**I**

**Overview**

# 1

## Introduction

### Hong W. Tan, Haruo Shimada, and Malcolm Palmatier

The opening up of new markets, foreign or domestic, and the organizational development from the craft shop and factory to such concerns as U.S. Steel illustrate the same process of industrial mutation . . . that incessantly revolutionizes the economic structure *from within,* incessantly destroying the old one, incessantly creating a new one. This process of Creative Destruction is the essential fact about capitalism.

—Joseph A. Schumpeter, *Capitalism, Socialism, and Democracy* (1942)

To the Honorable Members of the Chamber of Deputies: We are suffering from the ruinous competition of a foreign rival who apparently works under conditions so far superior to our own for the production of light that he is flooding the domestic market with it at an incredibly low price. . . . This rival . . . is none other than the sun. . . . We ask you to be so good as to pass a law requiring the closing of all windows, . . . openings, holes, chinks, and fissures through which the light of the sun is wont to enter houses, to the detriment of the fair industries with which, we are proud to say, we have endowed the country, a country that cannot without betraying ingratitude, abandon us today to so unequal a combat.

Signed: Candle Makers

—Frédéric Bastiat, *Economic Sophisms* (~1845-1848)

Schumpeter's familiar expression "Creative Destruction" possesses considerable explanatory power for the complex weave of forces that generate change in the economic fabric of nations. It says, about certain firms and industries, that trouble, decline, and perhaps even removal from the marketplace are events serving some larger societal purpose. Not merely destruction, mind you, but *creative* destruction: creation of "new consumers' goods, new methods of production, new markets, and new forms of industrial organization." It is a powerful, Darwinian concept, one that assents to the place of decline in the economic scheme of things, while recognizing the sustaining effects of the new and innovative. This continuing and dynamic process of "industrial mutation" he names the essential fact about capitalism.

So much for the larger view. The other extreme—the plea for protection, for preservation of the weak and evidently declining industry of candlemaking—is tellingly set forth in Bastiat's wry petition. To whom, or to what, do the Candle Makers turn when their craft is threatened by a "foreign rival" with superior facilities able to overwhelm local markets with reduced prices? To government ("Chamber of Deputies"), of course—and with an absurd, but apparently heartfelt, request. We may assume that the Deputies temporized and (rightly) did nothing in this case. In many cases, however, governments respond with subsidies, cartels, tariff barriers, import quotas, or "voluntary" export restraint (VER) agreements, to name just a few of the devices used to tilt the playing field in favor of domestic producers.

These two epigraphs contain elements of the arguments presented in this volume. The overarching proposition in Schumpeter is that the birth, heyday, and decline of whole industries is an intrinsic part of the capitalist system and, indeed, is the source of an economy's dynamism and well-being. One view, then, is to let the workings of the marketplace take its course; when the decline and eventual extinction of an industry is finally indicated, it will come, and with no regrets. A competing view is that completely market-based adjustment may not be economically optimal, or even socially or politically desirable. Compensation to losers (the Candle Makers) may be justified on moral and equity grounds, since society as a whole benefits from free trade and free markets, while the costs of adjustment fall on specific groups. Market imperfections and market failures would also justify intervention to smooth the flow of capital and labor resources from declining to growing sectors. Finally, on political grounds, providing temporary "breathing room" for industries to adjust may be a small price to pay when the alternative to inaction is more widespread, permanent protectionist legislation.

The points of view expressed above raise a number of issues about the proper extent of government intervention—of the visible hand—in the free market process. First, in the absence of any intervention, how well does the marketplace work? What do firms and workers do to adjust to loss of competitiveness and decline, how successfully do they adapt, and are there important market failures that constrain their adjustment responses? Second, if governments do intervene, what form should such interventions take? What criteria should be used in deciding among alternative policies and in evaluating their efficacy? Third, might we expect policies toward troubled industries to differ across nations. How effective, in practice, have different national strategies been in facilitating industrial adjustment or in addressing attendant inefficiencies? Finally, what insights may be gained by comparing different national experiences with troubled industries? Are policy lessons learned in one national context transferable to another?

These issues are the motivation for this book, which relates the national means of coping with troubled industries in the United States and Japan. It begins with broad theoretical studies of firm adjustments and government intervention to restructure whole industries. The discussion considers the economic rationale for government intervention, and the need for policy-makers to weigh the trade-offs between allocative and technical efficiency, and between producer and consumer surplus. The text then examines actual U.S. and Japanese policies toward troubled manufacturing industries over the past two decades. While there are broad similarities, national differences emerge: U.S. reliance on trade policies and import relief; and Japanese preferences for domestic-oriented policies and cartel actions.

The U.S.-Japan comparisons are then extended to the patterns of adjustment in labor and capital markets, to research and development strategies, and to case studies of specific troubled industries. They not only reveal broad national differences, but also industry-level similarities in the speed of employment adjustment and job attachment, and in the way capital-labor ratios respond to relative price changes. The organization of industrial research and development is then compared, and the different roles of corporate strategy and government policy in the two countries are discussed. The text concludes with case studies drawn from U.S. and Japanese troubled industries in machine tools, cement, and industrial fasteners. These case studies serve to draw together the interplay of government policies and private responses that shape the actual adjustment experiences of troubled industries in the two countries.

In the following sections we elaborate on each of these studies, how they address the issues described above, and their main findings. From this, we draw some comparative conclusions about industrial restructuring and government policies toward troubled industries in the two countries and their implications for both U.S.-Japan relations and the international trading system.

## OVERVIEW OF THE BOOK

### The Analytic Framework

What does economic theory have to say about the behavior of firms in an industry facing secularly declining demand? Under what conditions would the laissez faire market outcome not be economically optimal, and thus warrant government intervention? If governments do intervene, what guidance can theory provide about the choice of policies? The first three chapters together provide an analytic framework for studying the adjustment behavior of firms and evaluating alternative policies toward troubled industries.

In Chapter 2, McMillan reviews the theoretical literature on how intra-industry adjustments take place in declining industries. When an industry is characterized by excess capacity and declining demand, and there is a flow cost to maintaining capacity, which firm exits or reduces excess capacity first, the larger firm or the smaller one? Theory suggests that larger firms bear a disproportionately large share of the burden of adjustment, and McMillan provides evidence consistent with this prediction. He notes, however, that discreteness in the reduction of capacity—as in closing whole plants—can lead to quite complex patterns of industry shrinkage, and scale economies (or cost differences among firms) can provide a force in the opposite direction, tending to induce early exit of small and less cost-efficient firms. These hypotheses are explored in the case studies in Part V of this book.

McMillan discusses a variety of reasons why the price system may not produce optimal adjustments. Among these, the two leading causes of market failure appear to be labor market friction and technical inefficiency arising from the incomplete use of productive capacity. Labor market friction, such as sticky wages, high search costs, and externalities in search, gives rise to excessive or structural unemployment. Such friction is one rationale for government provision of adjustment assistance to workers, in the form of job search assistance, retraining in the United States, or, in the case of Japan, subsidies to employers that hire displaced workers or that accept workers directly from contracting industries.

Distortions can also arise in an imperfectly competitive declining industry. The laissez faire outcome is not technically efficient when average costs vary across firms. Both high- and low-cost firms produce less than their capacity, while technical efficiency requires the cost-efficient firm to produce up to its capacity and the less efficient firm to produce the residual. Targeted subsidies, relaxation of antitrust prohibition of mergers, or

Japanese-style recession cartels may increase technical efficiency, *provided* that production is shifted toward lower cost plants and that the import share of the market is large enough to protect consumers against monopolistic pricing by the domestic industry. In practice, these conditions may not be met (for example, see the Sekiguchi chapter on allocation of capacity reduction targets in Japanese cartels or the Mutoh chapter on privately negotiated import restraints in the Japanese cement industry).

Chapters 3 and 4, by Terasawa and Gates, address the issue of the appropriate choice of policy instruments. They develop a model of an oligopolistic industry composed of Nash firms with diverse production costs and excess capacity, with entry and exit of firms as well as foreign competition. (Nash firms produce their profit maximizing output under the assumption of a given output level from all other competing firms.) Within this framework, they evaluate the social welfare effects of alternative government policies on domestic producers and consumers and foreign producers. Policies that improve social welfare are not always pursued, however; lobby groups and governments may adopt alternative, suboptimal policies that benefit some groups at the expense of others. The authors highlight these trade-offs using numerical simulations of hypothetical distributions of production costs in both domestic and foreign firms.

Terasawa and Gates consider four broad kinds of policies. First, they note that policies that raise import prices (e.g., tariffs) decrease imports and, through lower consumption, reduce allocative efficiency and consumer surplus. Domestic output is increased, but technical efficiency falls because output rises proportionately more for less efficient firms. The result is a transfer of income from consumers and foreigners to domestic producers. Second, policies that restrict imports (e.g., import quotas) have similar effects on prices and output, and on producer and consumer surplus. However, they transfer income from government to foreign producers, who naturally find them more attractive than the alternative tariff policy. A third group of policies—e.g., price subsidies, public investments in R&D, and tax incentives—reduces the cost of production. They increase output and reduce price, thus raising allocative efficiency, and result in a transfer of producer surplus from foreign to domestic sources. How technical efficiency fares will depend upon whether policies favor the cost-efficient firms (improves technical efficiency) or the less efficient firms (reduces it). Finally, Terasawa and Gates consider policies that relax antitrust regulation, thereby enabling firms to capture economies of scale. Internal growth raises allocative efficiency, because of output increases and price decreases, as well as technical efficiency, from growth in the more efficient firms. Mergers raise technical efficiency but may reduce allocative efficiency, especially if scale economies are overshadowed by reduced output from a smaller number of firms.

In general, the authors conclude that policies that subsidize production or relax antitrust regulation are generally preferable to those that restrict imports. In some situations, combined strategies such as a mixed tariff/subsidy policy may actually improve social welfare more than a pure strategy. However, the preferred policy will depend in large part upon the specific characteristics of the industry and both domestic and foreign producers. For example, suppose that U.S. antitrust regulation prevented domestic producers from capturing scale economies enjoyed by foreign producers. While import relief policies would help domestic firms compete, and targeted production subsidies might offset the cost difference, the problem could be directly eliminated by relaxing U.S. antitrust laws, assuming that sufficient domestic or international competition existed to preclude collusion.

In Chapter 4, Terasawa and Gates incorporate two additional features into their model: (1) multiproduct firms and (2) a labor constraint. In the first case, firms are assumed to produce two products, X, which is declining in demand, and Y, whose demand is constant. The costs of producing X and Y are interrelated because of a fixed input (such as management) used in producing both products. The second case involves a labor constraint, perhaps from an agreement with the union, which prohibits the firm from reducing its workforce below some floor. When it reaches this floor, the firm must allocate labor between its two products so as to maximize total profits. These extensions enrich the realism of the model and yield much more complex patterns of firm adjustment (other than exit) than those suggested by the more simple models typically considered.

The results for the model with multiproduct firms are generally similar to those for the single-product firm. As demand for X declines, industry output and prices fall. Individual firms reduce output, and some firms exit industry X (but continue to produce Y). However, the proportionate decrease in output is most pronounced for the less efficient firms, so technical efficiency in the production of X increases. Production costs in industry Y also decrease as more of the fixed resource is devoted to the production of Y. This results in increased output of Y, reduction in its price, and an increase in allocative efficiency. These analyses suggest that cross-industry effects must be considered if firms produce in more than one market (as is often the case) and that policymakers must take these effects into account before implementing industry-specific policies.

The presence of a labor constraint produces the most striking change. When Firm 2 has a labor constraint, it becomes less sensitive to the declines in demand for X. In effect, the labor constraint forces the burden of adjustment onto other firms, especially the less efficient firms in the industry. Firm 2's output of X and its market share are both larger than they might be without the labor constraint. Profits for the constrained firm actually increase when the decline in demand is moderate, while profits of other firms decline. Thus, labor constraints can shape how different firms within an industry adjust (for example, see the Seike-Tan chapter on workforce adjustment), or, when labor constraints are more binding on foreign (say Japanese) than on domestic firms, determine whether domestic or foreign firms bear the brunt of output adjustments to declining demand.

## Policies toward Troubled Industries

How do U.S. and Japanese troubled industry policies stack up, in practice, against the kinds of policies suggested by theory? Are there differences in the policies adopted in the two countries, and why? Chapters 5, 6, 7, and 8 provide broad overviews of U.S. and Japanese policies toward troubled industries and detailed analyses of import relief petitions in the United States and cartel actions in Japan. Taken together, they provide numerous insights into the similarities and differences in policy approaches taken by the two countries.

Tan, in Chapter 5, provides an overview of U.S. policies toward troubled industries, describing not only those on trade policies (the primary policy instrument), but also on domestic policies, such as Trade Adjustment Assistance (TAA), displaced-worker programs under the Job Training and Partnership Act (JTPA), plant-closing legislation, and, more recently, "Super-301"action against restrictive trade practices abroad. Trade policies to assist troubled industries are of two types: (1) the "low-track" approach through escape-clause actions and antidumping and countervailing duty statutes, and (2) the "high-track" approach through bilateral or multilateral negotiations to restrict imports, or through tariffs. The chapter traces the development of these domestic and trade policies over the 1970s and 1980s, including changes to the policies under the 1988 Omnibus Trade and Competitiveness Act.

In general, the United States has no comprehensive set of policies targeted at specific troubled industries, as Japan does; instead, it relies on a patchwork of statutes in U.S. trade law that provides import relief to beleaguered industries and on domestic-oriented adjustment policies to retrain and facilitate the relocation of labor and to regulate plant closings. The U.S. preference for trade policy appears to stem from an ideology of nonintervention (if firms get in trouble, that is their worry); from the view that free markets have less acceptance in international trade than in domestic trade; and from the strictures of the federal budget deficit (unlike domestic assistance programs, trade restrictions take an off-budget form). Trade protection measures are also attractive politically: they provide a ready answer to trade-impacted industries; they spread the costs widely to many consumers; and they "compensate" foreign producers through valuable quota rents. But these are shortsighted solutions; they tax emerging domestic industries that use the products protected and confer rents on foreign producers, thus enhancing their competitive position.

In Chapter 6, Sekiguchi provides a detailed overview of government adjustment assistance policies in Japan. Following the sharp yen appreciation from the oil crises, the government prepared (in 1978) the Law for Adjustment Assistance for depressed industries in fourteen sectors. A broad array of domestic-oriented programs was provided to assist designated sectors—cartels for joint capacity reduction, subsidies, loan guarantees, tax relief, and income support and retraining for displaced workers. A second round of adjustments came five years later, when the Ministry of International Trade and Industry (MITI) enacted the Structural Improvement Law (1983) covering 22 sectors, and strengthened financial incentives to invest in specific depressed regions. MITI revised this law again in 1988, enacting the Adjustment Facilitation Law, which focused on equipment to be scrapped rather than on specific sectors. Some components of the 1988 law, notably those which promote regional development, have become permanent.

Japan's policies have generally focused on domestically oriented measures rather than import restrictions. Persistent pressures on Japan (since the mid-1960s) to liberalize its imports and open its markets, coupled with large current account surpluses in the 1980s, would have made it difficult for Japan to impose new import barriers to help troubled industries. In contrast to the United States, the government (MITI) has played an activist role (through administrative guidance and financial incentives) in coordinating sector-specific adjustment plans, in assisting small firms, and in encouraging investments in industrially depressed regions.

Chapter 7, by Tan and Lichtenberg investigates the economic determinants and outcomes of import relief actions—antidumping, countervailing duties, and escape-clause petitions—in the United States. Import relief petitions filed by U.S. manufacturing firms have increased dramatically since the 1970s, a threefold increase in petitioning in the case of antidumping petitions against imports allegedly sold in the United States at less than fair value. To date, relatively little is known about what has caused this surge in petitioning activity, about the petitioning process itself, the agencies that administer these policies, and their effectiveness in facilitating industrial adjustment. To study these issues, Tan and Lichtenberg use time-series industry-level production data linked to information on import relief petitions compiled from records of the Department of Commerce and the U.S. International Trade Commission (ITC).

Their econometric analyses of the determinants of petitioning suggest the following. First, the industries that petition are characterized by high and rising import penetration ratios, large employment and output loss, and depressed profitability. These characteristics are consistent with the criteria used by the ITC to determine material injury. Second, capital-intensive and highly unionized industries are more likely to petition than others, possibly reflecting the higher costs of scrapping excess capacity and of displacing high-wage jobs in these industries. Finally, they find some support for the hypothesis that revisions in U.S. trade laws have contributed to the increase in the number of petitions filed over time. The 1974 Trade Act targeted escape-clause petitions, and the number of such petitions rose after 1974; similarly, the number of fair-trade petitions increased after enactment of the 1979 Trade Agreements Act.

Tan and Lichtenberg also investigated the role of the ITC by conducting before and after comparisons of the time paths of key variables for petitioning and nonpetitioning industries. First, prior to petitioning, the industries whose petitions were rejected by the ITC experienced smaller increases in import penetration than, and similar output and employment growth to that of, nonpetitioners. However, industries with affirmative petition outcomes experienced rapidly accelerating penetration by imports and sharp declines in employment and output growth. These findings suggest that the ITC is able to discriminate between worthy and more frivolous petitions. Second, affirmative decisions by the ITC appear to provide time for troubled industries to adjust by moderating subsequent trends in these key variables. Finally, they note that these indicators were unchanged or even worsened for industries whose petitions were withdrawn, suspended, or terminated by the ITC. It has been argued that these petitions represent collusive efforts by the domestic industry to enforce price discipline among foreign competitors. If so, such efforts apparently do not have a sustained effect; while profits may recover temporarily, these industries as a group continue to experience high levels of import competition, output loss, and workforce reductions.

In Chapter 8, Sekiguchi provides a focused examination of Japanese cartels as a policy instrument for facilitating industrial adjustment to declining demand. The law provides for two legal exceptions to the general prohibition on cartels: first, *recession cartels* (legalized in the Antitrust Law of 1953) to solve temporary or cyclical problems of overproduction; and, second, *designated cartels* (provided by the 1978 and 1983 adjustment assistance laws) to facilitate joint capacity reductions in structurally depressed industries. On the basis of case studies, Sekiguchi provides a critical review of cartels, their consequences for technical efficiency, and the political economy behind their use and implementation.

Until 1978, producers were permitted to form temporary recession cartels upon approval of the Fair Trade Commission (FTC), if firms faced the possibility of bankruptcy because of depressed prices and were unable to resolve the issue through their individual efforts. Recession cartels were quite frequent in the 1950s and 1960s, especially during recessions, but their numbers declined over time as they became less effective. For the most part, this was due to the growing integration of the domestic market into the international economy; cartel efforts to prop up prices became less successful as import competition grew. As the experience of the craft paper industry demonstrates, two recession cartels formed in this industry—in 1978–79, and again in 1981—were largely unsuccessful in arresting large declines in profits. Subsequently, the industry was designated for adjustment assistance, and a cartel was formed between 1983 and 1986 to scrap excess capacity.

Unlike recession cartels, designated cartels under both the 1978 and the 1983 laws were to be used to reduce excess capacity in declining industries. How successful were these cartels? According to Sekiguchi, there were no significant differences in capacity reduction between those industries that formed a cartel and those that did not. Furthermore, capacity reduction may have come at the expense of technical efficiency; most likely, allocation of capacity reduction targets was based more on equity than on efficiency criteria, with larger (and low cost) firms bearing the brunt of adjustment. How do we explain this target allocation mechanism? Sekiguchi suggests several possible explanations. First, large firms are better able than small firms to find employment for displaced workers. Second, as leaders of industry associations, large firms are willing to bear a larger share of adjustment costs in return for political gains (pressure from MITI was another factor, as suggested by the critical comments of key Japanese industrialists who attended the conference). Finally, the government is more inclined to assist smaller firms whose workers represent a sizable, and potentially important, swing vote.

## Labor, Capital, and Technology

How do industries facing loss of competitiveness and declining demand adjust, how rapidly do they adjust, and what factors constrain their responses? Are patterns of adjustment very different in the United States and Japan, and why? Chapters 9 and 10 address these issues by looking at labor and capital markets and by comparing patterns of adjustment across the same manufacturing industries in the two countries. Chapter 9 examines the role of employment practices in shaping the speed and patterns of workforce adjustment; Chapter 10 compares the way that U.S. and Japanese industries have altered their use of capital and labor in response to changes in the relative prices of these inputs. Chapters 11 and 12 focus on the corporate R&D activities and their implications for innovativeness and industrial adjustment in the two countries.

In Chapter 9, Seike and Tan examine the impact of job security practices on the speed of employment adjustment, which is faster in the United States than in Japan. This issue is critical in understanding how workforce adjustments are managed in the two countries and what kinds of policies are used by each government to facilitate labor market adjustments. Lifetime employment practices in Japan are thought to be responsible, at least in part, for the willingness of workers to accept greater wage flexibility and for the greater emphasis that employers place on internal restructuring and worker reallocations before finally resorting to layoffs. Many U.S. companies also have long-term employment practices; during downturns, many have gone to extraordinary lengths not to lay off workers. The main difference is one of degree; industries in both countries turn out to be strikingly similar in their patterns of workforce adjustment, use of labor contracts, and long-term jobs.

The authors begin by comparing the speed of workforce adjustments in several U.S. and Japanese manufacturing industries. They conclude that while Japanese employers are generally slower to reduce the size of their workforce in response to output changes, there are strong cross-national similarities in the relative speeds of employment adjustment by different industries. Industries that respond rapidly do so in both countries, as do those that respond slowly to output shocks. This suggests that labor flexibility is determined to a large extent by technological factors common to industries in both countries.

If technology shapes training requirements, and if training is facilitated by the guarantee of job security, then industries with high training requirements will tend to be characterized by labor contracts (such as a lifetime employment guarantee) that reduce labor turnover. To test this hypothesis,

Seike and Tan estimate the duration of completed manufacturing jobs in Japan and the United States for roughly comparable industries. They find strong similarities in the distribution of long-term jobs across industries in the two countries. Next, they assemble evidence to show that U.S. private pension plans (severance pay systems in Japan) are effective in inhibiting labor turnover. Furthermore, the use of turnover-inhibiting compensation schemes, as measured by pension coverage rates, are very similar across industries in the two countries. The difference is that overall pension coverage rates are much higher in Japan, which might explain lower overall rates of job turnover in Japan as compared to the United States.

In Chapter 10, Yonezawa takes a similar tack in studying the speed of adjustments of factor proportions (capital-labor ratios) to changes in the relative prices of capital and labor inputs in comparable industries in the two countries. Using a simple neoclassical production model, the author examines the adjustment responsiveness of U.S. and Japanese manufacturing industries to changing wage and rate-of-return signals. In the model, producers intent on maximizing profits are induced to alter factor proportion—of labor and capital—in response to changes in relative factor prices (wage rate and rental rate). Firms that do not adjust their factor proportions in this manner stand to lose competitiveness over the long run.

The ratios of capital and labor (i.e., capital intensity) are studied for 35 manufacturing industries between 1967 and 1986 and related to changes in the relative factor prices (the wage-rental ratio). Producers using a well-behaved production function can quickly adjust their capital intensity whenever the ratio of factor rewards changes. Less well-behaved production functions have consequences for how smoothly the ratio changes. For both countries, Yonezawa finds that movements over time in the two variables appear to be positively related, as the model predicts. However, a comparison of elasticities of substitution indicates well-behaved response patterns in Japan, but somewhat slower responses to factor price signals in the United States. Generally, adjustment responses of U.S. manufacturers are less sensitive to changing price signals than those of Japanese firms. Yonezawa attributes some of these U.S.-Japan differences to greater access to capital markets in Japan. Measurement error and sticky factor prices (e.g., multiyear labor contracts in the United States) are other potential explanations for these results.

Research and development (R&D) activities are intimately linked to industrial restructuring, both as a cause of an industry's loss of international competitiveness and, especially in the case of troubled industries in Japan, as a strategy for responding to declining demand. The next two chapters—by Alexander in Chapter 11 and Wakasugi in Chapter 12—compare patterns of

R&D expenditures, innovation styles, and government policies toward technology in the United States and Japan. They touch on the distinctive composition of U.S. and Japanese corporate R&D expenditures, the relative strengths of each country in different parts of the innovation process (the United States in basic research and product development, Japan in process innovation), and the implications of these cross-national findings.

Alexander and Wakasugi highlight several distinctive innovation styles in the two countries. First, more than 75 percent of total Japanese R&D expenditures are made by private firms, only some 19 percent by the government. The proportions, by contrast, are divided nearly evenly in the United States. Second, U.S. firms put about two-thirds of their R&D funds into improved *product* technology and one-third into improved *process* technology; among Japanese firms, these proportions are reversed. Third, the traditional strengths of U.S. firms in pursuing new products and new technologies are matched by the organizational innovations of many Japanese firms in adapting and improving upon technology developed by others. Compared with their U.S. counterparts, Japanese firms spend less time and money to commercialize externally developed technologies.

What accounts for these distinctive national innovation styles? A contributing factor, according to Alexander, is differences in patterns of development in postwar Japan and America. The size of the domestic U.S. economy allows many industries to take advantage of economies of scale, to focus on developing new products and new markets rather than concentrating on cutting costs. In Japan, by contrast, competition to gain market share in a small domestic market drives firms to search for cost efficiency (even with small production runs) as a means toward profitability. In this environment, it makes sense for Japanese firms to draw on foreign technology, rather than develop it internally, and to meet competitive challenges through incremental improvements and R&D, cost-reducing innovations, and fast development times.

Another factor, stressed by Wakasugi, is differences in corporate management styles. Unlike U.S. firms, where R&D and production departments tend to be compartmentalized, R&D divisions in Japanese firms are very closely integrated with production and marketing functions; these contacts provide the ideas for a greater proportion of their R&D projects than in U.S. firms. The flow of ideas between upstream and downstream activities is also fostered by the practice of frequent intrafirm job rotation of personnel, including engineers, across different functional departments. Another consequence of job rotation is multiskilling, the development of expertise and problem-solving abilities in a wide variety of tasks. These management practices, while in no way unique to Japan (witness the diffusion of just-in-time methods to the United States), are thought to account for a large part of Japan's cost and time advantage in introducing innovations.

## Industry Case Studies

Thus far, the discussion of theory, government policies, and private sector adjustments has proceeded at a fairly high level of aggregation—across industries or factor markets. This aggregation, especially at the two-digit Standard Industrial Classification (SIC) level, conceals a great deal of diversity: in the degree of competitiveness at the four- or five-digit SIC industry levels, and in the diversity of adjustment responses of different firms in the same industry. The final three chapters provide in-depth case studies on selected U.S. and Japanese troubled industries. The chapters on U.S. machine tools and the Japanese cement industry describe the interplay between industry restructuring efforts and government policies. The final chapter takes the analysis down to the plant level. Data from the U.S. machine tool, hydraulic cement, and industrial fasteners industries are used to study patterns of firm entry and exit and import relief petitions.

In Chapter 13, Alexander describes adaptations to change in the U.S. machine tool industry and evaluates the effects of government policies on the restructuring of the industry. A highly cyclical industry, domestic machine tool demand has experienced a secular decline owing to the substitution of nonmetallic materials for metals, the development of alternative metal-forming technologies, the declining output of products that were heavy users of machined parts, and the increased productivity of numerically controlled (NC) machine tools. Japanese firms have adapted more rapidly than American firms to these technological and market changes. Aided by an overvalued dollar, imports have dominated the U.S. market increasingly, with imports rising from around 10 percent in the late 1960s to 50 percent in the 1980s.

How did the U.S. machine tool industry respond? Consistent with theory (see McMillan, Chapter 2), large firms were more severely affected by declining demand than small ones. The number of large firms fell from 77 to 25, while the number of smaller companies rose. Machine tool companies also underwent vertical disintegration—the outsourcing of components and specialized parts—with the result that many companies became assembly and design concerns. What explains the sluggish U.S. response? Alexander identifies several factors: insufficient financing, particularly for small firms that make up the industry; the relative insulation of the industry from world markets; exchange rates that penalized U.S. exports; and failure to reinvest in new equipment and products. The wave of mergers in the 1970s and early 1980s—possibly motivated more by the attraction of cash flow than the possibility of improving operations—may also have contributed to low rates of capital investment and R&D.

Government assistance for the machine tool industry emphasized import relief over positive adjustment assistance. In 1986, the U.S. Department of Commerce accepted an industry petition for relief on national security grounds. The United States then sought voluntary export restraint (VER) agreements on 17 types of machine tools from Japan (the largest importer), Taiwan, Germany, and Switzerland (the latter two countries refused). These agreements limited imports of NC machine tools to their 1981 market share and other machine tools to their 1985 share. Mirroring the experience with automobiles, the number of units shipped by Japan dropped in designated categories, exports expanded in other categories not covered by VERs, and production shifted increasingly to U.S. facilities. The industry also got Trade Adjustment Assistance (TAA) in the form of income support, training, and job search assistance for displaced workers. However, out of 31 TAA petitions, the Department of Labor approved only 7 petitions covering 953 workers, or 40 percent of the total number of workers affected.

Mutoh examines the adjustment experience of Japan's cement industry in Chapter 14. The problems in this industry began in the 1980s, precipitated by several factors: declines in construction activity and technological changes in construction methods, including the use of new compounds. The resulting excess capacity, exacerbated by growing import competition from Korea and Taiwan, led to a variety of rationalization efforts by the five largest cement producers. In addition to capacity scrapping, these included reduced input and energy use; diversification into new lines of business; intensified R&D spending to develop new cement products; workforce reductions through both early and voluntary retirement and employee loaning; mergers and spin-offs of unprofitable business operations; and globalization through joint ventures and the establishment of overseas distribution networks.

The industry also sought, and got, government adjustment assistance. First, in mid-1983, a recession cartel was set up to restrict domestic sales and fix cement prices, although with limited success. Second, the industry was designated under the Structural Improvement Law of 1983 for adjustment assistance, and exempted from antitrust laws by the Fair Trade Commission (FTC). The resulting plan, for capacity scrapping and establishment of joint-sales enterprises, was partly successful in easing price competition.

Prices and profits rose, but excess capacity still persisted because of shrinking exports and rising imports from Korea and Taiwan. Finally, adjustment assistance for the industry continued under the Structural Adjustment Law of 1988. This included approval for joint production, joint sales, mergers, and capacity scrapping; loan guarantees to finance capacity scrapping and business conversions; and tax benefits such as accelerated depreciation and exemption from and reductions in a variety of taxes.

Government policies, designated cartels in particular, appear to have facilitated the orderly reduction of excess capacity, as well as the scrapping of the least efficient kilns. Mutoh notes, however, that policies that facilitate cooperation among producers run the risk of promoting collusive and competition-restricting practices by cartel members. As examples, he cites the voluntary export restraint agreement negotiated by the manufacturer's association in 1986 to limit imports from Korea, the establishment of a joint storage facility that could (potentially) monopolize the regional cement market, and restrictive practices by the majors toward domestic ready-mix concrete firms using imported cement. His conclusion is that careful FTC scrutiny of such arrangements, as occurred in 1988, is needed to balance the use of cartel policies in Japan.

In Chapter 15, Tan and Lewis use time-series plant-level data to study patterns of firm entry and exit and firm behavior in petitioning for import relief. This focus on the individual establishment is motivated by the perception that labels, such as "troubled" or "declining" industry, mask very considerable diversity among firms in a given industry. Some firms are more competitive than others; some respond successfully to declining demand, while others fail to do so and ultimately exit the industry. What insights do plant-level data provide about the process of intra-industry restructuring in U.S. troubled industries? Which firms petition for import relief, and why? To address these questions, Tan and Lewis use panel data on individual plants in three selected industries—machine tools, hydraulic cement, and industrial fasteners. These data, from the Longitudinal Research Database (LRD), were analyzed at the Center for Economic Research, U.S. Census Bureau. For the analysis of petitions, the LRD data were linked to names of firms in the cement industry filing antidumping petitions with the International Trade Commission in the 1970s and 1980s.

The process of intra-industry restructuring in these three industries is studied by tracking individual plants over five census years—1963, 1967, 1972, 1977, and 1982. For each industry, Tan and Lewis compute several measures to characterize the plants that enter and exit the industry over this period. These include intercensal rates of plant entry and exit and the average sizes (number of employees and value of shipments) of entering, incumbent, and exiting plants. They also estimate a four-factor production function (with capital, labor, raw materials, and energy) to derive plant-level estimates of the relative efficiency of entrants, incumbents, and exits in each industry.

These data suggest several general conclusions about the intra-industry restructuring process. First, aggregate industry measures (even at the five-digit SIC level) conceal a great number of firm entries and exits—many new plants enter the industry even when overall demand is declining. Second, contrary to the theories reviewed by McMillan, exits tend to be concentrated among smaller firms, while new entrants tend to be somewhat larger than exiting firms. Finally, exiting firms have lower levels of efficiency compared with incumbents; although initially less efficient, entrants subsequently improve their efficiency, possibly through learning by doing. In short, U.S. troubled industries appear to restructure both through higher rates of firm exit than entry and through the departure of smaller and less efficient firms and their replacement by larger and (eventually) more efficient ones.

The second part of the Tan-Lewis chapter focuses on the behavior of firms in the cement industry that petitioned for import relief. Firms that participated in five import relief petitions between 1975 and 1984 were identified and linked to plant-level data in the LRD. Petitioning firms were divided into three groups—petitioners in the 1970s, petitioners in the 1980s, and petitioners in both periods—and compared with the population of firms that did not join in these petitions. Which firms petitioned? The analyses suggest that petitioners tend to be larger firms, both in terms of the number of plants operated and in terms of shipments, and firms that pay higher wages. Furthermore, with the exception of firms that petitioned in the 1980s, petitioning firms tend to be less efficient (as measured by a production function) relative to those that did not petition; not surprisingly, the least efficient firms were those that petitioned in both periods.

When do firms file petitions? By tracking levels of efficiency over time, the authors conclude that the timing of petitions generally coincides with large observed declines in measured levels of relative efficiency. Thus, firms that file industry petitions tend not to be representative of the industry; they tend to be less efficient on average. But, because they have a greater stake in restricting imports, large multiplant firms are more willing to incur the costs of filing petitions, even though other firms may benefit ("free-ride") from their actions.

## SUMMARY AND IMPLICATIONS

We derive a number of analytic and policy conclusions from the analytic chapters.

1.  In both the United States and Japan, a great deal of adjustment takes place through the marketplace without any significant intermediation by governments. As industries lose competitiveness, firms scrap excess productive capacity, reduce wages and lay off workers, change to new product lines, outsource to less costly domestic or overseas suppliers, or exit the industry (see Chapters 11 and 14). This process of industrial downsizing is a dynamic one, with new and more efficient firms entering the industry even as less efficient ones exit; the outcome is a smaller, more competitive industry (Tan and Lewis, Chapter 15). In both countries, the vast majority of workers displaced by plant closings or layoffs subsequently find employment without any government assistance, such as that provided by Title III programs in the United States and JS-Cards in Japan (see Chapters 5 and 6).

2.  One important difference between the two countries is the way in which employment adjustment is effected: a greater emphasis on intrafirm or intragroup job reassignments in Japan, and greater reliance on interfirm reallocation through the labor market in the United States. Because lifetime employment practices are generally more widespread in Japan, especially among large firms, employers tend to move workers within the firm (or to related firms) and adjust labor costs through reduction in real wages; there is less wage flexibility in the United States, so labor cost adjustments tend to occur through workforce reductions. This is consistent with the findings of other comparative U.S.-Japan studies, and with the evidence provided by Seike and Tan that the speed of employment adjustment to output shocks is much faster in Japan than in the United States.

3.  Another difference emerges from evidence that the restructuring process may emphasize the survival of firms more in Japan than in the United States. Several Japanese industrialists noted that lifetime employment practices often preclude plant closure except as a last resort. Employers, abetted in part by government policies (see Chapter 8), go to extraordinary lengths to avoid closing down firms— diversifying their product lines, investing heavily in R&D to develop new products, retraining workers, and spinning off whole divisions.

This point is supported by evidence from the Japanese cement case study (see Chapter 14), and by the extensive efforts of several Mitsubishi plants to switch (convert) to new product lines within the same plant. However, there are limits to what firms can do, as exemplified by the unprecedented 1993 decision of Nissan to close its Zama plant. Whether or not plant closures are more common in the United States than in Japan, and why, is an issue that needs further quantification and analysis.

4. Though important, these national differences should not be exaggerated. As in Japan, many industries and firms in the United States provide employment security to workers, a significant proportion of whom have long job-tenure (see Chapter 9). Perhaps more striking is the fact that industries that emphasize long-term job attachment have similar characteristics in both countries. Common industry attributes—such as rapid technological change, high rates of output growth, low cyclical variability, and skill-intensive production— may create demand for long-term employment stability; thus, in both countries, firms in these industries are much more likely to introduce deferred compensation schemes to reduce labor turnover. This suggests that the practice of lifetime employment in Japan (or for that matter, in the United States) is not culturally determined; rather, it may be an economically rational device that employers in both countries use to stabilize employment and encourage worker training. However, protracted slumps in economic activity can lead firms to jettison implicit or explicit employment guarantees. Witness the mass layoffs by large U.S. corporations, such as IBM, and calls by the Ministry of Labor for large Japanese companies to retain redundant employees.

5. Both the United States and Japan have used broadly similar *domestic* policies to assist workers, firms, and impacted communities. In both countries, displaced workers are provided income maintenance, retraining, counseling, and job search assistance. Unlike the case in the United States, however, which relies on public or private providers, worker assistance in Japan operates largely through retraining subsidies to firms that retrench workers and to those that hire displaced workers. Assistance to firms includes accelerated depreciation, loan guarantees, and consulting services for restructuring. The major beneficiaries in the United States are trade-impacted firms under the Trade Adjustment Assistance (TAA) Act; in Japan, they are firms in designated industries or regions. In Japan, assistance to industrially

depressed regions is substantial, and is larger today than industry-based programs. In the United States, although aid to communities may exist on the books, no programs were ever approved as part of the TAA. (There have been some community-based programs, however, such as the Downriver demonstration project.)

6. National differences in policies toward troubled industries are more pronounced than their similarities. The United States has tended to rely on providing import relief through trade laws—the escape clause, and antidumping and countervailing statutes—and on the International Trade Commission (ITC) to handle complaints of unfair trade or injury from impacted industries (see Chapter 5). In cases involving major industries, such as carbon steel, textiles, footwear, automobiles, and semiconductors, the United States has provided special protection—on a case-by-case basis—by negotiating bilateral and multilateral agreements with exporting countries.

   Japan, for its part, has relied more on domestic-oriented policies: cartels for capacity scrapping and price support, exemption from antimonopoly law, joint marketing and distribution arrangements, tax relief, subsidies, and low interest loans (see Chapter 6). Although it has safeguard and antidumping statutes, Japan has been constrained by huge current-account surpluses (and by pressure from other developed economies) not to restrict imports. In the recent past, however, a number of industry associations have privately negotiated "voluntary" bilateral agreements with their counterparts in Pakistan, Korea, and Taiwan to restrict exports of textiles, apparel, knitwear, and cement to Japan.

7. How effective have Japanese and U.S. policies been? Several Japanese industry leaders were openly critical of MITI's cartel policies for joint capacity reduction. Because targets for scrapping tend to be set in proportion to firm size, scaling down each firm by an equal proportion has meant that the larger (more efficient) firms have borne the burden of adjustment, while inefficient firms have survived and their adjustment (and possible exit from the industry) has been delayed. While such policies may have been effective in terms of achieving a goal—capacity reduction of the industry as a whole— they have not been economically efficient in terms of technical efficiency, or production, in the most efficient (least-cost) firms (see Chapters 3 and 4).

8. The U.S. fair trade and escape-clause laws appear to have been effective in buying time for trade-impacted industries to adjust. Tan

and Lichtenberg (Chapter 7) arrive at several conclusions. First, they suggest that the ITC is able to discriminate between deserving petitions and those without merit. Affirmative determinations appear to have arrested increases in import penetration, to have moderated output and employment losses, and to have improved profitability for this group of petitioners. For industries withdrawing petitions before a final determination—they may receive special protection from the executive or legislative branches of government—profits tend to recover, at least temporarily; however, as a group, they continue to experience both high and rising levels of import competition, output loss, and continued workforce reductions.

9. An important policy concern is that government assistance, once given, is difficult to withhold. In this regard, the U.S. and Japanese policy record is mixed. In the United States, there is evidence that many industries covered by safeguard actions successfully downsized and "graduated," in the sense of not requiring further assistance. Special protection for other troubled industries, such as textiles and steel, however, have been longer lasting. In Japan, since the late 1970s, the scope of industries covered by "temporary" restructuring measures has expanded greatly. While several have graduated, many industries continue to be designated for assistance under subsequent laws, and new industries are added. The 1988 law shifted the focus from designated industries to specific types of machinery to be scrapped, but these cover many of the same industries from the previous five-year program. Furthermore, region-based assistance programs have now been made a permanent part of this law (see Sekiguchi, Chapter 6).

10. Policies in both countries are potentially open to abuse by industries seeking to preserve monopoly "rents." In Japan, the cartel laws—to coordinate joint capacity scrapping or to establish joint production and sales companies—provide an environment that is conducive to price-fixing and output restraint by cartel members. Sekiguchi argues that cartels are effective only to the extent that imports can be restrained; the evidence that cartels restrict imports, either directly or indirectly through informal trade barriers, is mixed. Some instances of collusive arrangements with foreign suppliers to restrict imports to Japan have been documented (for example, see Chapter 14).

Similarly, in the United States, the act of filing a petition under the "fair trade" laws (and not the ITC's final determination itself) could have a threatening effect, and may result in tacit collusion with foreign exporters to raise prices and/or reduce output. Extant knowledge about this issue, however, is scanty. Fair trade laws also tend to invite further petitions, directed against other countries and other products not covered by countervailing duties and subsidies. Finally, as has happened with specialty steels, a trade-impacted industry can overwhelm the ITC with the simultaneous filing of a large number of multicountry, multiproduct antidumping petitions, and precipitate intervention by the executive or legislative branches of government.

11. In light of these comparative findings, what can we say about prospects for the future? It is clear that the problems of structural adjustment for troubled industries in Japan and the United States will persist into the 1990s. Furthermore, these problems are likely to increase rather than to diminish. In both countries, a growing number of mature industries will face difficult adjustment problems: from the protracted U.S. recession and the bursting of the Japanese financial "bubble," from diminished exports induced by the worldwide economic slowdown, from relocation of plants offshore to take advantage of low labor costs or to circumvent import restrictions, and from growing import competition by low-cost producers in newly industrialized and developing economies.

12. How policymakers respond to the problems of troubled industries in the two countries will have important implications for U.S.-Japan relations and for the international trading system. Extrapolating current policies into the future, one might expect rising numbers of import relief petitions from U.S. industries, growing demands on the U.S. government to provide (or extend) special protection outside the GATT framework, and increased pressure on foreign governments for more open markets and a "level playing field." In Japan, one might expect adjustment assistance to be provided to a growing number of industrial sectors and depressed regions. As imports encroach on domestic markets, distressed industries will be tempted, increasingly, to emulate the United States and resort to safeguarding and antidumping actions, or to privately negotiated VERs with foreign countries. In 1993, Japan imposed for the first time antidumping duties on more than 100 Chinese ferroalloy exporters. Previous antidumping lawsuits, against South Korea (1982 and 1988) and against Norway and France (1984), were withdrawn after foreign exporters agreed to raise prices or restrict exports to Japan. Both trends, if unchecked, could have a chilling impact on U.S.-Japan relations, on trade with newly industrializing and developing countries, and on the GATT system.

13. What do the comparative findings suggest about U.S. and Japanese policies toward troubled industries? On the broadest level, they suggest that governments have to get their macroeconomic policies right: sound fiscal policies for economic growth, which facilitates restructuring and the transfer of resources to growing sectors; monetary policies consistent with balance-of-payments equilibrium and exchange rates that do not penalize producers; and policies that provide incentives for saving, capital formation, research and development, and worker training.

14. Further, the findings suggest the need for a closer adherence to Organization for Economic Cooperation and Development (OECD) guidelines for "positive adjustment policies"—that is, policies that preserve market competition, that are temporary, that are transparent in their objectives and methods, and that speed up rather than retard adjustment. Measured against this yardstick, the record of both governments is mixed. In the choice of policy instruments, the United States should move away from trade protection toward more domestically oriented policies—targeted subsidies, relaxation of anti-monopoly laws, job search assistance, and worker retraining. Japan's sector-specific policies—capacity reduction cartels and joint-sales arrangements—may encourage collusive activities, and should be accompanied by stronger, and more vigorously enforced, antitrust laws.

**II**
—

**Theoretical Models of Troubled Industries**

# 2

# The Analytics of Industrial Restructuring

## John McMillan

### INTRODUCTION

The decline of industries is nothing novel or unusual; Joseph Schumpeter (1950) emphasized that capitalism is a dynamic process, characterized, in his famous phrase, by a "process of creative destruction." Schumpeter is worth quoting on this point, for he gives an eloquent introduction to the subject of industrial restructuring. Capitalism "is by nature a form or method of economic change and not only never is but never can be stationary. . . . The fundamental impulse that sets and keeps the capitalist engine in motion comes from the new consumers' goods, the new methods of production or transportation, the new markets, the new forms of industrial organization that capitalist enterprise creates." The history of capitalist economies demonstrates a "process of industrial mutation . . . that incessantly revolutionizes the economic structure *from within,* incessantly destroying the old one, incessantly creating the new one" (pp. 82–83, emphasis in the original).

For the economy's resources of capital and labor to be freed to move to new and more productive uses, industries that have lost their competitiveness must be allowed or encouraged to shrink, or even die. The health of any economy depends on the smoothness of interindustry adjustments.

Industrial-organization economists have given much attention to firms' decisions to enter an industry and to the barriers that can hinder entry, but relatively little attention to the concomitant phenomenon of exit. The word "entry" commands numerous page references in the indexes of most indus-trial-organization textbooks; but neither "exit" nor "declining industry" appears there. A small, yet growing theoretical literature exists, however, on declining industries; see the bibliography below.

Theoretical analysis serves two functions for a policy analyst. It can suggest new questions to ask of the data; and it can provide a taxonomy of the issues. This chapter offers an expository survey of the theoretical research on declining industries, focusing on empirical implications. The section that follows consists of a positive analysis, examining the logic of the exit decision. This is succeeded by a normative analysis, developing a classifi-cation of the theoretical rationales for government intervention. The conclu-sions of this chapter are framed as questions for empirical research.

## THE LOGIC OF THE EXIT DECISION

A set of experiments reported in the journal *Animal Behavior* (Baldwin and Meese, 1979) provides a lesson for students of declining industries. Two pigs, one dominant and the other subordinate, were put in a box. A lever located at one end of the box, when pressed, dispensed food at the other end. Thus, the pig that pressed the lever had to run to the other end; by the time it got there, the other pig had eaten some of the food. The dominant pig was able to prevent the subordinate pig from eating any of the food when both were at the food. Which pig would press the lever? The experimenters found that the dominant pig usually pressed the lever. This represented, in fact, rational behavior by each of the pigs. The subordinate pig gained nothing, in return for its effort, if it pressed the lever, yet received some food if it did not. Regardless of what the dominant pig did, the subordinate pig's best action was not to press the lever. Eventually, the dominant pig learned that it would get some food only if it pressed the lever itself. Thus, in this situation, weakness is strength.

Firms in a declining industry are in a similar situation to that of the pigs; each firm would like its competitors to reduce their capacity, just as each pig wants the other to push the lever. As we shall see, there is a sense in which larger firms, like the dominant pig, are relatively disadvantaged. Take the example of a duopolistic industry facing declining demand. The two firms are of different initial sizes. Capacity is maintained by flow cost, which is incurred each period.

First, let us consider a deliberately unrealistic case, in order to develop some feeling for the logic of the exit decision. Following Ghemawat and

Nalebuff (1985), we suppose that exiting is an all-or-nothing situation: each firm must either exit or maintain its existing capacity, bearing in mind that reentry is very costly. Maintenance of capacity is subject to constant returns to scale; that is, the cost of maintaining capacity is proportional to capacity. The two firms are identical except that they have different capacities. Then, as Ghemawat and Nalebuff (1985) indicate, the larger firm exits first.

The logic of this action, which is essentially the same as the logic of the pigs game, is seen by first considering how either firm would behave if it were a monopolist. A monopolist exits rationally at the time when its instantaneous profit turns negative. The larger the firm's capacity, the earlier this time occurs because the combination of capacity-maintenance costs with demand is negatively sloped. Let $t$ denote the time at which the larger firm would exit if it were a monopolist. Now, return to considering our duopolists. Suppose that we have reached time $t$ and that both firms are still producing (although, as we shall see, this situation will not actually be reached). Then, it is rational for the larger firm to exit, since the other firm is producing as well and has already passed the point at which its flow profit is negative. However, the smaller firm knows that its rival is sure to exit at $t$ at the latest. Thus, it knows that if it waits until time $t$, it will become, for a while, a profitable monopolist. The smaller firm, having the lower capacity-maintenance costs, can afford to wait for its larger rival to exit. As a result, the larger firm bears a disproportionate share of the burden of the industry's shrinkage.

Now, change the model by assuming, more realistically, that capacity can be reduced bit by bit. For example, each firm can shrink its capacity when demand declines by shutting down some of its plants. In this case, the larger firm starts to reduce capacity first; when it reaches the capacity of the smaller firm, the two shrink in tandem (Ghemawat and Nalebuff, 1987a; Whinston, 1988). Here, the logic is essentially similar to that of the previous example. To oversimplify the foregoing argument, both firms benefit if either one reduces its capacity. But the bigger firm benefits more, and so has a stronger incentive to shrink.

Three caveats must be added. First, economies of scale in the maintenance of existing capacity provide a force in the opposite direction to this strategic effect, tending to induce early exit of small firms. Thus, if average costs are falling, whether the greater burden of the industry's decline falls on large or on small firms depends on which of the two effects is the more pronounced (Ghemawat and Nalebuff, 1985). Next, the second model assumes that small capacity reductions are feasible. But if the process of capacity reduction consists of closing whole plants, there is an inherent discreteness to capacity reduction. When this discreteness is explicitly accounted for in the modeling, and when plant sizes differ from firm to firm, the clear-cut prediction that the larger firm shrinks first can be overturned; the predicted pattern of industry shrinkage can be quite complex (Whinston, 1988). Finally, the foregoing models assume that industry demand declines continuously and predictably. If, instead, it declines in jumps and randomly, there may be multiple equilibria, in which case either firm might exit first (Huang and Li, 1986; Fine and Li, 1989).[1]

What is the empirical content of these theories of industry decline? The Ghemawat-Nalebuff (1985, 1987a) model and, qualifiedly, the Whinston (1988) model predict that larger firms bear a disproportionate share of the costs of adjustment to declining demand. This is a testable hypothesis. Some empirical examples of this type of behavior from U.S. industry are given by Ghemawat and Nalebuff (1987a). For example, in 1967 the soda-ash industry consisted of five firms. By 1978 only one plant remained. This is consistent with the theory, "First, each of the three multi-plant firms closed a plant before either of the two single-plant firms. Second, none of the five firms dropped out of the market until all firms were down to one plant apiece" (Ghemawat and Nalebuff, 1987a, p. 6). Econometric tests are conducted by Deily (1985), Ghemawat (1985), and Londregan (1986b) (all reported by Ghemawat and Nalebuff, 1987a). In the U.S. integrated steel industry in 1962–79, larger firms invested less in replacement (Deily 1985). In declining industries in the U.S. primary-metal sector in 1977–82, larger firms shrunk proportionately faster than smaller firms (Londregan, 1986b). And in U.S. manufacturing (generally in 1967–77), declines in industry output were associated positively with decreases in industrial concentration (Ghemawat, 1985).

Whinston (1988), however, offers an empirical counterexample to the Ghemawat-Nalebuff theory. In the U.S. lead-based-gasoline antiknock-additive industry's post-1975 decline, the two smallest firms were the first to exit. Another counterexample may be the U.S. automobile industry, in which the two smallest firms, American Motors and Chrysler, suffered from the decline in the domestic industry's demand. A study by Lieberman (1989) of the U.S. chemical industry offers mixed support for this theory. On one hand, consistent with the theory, among those firms that stayed in the industry, larger firms cut more capacity than smaller firms did. On the other hand, smaller firms were disproportionately among those that exited. The latter finding can be explained on efficiency grounds: the smallest firms are likely to have the highest costs.

The Japanese shipbuilding industry faced a collapse of world demand in the 1970s. The Ministry of Transport (MOT) designed a stabilization plan for the industry based on a ten-year forecast of demand. According to Uekusa (1987, p. 495),

The MOT's capacity reduction plan called for the 61 companies with docks able to build ships over 5,000 GT [gross tons] to dispose of 35 percent of their total capacity. Because of differences in the disposal ratio, the seven largest companies would dispose of 40 percent, the 17 larger medium-size companies of 30 percent, the 16 smaller medium-size companies of 27 percent, and the other 21 smaller companies of 15 percent. The companies involved agreed to these ratios.

Thus, bigger firms were expected to shrink proportionately more than smaller firms. This does not provide a literal test of the Ghemawat-Nalebuff model, because that model depicts firms' voluntary adjustments in the absence of government intervention. Some indirect corroboration is provided by this case, however, because the MOT's plan actually worked. By 1982, four years after the plan was implemented, the industry as a whole had scrapped 5 percent *more* capacity than the plan required. The largest companies shrank by 99 percent of the amount the plan called for and the larger medium-sized and smaller medium-sized companies by 119 percent of the planned shrinkage. Only the group of the 21 smallest companies shrank by significantly less than required by the plan, reducing their capacity by 81 percent of the planned amount (despite the fact that their assigned shrinkage rate was by far the smallest). Evidently, the pattern of shrinkage mandated by the MOT, with the largest firms shrinking the most, was not inconsistent with each firm's perception of its self-interest. Furthermore, although the plan was formally the MOT's, it was initiated by the firms themselves and, at least to some extent, reflected the firms' own wishes.

## RATIONALES FOR GOVERNMENT INTERVENTION

To move from positive to normative analysis, what justifies active public policy toward declining industries? And what does economic theory suggest are the most effective policies?

Adam Smith, in his most often-quoted passage, argues that the price system can serve, like an invisible hand, to align individuals' self-interests with the interest of society as a whole. One of the most impressive findings of modern economic theory is the Fundamental Theorem of Welfare Economics, which shows a precise, albeit special, sense in which Smith's insight is logically valid. This theorem explains that under certain precisely specified conditions, a laissez-faire economy will reach a Pareto-efficient outcome, that is, a situation such that no citizen can be made better off without some other being made worse off (Debreu, 1959, Chapter 6). In showing elegantly the remarkable ability of the price system to coordinate the separate decisions of millions of individuals, this theorem reveals simultaneously the limits of the market mechanism. This theorem holds under certain assumptions, which essentially define a frictionless market. To the extent that these assumptions are not satisfied by an actual economy, the presumption that the market works efficiently breaks down; thus, the theorem provides a prima facie case for government intervention to improve the market's performance.[2]

Various kinds of distortions affect declining industries and conceivably prevent the market from achieving an efficient transition. The theory of welfare economics suggests several potential justifications for government policy toward declining industries, including the existence of market imperfections such as: inadequate mobility of capital, stickiness of factor prices, distortive taxation, and the oligopolistic nature of the declining industry; the government's acting as insurer against economy-wide risks; and the perception that a laissez-faire economy would produce an unfair distribution of income. I shall examine these rationales for government intervention in turn.

### Labor-Market Distortions

The market that looks the least like the frictionless markets posited in the Fundamental Theorem of Welfare Economics is the labor market. Because wages are sticky and/or displaced workers face high search costs for new jobs, there can be excessive unemployment, either temporary or permanent. Neary (1982) models the case of sticky wages and shows, by a standard second-best argument, that this distortion can be addressed by government intervention in the labor market in the form of adjustment assistance. Diamond (1984) and Howitt and McAfee (1987) show that when workers displaced from a declining industry face search costs for new jobs and when firms in the expanding industries face costs of recruiting workers, there is an externality. Agents on one side of the market would benefit if the agents on the other side searched more intensely, but none of the agents has an incentive to consider the benefits that their search decisions convey to the agents on the other side. As a result, too little search takes place. The free-market equilibrium occurs at a level of aggregate economic activity. This model suggests, therefore, there is a role for government policy to move the economy away from Pareto-dominated equilibria.

Riordan and Staiger (1988) develop a model in which the labor-market distortions are still more severe. Current employers are modeled as better informed than potential employers about individual workers' productivities.

As a result, workers who are laid off from a declining industry may not be rehired. There is an adverse-selection problem. Higher-quality workers who are laid off cannot prove their quality to potential employers; an employer cannot distinguish between lazy and unlucky, unemployed workers. Thus, the shrinkage of an industry creates unemployment that is structural rather than transitory. In the Riordan-Staiger model, this adverse-selection problem is mitigated by a government provision of adjustment assistance for workers who leave the declining industry.

Japanese policies may mitigate this adverse-selection problem. When the steel industry contracted, Nippon Steel moved into the leisure industry, retraining its existing work force. Its workers were not forced to go into the labor market in order to move from the declining sector to the expanding sector; therefore, they escaped the stigma of unemployment.

### Capital-Market Distortions

Another possible source of market imperfections is the capital market. Mussa (1982) models capital as being immobile in the short run, but mobile, with an adjustment cost, in the long run. He isolates three potential sources of the market's failure to induce the optimal rate of capital movement out of the declining industry and into other activities. First, some distortion might affect the price of labor or capital services, such as a tax on factor income. In this case, an optimal intervention takes the form of the government's granting of an investment tax credit for adjustment costs. Second, there could be a divergence between private and social discount rates. It might be, for example, that the market places too little weight on the interests of future generations. Optimal policy, in this case, would be some government subsidy to capital movements. Third, capital owners may have irrational expectations about future benefits from the capital movement. This, however, seems to be a tenuous basis for policy, unless some convincing argument can be found for why the government is better informed than the private sector about future profitability.

### Imperfect-Competition Distortions

For another example of market imperfection, we consider the effects if the declining industry is oligopolistic. Ghemawat and Nalebuff (1987b) (see also Terasawa and Gates, 1994) develop a model of an industry consisting of two firms; because demand has already declined, there is excess capacity. Each firm can produce, at constant returns to scale, up to its capacity limit; one firm has a lower average cost than the other. In a laissez-faire equilibrium of this depressed industry, it can be shown that both firms are producing, but each has excess capacity.

Consider two measures of efficiency. *Allocative efficiency* is the familiar notion of efficiency, measuring, for example, the losses in consumer welfare from a monopolistically low output. *Technical efficiency* measures whether any given output level is produced at minimum possible cost. An immediate result in the Ghemawat-Nalebuff model is that the laissez-faire outcome is not technically efficient. This is because competitive forces induce both firms to produce less than their capacity. But technical efficiency requires that the more efficient firm produce up to its capacity and that the less efficient firm produce the residual. This suggests a role for government intervention to enhance technical efficiency. What is the best form of intervention?

One policy that is theoretically simple (though not necessarily easy to implement) is targeted subsidies. In particular, Ghemawat and Nalebuff show that technical efficiency is increased (without any loss of allocative efficiency) by a policy that gives the efficient firm a per-unit subsidy and assesses an equal per-unit tax on the inefficient firm.

The political environment, however, may be such that any subsidy must be offered equally to all firms. Under the assumptions of Ghemawat and Nalebuff, an untargeted subsidy can be shown to decrease technical efficiency. But the untargeted subsidy simultaneously causes industry output to increase. Because the oligopolistic industry produces too little from the perspective of allocative efficiency, the subsidy has the effect of raising allocative efficiency. Thus, the net welfare effect of the untargeted subsidy cannot be predicted by theory. Which effect is the larger in any particular case and whether the net change in welfare is positive are empirical questions.

If the declining industry faces import competition, a tariff in this model has the effect of reducing the technical efficiency of the domestic producers. This happens because the tariff raises the domestic price and thereby reduces purchases of the item. Under the assumptions of this model, the tariff reduces sales of the domestic industry along with sales of imports. Considerations of profit induce the bigger and more efficient domestic firm to cut its output by a bigger proportion than the smaller domestic firm would. This technical-efficiency loss from the tariff adds to the familiar allocative-efficiency loss suffered by the consumers who pay higher prices; so the model predicts an unambiguous welfare loss from the tariff policy. A common U.S. policy toward declining industries is to impose trade restrictions. It is standard in empirical studies of trade restrictions to estimate allocative-efficiency losses.

In addition, the foregoing model suggests that empirical researchers should attempt to estimate the size of the technical-efficiency losses.[3]

The final policy examined by Ghemawat and Nalebuff is the merger of the firms in the troubled industry. Merging increases technical efficiency relative to the laissez-faire situation because the merged firm, unlike the laissez-faire market, produces as much as is feasible in the lowest-cost plant. (Note that this argument does not rely on scale economies.) The merger has an unfortunate allocative-efficiency effect, however; the merged firm might exploit its monopoly position by cutting back production. In the model of Dutz (1988), the industry contains three or more firms. Dutz shows that if demand is low enough for all firms to have excess capacity before a merger, then the technical-efficiency effects outweigh the allocative-efficiency effects, resulting in a desirable merger, from society's perspective. Consequently, when the merged firm decreases its output, the other firms, not party to the merger, increase their outputs, mitigating the allocative distortions from the merger. In a somewhat different model (in which the firms do not have capacity constraints but instead face increasing marginal production costs), McAfee and Williams (1987) develop a simple test for judging whether a proposed merger will increase welfare, based on easily observable variables. In this model, as a result of a merger, industry output falls; output and market share of the nonmerging firms rise; and the merged firm's output is less than the sum of its component firms' former outputs.

According to the analyses of Dutz (1988), Ghemawat and Nalebuff (1987b), and McAfee and Williams (1987), merging the firms in a declining industry increases technical efficiency to the extent that, after a merger, production is shifted into the low-cost plants. The empirical economist investigating the significance of this effect might look for evidence at the size and direction of any post-merger reallocations of production. Dutz (1988) finds case-study evidence that production reallocations following mergers increased technical efficiency in the U.S. steel, railroad, milk, beer, and auto-parts industries. An observable measure of the allocative-efficiency losses from a merger, not examined by Dutz, is any rise in output price and consequent reduction in industry sales following the merger. McAfee and Williams (1987) suggest that the welfare consequences of a merger can be judged by looking at pre-merger prices, demand elasticities, and firms' market shares.

The same issues that mergers present arise when considering the Japanese experience with recession cartels. By using the Dutz, Ghemawat-Nalebuff, or McAfee-Williams model, the effects of a recession cartel on welfare can be deduced from answering the following questions. What reallocations of production among firms followed the formation of a recession cartel? Is there any evidence that recession cartels have shifted production toward the more efficient producers, increasing allocative efficiency? Did the price of the industry's outputs rise, indicating a reduction in quantity consumed and therefore an allocative-efficiency loss? Or was there enough competition from imports to prevent such an allocative-efficiency loss? What was the effect of the recession cartel on market shares both among domestic firms and between the domestic industry and imports?

Mankiw and Whinston (1986) and Whinston (1988) show the existence of another distortion in an imperfectly competitive industry, arising from the logic of the exit decision: firms tend to reduce their capacity too soon. In the case of two firms (one larger than the other), the larger firm exits when the market price just equals its average cost, and then the market price immediately jumps. But social welfare would be higher if the firm stayed in the market a little longer. This is illustrated by an example from Tirole (1988, p. 313). Suppose that there are two consumers, each desiring only one unit of the item per time period, and valuing the item at $V_1$ and $V_2$, respectively, with $V_1 < V_2$. If $V_2$ is sufficiently larger than $V_1$ (specifically, $V_2 > 2V_1$), then the firm that remains a monopolist after its rival has exited maximizes its profit per period by charging a price equal to $V_2$ and, as a result, selling only to the high-valuation consumer. Charging $V_1$ and servicing both consumers would maximize social welfare, but since the monopolist (assumed to be unable to price-discriminate) would then capture only part of the consumer surplus, it has no incentive to do so. Provided that the flow cost of maintaining capacity is low enough, the social-welfare calculation calls for a later exit than the private-profit calculation induces. In principle, a subsidy offered to the firm that would otherwise exit could be used to correct this early exit bias. Price rises following the exit of firms are partial evidence of such an effect.

## Insurance and Redistribution

Still another rationale for government intervention is the government's acting as insurer against economy-wide risks (Dixit, 1987; Grossman and Eaton, 1985; Hillman, 1977; Newbery and Stiglitz, 1984). Workers and shareholders are risk-averse, so it is efficient to shelter them from any risks associated with changes in competitiveness across industries. Insurance, however, raises the problems of adverse selection and moral hazard: that is, any provision of insurance changes the insuree's incentives. Private insurance markets, as a result, may not be effective in coping with these risks. Thus, a government policy of routinely bearing some of the adjustment costs might be justified on insurance grounds. Such an argument, however, must face up to the fact that the government itself, like private insurers, is subject to moral hazard and adverse selection.

An important caveat to the Fundamental Theorem of Welfare Economics is that Pareto efficiency is a very limited welfare criterion. Many different outcomes are Pareto-efficient, including some that have quite inegalitarian distributions of income. Even if the market works without friction of any kind, so that Pareto efficiency is achieved, society may choose to overrule the market, on the grounds that the outcome generated, although Pareto-efficient, is unfair. People are harmed by the decline of an industry. The equity argument for policy toward declining industries is examined by Aho and Bayard (1984) and Diamond (1982). If workers in the declining industry are generally poorer than taxpayers (although Aho and Bayard question the empirical validity of this assumption), then there may be an equity argument for subsidies to redistribute income. There is, however, a trade-off between equity and efficiency. If the declining industry is subsidized, the firm's exit decisions are distorted, and exit from the industry is inefficiently reduced. If the workers' moving costs are subsidized, an inefficiently large number of workers will exit from the industry.

## Limits to Intervention

So far, we have examined only the potential benefits of government intervention; we must also note that there are costs, which can be large. Intervention can distort incentives; aid for firms and/or workers in declining industries may reduce their incentives to make the appropriate adjustments. Since any firm is likely to be better informed of the day-to-day details of its costs and demands than the government, the general theory of government regulation (Baron 1988) illustrates the limits of government policy—that the government does not have all the information it needs to design the ideal policy. This means that some of the prescriptions that emerge from the above-cited models, based on the unrealistic assumption that the policy's designer has all necessary information, cannot be implemented in practice. Before they can provide a sound basis for policy advice, the models need to be extended to account explicitly for any disparity in information between the government and the firms. Undoubtedly, such a modeling exercise will reveal that certain policies are not *incentive-compatible;* that is, the firms can use their informational advantages essentially to subvert the policies (McMillan, 1989).

Finally, to revert from normative to positive analysis, government policy in practice reflects political realities more than it reflects the ideals of welfare economics. The political economy of intervention in declining industries (the incentives of political actors) must be examined for any study to be policy-relevant. This is, of course, not unrelated to the point made above about the redistributional consequences of any policies toward industry; the potential gainers and losers from alternative policies can be expected to engage in political activity over the choice of policy (compare Aho and Bayard, 1984; Bhagwati, 1982; Feenstra and Lewis, 1991; Hillman, 1982; Hillman and Urspring, 1988).

The various arguments summarized in this section show that a theorist may easily construct a long list of theoretically valid reasons why an adjustment mediated by market forces might be suboptimal and, therefore, why government policy toward declining industries may be warranted. But the more important and challenging question about rationales for government intervention is empirical, not theoretical: how large are the distortions? Theory cannot establish whether any particular market failure is large enough to warrant that the benefits of government intervention outweigh the costs.[4] Also, theory shows that it is important to be specific about the rationale for intervention in any particular case because the appropriate policy varies according to why the intervention is needed. Some existing policies are directed at labor, others at capital (see Sekiguchi, 1994, and Tan, 1994, on Japanese and U.S. policies, respectively).

In practice, which of the many foregoing rationales for intervention are the most significant? In the absence of rigorous empirical studies of the sort just advocated, casual empiricism suggests that the two leading sources of market failure would seem to be labor-market friction and technical inefficiency arising from the incomplete use of productive capacity. Labor-market friction implies government provision of some form of adjustment assistance for workers. Technical inefficiency perhaps indicates the use of Japanese-style recession cartels or some relaxation of antitrust prohibitions of mergers, provided that the import share of the domestic market is large enough to protect consumers against monopolistic pricing by the domestic industry.

Finally, I should note that in practice, much of the adjustment that takes place in any market economy is mediated successfully by the market. Despite the foregoing arguments for intervention, changes in relative prices do induce resources to move to more productive uses.

## CONCLUSION

Theoretical analysis can raise questions, but these questions must be answered by detailed empirical analysis before the exercise becomes policy-relevant. In the descriptive theories of the exit decision discussed above, the precise phasing of the exit process depends on details of the modeling assumptions. But the following broad conclusion seems to hold: larger firms are relatively disadvantaged during the process of industry decline. This suggests some questions for the empirical researcher. What in fact has been the pattern of exit in past cases of industrial decline? In the absence of government intervention, do larger firms choose to decline faster than smaller firms, as theory predicts? If so, what does this suggest about the type of government policy to be applied to current or future declining industries, given that any policy seriously at odds with the firms' interests is likely to fail?

The prescriptive analyses provided in the text serve to narrow the focus of the empirical researcher's questions about the rationale for government intervention in any particular industry. In precisely what respect, if any, is the price system sending firms and/or workers the wrong signals? Which, if any, of the rationales for intervention provided here applies in this case? Does assisting the industry necessarily mean harming consumers? How great are the potential benefits and costs from government intervention in this industry? Do the benefits outweigh the costs? What is the most   direct and cost-efficient way to address this particular distortion? Asking these questions about policies implemented in the past might help improve policy design for the future.

---

### NOTES

1. The models assume that costs depend only on capacity. In practice, some firms are inherently more efficient than others. Moreover, if firms do differ, then each is likely to be better informed about its own costs than about its rivals' costs. The effects on the exit decision of cost information being private are modeled by Fudenberg and Tirole (1986). (See also Tirole, 1988, pp. 380–384; and Wilson, 1988.) Assume that each firm has economies of scale in production due to a fixed cost incurred in each period that production takes place, the size of which is known only to the firm itself. Because of a decline in industry demand, the fixed costs are now so high, relative to demand, that it is unprofitable for both firms to be active; the industry has become a natural monopoly. A war of attrition results, with both firms losing money until one leaves. Fudenberg and Tirole show that this Darwinian competition succeeds in selecting the efficient firm: the higher-cost firm rationally exits first. But because it does not know its rival's cost, it engages for some time in mutually damaging competition in the hope that it will be the firm that survives to earn the monopoly profits. Suffering these losses is the only way the low-cost firm can credibly establish its cost advantage: if, for

example, the firms tried to negotiate which would remain in the market, each would have an incentive to exaggerate its own efficiency. The Ghemawat-Nalebuff and Whinston models, in contrast, assume that the firms know each others' costs, so they have no incentive to continue producing after their instantaneous profits become negative. Models examining other aspects of the strategy of exit are Caves and Porter (1976), Eaton and Lipsey (1980), Frank (1988), Friedman (1979), Londregan (1986a), and Porter (1980).

2. The prima facie caveat should be stressed: whether the benefits from intervention outweigh the cost in any particular case cannot be established by theoretical arguments but only by a detailed examination of the facts.

3. The allocative-efficiency losses alone can be startlingly high. A U.S. Federal Trade Commission study, for example, estimates the annual cost to the United States of its own trade restrictions to be almost $13 billion. Automobile quotas cost an estimated $200,000 per job saved; textile quotas $40,000 per job saved; and steel quotas $80,000 per job saved (Tarr and Morkre, 1984).

4. Techniques for measuring distortions have been developed by Shoven and Whalley (1984).

## BIBLIOGRAPHY

Aho, Michael C., and Thomas O. Bayard (1984). "Costs and Benefits of Trade Adjustment Assistance," in R. Baldwin and A. R. Krueger (eds.), *The Structure and Evolution of Recent U.S. Trade Policy.* Chicago: University of Chicago Press.

Baldwin, B. A., and G. B. Meese (1979). "Social Behavior in Pigs Studied by Means of Operant Conditioning." *Animal Behavior* 27: 947–957.

Baron, D. (1988). "Design of Regulatory Mechanisms and Institutions," in R. Schmalensee and R. Willig (eds.), *Handbook of Industrial Organization.* Amsterdam: North-Holland.

Bhagwati, J. (1982). "Shifting Comparative Advantage, Protectionist Demands, and Policy Response," in J. Bhagwati (ed.), *Import Competition and Response.* Chicago: University of Chicago Press.

Caves, R., and M. Porter (1976). "Barriers to Exit," in R. Masson and D. Qualls (eds.), *Essays on Industrial Organization in Honor of Joe Bain.* Cambridge, Mass.: Ballinger.

Debreu, G. (1959). *Theory of Value: An Axiomatic Analysis of Economic Equilibrium.* New Haven: Yale University Press.

Deily, M. E. (1985). "Capacity Reduction in the Steel Industry." Ph.D. dissertation, Harvard Business School.

Diamond, P. A. (1982). "Protection, Trade Adjustment Assistance, and Income Distribution," in J. Bhagwati (ed.), *Import Competition and Response*. Chicago: University of Chicago Press.

——— (1984). *A Search Theoretic Approach to the Micro Foundations of Macroeconomics*. Cambridge, Mass.: MIT Press.

Dixit, A. (1987). "Trade and Insurance with Moral Hazard." *Journal of International Economics* 23: 201–220.

Dutz, M. A. (1988). "Horizontal Mergers in a Declining Industry: Theory and Evidence." Unpublished paper, Princeton University.

Eaton, B. C., and R. G. Lipsey (1980). "Entry Barriers Are Exit Barriers: The Durability of Capital as a Barrier to Entry." *Bell Journal of Economics* 11: 721–729.

Feenstra, R. C., and T. R. Lewis (1991). "Negotiated Trade Restrictions with Private Political Pressure." *Quarterly Journal of Economics* 106: 1287–1308.

Fine, C., and L. Li (1989). "A Stochastic Theory of Exit and Stopping Time Equilibria." *Games and Economic Behavior* 1: 40–59.

Frank, M. Z. (1988). "An Intertemporal Model of Industrial Exit." *Quarterly Journal of Economics* 103: 333–344.

Friedman, J. W. (1979). "Noncooperative Equilibria for Exit Supergames." *International Economic Review* 20: 147–156.

——— (1983). *Oligopoly Theory*. Cambridge: Cambridge University Press.

Fudenberg, D., and J. Tirole (1983). "Capital as Commitment: Strategic Investment to Deter Mobility." *Journal of Economic Theory* 31: 227–250.

——— (1986). "A Theory of Exit in Duopoly." *Econometrica* 54: 943–961.

Ghemawat, P. (1985). "Concentration in Decline." Unpublished paper, Graduate School of Business Administration, Harvard University.

Ghemawat, P., and B. Nalebuff (1985). "Exit." *RAND Journal of Economics* 16: 184–194.

——— (1987a). "The Devolution of Declining Industries." Woodrow Wilson School Discussion Paper 120, Princeton University.

——— (1987b). "Excess Capacity, Efficiency, and Industrial Policy." Woodrow Wilson School Discussion Paper 134, Princeton University.

Gray, H. Peter (1973). "Senile Industry Protection: A Proposal." *Southern Economic Journal* 40 (April): 569–574.

Grossman, G. M., and J. Eaton (1985). "Tariffs as Insurance: Optimal Commercial Policy When Domestic Markets Are Incomplete." *Canadian Journal of Economics* 18: 258–272.

Hillman, A. L. (1977). "The Case for Terminal Protection for Declining Industries." *Southern Economic Journal* 44: 155–160.

——— (1982). "Declining Industries and Political-Support Protectionist Motives." *American Economic Review* 72: 1180–1187.

Hillman, A. L., and H. W. Urspring (1988). "Domestic Politics, Foreign Interests, and International Trade Policy." *American Economic Review* 78: 729–744.

Howitt, P., and R. P. McAfee (1987). "Costly Search and Recruiting." *International Economic Review* 28: 89–107.

Hopenhayn, H. (1986). "A Competitive Stochastic Model of Entry and Exit to an Industry." Paper, University of Minnesota.

Huang, C. F., and Lode Li (1986). "Continuous Time Stopping Games." Working Paper 1796–86, Sloan School of Management, Massachusetts Institute of Technology.

Kreps, D., and J. Scheinkman (1983). "Quantity Precommitment and Bertrand Competition Yield Cournot Outcomes." *Bell Journal of Economics* 14: 326–337.

Kreps, D., and A. M. Spence (1984). "Modeling the Role of History in Industrial Organization," in G. Fiewel (ed.), *Contemporary Issues in Modern Microeconomics*. London: Macmillan.

Lieberman, M. B. (1989). "Exit from Declining Industries: 'Shakeout' or 'Stakeout'?" Research Paper No. 1043, Graduate School of Business, Stanford University.

Londregan, J. (1986a). "Entry and Exit over the Industry Life Cycle." Paper, Princeton University.

——— (1986b). "Essays on the Industry Life Cycle." Ph.D. dissertation, Princeton University.

Mankiw, N. G., and M. D. Whinston (1986). "Free Entry and Social Inefficiency." *RAND Journal of Economics* 17: 48–58.

McAfee, R. P., and M. A. Williams (1987). "Horizontal Mergers and Antitrust Policy." Unpublished paper, U.S. Department of Justice.

McMillan, J. (1989). "Adverse Selection and the Limits of Trade Policy," in Ryutaro Komiya (ed.), *Kokusaika suru Kigyo to Sekai Keizai*. Tokyo: Toyo Keizai (in Japanese).

Mussa, M. (1982). "Government Policy and the Adjustment Process," in J. Bhagwati (ed.), *Import Competition and Response*. Chicago: University of Chicago Press.

Neary, J. P. (1982). "Intersectoral Capital Mobility, Wage Stickiness, and the Case for Adjustment Assistance," in J. Bhagwati (ed.), *Import Competition and Response*. Chicago: University of Chicago Press.

Newbery, D. M. G., and J. E. Stiglitz (1984). "Pareto Inferior Trade." *Review of Economic Studies* 51: 1–12.

Porter, M. E. (1980). "Competitive Strategy in Declining Industries," Ch. 12 of *Competitive Strategy*. New York: Free Press.

Riordan, M. H., and R. W. Staiger (1988). "Sectoral Shocks and Structural Unemployment." Unpublished paper, Stanford University.

Schumpeter, J. A. (1950). *Capitalism, Socialism and Democracy,* 3d edition. New York: Harper.

Sekiguchi, Sueo (1994). "An Overview of Adjustment Assistance Policies in Japan," Ch. 6 of this volume.

Sheard, Paul (1987). "How Japanese Firms Manage Adjustment: A Case Study of Aluminum." *Pacific Economic Paper No. 151,* Australia-Japan Research Center, Australian National University.

Shoven, J., and J. Whalley (1984). "Applied General Equilibrium Models of Taxation and International Trade." *Journal of Economic Literature* 22: 1007–1051.

Tan, Hong W. (1994). "Policies toward Troubled Industries in the United States: An Overview," Ch. 5 in this volume.

Tarr, D. G., and M. E. Morkre (1984). *Aggregate Costs to the United States of Tariffs and Quotas on Imports.* Washington, D.C.: Federal Trade Commission.

Terasawa, Katsuaki, and William R. Gates (1994). "Public Policies toward Troubled Industries: A Theoretical Framework," Ch. 3 in this volume.

Tirole, J. (1988). *The Theory of Industrial Organization.* Cambridge, Mass.: MIT Press.

Uekusa, Masu (1987). "Industrial Organization: The 1970s to the Present," in K. Yamamura and Y. Yasuba (eds.), *The Political Economy of Japan.* Stanford: Stanford University Press.

Whinston, M. D. (1988). "Exit with Multiplant Firms." *RAND Journal of Economics* 19: 568–588.

Wilson, Robert (1988). "Entry and Exit," in G. Fiewel (ed.), *Imperfect Competition Revisited.* London: Macmillan.

# 3

## Public Policies toward Troubled Industries: A Theoretical Framework

Katsuaki L. Terasawa and William R. Gates

### INTRODUCTION

**A**s foreign producers capture a growing share of a domestic market, pressure builds for the government to assist troubled domestic producers. Several public policies are available for this purpose; including import price restrictions, import quantity restrictions, domestic production subsidies, and relaxed antitrust enforcement. Different public policies impinge differently on both consumers and producers. These impingements should be considered in selecting appropriate government policies.

Four factors will be considered here: technical efficiency, allocative efficiency, consumer surplus, and producer surplus. Technical efficiency is determined by total industry production costs. It is maximized when industry production costs are minimized for a given level of industry output. Allocative efficiency is determined by total industry output. It is maximized when industry output reaches the level where the price equals industry marginal cost. Consumer surplus is the net value received by consumers from a product (i.e., total value received minus the price paid). Consumer value is measured graphically as the area under the demand curve. Thus, consumer surplus is the area between the demand curve and a horizontal line denoting market price as output varies from zero to the total quantity consumed. Finally, producer surplus is revenue minus variable operating costs, measured as the area between curves representing market price and marginal operating costs as output varies from zero to the total quantity consumed. If the number of firms is constant, producer surplus increases with technical efficiency. All four of these factors should be considered in selecting public policies.

This chapter examines a simple oligopolistic industry model that can evaluate public policies supporting troubled industries. The model can analyze the impact of public policies on allocative efficiency, technical efficiency, and consumer and producer surplus. The model features Nash firms with excess capacity and diverse production costs, as in the framework developed by Ghemawat and Nalebuff (1987).[1] It also incorporates the impact of new entry and cost reducing technical changes (resulting from research and development).

The model characteristics are summarized in the following section. The chapter then examines market equilibrium in the absence of government intervention, and the impact of entry on allocative and technical efficiency. Against this background, public policies in support of troubled industries are analyzed; including import price and import quantity restrictions, domestic production subsidies (embracing direct price subsidies and publicly funded research), and relaxed antitrust enforcement. Combinations of these policies are considered in an attempt to identify a "preferred" policy option. Next, government policies are evaluated for both allocative and technical efficiency, as well as for their distributional effects on consumer and producer welfare. Distributional issues affect equity, which in turn affects political feasibility. We offer preliminary conclusions in the final sections.

## THE MODEL

Consider an industry with n firms. Each firm's total cost is a function of output, $q_i$. For simplicity, assume that each firm's total cost $C_i(q_i)$, is linear in output, $q_i$, for $i = 1, 2, ..., n$. Thus,

$$C_i(q_i) = c_i \cdot q_i \qquad q_i \in [0, k_i] \qquad (1)$$

where $c_i$ is Firm i's constant marginal cost and $k_i$ is a capacity limit. For expositional clarity, firms are ranked by technical efficiency. Relative technical efficiency is determined by relative marginal cost. More efficient firms have a lower index number. Thus, Firm 1 is the most technically efficient producer, Firm n is the least technically efficient. In other words, $c_i \leq c_{i+1}$ for $i = 1, ..., n-1$. Finally, the industry's technical efficiency can be measured by average industry production costs because there are no fixed production costs.

Consumer demand is given by an inverse demand function:

$$P = P(Q) \tag{2}$$

where P denotes market price and Q is total domestic industry output $(Q = \sum_{i=1}^{n} q_i)$.     Demand is price-sensitive and sufficient to support n firms. Thus

$$dP(Q) / dQ < 0 \tag{3a}$$

$$\lim_{Q \to 0} P(Q) > c_n \tag{3b}$$

Several constraints are imposed on costs and demand to ensure that the industry has the desired properties. First, the capacity restriction, $k_i$, ensures excess capacity. If all firms produce up to their capacity, market price drops below marginal cost for all firms. Mathematically,

$$P\left(\sum_{i=1}^{n} k_i\right) < c_1 \tag{4a}$$

At this price, production is infeasible for even the most efficient firm. Second, Hahn's stability condition is imposed to guarantee a well-behaved noncooperative equilibrium.[2] Specifically,

$$dP(Q) / dq_i + q_i\left(d^2 P(Q)/dq_i^2\right) \le 0, \quad i = 1, ..., n \tag{4b}$$

Finally, the following demand/cost conditions are assumed to ensure that n firms are active in the market:[3]

$$P(Q[i]) > c_{i+1}$$

$$P(Q[n]) < c_{n+1} \qquad\qquad i = 1, ..., n-1 \tag{4c}$$

where $Q[i] = \sum_{j=1}^{i} q_j$ is the sum of outputs for Firms 1 through i, and $P(Q[i])$ is the equilibrium industry price (with $n = i$).

Conditions (4a) through (4c) ensure that profit maximization leads to a stable n-firm equilibrium, and that the industry has excess capacity. To illustrate, assume that n is greater than two. Condition (4c) precludes any equilibrium based on fewer than n firms. If $i = 1$, there is a monopoly. The monopoly price is $P(Q[1])$, where [1] denotes the single-firm case. However, $P(Q[1]) > c_2$ for $n > 1$, according to Eq. (4c). Thus, Firm 1 cannot charge the monopoly price without losing the entire market to Firm 2. Similarly, Firms 1 and 2 cannot charge the duopoly price $P(Q[2])$—where [2] denotes the two-firm case—without losing the market to Firm 3. This process continues until there are n active firms, and $P(Q[n])$ is the equilibrium market price. Conditions (4a) and (4b), respectively, ensure that this equilibrium involves excess industry capacity and is stable.

With excess production capacity, the actual industry marginal cost curve is higher than it would be if all firms produced to their capacity. Thus, actual output is less than the output that maximizes allocative efficiency and consumer surplus. In this case, increases in industry output raise both allocative efficiency and consumer surplus.

## MARKET EQUILIBRIUM WITHOUT GOVERNMENT INTERVENTION

Under the assumptions in the previous section, a unique equilibrium exists where firms independently choose their output, assuming that the other firms' output is fixed. Firm i's problem is to choose its profit-maximizing output level, $q_i$.[4] Firm i's decision can be characterized as maximizing:

$$\pi_i = P(Q) \cdot q_i - c_i \cdot q_i \qquad (5)$$

The first- and second-order conditions for profit maximization are:

$$P(Q) + P'(Q) \cdot q_i = c_i \qquad (6a)$$

$$2P'(Q) + P''(Q) \cdot q_i < 0 \qquad (6b)$$

Assuming that Hahn's stability condition (4b) is satisfied, equilibrium industry output is derived by summing Eq. (6a) over all n firms. This yields:

$$n \cdot P(Q) + Q \cdot P'(Q) = C \qquad (7)$$

where C is the sum of marginal costs across the n firms, $C = \sum_{i=1}^{n} c_i$

Figure 3.1 illustrates graphically condition (7) for n = 1, 2, and 3. If n = 1, the firm is a monopolist. To maximize profits, the monopolist produces where its marginal cost equals the industry marginal revenue (i.e., $P(Q) + P'(Q) \cdot Q = C = c_1$). In Figure 3.1(A), the monopoly price and output are given by P[1] and Q[1], respectively.

With n = 2, marginal revenue for both firms is determined by the total output from both firms. Furthermore, as one firm changes its output, the other firm responds by changing its output as well. Each firm's marginal revenue must include the impact of changes in both firms' outputs on industry price. As indicated by Eq. (7), this occurs where $2P(Q) + P'(Q) \cdot Q = C = c_1 + c_2$. In Figure 3.1(B), the duopoly price and output are given by P[2] and Q[2], respectively. The outputs for Firms 1 and 2 are indicated by $q_1[2]$ and $q_2[2]$, respectively.

As discussed below under "Effects of New Entry," industry output increases when the second firm enters the industry (Q[2] > Q[1]), lowering industry price. As industry price drops, Firm 1 will reduce its output ($q_1[1]$ > $q_1[2]$). The second firm's output is the sum of these two effects (i.e., $q_2[2] = \{Q[2] - Q[1]\} + \{q_1[1] - q_1[2]\}$). Figure 3.1(C) indicates that this pattern continues when n = 3. P[3] and Q[3] denote the three-firm equilibrium industry price and output, while $q_1[3]$, $q_2[3]$, and $q_3[3]$ denote the output for Firms 1, 2, and 3, respectively.

## Allocative and Technical Efficiency: Consumer and Producer Surplus

If marginal costs are constant, a mean-preserving change in costs across firms will not change total industry output.[5] This is illustrated by Eq. (7). Industry output is determined by C, the sum of the firms' marginal costs. A mean-preserving change in the firms' marginal costs, $c_i$, will not affect the sum of the marginal costs, so long as the number of active firms does not change. Thus, industry output is unaffected. For example, suppose that n = 2. A change in the distribution of marginal costs from $c_1 = 2$, $c_2 = 5$ to $c_1 = 3$, $c_2 = 4$ will not change the mean (3.5) or sum (7) of the marginal costs. Thus, total industry output and price remain the same. If total output does not change, the level of allocative efficiency and consumer surplus does not change either.

In contrast to allocative efficiency, technical efficiency and producer surplus are affected by mean-preserving changes in firms' costs. A firm's output is determined by market price and the firm's marginal cost. A change in the firm's marginal cost changes its output, even if industry output and price are unaffected.

This is illustrated by rearranging Eq. (6a):

$$q_i = (P(Q) - c_i) / (-P'(Q)) \qquad (6a')$$

Given the industry output ($Q$) and price ($P(Q)$), Firm $i$'s output is determined by its marginal cost ($c_i$). Its output will be larger as its marginal costs decrease, and smaller as its marginal costs increase. Thus, the distribution of output across firms is affected by the distribution of marginal costs across firms. Technical efficiency and producer surplus are determined, in part, by the distribution of output across firms. Thus, they are both affected by the distribution of marginal costs.

Among cost distributions with the same mean ($C/n$), technical efficiency and producer surplus are maximized by maximizing $\sum c_i^2$, the sum of the squared marginal costs.[6] For example, consider three cost distributions A = (1, 3, 5), B = (1.1, 2, 5.9), and C = (3, 3, 3). Distribution A, with the squared sum of 35, is more efficient than C, with the squared sum of 27. Distribution B, with the squared sum of 40, is more efficient than A. In fact, B is the most efficient distribution.

These observations have obvious policy implications. In choosing among policy alternatives that shift the cost distribution, the alternative that minimizes the sum of marginal costs is the most effective at increasing allocative efficiency and consumer surplus. Moreover, if the alternative policies all result in the same level of allocative efficiency (i.e., if $C = \sum c_i$ is the same), then the policy that maximizes the sum of the squared marginal costs has the highest technical efficiency and producer surplus.

## EFFECTS OF NEW ENTRY

To provide a framework for analyzing policies to support troubled industries, it is useful to understand the effects of entry by new foreign producers and domestic competitors on domestic markets. In particular, what impact does domestic and foreign entry have on efficiency and surplus value?

### Figure 3.1
### Equilibrium industry output

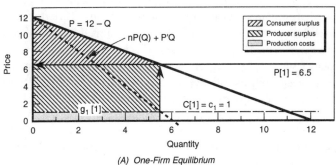

*(A) One-Firm Equilibrium*

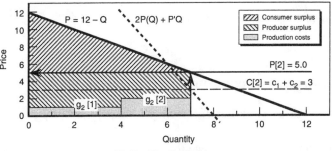

*(B) Two-Firm Equilibrium*

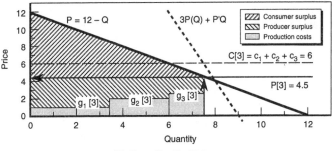

*(C) Three-Firm Equilibrium*

## Domestic Entry, Allocative Efficiency, and Consumer Surplus

First, consider the effects on allocative efficiency and consumer surplus when a new domestic firm enters the industry. The impact of entry is determined by the interaction of supply and demand. If industry output increases and demand is downward-sloping, market price decreases. This increases allocative efficiency and consumer surplus. Alternatively, if entry reduces industry output, market price increases and both allocative efficiency and consumer surplus decrease.

To determine the impact of entry on industry output, consider the case where the entrant is the least efficient (marginal) firm.[7] For a firm to enter an industry, its marginal cost ($c_e$) must be lower than the prevailing price (i.e., $c_e < P[n]$, where there are n firms). If the new entrant is the marginal firm, the entrant's marginal cost must satisfy :

$$P(Q[n]) > c_e = c_n \qquad (8a)$$

From Eq. (7), the n-firm (pre-entry) equilibrium output is:

$$n \cdot P(Q[n]) + P'(Q[n]) \cdot Q[n] = C[n] \qquad (8b)$$

Similarly, the n + 1 firm (post-entry) equilibrium output is:

$$(n + 1) \cdot P(Q[n+1]) + P'(Q[n+1]) \cdot Q[n+1] = C[n] + c_e \qquad (8c)$$

Combining Eqs. (8a), (8b), and (8c) yields:

$$n \cdot P(Q[n]) + P'(Q[n]) \cdot Q[n] > \qquad (8d)$$
$$n \cdot P(Q[n+1]) + P'(Q[n+1]) \cdot Q[n+1] + \{P(Q[n+1]) - P(Q[n])\}$$

$Q[n]$ can be compared with $Q[n+1]$ to determine the impact of entry on industry output. Suppose that $Q[n] = Q[n+1]$; then the right- and left-hand sides of Eq. (8d) are equal, contradicting the inequality. Thus, $Q[n] \neq Q[n+1]$. Alternatively, suppose that $Q[n] > Q[n+1]$. With downward-sloping demand, this implies that $P(Q[n+1]) > P(Q[n])$. In this case, the square-bracketed term would be positive. Moreover, the second-order condition for profit maximization requires that $d[n \cdot P(Q[n]) + P'(Q[n]) \cdot Q[n]] / dQ < 0$. If entry decreases industry output, then the second-order condition implies that

$$n \cdot P(Q[n]) + P'(Q[n]) \cdot Q[n] <$$
$$n \cdot P(Q[n+1]) + P'(Q[n+1]) \cdot Q[n+1]$$

Combining downward-sloping demand and the second-order condition yields:

$$n \cdot P(Q[n]) + P'(Q[n]) \cdot Q[n] <$$
$$n \cdot P(Q[n+1]) + P'(Q[n+1]) \cdot Q[n+1] + \{P(Q[n+1]) - P(Q[n])\}$$

This contradicts the initial assumption. Thus, $Q[n] < Q[n+1]$. As a result, entry increases industry output, reduces market price, and increases both allocative efficiency and consumer surplus.

### Domestic Entry, Technical Efficiency, and Producer Surplus

The impact of entry on technical efficiency and producer surplus is determined by the impact of entry on the output per firm and the relative efficiency of the entrant. If entry causes existing firms to reduce their output, technical efficiency and producer surplus tend to increase if lower-efficiency firms reduce their output proportionally more than higher-efficiency firms. Thus, technical efficiency and producer surplus depend, in part, on the impact of entry on the output per firm. (As discussed below, they also depend on the entrant's efficiency relative to that of existing firms.) Both proportional and absolute reductions in output per firm are considered.

Equation (6a′) can be used to determine the impact of entry on output per firm. This equation relates output per firm to industry price and the firm's marginal costs. In particular, Eq. (6a′) states that $q_i = \{P(Q) - c_i\}/\{-P'(Q)\}$. Differentiating (6a′) with respect to Q shows how an increase in total industry output affects output per firm:

$$dq_i \, / \, dQ = \{-P'(Q)^2 + (P(Q) - c_i)P''(Q)\} \, \{P'(Q)\}^2, \quad i=1, \ldots, n \qquad (9)$$

To sign $dq_i/dQ$, recall Hahn's stability condition: $P'(Q) + P''(Q) \cdot q_i < 0$. This can be rewritten as $P''(Q) < -P'(Q)/q_i$. Substituting (6a′) for $q_i$ in the stability condition yields: $P''(Q) < P(Q)'^2/(P(Q) - c_i)$. Substituting this inequality into Eq. (9) yields $dq_i/dQ < 0$. Thus, domestic entry reduces output per firm. This is consistent with the earlier result showing that entry increases industry output and decreases market price. As price decreases, output per firm should also decrease. The entrant's output comes from a combination of expanded industry output and reduced output per firm.

To examine the impact on output relative to the firm's efficiency, let r be the proportional production cutback:

$$r = [q_i[n] - q_i[n+1]] / q_i[n]$$

Substituting Eq. (6a') into this expression and simplifying yields:

$$r = 1 - \{P'(Q[n]) / P'((Q[n+1])\} \cdot P(Q[n+1]) - c_i\} / (P(Q[n]) - c_i)$$

Differentiating this expression with respect to $c_i$ shows how relative production cutbacks vary with marginal cost (i.e., technical efficiency):

$$dr / dc_i = \{P'(Q[n]) / P'(Q[n+1])\} \cdot P(Q[n])$$
$$- P(Q[n+1])\} / (P(Q[n]) - c_i)^2 \qquad (10)$$

If the demand curve is downward-sloping and $Q[n] < Q[n+1]$, this expression is always positive. Thus, the proportionate production cutback increases with marginal cost. Less efficient firms suffer proportionately greater production cutbacks than more efficient firms.

For reference, Figure 3.2 shows total industry output and output per firm as domestic firms enter the industry. In this figure, industry demand is $P = 12 - Q$ and the firms' costs are $c_1 = 1$, $c_2 = 2$, and $c_i = 3$ for $3 \leq i \leq n$. This figure illustrates that entry increases market output while reducing output per firm. Furthermore, the proportionate decrease in output per firm is larger for the less efficient firms relative to the more efficient firms.

Finally, the size of absolute production cutbacks across firms depends on the convexity of demand in price. To derive this result, let $q_i[n]$, $P(Q[n])$, and $C[n]$ denote the firm output, the industry price, and the total industry cost associated with an n-firm industry. Equation (6a') becomes $q_i[n] = \{P(Q[n]) - c_i\} / \{-P'(Q[n])\}$. This equation can be rewritten to show the $i^{th}$ firm's decrease in output as a domestic firm enters the industry:

$$q_i[n] - q_i[n+1] = \{-P'(Q[n+1]) \cdot (P(Q[n]) - c_i) \qquad (11)$$
$$+ P'(Q[n]) \cdot (P(Q[n+1]) - c_i)\} / \{P' Q[n]) \cdot P'(Q[n+1])\}, i = 1, ..., n$$

A similar relationship pertains to Firm j. To find the relationship between the absolute cutback in production and technical efficiency, the change in production for Firm j can be subtracted from the change in production for Firm i (where i<j). Using Eq. (11) for both Firms i and j yields:

$$\{q_i[n] - q_i[n+1]\} - \{q_j[n] - q_j[n+1]\}$$
$$= (c_j - c_i) \cdot \{P'([n]) - P'(Q[n+1])\} / \{P'(Q[n+1]) \cdot P'(Q(n))\}$$

The sign of the right-hand side (RHS) of this equation depends on the shape of the demand curve. Specifically,

$$\begin{aligned}
\text{RHS} > 0 &\qquad \text{for } P'' < 0 \\
\text{RHS} = 0 &\qquad \text{for } P'' = 0 \qquad\qquad (12)\\
\text{RHS} < 0 &\qquad \text{for } P'' > 0
\end{aligned}$$

Equation (12) states that the absolute reduction in output is larger for the more efficient firms, relative to the less efficient firms, if demand is concave in price. The absolute reduction in output is smaller for the more efficient firms, relative to less efficient firms, if demand is convex in price. Firms reduce output equally, in absolute terms, if demand is linear. In sum, entry reduces output per firm for all firms in the industry. Furthermore, the relative cutbacks are greater for the less efficient firms than for the more efficient firms. Finally, the absolute reduction in output depends on the convexity of the demand curve.

Considering this, the effects on technical efficiency are not clear-cut. The price decline caused by entry forces proportionately more production cutbacks on the less efficient firms. This improves technical efficiency. However, this positive effect must be balanced by the potentially negative effect of the entrant's production. On one hand, if the entrant's marginal cost is higher than that of all existing firms (i.e., if the entrant is the least efficient firm), then technical efficiency clearly suffers. On the other hand, entry improves technical efficiency if the entrant is the most efficient firm. For intermediate cases, technical efficiency depends on the relative magnitudes of these two effects. If the positive effects of larger production cutbacks by the less efficient firms outweigh the negative effects of the new entrant's production, technical efficiency increases. Conversely, if the negative effect outweighs the positive effect, technical efficiency decreases. As explained earlier, the net impact on technical efficiency can be measured by the change in average industry production costs.

Technical efficiency has direct implications for producer surplus. If entry decreases technical efficiency, producer surplus will also decrease. The reverse, however, is not always true—entry also reduces market price. To increase producer surplus, the gains in technical efficiency (decrease in average industry costs) would have to be greater than the decrease in market price.

### Domestic Entry: A Numerical Example

To illustrate this section's results, consider the effects of entry for three different demand curves. In case 1, demand is convex in price (i.e., $P'(Q) <$

**Figure 3.2**
**Entry, industry output, and output per firm**

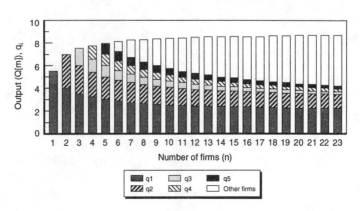

0, and $P''(Q) > 0$). In case 2, demand is linear in price (i.e., $P'(Q) < 0$, and $P''(Q) = 0$). In case 3, demand is concave in price (i.e., $P'(Q) < 0$, and $P''(Q) > 0$). In each case, changes in industry output and price, in firm output and profits, and in average industry costs are calculated as the number of firms expands from $n = 2$ to $n = 3$.

For reference, the numerical examples are summarized in Table 3.1. According to Eq. (8d), entry should increase industry output and reduce market in all cases, thereby increasing both allocative efficiency and consumer surplus. According to Eq. (10), Firm 2 should reduce output proportionally more than Firm 1 in all cases. According to Eq. (12), Firm 2 should reduce output by a greater absolute amount than Firm 1 if demand is convex. The opposite should occur if demand is concave. If demand is linear, the decrease in output should be the same for all firms.[8] Finally, because the entrant is the least efficient firm in all three cases, technical efficiency (average industry cost) and producer surplus (profit) should decrease in all cases. According to Table 3.1, the numerical results verify all of the theoretical predictions.

### Foreign Entry

Foreign competition has exactly the same effect on allocative efficiency and consumer surplus as domestic entry. Foreign entrants improve allocative efficiency and consumer surplus by increasing equilibrium output, which reduces market price. However, in contrast to domestic entrants, foreign competition unambiguously improves domestic technical efficiency. As with

**Table 3.1**
**Numerical results for domestic entry**

| | Case 1 $P = Q^{-1/2}$ | | | Case 2 $P = 12 - Q$ | | | Case 3 $P = (100 - Q^2)^{0.5}$ | | |
|---|---|---|---|---|---|---|---|---|---|
| Demand | | | | | | | | | |
| Shape | Convex | | | Linear | | | Concave | | |
| $c_1^a$ | 0.270 | | | 1.429 | | | 3.534 | | |
| $c_2^a$ | 0.297 | | | 1.571 | | | 3.887 | | |
| $c_3^a$ | 0.324 | | | 1.714 | | | 4.240 | | |
| Entry | Before | After | % Change | Before | After | % Change | Before | After | % Change |
| $Q^b$ | 7 | 7.876 | 13 | 7 | 7.821 | 12 | 7 | 7.454 | 6 |
| $P(Q)$ | 0.378 | 0.356 | − 6 | 5 | 4.179 | −16 | 7.141 | 6.666 | − 7 |
| $q_1^c$ | 4 | 3.818 | − 5 | 3.571 | 2.75 | −23 | 3.68 | 2.8 | −24 |
| $q_2^c$ | 3 | 2.623 | −13 | 3.428 | 2.607 | −24 | 3.320 | 2.484 | −25 |
| $q_3^c$ | — | 1.435 | — | — | 2.464 | — | — | 2.169 | — |
| $\pi_1$ | 0.43 | 0.33 | −24 | 8.58 | 7.01 | −18 | 13.28 | 8.77 | −34 |
| $\pi_2$ | 0.24 | 0.16 | −36 | 4.08 | 3.02 | −26 | 10.8 | 6.9 | −36 |
| $\pi_3$ | — | 0.05 | — | — | 0.72 | — | — | 5.26 | — |
| $\pi_T$ | 0.67 | 0.53 | −21 | 12.66 | 10.74 | −15 | 24.08 | 20.94 | −13 |
| Average cost | 0.282 | 0.289 | 2.6 | 6.691 | 6.848 | 2.4 | 3.702 | 3.858 | 4.2 |

[a] $c_2$ and $c_3$ are set 10 percent and 20 percent above $c_1$, respectively.
[b] From Eq. 7. Parameters are selected so that preentry output is seven in all three cases.
[c] From Eq. 6a.

domestic entry, the price reduction caused by foreign competition forces proportionately more production cutbacks on the less efficient domestic firms. There is, however, no offsetting decrease in domestic technical efficiency from the entrant's production. Thus, domestic technical efficiency improves unambiguously. In fact, the more efficient the foreign entrant, the larger the gains in both allocative and technical efficiency.

Foreign entry, however, creates difficult political and distributional issues. Foreign competition reduces market price and forces production cutbacks on existing domestic firms. This reduces domestic profits and may create pressure for protectionist trade policies. The more efficient the foreign producer, the stronger the impact. Public policies to protect domestic producers must balance the domestic producers' losses against both the consumers' gains (i.e., increases in both allocative efficiency and consumer surplus) and the increase in domestic technical efficiency.

## PUBLIC POLICIES

Several public policies are designed to assist troubled industries. Four groups of policies are considered here: import price restrictions, import quantity restrictions, domestic sales or production subsidies, and domestic market structural changes. Import price restrictions include tariffs and various other import duties. Import quantity restrictions include formal quotas, orderly marketing arrangements (OMAs), voluntary restraint agreements, and voluntary export restraints. Domestic sales or production subsidies include direct price subsidies, government-funded research activities, accelerated depreciation, and trade adjustment assistance programs. Finally, domestic market structural changes include policies that weaken antitrust regulations for troubled industries, liberalizing merger guidelines and allowing firms to cooperate in research or manufacturing.

### Import Price Restrictions (Tariffs and Duties)

Over the past decade, U.S. government agencies have taken an increasingly sympathetic view when domestic producers complain about foreign dumping in the United States or about foreign government export subsidies. As a result, antidumping and countervailing duties have become increasingly popular. For example, Table 3.2 shows the increase in antidumping petitions between 1980 and 1985. Dumping duties are one form of import price restrictions.

**Table 3.2**
**Summary of U.S. antidumping cases**

| Result of Case | 1980 | 1981 | 1982 | 1983 | 1984 | 1985 | Total |
|---|---|---|---|---|---|---|---|
| Dumping duties | 10 (27%) | 5 (33%) | 13 (20%) | 19 (41%) | 10 (14%) | 25 (40%) | 82 (27%) |
| Petitions rejected | 9 (24%) | 6 (40%) | 21 (32%) | 5 (11%) | 43 (58%) | 20 (32%) | 104 (35%) |
| Petitions withdrawn | 18 (49%) | 4 (27%) | 31 (48%) | 22 (48%) | 21 (28%) | 18 (29%) | 114 (38%) |
| Total cases[a] | 37 | 15 | 65 | 46 | 74 | 63 | 300 |

[a]The 1986 figure for total number of petitions is close to 100.
*Source:* Thomas J. Prusa (1988), "Why Are So Many Antidumping Cases Withdrawn?" Stanford University, Working Paper, April 12.

Equation (7) can be rewritten to show the impact of import price restrictions on domestic equilibrium output:

$$(n + m)P(Q[n + m]) + Q[n + m] \cdot P'(Q[n + m]) = C[n + m] + t \cdot m \qquad (13)$$

where n and m denote the number of domestic and foreign firms, respectively; C[n + m] denotes the sum of the marginal costs for all firms; and t denotes the marginal import tariff/duty. From Hahn's stability condition, the left-hand side of Eq. (13) increases as quantity decreases. Thus, an increase in tariffs/duties reduces Q. In turn, P increases.[9]

The precise relationship between import tariffs and domestic market prices can be found by solving Eq. (13) for dP/dt.

$$dP / dt = m / (n + m + 1 + Q \cdot P'' / P') \qquad (14)$$

Equation (14) shows that the price increase is greater as demand becomes more convex (i.e., $P'' > 0$) and as the domestic industry becomes more concentrated (i.e., fewer domestic firms, n). Furthermore, as long as domestic costs have the same mean, the distribution of domestic production costs has no effect on the increase in market price.[10]

Restricting import prices effectively increases foreign production costs; thus, price restrictions decrease imports. This raises domestic market prices and reduces consumption. Domestic production, however, increases with market prices. To evaluate the implications of this public policy, it is important to consider both efficiency and domestic surplus.

Import price restrictions reduce technical and allocative efficiency and consumer surplus, but they increase producer surplus. As shown above, tariffs/duties reduce industry output and increase industry price. This reduces allocative efficiency and consumer surplus. Technical efficiency is reduced because import price restrictions increase output proportionately more for less efficient firms. Although technical efficiency decreases, producer surplus increases because import price restrictions raise both price and domestic output. In fact, the absolute profit gains are larger for the more efficient firms despite the shift in relative output per firm to the less efficient firms. Domestic producers gain at the expense of domestic consumers and foreign producers.

In contrast to perfect competition, the import price restriction that maximizes the domestic surplus value is not generally zero for oligopolistic competition. To maximize total domestic surplus, the government could select t to maximize:

$$\int_0^Q P(x)\,dx - \sum_{i=1}^n c_i \cdot q_i - (P(Q) - t)\sum_{j=1}^m q_j \qquad (15)$$

subject to $(n + m) \cdot (Q) + Q \cdot P'(Q) = C[n + m] + t \cdot m$, where indexes i and j denote domestic and foreign producers, respectively. The first term in the maximization calculates the area under the demand curve as output varies from zero to the total industry output. The second term calculates total domestic production costs. The difference between these two terms is consumer and producer surplus plus foreign revenues. The third term subtracts foreign revenues and adds tariff revenues. This yields total domestic surplus.

To solve for the domestic surplus-maximizing value of t, Eq. (15) can be differentiated with respect to t and set equal to zero. Assuming a linear demand, the domestic surplus-maximizing import price restriction is:

$$t = n \cdot P(Q[n + m]) / (1 + n) - Q[m] \cdot P'(Q[n + m]) / m - C[n] / (1 + n) \qquad (16)$$

The optimal t increases as the sum of domestic marginal costs, C[n], decreases. It also increases as demand becomes more inelastic and as initial imports, Q[m], increase.[11]

To illustrate, suppose that demand is given by $P = 12 - Q$. Also suppose that there are three producers, with $c_1 = 1$, $c_2 = 2$ and $c_3 = 3$. Firm 1 is a foreign producer and Firms 2 and 3 are domestic producers. From Eq. (16), the surplus-maximizing level of t is $t = (19 - 2Q + 3q_1)/3$. To find the optimal t, both Q and $q_1$ must be expressed in terms of t. Equation (7) relates total industry output to marginal production costs (including tariffs). So, $Q = 7.5 - 0.25t$. Plugging this result into Eq. (6a') implies that $q_1 = 3.5 - 0.75t$, where the price received by foreign producers is $P(Q[n + m]) - t$. Substituting these values for Q and $q_1$ back into Eq. (14), the domestic-surplus-maximizing tariff is $t = 58/19 = 3.05$.

Table 3.3 compares pre- and post-tariff industry output and price, output and profits per firm, domestic consumer and producer surplus, total domestic surplus (including tariff revenues), and average domestic costs. As expected, the tariff reduces industry output and increases price. This reduces allocative efficiency and consumer surplus. In contrast to industry output, domestic output increases; however, market share shifts toward the less efficient domestic producer, decreasing technical efficiency (increasing average domestic cost). Furthermore, profits increase for both domestic producers, but the increase is relatively larger for the more efficient firm. In all cases, the numerical results are consistent with the theoretical predictions. Even if import price restrictions increase total domestic surplus, they transfer income from consumers to producers. Thus, import price restrictions must balance consumer losses and producer gains.

**Table 3.3**
**Numerical results for import price restrictions**

| Demand | \multicolumn{3}{c}{$P = 12 - Q$} |
|---|---|---|---|
| $c_1$ | | 1 | |
| $c_2$ | | 2 | |
| $c_3$ | | 3 | |
| Tariff | Before | After | % Change |
| Q | 7.5 | 6.74 | − 10 |
| P(Q) | 4.5 | 5.26 | 17 |
| $q_1$ | 3.5 | 1.21 | − 65 |
| $q_2$ | 2.5 | 3.26 | 31 |
| $q_3$ | 1.5 | 2.26 | 51 |
| $\pi_1$ | 12.25 | 1.47 | − 88 |
| $\pi_2$ | 6.25 | 10.65 | 70 |
| $\pi_3$ | 2.25 | 5.12 | 128 |
| $\pi_D = \pi_2 + \pi_3$ | 8.5 | 15.77 | 86 |
| Consumer surplus | 28.13 | 22.69 | − 19 |
| Tariff revenues | 0 | 3.70 | — |
| Domestic surplus $= \pi_D + CS + TR$ | 36.63 | 42.16 | 15 |

## Import Quantity Restrictions (Quotas/OMAs)

Import quantity restrictions are an alternative to import price restrictions, reducing the total supply in the domestic market. As with import price restrictions, this form of reduction increases market price. If quantity restrictions allow the same level of imports as price restrictions, both policies have the same impact on equilibrium output and market price. Domestic producers respond to higher domestic prices by increasing their output. As long as price rises to the same level, it is irrelevant whether the increase in domestic price results from import price or quantity restrictions; domestic producers are indifferent to the two policies. Similarly, consumers are indifferent to the two policies if both have the same impact on equilibrium output and price. In this case, import price and quantity restrictions have the same impact on allocative and technical efficiency and on consumer and producer surplus.

The main difference between the policies concerns the foreign producers' profits and the domestic government's tax revenue. With import price restrictions, the tariff or duty is subtracted from the higher domestic price in calculating the foreign producers' revenues. The domestic government receives the tariff/duty revenues. With import quantity restrictions, there is an income transfer from the domestic government to the foreign producers. Because of this income transfer, there is likely to be less foreign resistance (and threats of retaliation) to import quantity restrictions, especially so-called voluntary restraints.

## Subsidies

The third government policy to assist troubled industries involves production subsidies (i.e., government actions that reduce domestic production costs). This group includes direct price subsidies, government investments in commercial research and development, and special tax incentives, including accelerated depreciation.

All of these policies increase equilibrium output and reduce market price. To illustrate, let $s_i$ be the subsidy for Firm i. If there are n domestic firms, the total subsidy is

$$S = \sum_{i=1}^{n} s_i$$

According to Eq. (7), the equilibrium industry output is:

$$(n + m)P(Q[n + m]) + Q \cdot P'(Q[n + m]) = C[n + m] - S \qquad (17)$$

where n and m denote domestic and foreign producers, respectively. According to Hahn's stability condition, the left-hand side of Eq. (17) is decreasing with respect to Q. Thus, an increase in S will increase Q. With downward-sloping demand, an increase in Q will decrease market price. If domestic sales and production subsidies increase industry output and reduce market price, they also increase allocative efficiency. To verify this result, Eq. (17) can be differentiated with respect to S to show explicitly the impact of a change in S on market price. Specifically:

$$dP / dS = (-1) / (n + m + 1 + Q \cdot P'' / P') < 0 \qquad (18)$$

According to Eq. (18), the price decrease, and hence the increase in allocative efficiency, is more pronounced if demand is more convex and there are fewer firms in the industry.

Effects on technical efficiency are more complex. Domestic production subsidies may not affect costs equally for all domestic firms. Some policies may reduce costs more for efficient firms; others may have the opposite effect, or may affect all firms equally. For example, if each domestic producer receives the same per-unit production subsidy, increases in production will be proportionately greater in less efficient firms. This will decrease technical efficiency. Conversely, if the per-unit production subsidy increases with the firm's efficiency, technical efficiency could improve.

Subsidies that are directed toward more efficient firms may be politically controversial. Therefore, targeting would probably have to be subtle or disguised. For example, employment adjustment assistance subsidizes employers' costs of layoffs and new hires. These subsidies help all firms at the time of adjustment. Innovative use of these subsidies, however, could help expand the production of efficient firms relative to less efficient firms, improving domestic technical efficiency. For example, Eq. (12) states that foreign entry causes a smaller absolute change in output for more efficient firms if demand is convex in price. If demand is convex, efficient firms can be targeted by decreasing the firm's employment adjustment assistance as the number of layoffs or new hires increases.

With regard to surplus value, a production subsidy increases domestic surplus, as long as market price after the subsidy is higher than domestic marginal cost. A subsidy reduces price and increases output, increasing consumer surplus. At the same time, the subsidy enables domestic production to replace foreign imports. This transfers producer surplus from foreign to domestic producers. Equation (15) can be rewritten to show how to find the domestic welfare-maximizing subsidy. To maximize surplus value, the government should select $s_1, s_2, \ldots, s_n$ to maximize:

$$\int_0^Q P(x)\, dx - \sum_{i=1}^n c_i \cdot q_i - \sum_{j=1}^m P(Q) \cdot q_j \qquad (19)$$

subject to $S = \sum_{i=1}^n s_i$, and $(n + m) \cdot P(Q) + Q \cdot P'(Q) = C[n + m] - \sum_{i=1}^n s_i$, where n and m are domestic and foreign producers, respectively. To minimize tax distortions, funding for the subsidy may be collected either by lump-sum taxes, by corporate profits taxes, or by personal income taxes.

Research and development (R&D) subsidies are a special class of subsidy that can also reduce production costs. The impact on production costs across firms may vary with the type of R&D. For example, improvements in labor productivity may reduce costs proportionately across firms, while a process innovation that eliminates certain production steps may lead to an equal absolute cost reduction across firms. In general, R&D-induced cost reductions can be expressed as a combination of these two effects. If R is the cost reduction due to R&D, then:

$$R_i = a + b \cdot c_i \qquad (20)$$

where a denotes the absolute cost reduction and b denotes the proportionate cost reduction.

The impact of absolute and proportionate cost reductions on a firm's total profits depends on the firm's efficiency. More efficient firms (i.e., firms with a lower $c_i$) receive a larger increase in profits from an equal absolute cost reduction. Equal absolute cost reductions increase per-unit profits equally for all firms. Output is larger, however, for the more efficient firms; thus, their total profits will increase by more for the same absolute cost reduction.

Conversely, a proportionate cost reduction may have a greater absolute effect on less efficient firms. If costs decrease by the same proportion for all firms, the absolute decrease in costs is greater for less efficient firms. Thus, they experience a greater absolute increase in per-unit profits. Furthermore, less efficient firms increase their output relative to more efficient firms because of their greater absolute cost reduction. In fact, output may decrease for the more efficient firms as less efficient firms capture more of the market.

**Table 3.4**
**The effects of proportionate and absolute cost reductions**
(Illustrative example)

| Demand | $P = 12 - Q$ | | |
|---|---|---|---|
| | Base Case | Reduction in $c_i = 50\%$ | Reduction in $c_i = 0.5$ |
| $c_1$ | 1 | 0.5 | 0.5 |
| $c_2$ | 5 | 2.5 | 4.5 |
| $Q^a$ | 6 | 7 | 6.33 |
| $P(Q)$ | 6 | 5 | 5.67 |
| $q_1{}^b$ | 5 | 4.5 | 5.16 |
| $q_2{}^b$ | 1 | 2.5 | 1.16 |
| $\pi_1$ | 25 | 20.25 | 26.69 |
| $\pi_2$ | 1 | 6.25 | 1.36 |

[a]From Eq. 7.
[b]From Eq. 6a.

Both of these factors increase profits for less efficient firms relative to more efficient firms. Less efficient firms, however, have a lower production volume. This may offset, at least in part, the advantage that less efficient firms derive from proportionate cost reductions.

To illustrate, Table 3.4 compares a proportional and an absolute cost reduction. Suppose that industry demand is given by $P = 12 - Q$ and there are two firms in the industry. The federal government is considering two different R&D projects to reduce production costs in this industry. One project reduces all firms' production costs by the same percentage, while the other reduces all production costs by the same absolute amount. The example was constructed so that the most efficient firm's production costs are the same in either case. However, according to the results in Table 3.4, different projects have different effects on the two firms. The less efficient firm's profits increase in both cases, but they increase by more with the proportional cost reduction. However, the most efficient firm's profits actually decrease with the proportional cost reduction. Thus, Firm 1 is unlikely to support this research effort. Support for government-sponsored R&D may depend crucially on the nature of the expected research results.

The differing effects of absolute and proportionate cost reductions have policy implications for government-sponsored R&D. Suppose that a government research consortium develops a process technology that proportionately reduces production costs for all consortium members. It is possible for less efficient firms to receive a larger relative benefit from that development, in terms of both production volume and total profits. Thus, the more efficient firms are not likely to support this type of R&D project.

## Market Structure

An alternative government policy frequently suggested to help industries troubled by foreign competition is to relax antitrust regulation. Allegedly, this enables firms to capture greater economies of scale, either through mergers or through internal growth (to the extent that fear of antitrust action constrains internal growth). The oligopolistic industry model developed here can be used to examine the impact of mergers and internal growth on allocative and technical efficiency.

First, consider internal growth. If this growth enables domestic firms to capture economies of scale (i.e., if it reduces $c_i$ for domestic firms), it will raise both allocative and technical efficiency. As $c_i$ decreases for domestic firms, equilibrium industry output increases and market price decreases. This in turn increases allocative efficiency and consumer surplus. At the same time, production shifts from foreign producers and domestic firms whose costs have not changed to domestic firms with decreasing production costs. This increases domestic technical efficiency and domestic producer surplus. Thus, allocative efficiency, technical efficiency, and domestic surplus value all increase.

This result holds even if the number of firms decreases (i.e., if some firms are driven out of the industry). If there were n firms in the industry before antitrust laws were relaxed, then $P > c_n$. If the least efficient firm is driven from the industry, then the growth in output from the expanding firms must have been sufficient to drive P below $c_n$. Thus, allocative efficiency will increase even though the number of firms decreases. Technical efficiency and domestic surplus value still increase for the same reasons as cited above. Internal growth to capture economies of scale unambiguously has net positive benefits for domestic consumers and producers.

In contrast, mergers increase domestic technical efficiency and producer surplus (as domestic production costs decrease), but they may decrease allocative efficiency and consumer surplus. As firms merge to capture economies of scale, their production costs decrease. However, there are fewer firms in the industry, even if P still exceeds $c_n$. These two changes have offsetting effects on industry output. The net effect on market price, allocative efficiency, and consumer surplus depends on whether the economies of scale are sufficient to offset the reduction in the number of firms. Equation (7) can be used to show industry output before and after two domestic firms merge (denoted Q[B] and Q[A], respectively). After some simplification, industry output will be the same before and after the merger if:

$$Q[B] = Q[A] \rightarrow c_i + c_j - c_{ij} = P(Q)$$

where i and j are the firms that merge and $c_{ij}$ represents their post-merger costs. Thus, the change in total industry costs because of the merger must equal industry price. If economies of scale are modest and the net change in industry price is less than this amount, industry output will decrease. If economies of scale are significant and the net change in industry price is greater than this amount, industry output will increase.

The impact of mergers on the volume of imports depends largely on the change in industry output and market price.[12] Equation (6a') can be used to show a representative foreign producer's output before and after relaxing domestic antitrust laws (denoted $q_j[B]$ and $q_j[A]$, respectively). After some simplification, the change in the foreign producer's output can be written as:

$$q_j[B] - q_j[A] = [\{P(Q[B]) - c_j\}P'(Q[A])$$
$$- \{P(Q[A]) - c_j\}P'(Q[B])] / P'(Q[A])P'(Q[B])$$

The sign of the numerator determines whether the foreign producer's production increases or decreases. If demand is linear, then $P'(Q[A]) = P'(Q[B])$. In this case, $q_j[B] < q_j[A]$ if $P(Q[B]) < P(Q[A])$. In other words, if market price increases because of domestic mergers, foreign production will increase. Conversely, if economies of scale are strong enough that domestic mergers reduce market price, foreign production will decrease. If demand is not linear, the change in foreign production depends both on the change in market price and on the shape (convexity) of the demand curve.

For example, consider an industry with linear demand given by $P = 12 - Q$. Assume that there are three firms, and that Firm 1 is a foreign producer. If the domestic producers merge, the net effect on domestic consumers and domestic and foreign producers depends largely on the reduction in domestic production costs after the merger. As Table 3.5 indicates, mergers always increase technical efficiency and producer surplus. However, if domestic production costs decrease modestly (i.e., $c_i + c_j - c_{ij} < P(Q)$), industry output decreases and market price increases. This decreases allocative efficiency and consumer surplus, while foreign output and profits increase. Alternatively, if the reduction in domestic production costs is significant (i.e., $c_i + c_j - c_{ij} > P(Q)$), industry output increases and

**Table 3.5**
**Effects of mergers**

| Demand | P = 12 − Q | | |
| | Base Case | Modest Economies of Scale ($C_{23} = 1.5$) | Large Economies of Scale ($C_{23} = 0.2$)* |
| --- | --- | --- | --- |
| $c_1$ | 1 | 1 | 1 |
| $c_2$ | 2 | 1.5 | 0.2 |
| $c_3$ | 3 | — | — |
| $Q^a$ | 7.5 | 7.17 | 7.6 |
| $P(Q)$ | 4.5 | 4.83 | 4.4 |
| $q_1{}^b$ | 3.5 | 3.83 | 3.4 |
| $q_2{}^b$ | 2.5 | 3.33 | 4.2 |
| $q_3{}^b$ | 1.5 | — | — |
| $\pi_1$ | 12.25 | 14.69 | 11.56 |
| $\pi_2$ | 6.25 | 11.11 | 17.64 |
| $\pi_3$ | 2.25 | — | — |
| $\pi_D = \pi_2 + \pi_3$ | 8.5 | 11.11 | 17.64 |
| Consumer surplus | 28.13 | 25.68 | 28.88 |
| Domestic surplus = $\pi_D$ + CS | 36.63 | 36.79 | 46.52 |

*With $C_{23} = 0.5$, the output remains the same as pre-merger.
[a]From Eq. 7.
[b]From Eq. 6a'.

market price decreases. In this case, allocative efficiency and consumer surplus increase, while foreign output and profits decrease.

Unfortunately, the net effect of a merger on allocative efficiency, consumer surplus, foreign output, and foreign profits cannot be determined *a priori*. With a straight-line demand, the net change in domestic surplus is related to the reduction in domestic production costs. For small reductions in cost, gains from economies of scale are insufficient to counterbalance the reduction in the number of firms. Market price increases, reducing consumer surplus, but profits do not increase enough to offset the consumers' loss. As the cost reduction increases, market price falls. This reduces the loss in consumer surplus and increases producer profits. If market price falls below its pre-merger level, consumer surplus actually increases. For reference, Figure 3.3 illustrates the relationship between $C_{23}$ and domestic surplus for P = 12 − Q and ($C_1 = 1, C_2 = 2, C_3 = 3$). The gain from the merger is plotted as a function of $C_{23}$.

**Figure 3.3**
**Economies of scale and domestic surplus value**

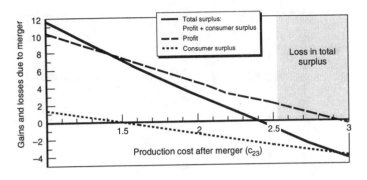

### Combined Strategy

In some cases, combining policies may provide a more efficient and politically viable solution. It is impossible to find a general expression for the optimal combination of policies, but an example can be used to illustrate the benefits of a combined strategy. Import price restrictions can be compared with a strategy combining import price restrictions and a domestic production subsidy. The combined strategy provides domestic producers greater relief for the same, or a lower, cost to society.

To illustrate, consider an industry with a linear demand given by $P = 12 - Q$. Assume that there are two firms, where Firm 1 is a foreign producer. The government, which wants to help the domestic producer, is trying to decide between a tariff and a mixed tariff/subsidy strategy.[13] Table 3.6 compares the results of these two strategies. The combined strategy improves allocative efficiency, domestic consumer surplus, domestic producer profit, and foreign producer profit. This strategy may be globally efficient if the foreign firm is less efficient than the domestic firms. In this case, the combined strategy will encourage the more efficient (domestic) firm to increase output relative to the less efficient (foreign) firm.

### CONCLUSIONS

This chapter has presented a stylized framework of troubled industries characterized by oligopolistic competition, diverse production costs, excess capacity, and foreign competition. Different public policies to help these

Table 3.6
Tariff versus combined tariff/subsidy

| Demand $c_1$ $c_2$ | $P = 12 - Q$ 2 4 | | | Percent Gain from Combined Strategy over Tariff Strategy |
|---|---|---|---|---|
| | Base Case | Tariff Strategy $t = 3$ | Combined Strategy $t = 3$ | |
| $Q^a$ | 6 | 5 | 5.90 | 18 |
| $P(Q)$ | 6 | 7 | 6.10 | -13 |
| $q_1^b$ | 4 | 2 | 2.60 | 30 |
| $q_2^b$ | 2 | 3 | 3.29 | 10 |
| $\pi_1$ | 16 | 4 | 6.78 | 70 |
| $\pi_2 = \pi_D$ | 4 | 9 | 10.83 | 20 |
| Consumer surplus | 18 | 12.5 | 17.38 | 39 |
| Tariff revenues | 0 | 6 | 3.91 | |
| $S$ (Subsidy) | 0 | 0 | 3.91 | |
| Domestic surplus = $\pi_D + CS + TR - S$ | 22 | 27.5 | 28.21 | 2.5 |

[a]From Eq. 7.
[b]From Eq. 6a.

industries were analyzed to determine the implications for allocative and technical efficiency and for consumer and producer surplus. Four policies were analyzed: import price restrictions, import quantity restrictions, domestic production subsidies, and relaxed antitrust enforcement. The primary results are summarized in Table 3.7.

Import quantity restrictions, particularly voluntary export restraints, orderly marketing arrangements, and other "voluntary" quantity restrictions, have become increasingly popular in recent years. This popularity results largely from their political convenience (i.e., less foreign resistance). Despite their political popularity, import quantity restrictions have adverse effects on allocative and technical efficiency and on consumer surplus. According to the criteria considered in Table 3.7, domestic production subsidies have the least undesirable economic outcomes. If subsidies can be targeted to the most efficient firms, they improve allocative and technical efficiency unambiguously. Both consumer and producer surplus also increase. Because all groups in the domestic economy receive a net benefit from this policy, it is

**Table 3.7**
**Public policies for troubled industries**

| Policy | Allocative Efficiency | Technical Efficiency | Consumer Surplus | Producer Surplus |
|---|---|---|---|---|
| Import price restrictions | Decrease | Decrease | Decrease | Increase |
| Import quantity restrictions | Decrease | Decrease | Decrease | Increase |
| Production subsidies | Increase | Ambiguous | Increase | Increase |
| Market structure | Ambiguous | Increase | Ambiguous | Increase |

less likely to receive internal opposition. The same desirable outcomes characterize policies to relax antitrust regulation, if economies of scale are significant. Finally, a combined strategy, such as tariff/subsidy policy, may dominate any single strategy.

Unfortunately, it is difficult to identify a single preferred policy, or combination of policies, to support troubled industries in all situations. Instead, the preferred policy, or combination of policies, will probably depend on the specific characteristics of both the industry and the domestic and foreign producers.

For example, suppose that foreign producers have a significant cost advantage owing to economies of scale, but that U.S. antitrust laws preclude domestic producers from capturing the same advantage. Import price or quantity restrictions would help domestic producers compete with foreign producers, but they would reduce allocative efficiency, technical efficiency, and consumer surplus. Furthermore, they would not directly address the cause of the problem, untapped domestic economies of scale. Domestic sales or production subsidies could also be used to compensate domestic producers for the cost difference. If the subsidies were targeted to the most efficient domestic producers, this policy would have a net positive benefit for domestic consumers and producers (although foreign producers would probably protest). Subsidies, however, would not address the underlying cause of the problem either. The problem could be directly eliminated if U.S. antitrust laws were relaxed (assuming that sufficient domestic and international competition remained to preclude tacit collusion). This would enable U.S. producers to reduce production costs by capturing the economies of scale. Relative to other government policies, both domestic consumers and producers would receive an equal or greater positive net benefit, government subsidies would not be required, and there would probably be less foreign resistance. In this case, relaxing antitrust regulations would in all likelihood be the preferred policy.

Thus, public policies to support troubled industries should also consider the specific cause of the problems affecting the troubled industry. Some policies might help alleviate the problem's symptoms—but not the underlying cause. The industry would remain dependent on government support. If government policies were to help eliminate the underlying cause of the problem, the industry could perhaps be weaned from government support.

---

## NOTES

1. Nash firms maximize their profits under the assumption of a given output from all other firms. As one firm adjusts its output, other firms respond by adjusting their outputs as well. Nash equilibrium occurs when each firm's assumptions are consistent with its competitors' actual output.
2. See Hahn (1962).
3. In this chapter, it is common knowledge that accommodation is the best response to entry. Predation and entry deterrence are not considered. For a discussion of common knowledge, see Aumann (1976) and Milgrom (1981). For a discussion of predation and entry deterrence, see Milgrom and Roberts (1982).
4. Because corporate profits taxes will not change the profit-maximizing output level, they have been omitted in this formulation.
5. See Dixit and Stern (1982) and Bergstrom and Varian (1985).
6. This can be seen as follows: Consider the industry costs, $TC = \sum c_i q_i$, where $q_i = (P - c_i)/(-P')$. Total cost can be rewritten as $TC = A\sum c_i - B\sum c_i^2$ where $A = (-P/P')$ and $B = (-1/P')$. For a given total industry cost, $\sum c_i$ is constant. A and B are also constants, so industry costs are minimizing $\sum c_i$.
7. This result can easily be generalized for a nonmarginal entrant with some care for the firms that may be forced to exit because of the entry. With the marginal entrant, no firms need to exit.
8. In fact, the increase in industry output just equals the decrease in output per firm when demand is linear. For example, when the second firm enters the industry, half its output comes from a decrease in demand, the other half from a decrease in Firm 1's output. In general, $1/n$th of the $n$th firm's output comes from an increase in industry output. The remainder comes from equal decreases in output for the existing $(n - 1)$ firms.
9. Prusa (1988) finds that domestic output and price can be affected by the mere threat of import tariffs/duties. Industry price frequently increases even when U.S.

producers withdraw the dumping petition before it reaches a final determination. Prusa notes that filing a petition creates a legal opportunity for domestic firms to negotiate private price/quantity agreements with their foreign rivals. In some cases, he finds that price and output may be more affected by these informal agreements than by government-imposed restrictions.

10. With linear demand, the price increase due to a tariff is completely determined by the number of firms, both domestic and foreign.

11. Because this is a partial equilibrium analysis, caution must be exercised in interpreting the results. The analysis does not consider possible foreign retaliation. Overt import price restrictions (e.g., tariffs) are likely to invite foreign retaliation. In contrast, antidumping duties or countervailing duties may be less likely to invite retaliation.

12. In their econometric study of U.S.-Japanese trade, Audretsch and Yamawaki (1988) find that a tax depreciation subsidy, which reduces production costs, helps to reduce imports, but that cartelization does not.

13. By assumption, the mixed strategy is calculated so that the tariff revenue covers the subsidy costs.

## BIBLIOGRAPHY

Audretsch, D. B., and H. Yamawaki (1988). "R&D Rivalry, Industrial Policy, and U.S.-Japanese Trade." *Review of Economics and Statistics,* vol. LXX, 438–447.

Aumann, R. (1976). "Agreeing to Disagree." *Ann. Statist.,* vol. 4, 1236–1239.

Bergstrom, T. C., and H. R. Varian (1985). "When Are Nash Equilibria Independent of the Distribution of Agents' Characteristics?" *Review of Economic Studies,* vol. 52, 715–718.

Dixit, A. K., and N. Stern (1982). "Oligopoly and Welfare: A Unified Presentation and Application to Trade and Development." *European Economics Review,* vol. 19, 123–143.

Ghemawat, P., and B. Nalebuff (1987). "Excess Capacity, Efficiency, and Industrial Policy." Woodrow Wilson School Discussion Paper 134, Princeton University.

Hahn, F. H. (1962). "The Stability of the Cournot Oligopoly Solution." *Review of Economic Studies,* vol. 29, 329–332.

Milgrom, P. (1981). "An Axiomatic Characterization of Common Knowledge." *Econometrica,* vol. 49, 219–222.

Milgrom, P., and J. Roberts (1982). "Limit Pricing and Entry Under Incomplete Information: An Equilibrium Analysis." *Econometrica,* vol. 50, 443–459.

Prusa, T. J. (1988). "Why Are So Many Antidumping Cases Withdrawn?" Stanford University, Working Paper, April 12.

# 4

## Multiproduct Firms, Labor Fixity, and Firm Adjustment Responses

Katsuaki L. Terasawa and William R. Gates

International competition is characterized by oligopolistic industries composed of multiproduct firms competing simultaneously in several industries. Frequently, cost interdependencies exist between a firm's outputs in different industries. Furthermore, firms have differing views concerning the variability of labor in the production process, some firms viewing labor as a variable input, others not. Some firms may act as if a constraint operates on the minimum quantity of labor hired. Once the optimal quantity of labor reaches this minimum level, labor is considered, essentially, a fixed cost of production. Foreign firms competing in U.S. markets (e.g., Japanese firms) are frequently thought to provide employees with a lifetime employment commitment, effectively creating a minimum labor constraint.

A multiproduct firm model is developed here to characterize this industry structure. The model is used to examine the impact of a reduction in demand on industry and firm output, both with and without a labor constraint. Finally, the authors discuss, in the context of the model, policy implications for declining domestic industries facing international competition.

## OLIGOPOLISTIC INDUSTRIES WITH MULTIPRODUCT FIRMS

Oligopolistic firms frequently produce products for multiple markets, and production costs in these industries may be interrelated. Furthermore, some producers (typically, foreign ones) may consider labor to be a fixed input. An oligopolistic industry model involving multiproduct firms and minimum labor requirements is required to reflect these complexities. The objective is to develop a model that captures, with greater accuracy than at present, the impact of public policies to assist troubled industries. It may be possible to use this model to examine other policies, such as the optimal blend of government- and firm-financed labor training programs.

### The Multiproduct-Firm Model with Labor Constraints

Consider an industry with n firms. Firm i's total production costs are given by $c_i(x_i, y_i)$, where $x_i$ and $y_i$ are the firm's output in Industry X and Industry Y, respectively. Then:

$$c_i(x_i, y_i) = a_i x_i + b_i y_i + d_i x_i y_i, \quad i = 1, 2, ..., n \qquad (1)$$

In this cost function, the firm's marginal production costs in Industry X and Industry Y, respectively, are given by:

$$MCx_i = a_i + d_i y_i \qquad (2)$$

$$MCy_i = b_i + d_i x_i \qquad (3)$$

where $a_i, b_i, d_i \geq 0$. Thus, marginal costs are constant in both industries, given the level of output in the other industry.[1]

Costs in Industries X and Y are interrelated through the term $(d_i x_i y_i)$. This term can represent a fixed factor of production that is used competitively in the production of both x and y (e.g., management or some similar overhead factor).[2] In this characterization, the firm's marginal cost in Industry X increases (decreases) as the firm's output in Industry Y increases (decreases). In other words, as the firm increases its output of y, more of the joint input is devoted to that industry. The marginal cost of x increases as the firm's output of y increases, because the production of x receives less of the joint production factor.

The consumers' inverse demand functions for X and Y are given by:

$$P_X = P(X) \qquad (4)$$

$$P_Y = P(Y) \qquad (5)$$

where $P(X)$ and $P(Y)$ denote the price functions and $X$ and $Y$ stand for total outputs in Industry X and Industry Y, respectively. So,

$$X = \sum_{i=1}^{n} x_i \quad \text{and} \quad Y = \sum_{i=1}^{n} y_i$$

Demand is assumed to be price-sensitive and sufficient to accommodate n firms. Thus:

$$dP(Q) / dQ < 0$$

and

$$\lim_{Q \to 0} P(Q) > MCq_n, \quad \text{where } Q = X, Y; q = x, y$$

Under these assumptions, a unique Nash equilibrium exists where firms simultaneously choose their output levels, $x_i$ and $y_i$, assuming certain levels of output by the other firms in both industries. The problem for Firm i is to choose its output level, $x_i$ and $y_i$, to maximize its total profits:

$$\pi_i = P(X)x_i + P(Y)y_i - c_i(x_i, y_i) \tag{6}$$

In some cases, the firm's output decisions may be further affected by a constraint on the quantity of labor hired. If applicable, the labor constraint is $l_{ix} + l_{iy} \geq L_{i0}$, where $l_{ix}$ is the quantity of labor used by Firm i in the production of $x_i$, $l_{iy}$ is the quantity of labor used by the firm in the production of good $y_i$, and $L_{i0}$ constrains the minimum total quantity of labor used by the firm. If demand decreases in one of the firm's markets, the firm can reduce the quantity of labor hired until the total quantity of labor hits the labor constraint. After this point, the firm cannot reduce the quantity of labor hired. Instead, the firm will allocate labor between its two products so as to maximize its total profits.[3]

Assuming Cournot-Nash behavior (i.e., each firm maximizes total profits, where the other firms' outputs in both industries are given), the equilibrium output for all firms in both industries must be determined simultaneously. The analysis is complicated by the circumstance that the number of firms changes as demand expands and contracts. As a result, a detailed description of the mathematical results is not presented here. Instead, we discuss below the results for an illustrative case.

## Multiproduct Firms with Linear Demand

To illustrate this model, consider a case where the demand for X and Y is linear and equal to:

$$P(X) = A - BX \tag{7}$$

$$P(Y) = C - DY \tag{8}$$

The demand for Y remains constant throughout this analysis ($C = 20$, $D = 1$). The demand for X varies to reflect an industry experiencing declining demand. The slope remains constant, $B = 0.5$; but A decreases from an initial value of 12, by increments of 2, until reaching 6. As the demand curve shifts left, the number of firms producing X may decrease. Production costs vary across firms. The values for $a_i$, $b_i$, and $d_i$ are given in Table 4.1. Firm 1 is the most efficient producer in both industries. Firm 2 is the second most efficient producer. Firms 3 through 6 are identical, so they produce equal outputs in both industries.[4] Similarly, Firms 3 through 6 enter and leave the industry at the same time (i.e., as demand contracts, the number of firms drops from six to two). Finally, Firm 2 is assumed to be a foreign producer; all other firms are domestic producers. The labor constraint is relevant only for the foreign producer. When applicable, the labor constraint is given by $l_{2x} + l_{2y} \geq 10$, with $l_{2x} = 2x_2$, and $l_{2y} = y_2$.

## ENTRY OF FIRMS

To provide a framework for analyzing the impact of declining industry demand, it is useful to understand how consumers and producers are affected by entry into industries such as those described here. Entry will affect allocative efficiency (as determined by total industry output), technical efficiency (as determined by average industry production costs), market share, and consumer and producer surplus (producer surplus is equal to producer profits, assuming no fixed costs). According to Terasawa and Gates (1994), the specific results depend on the entrant's characteristics relative to the industry. They also depend on whether the entrant is a domestic or a foreign firm. In fact, the general results for multiproduct oligopolistic firms are consistent with our earlier results for oligopolistic industries with single-product firms.

To illustrate the effects of entry on oligopolistic industries with multiproduct firms, assume a high demand for Industry X (i.e., A = 12) and entry

## Table 4.1
## Production cost parameters

| Parameter | Firm 1 | Firm 2 | Firm i (i = 3, 4, 5, 6) |
|-----------|--------|--------|--------------------------|
| $a_i$ | 2.0 | 2.5 | 3.5 |
| $b_i$ | 3.0 | 4.0 | 5.0 |
| $d_i$ | 0.025 | 0.025 | 0.025 |

of firms into the industry in the order of decreasing efficiency (i.e., the most efficient firms enter the industry first). The model described above can show the impact of entry, in both industries (X and Y), on market prices (hence industry output), market share, average costs, industry profits, and consumer surplus. These factors are compared as the number of firms expands from one to six.[5]

In general, entry increases industry output.[6] If demand is downward sloping, entry decreases market price and increases both allocative efficiency and consumer surplus. At the firm level, entry decreases output per firm for the existing firms. Proportionate output reductions are greater for the less efficient firms relative to the more efficient ones. In other words, market share shifts toward firms with lower marginal costs. Thus, entry tends to increase domestic technical efficiency. If, however, the entrant is a domestic firm, this gain in efficiency has to be weighed against the entrant's relative efficiency. If the entrant is the most efficient domestic firm, domestic technical efficiency will increase overall. Conversely, if the entrant is the least efficient domestic firm, as assumed here, domestic technical efficiency will decrease on balance. For intermediate cases, technical efficiency depends on the relative magnitudes of these two effects. Finally, because entry reduces market price and output per firm, it also reduces producer surplus (profits).

Figure 4.1 shows the change in market price and average total cost as the number of firms increases.[7] As expected, this figure illustrates the point that entry increases industry output and decreases market price, thus increasing allocative efficiency. However, average production costs also increase, suggesting that technical efficiency decreases as less efficient firms enter the industry.

Figure 4.2 indicates that market shares for existing firms decrease as new firms enter the industry (i.e., market output increases by less than the output produced by the new entrant). Furthermore, the numerical results confirm that the decrease in market share is relatively larger for the less efficient firms. This shift in relative market shares helps increase technical efficiency. But Figure 4.1 indicates a net decrease in technical efficiency. This is as predicted because the entrants are less efficient than the existing firms.

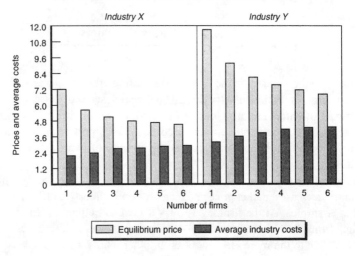

**Figure 4.1**
**Equilibrium prices and average industry costs**

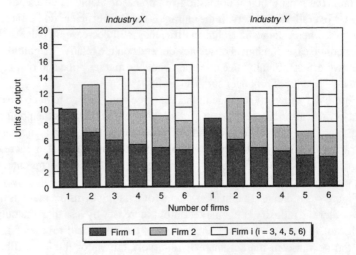

**Figure 4.2**
**Industry output and market shares**

**Figure 4.3**
**Industry profits and consumer surplus**

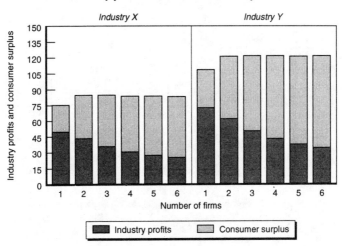

Finally, Figure 4.3 shows that entry into the industry reduces industry profits and raises consumer surplus. This is consistent with the trends in allocative and technical efficiency. However, Figure 4.3 also shows that maximizing total surplus, as measured by the sum of industry profits and consumer surplus, may require limiting the number of firms in each industry. Numerical results indicate that this occurs when n = 2 for Industry X, and when n = 4 for Industry Y.

## DECREASING DEMAND

Many industries in the United States face foreign competition and decreasing industry demand (i.e., "sunset industries"). Several public policies have been suggested to assist these industries, including import price and quantity restrictions, domestic-sales and production subsidies, and relaxed antitrust enforcement. To analyze the effects of these policies, it is important to understand the impact of declining industry demand, both on the industry as a whole and on individual firms.

If demand in Industry X decreases, the effects are felt in both Industry X and Industry Y. General impacts in both industries can be predicted, assuming normal-shaped supply and demand curves. Decreasing demand should reduce output and price in Industry X. As price decreases, individual firms also reduce their output, $x_i$, and some firms might leave the industry.

Figure 4.4
**Output in Industries X and Y: declining demand without labor constraint**

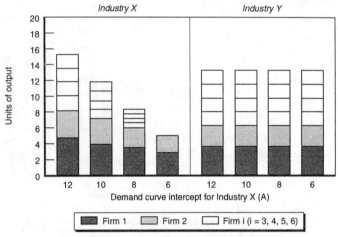

Furthermore, if the price decreases resulting from declining demand and entry have similar effects on output per firm, the proportionate decrease in output should be greatest for the less efficient firms. As relative market share shifts to firms with lower production costs, technical efficiency increases. Production costs within Industry Y should decrease with the demand for X. When firms produce less X, more of the joint input can be devoted to Y. This reduces Y's production costs, increasing the output of Y and decreasing market price.

The model and numerical example introduced above illustrate the effects of declining demand in Industry X, and verify the predicted results. Declining demand for X is modeled by sequentially decreasing the demand curve's intercept (i.e., A assumes the values 12, 10, 8, and 6). When A = 10, the labor constraint becomes binding on the foreign producer (Firm 2). For reference, results are compared both with and without the labor constraint.

Figures 4.4 and 4.5 show total output and each firm's market share as the demand for X decreases, ignoring the labor constraint for Firm 2. Figure 4.4 indicates that total output for good X decreases as predicted.[8] Furthermore, less efficient firms bear a disproportionate share of this decrease. In fact, Firms 3, 4, 5, and 6 leave Industry X when A falls from eight to six. To illustrate this trend more clearly, Figure 4.5 shows each firm's relative market share as demand decreases: the relative market shares for Firms 1 and 2 increase, with Firm 1's market share increasing the most. The relative

**Figure 4.5**
**Relative market shares in industries X and Y:**
**declining demand without labor constraint**

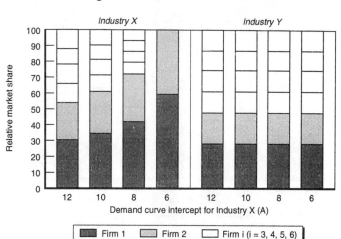

market shares for Firms 3, 4, 5, and 6 decrease with demand. This shift in relative market shares indicates that production decreases proportionately more in the less efficient firms. This is consistent with the predicted results.

Figures 4.6 and 4.7 demonstrate that the results are similar when Firm 2 is bound by a labor constraint, with one significant exception. If the demand for X decreases and Firm 2's labor force cannot be reduced, Firm 2 can either continue producing the same level of $x_2$ or shift labor to the production of $y_2$. In this example, $x_2$ remains essentially constant for A = 10 and 8. When A = 6, Firm 2 begins shifting labor to $y_2$. This is illustrated in Figure 4.6 by Firm 2's output in both industries. It is also illustrated in Figure 4.7 by Firm 2's relative market share in both industries.

The domestic producers are also affected by Firm 2's minimum labor constraint. To show this effect, Figures 4.8 and 4.9 directly compare the results for Industry X with and without a labor constraint.[9] As explained above, the minimum labor constraint makes Firm 2 less sensitive to decreases in the demand for X. Thus, the burden of adjustment in output is forced on the other firms in the industry. This can be seen both from comparative output data (Figure 4.8) and from relative market share data (Figure 4.9). Firm 2's output of X and its relative market share are both larger when the labor constraint is binding. Output and relative market share for domestic producers must compensate for the change in Firm 2's behavior. According to Figure 4.8, output

Figure 4.6
Output in Industries Y and X: declining demand with labor constraint

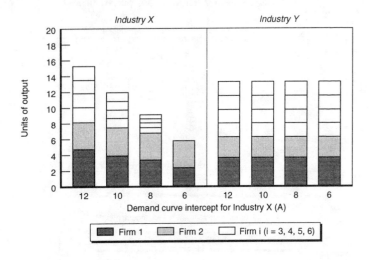

Figure 4.7
Relative market shares in Industries X and Y:
declining demand with labor constraint

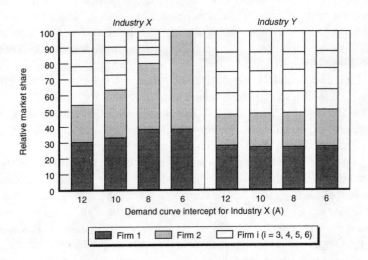

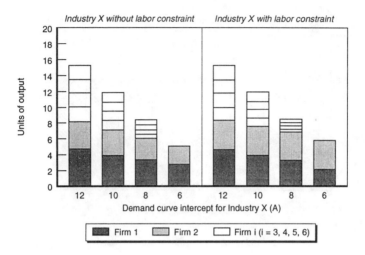

**Figure 4.8**
**Output in Industry X:**
**declining demand with and without labor constraint**

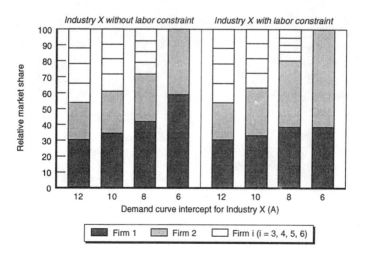

**Figure 4.9**
**Relative market shares in Industry X:**
**declining demand with and without labor constraint**

**Figure 4.10**
**Total production costs on Industry X:**
**declining demand with and without labor constraint**

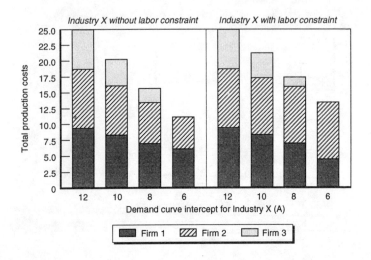

**Figure 4.11:**
**Profits in Industry X:**
**declining demand with and without labor demand constraint**

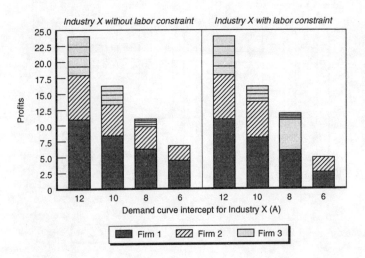

for the domestic firms is smaller when Firm 2 is constrained by a minimum labor requirement. From Figure 4.9, Firm 1's relative market share in Industry X increases less when Firm 2 is bound by a labor constraint, and the relative market shares for firms 3, 4, 5, and 6 decrease more quickly. Furthermore, the impact is relatively greater for the less efficient firms in the industry. If this should reflect foreign producers' responses to labor constraints, it would probably increase trade tensions.

Figure 4.10 compares production costs in Industry X with and without the labor constraint. It indicates that the labor constraint increases total industry production costs, reflecting an increase in Firm 2's total production costs. Total costs for the other firms decrease slightly owing to changes in both output and average costs. Domestic firms produce less where labor is constrained, and average costs decrease slightly.[10] Thus, the foreign labor constraint would increase domestic technical efficiency, while raising Firm 2's average costs.

Figure 4.11 shows firm and industry profits with and without the labor constraint. Profits for Firm 2 actually increase under the labor constraint when the demand decline is moderate (A = 10, 8), even though its average costs increase. Profits for the other firms decrease. This surprising result can be explained by considering the assumption that firms follow a Cournot-Nash strategy. The labor constraint forces Firm 2 to produce more than the Cournot-Nash output. In effect, the labor constraint forces Firm 2 to act like a Stackelberg industry leader. Firm 2 can successfully adopt the role of industry leader because the other firms are following Cournot-Nash behavior. In the leader-follower model, total industry profits can increase because the leader moves the industry toward the monopoly output. Furthermore, the leader's profits increase while the followers' profits decrease, relative to the Cournot-Nash case. These responses are consistent with the results in Figure 4.11, especially when A = 8, at the output level closest to the Stackelberg leader. They become less significant when A = 10 (not large enough output as the effective leader), or when A = 6. In the latter case, the labor constraint becomes too stringent and costly to gain from the "leadership."

## CONCLUSIONS

We have developed an oligopolistic industry model that includes multi-product firms and a minimum labor constraint for one firm. This model was used to examine the effects on individual firms and two industries when demand decreased in one market. When the labor constraint is not binding, the results of the model were roughly consistent with the earlier results for the single-product firm. When one firm faces a labor constraint, however, the results can change significantly. The constraint forces the firm to change its behavior from Cournot-Nash to pseudo-Stackelberg. Output adjustments are shifted to the other firms in the industry, and their profits are reduced correspondingly. In contrast, profits for the firm forced into the leader role, and for the industry as a whole, can increase. If foreign producers face a labor constraint, trade tensions are likely to rise and lead to cries for relief from foreign competition. However, these pleas should be considered carefully. Public policies to protect troubled industries—particularly import quantity and price restrictions, two commonly used policies—typically increase producer profits at the expense of consumer surplus (Terasawa and Gates, 1994). Producers, being concerned primarily with producer profits, may lobby for public policies that increase profits, even if the loss in consumer surplus exceeds the net gain in producer profits. Federal policymakers should ensure that public policies at least generate a net gain in total surplus.[11]

Furthermore, a minimum labor constraint may significantly mitigate the effect of public policies to protect troubled industries, a circumstance that may be felt in several industries if the firms involved are multiproduct firms. These cross-industry effects, which could be more significant than the effects on the targeted industry, should be considered before recommending a policy response.

This model introduces the possibility of interdependencies among the cost functions for a firm producing in multiple markets. Thus, policies implemented in one industry could have important secondary effects in other industries. These interactions may be exacerbated if some firms also face labor constraints. Again, such effects should be considered before implementing public policies to protect troubled industries.

---

## NOTES

1. Assuming constant marginal costs significantly simplifies the analysis and is consistent with the model originally developed by Ghemawat and Nalebuff (1987).
2. If $d_i$ is negative, we can conclude that there is a return to scope in the joint operation. In this paper, however, we examine only the case where $d_i > 0$.
3. The actual impact on the firm's output of x and y depends on the value of the joint production costs ($d_i x_i y_i$), the demand curves in both industries, and the other firms' reactions in both industries.
4. If all firms j, $j \geq 3$, have identical costs, there is no limit to the number of firms. However, expanding the number of firms significantly increases the expositional

complexity without changing the general results. Therefore, the number of firms is arbitrarily limited to six in this analysis.

5. With $A = 12$, the labor constraint for Firm 2 is not binding, and so is ignored.

6. These results are explicitly derived for single-product firms in Terasawa and Gates (1994). A similar approach can be used to derive the same results for multiproduct firms. This derivation is not included here.

7. The difference between price and industry average costs represents the industry's average unit profits.

8. There is also a slight increase in the output of Y resulting from the cost interactions between $x_i$ and $y_i$. Recall that, as the output of $x_i$ decreases, $MC_{y_i}$ also decreases. However, when $d_i = 0.025$, this impact is small.

9. Figure 4.8 combines the results for Industry X from Figures 4.4 and 4.6; Figure 4.9 combines the results for Industry X from Figures 4.5 and 4.7.

10. The decrease in average costs results in part from a decrease in the portion of joint costs allocated to X as $x_i$ decreases (see note 2).

11. The net change in total surplus is measured as the increase in producer profits less both the loss in consumer surplus and the cost of rent-seeking, lobbying activities. If such lobbying activities are expensive and represent a deadweight loss to society, the net surplus gain may be negative, even if the gain in producer profits exceeds the loss in consumer surplus.

### BIBLIOGRAPHY

Ghemawat, P., and B. Nalebuff (1987). "Excess Capacity, Efficiency, and Industrial Policy." Woodrow Wilson School Discussion Paper 134, Princeton University.

Terasawa, Katsuaki L., and William R. Gates (1994). "Public Policies toward Troubled Industries: A Theoretical Framework," Ch. 3 in this volume.

**III**
---

**Public Policies toward Troubled Industries**

# 5

## Policies toward Troubled Industries in the United States: An Overview

Hong W. Tan

### INTRODUCTION

**O**ver the past two decades, a growing number of U.S. industries have experienced severe and protracted contractions in demand, leading them to scrap obsolete capacity, to lay off workers, and to restructure production and firm organization. These include some industries that have lost cost competitiveness (textiles and apparel, nonrubber footwear, steel, and televisions); some that, although basically competitive, suffer from excess capacity because of a cyclical downswing in demand (such as automobiles); and, more recently, even some high-technology sectors, such as semiconductors, with excess capacity because of a rapid product cycle. Whatever the causes, and there are many, the consequences can be quite severe: low profits, idled capacity, and plant closings for employers; job-loss, unemployment, and lower-paying jobs for many workers with firm-specific skills; and disruption of local and regional economies heavily reliant on these industries for jobs and their tax base.

This chapter examines the most important policy instruments used in the United States to aid troubled industries, displaced workers, and hard-hit communities. In contrast to many other industrialized countries, such as present-day Japan,[1] the United States does not have a comprehensive set of policies targeted at specific troubled industries; instead, it relies on a patchwork of statutes in U.S. trade law that provide import relief to trade-impacted industries, as well as on a number of domestic-oriented adjustment policies to provide unemployment assistance and retraining, facilitate reallocation of labor, and regulate plant closings. Well-organized and politically powerful industrial sectors are sometimes able to bypass these routes and go directly to the administration and Congress for special assistance. Special assistance—such as the Chrysler bailout, the country-by-product Multifiber Agreement to limit textile and apparel imports, the trigger-price mechanism to set floor prices on steel imports, and voluntary export restraint agreements on Japanese automobiles—has been extended to industries on a case-by-case basis. A review of these cases, however, is beyond the scope of this chapter.

United States trade laws provide import relief to industries able to demonstrate that they have been severely injured by import competition. Through tariffs, countervailing duties, quotas, and "voluntary" export restraint agreements (VERs) negotiated with foreign suppliers, the United States provides trade-impacted industries with time to adjust, often through reductions in capacity and employment. These trade laws are of two types: escape-clause provisions and antidumping and countervailing statutes under the so-called Fair Trade Laws. A common feature of both sets of laws is the eligibility requirement that both injury and causation of injury by imports be demonstrated in an open forum. For completeness, I note that some industries have also sought assistance under Section 232 (the National Security Clause) of the U.S. trade law. Unlike the other routes to protection, here industries need not demonstrate unfair-trade practices, or even that imports caused injury to the industry; only that imports would impair (or threaten to impair) the national security.[2]

The United States also has several domestic policies to assist displaced workers, trade-impacted firms, and local communities—a fact not widely known. The Trade Adjustment Act (TAA) was enacted in 1962, in large part to gain the support of organized labor and employers for legislation to liberalize international trade. It is unique among trade laws of industrialized nations in targeting adjustment assistance at workers and firms injured by import competition. Since then, it has been largely supplanted by Title III of the Job Training and Partnership Act (JTPA). Title III provides retraining, job placement, and relocation assistance to a broader population of workers—those displaced by plant closings or permanent layoffs and the long-term unemployed—with individual states being responsible for the development and delivery of adjustment services. Several states have also enacted (or proposed) legislation to restrict (or delay) plant closings and mass layoffs. Provisions vary, but many call for advance notice of plant closings, mandatory severance pay or other income maintenance for displaced workers, and in some cases financial restitution to local communities.

The 1988 Omnibus Trade and Competitiveness Act modified many of these policies toward troubled industries. The escape clause now provides import relief contingent upon compliance with an industry adjustment plan, and is time-degressive to encourage adjustment and restructuring. Relief is made more certain by the automatic triggering of expedited TAA benefits to industries determined to be severely injured by imports. Although it was to have been slated for termination by the end of 1993, TAA will continue to provide adjustment assistance through a small uniform fee on imports. The Economic Dislocation and Worker Adjustment Assistance Acts significantly modify, and expand funding for, dislocated worker programs under Title III of the Job Training and Partnership Act. This act establishes federal and state dislocated-worker units capable of rapid-response delivery of adjustment assistance and, for the first time, mandates advance notice of plant closings and mass layoffs for larger establishments.

The sections that follow discuss U.S. trade policies toward troubled industries, important domestic-oriented policies, and recent modifications to these policies.

## IMPORT RELIEF THROUGH U.S. TRADE LAWS

Domestic industries severely affected by foreign trade have had recourse to import relief under several U.S. trade laws. The most important of these are the escape-clause (or "safeguard") provisions contained in Section 201 of the 1974 Trade Act, and the antidumping and countervailing-duty statutes that make up the Fair Trade Laws. Over time, troubled American industries have come to rely less on escape-clause petitions—where import relief has been uncertain—and more on antidumping petitions. Several factors—the lower causation test for injury, a shortened time limit for determinations of dumping margins and injury, and greater certainty of protection once petitions are approved—have also made petitions under the Fair Trade Laws more attractive than escape-clause action.

### Escape Clause

The idea, widely accepted, that domestic industries adversely affected by international trade require time to adapt is embodied in the safeguard provision (Article XIX) of the General Agreement on Tariffs and Trade

(GATT). The U.S. Congress enacted the first escape clause in 1951, requiring the Tariff Commission (later the International Trade Commission, or ITC) to initiate an investigation when petitioned by a trade-impacted industry, and, if an affirmative determination was made, to recommend to the president appropriate remedies to provide import relief (primarily through tariffs). The president had 60 days to implement the recommended remedy, or, if he decided that it was not in the national interest, to advise Congress on why he had not done so. From 1951 to 1962, the Tariff Commission returned affirmative decisions in 35 percent of petitions; of these, 37 percent were granted relief by the president.

*Evolution:* In 1962, and again in 1974, the escape clause underwent several important modifications: a tightening of "injury" criteria in 1962, followed by a relaxation in 1974. The amendments had a large effect not only on the number of petitions filed under the escape clause, but also on the number receiving affirmative findings from the ITC. Table 5.1 shows that the number of petitions fell from 116 petitions filed between 1951 and 1962 to 40 filed in the comparable 11-year period 1963–74. The relaxed criteria after 1974 resulted in a marginal rise in the number of Section 201 petitions (to 57). Many petitioners were, by this time, seeking import relief under alternative unfair-trade routes (see below). These modifications were made in response to concerns about how best to relieve political pressure for protectionist legislation from trade-impacted industries.[3]

As part of the 1962 Trade Expansion Act, the criteria for relief under the escape clause were significantly tightened. Whereas earlier petitions had only to demonstrate that imports were an important cause of injury, the 1962 amendments now required demonstration (1) of an absolute (not just relative) increase in imports, (2) that increased imports were causally related "in major part" to trade concessions, and (3) that imports were "the major factor" causing or threatening to cause serious injury to the industry. The "major

**Table 5.1**
**Determination under the escape clause**

| Escape-Clause Petitions | 1951–1962 | 1963–1974 | 1975–1985 |
|---|---|---|---|
| Cases before ITC | 116 | 40 | 57 |
| Affirmative injury | 41 | 8 | 33 |
| Fraction affirmative | .35 | .20 | .58 |
| Cases granted relief | 15 | 2 | 14 |
| Fraction granted relief | .37 | .25 | .42 |

*Source:* Lawrence and Litan (1986), Table 3–2, p. 40.

factor" meant that rising imports had to be more important than the combined effect of all other factors (such as falling demand, technological change, and change in tastes). The linkage between imports and trade concessions was particularly limiting because no trade concessions had been made since the last major round of tariff negotiations in the 1940s. Not surprisingly, the ITC made no affirmative decisions between 1963 and 1969; it was not until after tariff reductions negotiated in the Kennedy Round were implemented in 1969 that any affirmative determinations were made.

In 1974, in the wake of the severe recession induced by the oil crisis, Congress reversed itself and relaxed the criteria for escape-clause relief. Its intent was to make it easier for trade-impacted industries to seek temporary relief from imports, and to defuse support for overtly protectionist legislation, such as the proposed Burke-Hartke Bill.[4] The 1974 Trade Act removed the requirement that increased imports result from trade concessions and relaxed the injury standard to imports as "a substantial cause" of injury. "Substantial" cause is defined as one that is as important as, but not less important than, any other cause of injury. It also set new limits on relief—an initial five-year period with one extension of three years—and added expedited Trade Adjustment Assistance to the kinds of relief available under the escape clause.[5]

The relaxed criteria for escape-clause relief resulted in a significant rise in the percentage of affirmative decisions by the ITC—to 58 percent from 20 percent in the previous period. The president also approved a higher proportion of import relief recommendations from the ITC—42 percent as compared with 25 percent previously—and recommended expedited TAA in five cases.

*Discussion:* In general, the escape clause has performed reasonably well in providing temporary relief for industries seriously hurt by import competition. First, the ITC has demonstrated an ability to withstand political pressures for protection (Baldwin, 1985) and has recommended relief only when petitioners have demonstrated that serious injury occurred and that imports were the substantial cause of such injury to the industry. The ITC has consistently returned negative determinations in over 50 percent of escape-clause petitions. Second, the protection provided has generally been temporary. Of the 31 industries receiving escape-clause relief, only two industries—specialty steel and roofing materials—are still protected.[6] Furthermore, few industries receiving relief since 1975 have obtained it again, either through extensions of escape-clause protection or through subsequent petitions under the unfair-trade laws.[7] In contrast, protection granted outside the escape-clause provisions has tended to endure far longer than the five years of relief typical of most escape-clause cases.[8]

The time-limited nature of escape-clause relief appears to have resulted in considerable industry adjustment. Although there are exceptions (employment actually increased in the U.S. bicycle industry), most industries have responded by downsizing to the point where they can operate profitably without protection (Lawrence and Litan, 1986). In the 31 industries studied by Hufbauer, Berliner, and Elliott (1986), the number of production jobs almost always declined during the period of protection. Table 5.2, which summarizes their findings, indicates that employment in Carbon Steel III has declined by 10 percent annually since 1980; rubber footwear, glassware, industrial fasteners, and the auto industry all shed labor at rates in excess of 4 percent annually.

Escape-clause protection, however, has proved to be very costly to consumers. In seven escape-clause cases, Hufbauer, Berliner, and Elliott (1986) calculate that the costs to consumers averaged $340,000 per job "saved," ranging from $55,000 for each job in footwear to $1,000,000 in specialty steel. Because relief is often provided in the form of quotas rather than tariffs, the apparent trend in recent years, both domestic and foreign producers gain through higher prices.[9] They estimate the gains to domestic producers at about $4,000 to $20,000 per job annually; for foreign suppliers, the estimated quota rents total $200 million for automobiles, and may run as high as $2 billion annually for carbon steel.

Drawbacks of the escape clause—the low likelihood and uncertainty of relief—may have discouraged its use in recent years. One consequence is

**Table 5.2**
**Employment adjustment during period of protection**

| Industry | Employment Change[a] (%) | Industry | Employment Change[a] (%) |
|---|---|---|---|
| Book manufacturing | −2.2 | Carbon steel I | − 0.5 |
| Bexzenoid chemicals | −2.1 | Carbon steel II | 0.8 |
| Glassware | −4.0 | Carbon steel III | −10.4 |
| Rubber footwear | −4.5 | Ball bearings | − 0.4 |
| Ceramic articles | −3.3 | Specialty steel | − 1.3 |
| Ceramic tiles | −1.2 | Nonrubber footwear | − 1.5 |
| Textiles and apparel I | 0.0 | Color televisions | − 3.7 |
| Textiles and apparel II | −0.6 | CB radios | −15.2 |
| Textiles and apparel III | −1.6 | Industrial fasteners | − 5.3 |
| Orange juice | −4.0 | Automobiles | − 4.5 |
| Canned tuna | −2.2 | Motorcycles | 25.0 |

[a]Annual percentage change in employment between prerestraint and postrestraint years.
*Source:* Hufbauer, Berliner, and Elliott (1986), Table 1.3.

increased political pressure on Congress and the executive branch for protectionist remedies outside the escape-clause framework, as happened in 1980 after the automobile industry failed to demonstrate to the ITC that imports were the substantial cause of injury (Lawrence and Litan, 1986). The result was the negotiated (and costly) VER agreement with Japan to "voluntarily" limit automobile imports into the United States.[10] Another apparent result of the automobile case was a falloff in escape-clause activity—from 17 petitions in the three years prior to 1980, to 4 in the following three years. One view was that the ITC had resolved the "substantial cause" issue, namely, how to disentangle the effects of imports from other factors in such a way as to deny relief to cyclical industries such as the automobile industry.[11] Another contributing factor, to which I now turn, was changes in the antidumping and countervailing-duty statutes that made them more attractive alternatives to escape-clause action.

### Fair Trade Statutes

Industries injured (or threatened with injury) by imports may also seek relief under antidumping and countervailing-duty statutes in the Tariff Act of 1930. In these so-called Fair Trade Laws, the Department of the Treasury (and now the Department of Commerce) investigates complaints of dumping or government subsidization of exports, while the ITC determines whether material injury resulted from imports. Upon affirmative findings of *both* unfair-trade practices and material injury to the domestic industry, the U.S. Customs is instructed to impose a tariff or countervailing duty on the imported items to offset the effect of the unfair-trade practice.

Broadly speaking, dumping is defined as export sales at prices below that of sales in the home market or, under some circumstances, export sales that fail to cover a statutory measure of the producer's production costs. In a dumping complaint, import prices are compared with home market prices or the "fair value" of imports, and an antidumping duty equal to the dumping margin is assessed upon evidence of material injury to the U.S. industry. In situations where a foreign nation bestows a subsidy on a producer, and imports of this product cause injury to a U.S. industry, countervailing duties set equal to the amount of the subsidy are levied on the product when it enters this country. The rationale is that it would offset any unfair advantage accruing to a foreign producer owing to a government subsidy.

*Evolution:* Over time, the dumping and countervailing-duty statutes underwent several modifications that encouraged their greater use by troubled industries. First, the Trade Act of 1974 broadened the use of a "constructed value" criterion in determining dumping (Eichengreen and Van der

Ven, 1984). Under Section 205(b) of this act, the Treasury Department was instructed to disregard sales below cost in the home market "over an extended period of time and in substantial quantities" and to substitute constructed values in their place. Constructed values are prices that recover the costs of raw materials and fabrication, plus a minimum allowance of 10 percent for general expenses and 8 percent for profits. Since these statutory minimums made no provisions for the variation of profit margins over the business cycle, they increased the likelihood that marginal cost pricing during recessions would be construed as dumping.[12]

Additional changes were made to these statutes in the Trade Agreements Act of 1979. In this act, the United States agreed to adopt the higher "material injury" requirements of the 1979 GATT Antidumping and Subsidies Codes negotiated in the Tokyo Round, and to apply a uniform definition of subsidy to countries that were signatories to the GATT Subsidies Code.[13] Nonsignatories, however, would still be subject to countervailing duties, even without demonstration of material injury. To enhance the prospects for relief under the stricter injury standard, Congress shortened the time limits for antidumping and countervailing-duty determinations, and removed some restrictions on the use of constructed values in antidumping cases.[14] Another change was to shift antidumping and countervailing-duty investigations to the Commerce Department on the grounds that it would be more responsive to industry complaints than the Treasury Department (Borrus and Goldstein, 1987).

*Discussion:* These modifications probably contributed to the rise in the number of antidumping and countervailing-duty petitions filed. As shown in Table 5.3, the norm was 6 antidumping and 12 countervailing-duty petitions per year prior to 1974. In the most recent period, 1980–88, the average number of petitions filed had risen to just under 50 per year. Other factors contributed to this recent rise in activity under the unfair-trade statutes. I have already noted the difficulty of obtaining import relief under the escape clause, especially after the ITC's negative determination in the automobile industry's petition. Another related, but possibly more important, cause was the difference in the injury causation standards used in escape clause and unfair-trade petitions. Unlike escape-clause cases, where the "substantial cause" test of injury is required, the ITC needs only to determine that injury was caused "by reason of" imports in unfair-trade investigations. In other words, the ITC need not weigh relative causes of injury, only that the imports in question contributed, even minimally, to the depressed condition of the domestic industry.[15] This low-causation test certainly made antidumping and countervailing-duty petitions more attractive alternatives to escape-clause action.

**Table 5.3**
**Antidumping and countervailing-duty petitions**
(Per year)

| Period | Antidumping Petitions | Countervailing-duty Petitions |
|---|---|---|
| 1955–73 | 6 | 12 |
| 1974–79 | 13 | 37 |
| 1980–88 | 48 | 49 |

*Sources:* Baldwin (1984); ITC Antidumping and Countervailing-duty data base for 1980–88.

It has been suggested that trade-impacted industries may increasingly be using antidumping laws to extract concessions from foreign producers (Prusa, 1988). The act of filing a petition might lead to privately negotiated settlements between parties in which foreign producers agree to raise prices or to restrain exports. This might explain why large numbers of petitions are withdrawn before reaching a final determination. It may also explain why imports subject to antidumping petitions decline by the same proportion regardless of whether antidumping or countervailing duties are levied or petitions withdrawn (UNCTAD, 1984).

Finally, troubled industries may file antidumping petitions as a prelude to intensive lobbying of Congress and the Administration for special protection. The U.S. steel industry is notable in this regard. Between 1980 and early 1988, fully 209 out of 409 antidumping petitions and 200 out of 395 countervailing-duty petitions were related to steel and specialty steel products. Most of these petitions were terminated, either after a new Trigger Price mechanism for steel imports was implemented (1980), or after a series of voluntary restraint agreements (VRAs) were negotiated with major foreign suppliers (1982, 1984, and 1985).

For cases reaching a final determination, the Fair Trade Laws appear to ensure that only petitions with merit (that is, those that satisfy both unfair trade and injury criteria) receive import relief. Relief is by no means certain. Excluding cases terminated before a final determination is made, antidumping cases filed between 1980 and 1988 split roughly 50–50 between affirmative and negative determinations; in countervailing-duty cases, just over 40 percent of determinations were affirmative. A large part of this outcome is attributable to the system of checks inherent in dividing responsibilities for determining injury and unfair-trade practices between the ITC and the Commerce Department's International Trade Administration (ITA). To illustrate this point, Tables 5.4 and 5.5 show how final outcomes in anti-

**Table 5.4**
**Antidumping determinations, 1980–1988**

| Determination | ITC Preliminary Injury | | ITA Final Dumping[a] | | ITC Final Injury[b] | |
|---|---|---|---|---|---|---|
| | Cases | (%) | Cases | (%) | Cases | (%) |
| Affirmative | 306 | 80.9 | 186 | 89.8 | 116 | 66.3 |
| Partial affirmative | 3 | 0.8 | 1 | 0.5 | 13 | 7.4 |
| Negative | 69 | 18.3 | 20 | 9.7 | 46 | 26.3 |
| Suspended | 0 | | 5 | | 0 | |
| Terminated | 20 | | 45 | | 12 | |
| Outcome not available | 12 | | 52 | | 1 | |
| Total petitions | 410 | | 309 | | 188 | |

[a]Petitions with ITC preliminary affirmative or partial affirmative determinations only.
[b]Petitions with ITA final affirmative or partial affirmative determinations only.
*Source:* ITC data base.

dumping and countervailing-duty cases are shaped by each agency's determinations over the course of an investigation. These tables may be read as
decision-trees, with probabilities associated with each of three possible
outcomes—affirmative, partial affirmative (split vote), and negative. I exclude cases that are suspended,[16] terminated, or still in progress. First,
consider the antidumping determinations shown in Table 5.4. In preliminary
injury determination, the ITC screened out about 18 percent of the petitions
for not meeting injury standards. Of the 309 affirmative petitions passing the
preliminary screen, the ITA found evidence of dumping in 90 percent of the
cases and none in 10 percent. In its final determination, the ITC rejected 26
percent that did not meet the injury and causation criteria, even though it
found evidence of dumping. Thus, out of a total of 135 negative determinations—each of which would have led to rejection of the antidumping
petition—115 were made by the ITC and only 20 by the ITA. The low
number of negative determinations by the ITA is not surprising in view of
the *de minimus* standard (0.5 percent dumping margin) required for an
affirmative dumping finding.

Table 5.5 shows comparable figures for countervailing-duty cases. Recall
that only signatories of the 1979 GATT subsidies code are subject to the joint
oversight of the ITC and ITA; for nonsignatory countries, no injury determination is required and only the demonstrated presence of subsidies is
required to trigger countervailing duties. For the first group of signatory
countries, the ITA arrived at affirmative determinations in 89 percent of
cases, rejecting just 11 percent of all subsidy complaints. Of the 137

### Table 5.5
### Countervailing-duty determinations, 1980–1988

| Determination | Signatories to Subsidies Code | | | | Nonsignatories | |
| | ITA CV-Duty | | ITC Injury[a] | | ITA CV-Duty | |
| | Cases | (%) | Cases | (%) | Cases | (%) |
|---|---|---|---|---|---|---|
| Affirmative | 137 | 88.9 | 45 | 39.5 | 63 | 80.8 |
| Partial affirmative | 0 | 0.0 | 5 | 4.4 | 3 | 3.8 |
| Negative | 17 | 11.1 | 64 | 56.1 | 12 | 15.4 |
| Suspended | 3 | | 1 | | 9 | |
| Terminated | 21 | | 21 | | 11 | |
| Outcome not available | 114 | | 1 | | 12 | |
| Total petitions | 292 | | 137 | | 110 | |

[a]Petitions with ITA affirmative or partial affirmative determinations only.
*Source:* ITC data base.

affirmative ITA cases that were not suspended or terminated, the ITC found no evidence of material injury in over 55 percent of them. For cases brought against nonsignatories, only the ITA was involved and affirmative final determinations were returned in over 80 percent of cases.

Overall, the tables reveal that while existing unfair-trade statutes make it relatively easy to show dumping and subsidies (over 80 percent of cases succeed in doing so), they also tend to restrict relief to those industries that have been materially injured by imports (and other factors). In its injury investigations, the ITC has consistently returned affirmative determinations in about half of the cases.[17] Its voting record in unfair-trade cases is similar to that in escape-clause petitions (58 percent), which is surprising in view of the more stringent injury and causation standards used in Section 201 cases.

## DOMESTIC-ORIENTED ADJUSTMENT POLICIES

In addition to import protection, the United States provides assistance to workers, firms, and communities to help adjust to economic dislocation. These include Trade Adjustment Assistance (TAA), Title III of the Job Training and Partnership Act (JTPA), and legislation on plant closings. TAA specifically targets workers, firms, and communities affected by import competition. Since the 1980s, it has been largely supplanted by the Title III program, which extends income support, retraining, and other adjustment assistance to dislocated workers without regard to cause of dislocation. States have also enacted (or introduced) legislation to restrict or otherwise delay plant closings, and to require employers to provide advance notice of closings and permanent layoffs.

## Trade Adjustment Assistance (TAA)

The TAA Act, first enacted by Congress as part of the Trade Expansion Act of 1962, was intended to mitigate the adverse effects of trade liberalization on workers and firms in impacted industries. Organized labor, as well as many employers, supported trade liberalization in return for this legislation. In 1974, TAA coverage was expanded to include trade-impacted communities, although none so far has met the criteria for assistance under this act. Modified eligibility for workers and budget reductions since 1981 have resulted in a shrinkage in TAA assistance; although Congress reauthorized TAA in 1983 and 1986, the program was to have been slated for termination after 1993.

*TAA program features:* For workers meeting eligibility criteria, TAA provided a variety of allowances for income maintenance, job counseling, retraining, and relocation. Adjustment allowances primarily took the form of supplemental unemployment insurance payments, up to 65 percent of previous wages or up to a maximum of 65 percent of average weekly wages in manufacturing—whichever was lower (benefit levels were increased to 70 percent in 1974). Together with unemployment insurance (UI), income replacement with TAA could not exceed 75 percent of earnings in the previous job. This coverage could be received for up to 52 weeks, with an additional 26 weeks if the worker was enrolled in a certified training (or retraining) program.

Trade-impacted firms certified by the Commerce Department were eligible to receive technical and financial assistance (Lawrence and Litan, 1986). This included technical assistance for market research and engineering to help firms develop adjustment plans, loan guarantees (up to 90 percent of principal), direct loans (with maturities up to 25 years), and tax relief (carrybacks on operating losses for five rather than three years).

The 1974 legislation added assistance to communities that could demonstrate to the Commerce Department that imports contributed "importantly" to a significant proportion of layoffs in the local community. If the Department approved these plans, communities were eligible for technical assistance in developing adjustment plans, grants, or loans to improve local public works and attract new firms. To date, no TAA funds have been extended to communities (two trade-impacted communities applied for TAA assistance but were rejected). Heavy reporting requirements, coupled with difficulties in persuading local companies to provide the information needed for community-based petitions, were major reasons why this form of TAA was so little used.

*Adjustment assistance under TAA:* Table 5.6 gives information on adjustment assistance provided under TAA since its inception in 1962. TAA coverage and level of adjustment assistance varied greatly over this period, with the greatest use of TAA occurring between 1976 and 1980, when benefit payments to workers expanded by more than 50 times compared with the previous 13 years.

The initial TAA criteria were based on the escape-clause standards of the 1962 Trade Expansion Act. Petitioners had to persuade the Tariff Commission that imports had increased, that this increase resulted from trade concessions, and that the increase in imports was the major cause of injury to displaced workers. The causal linkage between imports and trade concessions was particularly restrictive, since the last major trade concessions took place in the 1940s. Not surprisingly, no one was certified under TAA between 1962 and 1969, and only after trade concessions from the Kennedy Round of negotiations took effect in 1968 did a somewhat larger number (35,000 workers between 1969 and 1975) receive certification.

Eligibility criteria were changed subsequently, first in 1974 and again in 1981. Paralleling modifications to the escape clause, the 1974 Trade Act substantially relaxed these criteria. The linkage between imports and trade concessions was dropped and the definition of causation was weakened to imports as an "important" cause of layoffs. These changes had a dramatic

**Table 5.6**
**Trade adjustment assistance 1962–1985**
(Assistance in millions of dollars)

|  |  | 1962–1975 | 1976–1980 | 1981–1985 |
|---|---|---|---|---|
| A. | Workers | | | |
|  | Number of workers certified | 58,899 | 1,313,349 | 179,689 |
|  | Benefit payments | 45.3 | 2,455.2 | 1,718.8 |
|  | Allowances | — | 2,433.0 | 1,656.0 |
|  | Training | — | 19.0 | 51.4 |
|  | Relocation | — | 2.6 | 10.1 |
| | | | | |
| B. | Firms | | | |
|  | Number of firms certified | 36 | 972 | 1,624 |
|  | Technical assistance | 1.2 (1969 on) | 53.4 | 79.9 |
|  | Financial assistance | 39.6 (1970 on) | 272.0 | 112.2 |

*Source:* Lawrence and Litan (1986), Table 3–6, p. 56.

effect on the number of workers certified—over 1.3 million were certified as eligible for TAA between 1976 and 1980. The second change, which came as part of the Budget Reconciliation Act of 1981, was motivated largely by the incoming administration's efforts to cut federal spending. In that act, the 1974 eligibility criteria were tightened so that imports again had to be a "substantial" cause of injury. This resulted in a dramatic decline in the number of workers certified, and although more firms were certified during this latter period, average disbursements per firm fell.

*Discussion:* Government intervention in TAA has been justified on equity, political, and efficiency grounds (Aho and Bayard, 1984). The first—equity—argues that workers displaced by foreign trade deserve to be compensated for losses in income, especially when government action in removing trade tariffs contributed to those losses. The second justification—political—argues that socially beneficial trade liberalization would be blocked politically by losers from trade liberalization. By compensating trade-impacted workers and firms, a targeted assistance program may offset political pressures to enact protectionist legislation. Finally, government intervention may be justified on efficiency grounds, arguing that adjustment is impeded by labor market imperfections and informational asymmetries (McMillan, 1990).

In assessing the validity of these three arguments, Aho and Bayard (1984) concluded that the political gains of TAA, in the form of the welfare benefits of freer trade, were enormous. They arrived at this conclusion by comparing the welfare loss and consumer costs of a tariff with the TAA payments in five industries where the president recommended expedited TAA rather than a 25 percent tariff. They were less sanguine, however, about the administrative costs, induced labor market inefficiencies, and inequities in the TAA program—for several reasons.

First, because of the injury and causation tests used to determine eligibility under TAA, certification was very slow, and benefits were often provided years after injury or after job displacement occurred. This is not surprising, inasmuch as the Department of Labor had to determine not only the merits of each petition, but also the particular categories of workers in an establishment that had been "injured" by imports. A General Accounting Office (GAO) study found that by the time TAA-certified workers received their first benefit payment, 71 percent of them were already back at work (GAO, 1980).

Second, the empirical evidence does not support the notion that TAA encouraged much labor market adjustment. Extended income replacement under TAA (up to 52 weeks) may have increased unemployment duration by providing insufficient incentives for workers to find new jobs. A Mathematica study (1979) found evidence of increased unemployment duration among TAA recipients, although this may have improved job search, as reflected in higher earnings or a lower likelihood of job separation in the post-displacement job. The Mathematica study, however, found no significant wage gains in subsequent jobs in a more recent cohort of TAA recipients.

Finally, on equity grounds, there appears to be little justification for categorical labor adjustment programs that discriminate between trade-impacted workers and those displaced for other domestic causes. In the studies cited above, TAA recipients were compared with a control group of workers receiving unemployment insurance payments. TAA recipients were somewhat older, more unionized, and less educated, and a higher fraction (81 percent) as compared with UI recipients (73 percent) expected layoffs to be temporary. The TAA group tended to have longer spells of unemployment, but this appears to have been induced by TAA's high income replacement. Overall, the TAA group resembled other displaced workers—they did not experience significantly higher earnings losses than the UI control group and large initial wage losses were found only among the permanently displaced TAA sample (28 percent of TAA recipients). It is this latter group of displaced workers who experienced the greatest problems in adjustment.

### The Displaced Worker Program of JTPA (Title III)

Title III of the Job Training and Partnership Act of 1982 shifted the focus of adjustment assistance from trade-impacted workers to all dislocated workers, irrespective of the reason for dislocation. The displaced-worker program of JTPA grew out of the perceived limitations of the TAA program, as well as out of growing concerns about plant closings and worker dislocation. Several surveys by the Bureau of Labor Statistics (BLS) served to focus policy attention on the dislocated worker problem, particularly the fact that, between 1979 and 1984, 5.1 million workers with more than three years of seniority were displaced from their jobs by plant closings, slack work, or elimination of job positions.[18]

This shift in focus was reflected in funding for the two programs. Between 1982 and 1986, $650 million in federal funds were made available through the Title III program. Total disbursements under Title III in 1985 were over $220 million, compared with just $53 million under TAA. The emphasis also shifted from income maintenance to training, counseling, job placement, worker relocation assistance, and other support services. Finally, Title III turned over to states many of the earlier federal responsibilities for designing and implementing dislocated worker programs—which population to target, how resources are distributed, and what services to provide.

Federal JTPA funds are allocated to states in two ways. Three-quarters of funds are allocated in proportion to a state's share of unemployed in the country, its share of the unemployed exceeding 4.5 percent of the civilian labor force, and its share of the long-term unemployed (defined as exceeding 15 weeks of unemployment). These federal funds are matched by states, with reductions for states with higher unemployment rates than the national average. The remaining 25 percent of funds is allocated to states at the Secretary of Labor's discretion.

*Discussion:* States have had considerable latitude in designing programs to help displaced workers. Consequently, there is great variation not only in Title III operators, but also in the populations served and the kinds of adjustment services provided. Title III projects are operated by Service Delivery Area–Private Industry Councils (SDA-PICs), educational institutions (primarily vocational and technical schools and community colleges), public organizations (including state and local employment service agencies), and private sector organizations, including unions and projects operated jointly by unions and employers.

Title III projects have several important characteristics, as noted in GAO (1986). First, the majority of projects (62 percent) were open to all eligible dislocated workers who applied for assistance, the remaining 38 percent being targeted toward specific populations, such as a group of displaced workers from a specific factory, or an entire industry facing large numbers of layoffs. Second, most Title III projects tended to be small, enrolling on average about 78 displaced workers; however, a few large projects (5 percent) served over 800 participants. Third, despite the mix of services provided by most projects, relatively few participants received training assistance—less than half reported any form of classroom training, on the job training (OJT), or remedial training. However, most participants received job placement assistance, 80 percent received job-counseling, and 60 percent received job-search assistance. The apparent preference of displaced workers for job search and OJT, rather than long-term retraining in educational institutions, suggests that many skills may not be firm-specific; skills may be generic and only require "certification" to be marketed to potential employers (Cook, 1987). Finally, relative to nationally representative samples of displaced workers, Title III projects tended to serve fewer older displaced workers (over 55 years), and more minorities and women. Furthermore, only a small fraction of displaced workers received assistance from Title III programs. Of the 2.3 million workers identified as displaced by the

BLS survey, the Title III program enrolled only about 130,000 such workers in program year 1984.

The great variability of projects, providers, and populations served makes it difficult to assess the effectiveness of the Title III program. The 1986 GAO study found an average placement rate of 69 percent, which compares favorably with the 55 percent placement rate in Community Education and Training Act (CETA) demonstration projects.[19] It should be noted, however, that the latter program served economically disadvantaged populations as distinct from those who participated in Title III programs. The average entry-level hourly wage for new jobs found by CETA participants was $6.61, which was generally lower than their prior wage and considerably lower (by over 20 percent) than the private-sector average hourly wage of $8.52.[20] The simple cross-tabulation of provider characteristics and project outcomes reported in the GAO study makes it difficult to compare the efficacy of alternative service providers. In general, private-sector providers reported both higher placement rates (71 percent) and wage levels ($7.62); projects that targeted special populations (such as workers involved in plant shutdowns) had somewhat lower placement rates (65 percent) but higher wage levels ($7.03). Projects that stress OJT tended to have higher placement rates, which is not surprising since program participation is linked to job placement; lower reported hourly wages may simply reflect job training financed through payment of lower entry wages.[21]

### State Legislation on Plant Closings

Concerns about worker displacement and the impact of plant closings on local communities gave rise in the late 1970s and 1980s to numerous legislative bills, both at the federal and the state level, to restrict plant closings and to make advance notification mandatory. Much of the initial push for federal legislation came from congressmen and senators in states with heavy regional concentrations of high-paying, unionized manufacturing jobs. Because many of these bills died in committee, supporters of plant-closing restrictions moved their political efforts to state capitals. There, a spate of bills having common objectives and similar features were introduced.

As of 1986, three states—Maine, Wisconsin, and Massachusetts—had passed advance notification laws, and similar proposals were pending in 38 other states. Maine required establishments with 100 or more employees to provide 60 days notification of relocation and terminations resulting in a substantial permanent reduction in operations. It mandated payment of severance pay equal to the product of average weekly pay and years of job tenure. Wisconsin made a 60-day advance notice mandatory. Michigan's Public Act 44 required employer notification so that the Michigan Department of Labor could offer state assistance to facilitate employee buyouts in situations where this was feasible (Gordus, Jarley, and Ferman, 1981).

Most of the state legislative proposals had several key features in common (McKenzie, 1984). First, with variations, the proposals tended to apply to larger firms with over 100 employees. Second, many required a one-year notification of plant closings; several bills even proposed a two-year notification period. Third, many incorporated mandatory severance pay or other forms of supplementary income maintenance, and several required continued health insurance coverage for laid-off workers. Fourth, several required the relocating company to make financial restitutions to the community, some in the form of a payment proportional to the annual wage bill, others as a fraction of tax revenues lost to the local government through relocation of the firm. Finally, most bills required the company to submit an "economic impact statement" to both its employees and responsible public officials.

*Discussion:* The first solid evidence on the extent of plant closings in the United States was provided by a 1986 GAO study. Based upon a random, stratified sample of firms experiencing a plant closing or mass layoff exceeding 20 percent of its workforce in 1983 and 1984, the GAO estimated that each year about 8,800 establishments with 50 to 99 employees and 7,400 establishments with 100 or more employees experienced a plant closing or permanent layoff, affecting about 1.3 million workers annually.[22] Table 5.7 indicates that the manufacturing sector, durables in particular, reported the highest rates of plant closings or mass layoffs, accounting for some 66 percent of all workers displaced in those two years.

Some of the major reasons given for plant closure or layoff concerned problems of competition in the marketplace (foreign competition is one factor). Over 35 percent of the 7,800 closures and permanent layoffs identified in establishments with 100 or more employees fell in industries that had been certified by the Department of Labor or the ITC as being hurt by international trade. These closures and mass layoffs affected about 436,000 workers, or some 40 percent of displaced workers.

In a related study, the GAO also found that most establishments (66 percent) provided their employees with at least 14 days of advance notice of pending plant closings or mass layoffs (GAO 1987). However, about one-third of the establishments provided no advance warning at all. Because they refer only to "specific notice" (in which a date of closing or termination is specified) and exclude "general notice," the GAO figures tend to understate the extent of advance notification. When the two are combined, the number of establishments giving some notice rises to 88 percent, with almost 60 percent providing more than two weeks notice (McKenzie, 1988). For a sample of somewhat larger establishments, the Conference Board study by Berembeim (1986) found that over half announced plant closings more than three months in advance.

There appears to be some agreement that advance notification would facilitate worker adjustment and reallocation of labor to other expanding industries (Office of Technology Assessment [OTA], 1987). Recent research by Addison and Portugal (1987) based on the BLS's January 1985 Current Population Survey of Displaced Workers shows that advance notification had a statistically significant effect on reducing the duration of unemployment—about 27 percent or, at the sample mean, by about four weeks. Another effect of advance notification, however, was to stimulate early job separations prior to plant closing; this accounted for a large part of the measured notification effect on unemployment duration.[23] This appears to confirm the OTA conclusion that loss of qualified manpower during notification may be a potentially serious cost of advance notification.

Advance notification also imposes costs on employers by raising the cost of adjustment to changes in demand. Other components of states' plant-closing legislation, such as provision of mandatory severance pay and extended health benefits, also add to employers' costs. McKenzie (1988) argues that if employees desire advance notice and severance pay, they should be willing to give up part of their current compensation for that guarantee. Making severance pay and other fringe benefits mandatory should, so the argument goes, result in pressure on employers to reduce

**Table 5.7**
**Plant closings, permanent layoffs, and worker displacement**

| Industry | Establishments with Closings or Mass Layoffs | Rate of Closings, Layoffs (%) | Number of Workers Displaced | Percent of Total Cases |
|---|---|---|---|---|
| Total | 7,790 | 7.8 | 1,048,600 | 100 |
| Manufacturing | 4,650 | 13.2 | 694,900 | 66 |
| Durable | 3,050 | 17.7 | 472,000 | 45 |
| Nondurable | 1,600 | 10.2 | 222,900 | 21 |
| Wholesale-retail | 690 | 3.6 | 69,200 | 7 |
| Services | 1,750 | 4.4 | 181,100 | 17 |
| Other industries | 700 | 12.4 | 103,400 | 10 |

*Source:* General Accounting Office (1986), p. 10.

current compensation to pay for these fringe benefits.[24] Furthermore, state efforts to retard plant closings and relocation may inhibit future plant openings and job creation in the state, and by making it more expensive to do business or stay in business, lead existing and potential employers to locate in other, lower-cost regions.

## RECENT DEVELOPMENTS AND CONCLUDING REMARKS

In the years ahead, U.S. adjustment policies will be shaped by several bills in the 1988 Omnibus Trade and Competitiveness Act. In this concluding section, I will review the modifications that this act makes to the troubled-industry policies described above, and to Section 301 of the 1974 Trade Act, which requires the administration to investigate allegations of unreasonable foreign business practices burdening U.S. commerce. Together, these new statutes provide some insights into the direction in which troubled-industry policy in the United States is headed.

### Changes to Trade Laws

The Omnibus Trade and Competitiveness Act modified the escape-clause provisions in several ways to "facilitate positive adjustment to import competition."[25] First, it appears to make relief conditional on compliance with an industry adjustment plan. Within 120 days of filing a Section 201 petition, petitioners are required to submit a plan for positive adjustment to import competition, after consultation with the USTR and other federal agencies to evaluate the adequacy of the proposals. During the period of import relief, the ITC is to monitor the progress made in implementing these plans and, after two years, to recommend reduction, modification, or termination of relief if it determines that the industry has not made adequate efforts to adjust. Past experience with conditionality provisions, such as the reinvestment requirements imposed on the steel industry by Congress, has not proved particularly effective.[26] It remains unclear just what form the industry adjustment plans envisaged in this new act will take.

Second, protection will be phased down during the period of relief, with the first reduction taking place at the end of three years. Such time-degressive relief should provide trade-impacted industries with incentives to begin adjustment early. In some earlier cases, the adjustment process was postponed so long that a huge chasm separated the U.S. industry from its foreign competitors, necessitating further extensions of import relief (Hufbauer, Berliner, and Elliott, 1986).

Finally, affirmative findings by the ITC would now automatically trigger expedited consideration for TAA benefits by the Department of Labor (for displaced workers) and the Department of Commerce (for firms), with no presidential action required. Previously, expedited TAA consideration was just one of several relief options that could be recommended by the president after an affirmative injury determination by the ITC. As noted above, the president did not always recommend relief and this uncertainty may have discouraged use of the escape clause in recent years. The automatic triggering of TAA relief would make it easier for lawmakers to fend off protectionist legislation sponsored by import-injured industries that failed to obtain relief.

A potentially more important change was the adoption of the so-called "Super-301" provision in the Omnibus Trade Act. This new law requires the administration to investigate a wide range of foreign business practices that burden U.S. trade, to identify the most important trade barriers in an annual National Trade Estimate, and to seek their removal. Should the unreasonable practices continue, it authorizes the president to retaliate against the offending country, or explain to Congress why no action was taken. The earlier Section 301 statute of the 1974 Trade Act gave the president considerable discretion in responding to industry claims of foreign trade barriers (Bello and Holmes, 1986); however, no retaliatory action was initiated by him between 1975 and 1985, even though 53 Section 301 petitions were filed over this ten-year period.

Although not immediately apparent, Super-301 is significant to U.S. troubled industries in several ways. First, many potential candidates for Super-301 action are the same countries whose industries have been major competitors of troubled U.S. industries. Retaliation by the United States would mean closure of domestic markets to imports from these countries. Second, the threat of retaliation itself may induce other countries to accept higher levels of U.S. exports in return for moderating their import levels into the United States.[27] These potential benefits might explain why organized labor and domestic-oriented industries were the main supporters of political efforts to enact Super-301 (Milner, 1989).

### Domestic-Oriented Policies

The Omnibus Trade Act also implemented several changes in the domestic-oriented policies described earlier. The 1988 Act reauthorized TAA—but only until 1993, after which the program was slated to be terminated. Other changes, such as the expanded funding for assistance to displaced workers and the plant-closing notification requirements, may signal the beginnings of a more coordinated labor market policy toward worker displacement.[28]

*Economic Adjustment and Worker Dislocation Act:* The 1988 Omnibus Trade and Competitiveness Act amended Title III of the Job Training and Partnership Act (JTPA) in a number of ways. First, it called for almost a billion-dollar budget for training, counseling, reemployment, and relocation assistance for displaced workers. As with the previous Title III program, 80 percent of the funds would be allocated to states, with a reserve of 20 percent for use at the discretion of the Secretary of Labor. Second, a federal Dislocated Worker Unit (DWU) would be established, with local counterparts in each state, to provide rapid response adjustment assistance to workers displaced by plant closings or mass layoffs. The DWU has several functions: to establish on-site contact with employer and workers after notification of plant closing or mass layoff; to provide information on job availability in the local labor market; to promote the creation of labor-management committees; and to collect information on worker displacement. Finally, it broadened the array of services to include entrepreneurial training to help program participants set up new businesses.

This act also includes several modifications intended to encourage greater (and earlier) use of training assistance. Experience under the previous Title III program revealed that limited income replacement was a major deterrent to retraining, leading many participants to choose job search and placement over training assistance. To encourage early participation in certified training programs, the act established time limits for enrollment in training—no later than the thirteenth week of receipt of unemployment insurance (UI) or the eighth week after notice is given that the layoff will exceed six months—to qualify for supplemental income support after the end of UI support. For these participants, income support is available to complete the training program, but at levels not to exceed the level of UI benefits.

*Worker Adjustment and Retraining Notification Act:* An integral part of the rapid response capability envisioned by the new Title III displaced worker program is advance notification of plant closings and mass layoffs. This is provided through the Worker Adjustment and Retraining Notification Act, implemented as Section 6401 of the 1988 Omnibus Trade and Competitiveness Act. Broadly, it mandates 60 days advance notification of plant closings and mass layoffs in firms with over 100 full-time employees.[29] Employers are required to serve written notice to worker representatives and to both the state Dislocated Worker Unit and local government officials. Notification would set into motion a coordinated, rapid delivery of adjustment assistance under Title III of JTPA. The act also specifies employer liabilities to workers (back pay) and to the state ($500 a day) for failure to provide advance notification.

A number of exclusions and exemptions, however, are permitted under this act. Specifically, employers are exempt when plant closings or layoffs do not result in (1) a break of employment exceeding six months and (2) affected workers are offered an opportunity to transfer to a different plant site. Other provisions permit employers to shut down plants prior to the end of the 60-day period if notification prevents employers from getting capital and business that would have allowed postponement of the shutdown, or if plant closing or mass layoffs were caused by business circumstances that were not reasonably foreseeable at the time notice was required. Closing of facilities, whether due to time-limited employment contracts, or to strikes and lockouts not intended to evade the intent of the act, are also exempt from notification requirements.

The Worker Adjustment and Retraining Notification Act did not implement some of the more onerous provisions contained in previous state plant closing legislation. The Act kept notification to 60 days (compared with one or two years in several state bills), and did not mandate payment of severance pay and other fringe benefits.

---

### NOTES

1. See Komiya, Okuno, and Suzumura (1988).
2. Section 232 petitions are rare, although several industries—petroleum, industrial fasteners, and machine tools—have sought import relief using this route. The 1986 partial affirmative finding for the National Machine Tool Builders Association petition was only the second case to win approval under the National Security Clause (see Alexander, 1990; Saxonhouse, 1986).
3. The Kennedy Administration sought broad authority to negotiate tariff reductions with the European Economic Community, and was concerned about the potentially disruptive effects on trade policy of tariffs granted under the escape clause. The Trade Expansion Act balanced tightened eligibility for escape relief with enactment of the Trade Adjustment Act.
4. If passed by Congress, the Burke-Hartke Bill would have rolled 1972 imports back to levels prevailing between 1965 and 1969.
5. By 1974, the president could extend import relief to successful petitioners in the form of tariffs, quotas, or orderly marketing arrangements (OMAs).
6. Recently, the U.S. heavy motorcycle industry requested that relief be ended early, because the industry had recovered.

7. One of the exceptions was the nonrubber footwear industry, which received escape-clause protection through import quotas between 1977 and 1981. Subsequently, in 1982 and 1983, it filed two petitions under the unfair-trade laws, but both were terminated. Two other escape-clause petitions followed in 1984 and 1985; the first returned a negative finding, but the ITC found affirmatively for the industry in 1985.

8. Examples include domestic shipbuilding (since 1920), automobiles (voluntary export restraints from Japan since 1981), meat (quotas since 1965), and textiles and apparel. Concerning textiles, what began as a voluntary export restraint (VER) agreement with Japan in 1957 has now grown into a country-by-product quota system negotiated under the Multifiber Agreement. For a more complete list, see Lawrence and Litan (1986), particularly Table 3-4.

9. Recently, the United States has relied more on voluntary quantitative export restraints than on tariffs to provide escape-clause relief. VERs are a way of circumventing Article XIX of GATT, which requires compensation to countries whose exports are subjected to tariffs invoked under the escape clause.

10. Other examples of VERs with Japan resulting from negative ITC determinations include bicycle parts, raincoats, porcelain tableware, and cast-iron joints.

11. Former commissioners involved in the case, however, assert that no such consensus existed in the ITC (Stern and Wechsler, 1986).

12. The 10-percent margin for general expenses also made no allowance for cross-national differences in cost structure.

13. "Material injury" is defined as "harm that is not inconsequential, immaterial, or unimportant." While this standard is hardly clear, it appears to raise the injury threshold from the *de minimus* standard that existed prior to 1979 (Borrus and Goldstein, 1987).

14. Antidumping investigations were to be completed within 140 to 190 days, down from 180 to 270 days; for countervailing-duty cases, the time limit was lowered to seven months from the previous one year.

15. See Applebaum and Kaplan (1987), p. 191.

16. An investigation is suspended when the government of the dumping country, or the exporters who account for substantially all of the merchandise, agree to stop exports to the United States within six months of the date of suspension, or to revise their prices promptly to eliminate any dumping margin.

17. In antidumping cases, the joint probability of an affirmative ITC decision in both preliminary and final determinations is 53 percent.

18. The BLS defines displaced workers as persons who lost their jobs because of plant closings, slack work, or elimination of a position or job, and who had significant attachment to their former position (three or more years of job tenure). To study the magnitude of displaced workers, two supplementary surveys—in January 1984 and January 1986—were sponsored by the Employment and Training

Administration. The first survey showed that, among those aged 20 and above, 13.9 million workers lost their jobs between January 1979 and January 1984; using the BLS definition, 5.1 million of these were displaced workers. In the second survey, spanning the period between 1981 and 1986, the number declined only slightly to 13.1 million. Of these, however, 10.8 million were permanently separated from their jobs and did not expect to be recalled.

19. See Abt Associates, "Serving the Dislocated Worker: A Report on the Dislocated Worker Demonstration Project," U.S. Department of Labor, Employment and Training Administration, 1983.

20. In his 1987 study of "successful" Title III projects, Cook reported wage replacement rates ranging from 62 to 89 percent, as compared with 70 percent for CETA demonstration projects.

21. The confounding effects of training on starting pay suggest that assessments of the impact of job displacement should focus not on entry-level pay but on long-term earnings growth in new jobs.

22. These extrapolations were based on a random sample of 2,400 establishments with 100 or more employees and 200 establishments with between 50 and 99 workers. They were drawn from a larger list of 28,000 establishments, provided by the Small Business Administration, that were thought to have experienced plant closings or permanent layoffs; closings and layoffs were confirmed through telephone calls.

23. One-fifth of workers who were at risk of layoff quit during the notification period, and their unemployment spells were significantly lower than those of workers who elected to stay.

24. However, as an empirical matter, the evidence on wage-fringe trade-offs is at best mixed.

25. Positive adjustment occurs when the industry is able to compete successfully with imports after termination of relief, and resources (including displaced workers) are transferred in an orderly fashion to other productive pursuits.

26. Lawrence and Litan (1986) argue that making relief contingent upon compliance with adjustment plans would probably retard adjustment and prolong government protection.

27. By making the threat of retaliation more credible, the Super-301 provision may accelerate the trend toward voluntary bilateral arrangements, such as the 1985 U.S.-Japan semiconductor agreement.

28. The 1988 Act implemented many of the recommendations of the Secretary of Labor's task force on economic adjustment and worker displacement, headed by Malcolm Lovell (1984).

29. Plant closings may be permanent or temporary, involving employment loss for 50 or more full-time workers over a month, but excluding employment terminations for cause, quits, or retirement. Layoffs exceeding six months, or reductions in

hours of more than 50 percent over a comparable period, are also to be included in this definition of mass layoff.

## BIBLIOGRAPHY

Abt Associates (1983). *Serving the Dislocated Worker: A Report on the Dislocated Worker Demonstration Project.* U.S. Department of Labor, Employment and Training Administration.

Addison, John, and Pedro Portugal (1987). "The Effect of Advance Notification of Plant Closings on Unemployment." *Industrial and Labor Relations Review,* vol. 41, no. 1, October.

Aho, Michael, and Thomas Bayard (1984). "Costs and Benefits of Trade Adjustment Assistance," in Robert Baldwin and Anne Krueger (eds.), *The Structure and Evolution of Recent U.S. Trade Policy.* Chicago: University of Chicago Press.

Alexander, Arthur (1990). *Adaptation to Change in the U.S. Machine Tool Industry and the Effects of Government Policy.* RAND, N-3079-USJF/RC, September.

Applebaum, Harvey, and Gilbert Kaplan (1987). *U.S. Trade Law and Policy.* Washington D.C.: Practicing Law Institute.

Baldwin, Robert (1984). "The Changing Nature of U.S. Trade Policy Since World War II," in Robert Baldwin and Anne Krueger (eds), *The Structure and Evolution of Recent U.S. Trade Policy.* Chicago: University of Chicago Press.

——— (1985). *The Political Economy of U.S. Import Policy.* Cambridge, Mass.: MIT Press.

Bello, Judith, and Alan Holmes (1986). "Section 301 of the Trade Act of 1974: Requirements, Procedures, and Developments." *Northwestern Journal of International Law and Business,* vol. 7, 633–665.

Berenbeim, Ronald (1986). *Company Programs to Ease the Impact of Shutdowns.* Washington, D.C.: The Conference Board.

Borrus, Michael, and Judith Goldstein (1987). "U.S. Trade Protectionism: Institutions, Norms, and Practices." *Northwestern Journal of International Law and Business,* vol. 8, no. 2, 328–364.

Cook, Robert (ed.) (1987). *Worker Dislocation: Case Studies of Causes and Cures.* Kalamazoo, Mich.: The W. E. Upjohn Institute for Employment Research.

Eichengreen, Barry, and Hans Van der Ven (1984). "U.S. Antidumping Policies: The Case of Steel," in Robert Baldwin and Anne Krueger (eds.), *The Structure and Evolution of Recent U.S. Trade Policy.* Chicago: University of Chicago Press.

General Accounting Office (1980). *Restricting Trade Act Benefits to Import Affected Workers Who Cannot Find a Job Can Save Millions.* Washington, D.C.: U.S. Government Printing Office.

—— (1986). *Dislocated Workers: Extent of Business Closures, Layoffs, and the Public and Private Response.* Washington D.C.: U.S. Government Printing Office, July.

—— (1987). *Plant Closings: Information on Advance Notice and Assistance to Dislocated Workers.* GAO/HDR-87–86BR, Washington, D.C.: U.S. Government Printing Office, April.

Gordus, Jeanne Prial, Paul Jarley, and Louis Ferman (1981). *Plant Closings and Economic Dislocation.* Kalamazoo, Mich: The W. E. Upjohn Institute for Employment Research.

Hufbauer, Gary Clyde, Diane Berliner, and Kimberly Ann Elliott (1986). *Trade Protection in the United States: 31 Case Studies.* Washington, D.C.: Institute for International Economics,.

Komiya, Ryutaro, Masahiro Okuno, and Kotaro Suzumura (eds.) (1988). *Industrial Policy of Japan.* New York: Academic Press.

Lawrence, Robert, and Robert Litan (1986). *Saving Free Trade: A Pragmatic Approach.* Washington, D.C.: The Brookings Institution.

Lovell, Malcolm Jr. (1984). "An Antidote for Protectionism." *The Brookings Review,* Fall, vol. 3, no. 1, 23–28.

Mathematica Policy Research Institute (1979). *Final Report: Survey of Trade Adjustment Assistance Recipients.* Report to the Office of Foreign Economic Research, Department of Labor.

McKenzie, Robert (1984). "Fugitive Industry: The Economics and Politics of Deindustrialization." Pacific Institute for Public Policy Studies, San Francisco.

—— (1988). *The American Job Machine.* New York: Universe Books.

McMillan, John (1990). *The Analytics of Declining Industries.* RAND, N-3080–USJF/RC, February.

Milner, Helen (1989). "The Political Economy of Specific Reciprocity: A Study of the Super 301 in U.S. Trade Law." Unpublished paper, New York: Columbia University.

Office of Technology Assessment (1987). *Plant Closing: Advance Notification and Rapid Response.* Washington, D.C.: U.S. Government Printing Office.

Prusa, Thomas (1988). "Why Are So Many Antidumping Cases Withdrawn?" Paper presented at a conference on "Designing Policies to Open Trade," University of California, Davis.

Report of the Secretary of Labor's Task Force on Economic Adjustment and Worker Dislocation (1986). "Economic Adjustment and Worker Dislocation in a Competitive Society." Washington, D.C., December.

Saxonhouse, Gary (1986). "The National Security Clause of the Trade Expansion Act of 1962: Import Competition and the Machine Tool Industry," in Gary

Saxonhouse and Kozo Yamamura (eds.), *Law and Trade Issues of the Japanese Economy*. Seattle: University of Washington Press.

Stern, Paula, and Andrew Wechsler (1986). "Escape Clause Relief and Recessions: An Economic and Legal Look at Section 201," in Gary Saxonhouse and Kozo Yamamura (eds.), *Law and Trade Issues of the Japanese Economy*. Seattle: University of Washington Press.

United Nations Conference on Trade and Development (UNCTAD) Secretariat (1984). *Protectionism and Structural Adjustment: Anti-Dumping and Countervailing Duty Practices*. Geneva: United Nations.

United States House of Representatives (1988). *Omnibus Trade and Competitiveness Act of 1988: Conference Report,* Report 100–576. Washington, D.C.: U.S. Government Printing Office.

# 6

# An Overview of Adjustment Assistance Policies in Japan

Sueo Sekiguchi

## INTRODUCTION

Industries go through life-cycles: sequences that vary with changing factor endowments, with technical progress, including the emergence of strong substitutes, and with exigencies of external trade, which accelerate the growth or decline of industries. Japan's coal and sulfur mining, for example, began to decline during the mid-1950s because of the substitution of petroleum products, and textile industries recorded excess capacity from the late 1950s onward because of competition by less-developed countries, import restrictions by importer countries, and a steady increase of wage rates.

Until the late 1960s, many of the policy instruments used to provide adjustment assistance to these declining industries depended on government control over external trade. For example, where external trade was restricted by high tariffs and direct controls, the government could slow down imports of competing products from abroad; where the government had leverage over private firms through the allocation of subsidies, it could guide them to operate in ways that the government desired. For workers employed in industries that could not compete internationally, adjustment assistance was provided to help displaced workers find new jobs in other sectors. As some industries were geographically concentrated, such assistance often took the form of assistance to specific areas, as in the case of coal-mining regions in the 1960s and 1970s.

## Overview of Developments Since 1971

After the dramatic appreciation of the yen in 1972 and 1973 (see Table 6.1), the cost of production in Japan increased significantly vis-à-vis that in most foreign countries. Japan's trade changed to an open and free regime, and tariff rates on imports were reduced substantially. Many manufacturing industries were forced to adapt to this new environment, and labor-intensive sectors were particularly hard-hit. Another important factor necessitating adjustment was the quadrupling of oil prices in 1974. To the extent that the oil crisis resulted in the depreciation of the Japanese yen, it also provided some relief to the labor-intensive sectors; petroleum, however, was not freely traded—because of both domestic and external factors—and industries that used oil intensively were affected severely.

Industrial adjustment became increasingly widespread among sectors at this time. In 1978 the government prepared a basic *Law for Adjustment Assistance* comprising four component laws: one for large corporations; one for small enterprises and regions where the impacted small firms were concentrated; one for assistance to workers in depressed industries; and one

### Table 6.1
### Features of the Japanese economy, 1971-1987: exchange rate, GNP, prices, and employment

|      | Exchange Rate (Yen/$) | GNP at 1980 Prices (Trillions of Yen) | Consumer Price Index (1980=100) | Manufacturing Employment (1980=100) |
|------|-----------------------|----------------------------------------|----------------------------------|--------------------------------------|
| 1971 | 349.3      —          | 158.8     —        | 45.0    —        | 112.8     —        |
| 1972 | 303.1  (−13.21)       | 172.3  (  8.50)    | 47.2  (  4.91)   | 110.7  (−1.86)     |
| 1973 | 271.7  (−10.38)       | 185.9  (  7.89)    | 52.7  (11.60)    | 111.0  (  0.27)    |
| 1974 | 292.0  (  7.50)       | 183.3  (−1.40)     | 64.9  (23.20)    | 109.9  (−0.99)     |
| 1975 | 296.7  (  1.61)       | 188.2  (  2.67)    | 72.5  (11.75)    | 104.7  (−4.73)     |
| 1976 | 296.5  (− 0.08)       | 197.2  (  4.78)    | 79.3  (  9.38)   | 102.6  (−2.01)     |
| 1977 | 268.5  (− 9.46)       | 207.7  (  5.32)    | 85.8  (  8.16)   | 101.7  (−0.88)     |
| 1978 | 210.4  (−21.63)       | 218.5  (  5.20)    | 89.4  (  4.20)   | 99.4  (−2.26)      |
| 1979 | 219.1  (  4.13)       | 230.1  (  5.31)    | 92.8  (  3.73)   | 98.9  (−0.50)      |
| 1980 | 226.7  (  3.47)       | 239.9  (  4.26)    | 100.0  (  7.74)  | 100.0  (  1.11)    |
| 1981 | 220.5  (− 2.73)       | 248.7  (  3.67)    | 104.9  (  4.95)  | 101.1  (  1.10)    |
| 1982 | 249.0  ( 12.94)       | 256.4  (  3.10)    | 107.8  (  2.73)  | 101.8  (  0.69)    |
| 1983 | 237.5  (− 4.65)       | 264.7  (  3.24)    | 109.8  (  1.89)  | 101.7  (−0.10)     |
| 1984 | 237.5  (  0.00)       | 278.1  (  5.06)    | 112.3  (  2.26)  | 103.0  (  1.28)    |
| 1985 | 238.5  (  0.43)       | 291.2  (  4.71)    | 114.6  (  2.05)  | 105.0  (  1.94)    |
| 1986 | 168.5  (−29.35)       | 298.5  (  2.51)    | 115.3  (  0.61)  | 105.7  (  0.67)    |
| 1987 | 144.6  (−14.17)       | 311.5  (  4.36)    | 115.4  (  0.05)  | 103.8  (−1.80)     |

*Note:* Figures in parentheses indicate percentage change from the previous year.
*Sources:* International Monetary Fund (IMF), *International Financial Statistics Yearbook,* June 1987 and 1988.

for assistance to workers in depressed regions. The division of administrative responsibilities and the sectionalism among government departments complicated these laws, making them difficult to understand (see "Prospects and Implications for Trade," below).

As most of the 1978 laws were time-limited—typically to five years—the government had to prepare a new set of laws in 1983 to assist these troubled industries. In doing so, it revised laws to make policy more anticipatory and crisis-preventing. I shall call these revised laws the *Adjustment Assistance Laws of 1983*. Assistance to workers through regions and industrial sectors was combined into one category, although a subsequent revision (1987) again divided them into two distinct categories.

An important external factor forced continued efforts for adjustment in 1983: the second oil crisis, during which the yen exchange rate was devalued. Later, in 1987, when the basic law for adjustment assistance was due to expire, oil prices remained low but the yen appreciated rapidly, rising to around 145 yen per U.S. dollar as compared with some 237 yen per dollar in 1983 (see Table 6.1). Thus, by 1987, adjustment became more critical to manufacturing industries in general. Tariff rates had already been lowered significantly; domestic manufacturers actively sought to maintain price competitiveness in their operations overseas; and government assistance emphasized adjustment as well as domestic investment in depressed regions. The basic Adjustment Assistance Laws were revised in 1987 and similar steps were taken by other ministries—collectively, here, the *Laws of 1987*.

### Definitions and Concepts

The term *adjustment* as used here refers to the reallocation of productive factors such as labor and capital. This reallocation can be intra- as well as interindustry, although interindustry reallocation has typically been the focus of theoretical research. In reality, intraindustry reallocation also plays an active role, for individual firms can grow even though the industry as a whole may experience declines in output and employment. For policymakers, however, reallocation of resources within an industrial sector is left largely to market forces, although the government may intervene in ways that run counter to the direction of market adjustment.[1]

The goal of adjustment assistance should be to facilitate the reallocation of factors and ensure their full efficient utilization in line with a free trade regime.[2] In this context, assistance to depressed regions may seem strange, but because of labor immobility and region-specific economies that shape industry-location decisions, it can be rational for the government to encourage capital to move into such regions. Because of labor immobility, wage rates may be relatively low and enterprises may find it profitable to relocate there. Moreover, heavy regional dependence on specific industrial sectors that have to shrink drastically can destroy the economic base of local communities, generating pressures for protection against foreign competition.

While adjustment problems are often triggered by foreign trade, competitiveness also depends on exchange rates and other factors. Adjustment assistance policies often assume in theory that the government can correctly predict the most efficient industry-mix in the international division of labor—surely a questionable assumption in view of the volatile fluctuations of exchange rates. Suppose that an industry is initially judged to be no longer viable at a 100 yen per dollar exchange rate and that the government encourages resources to flow out of this sector. Subsequently, the yen exchange rate falls to 150 yen per dollar. The factor responsible for eliciting adjustment assistance in the first place now implies that policy intervention is no longer warranted.[3]

The following section reviews industrial adjustment since the 1960s with emphasis on the most important factors affecting manufacturing industries. This review leads into a description of policy responses to the problems of troubled industries, and of the instruments used by the government in the three periods noted above. The final section summarizes the discussion of industrial adjustment policies and takes up possible implications of Japanese policies for international trade.

## DECLINE OF INDUSTRIES: CAUSES AND RESPONSES

In the 1960s the coal mining industry in Japan began a steady decline as petroleum replaced coal as an energy source. Sulfur mining also declined, as by-products of oil refining processes replaced mining as a source of that element. In this context, one can say that technological progress, including the emergence of strong substitutes, necessitated industrial adjustment. Still, textile industries had occasionally experienced cyclical downturns because of excess capacity created during phases of expansion. Although domestic manufacturers were able to maintain competitiveness within the domestic market when imports were negligible, their competitiveness declined in overseas markets as less developed countries caught up with Japanese manufacturers. The imposition of voluntary export restraint (VER) agreements by importing industrial countries added to the problems faced by this industry.[4]

To cope with these problems, the government intervened to moderate declines in demand by subsidizing the cost of adjustment. As oil imports were under quantitative controls, the government was able to control supply of the substitute. Following government directives, large users of coal as an energy source, such as utility companies, contributed funds to help subsidize adjustment. Using the allocation of import quotas as leverage, the government induced industry to comply with these adjustment plans. As for labor reallocation, the government promoted regional development programs to provide employment opportunities for those workers who could not move out of depressed regions.[5]

As for the textile industries, the government enacted laws giving itself the legal right to intervene, both to prevent construction of excess capacity and to control capacity operation rates. The *recession cartel,* first introduced in 1953 as a legal exception to the prohibition of cartelization, was now frequently used for joint reduction of production. As long as the foreign supply of exports to Japan was inelastic—the case in the 1960s—the recession cartel was an effective means of controlling supply.[6]

In 1971, when the yen appreciated for the first time in the postwar period, the government provided special relief for small-scale manufacturers without specifying industrial sectors. It justified this move by arguing that a 16.8 percent appreciation of the yen, from 360 yen to 308 yen per dollar at the time of the Smithsonian Agreement, was a burden that small manufacturers were not responsible for. The General Scheme of Tariff Preferences (GSP) was signed in the same year, and the government extended temporary relief to small-scale manufacturers who experienced difficulties as a result. In general, government policies toward small-scale manufacturers have always been complicated by the fact that the policies include both broad-based aid (protection against competition and subsidies as well) and targeted adjustment assistance.

In the 1970s, the adjustment difficulties were aggravated by two factors—dramatic increases in oil prices and yen appreciation. After the first oil crisis of 1974, many industrial sectors that used petroleum—directly or indirectly—were severely depressed. First, aluminum refining declined because the refining process was a heavy user of electricity, whose price skyrocketed from the oil embargo. Many synthetic fiber industries also contracted because the price of this key input increased. The shipbuilding industry, which had been a strong export sector and enjoyed the world's largest market share, was forced to reduce production—partly because of a contraction in worldwide demand and partly because orders were reallocated to domestic shipbuilders in Organization for Economic Cooperation and Development (OECD) countries.

In the past, changes in the yen exchange rate had often absorbed the impact of higher oil prices. The yen reached a peak of some 270 yen per dollar in 1973, when major nations adopted a floating exchange rate system, but it fell to nearly 300 yen per dollar immediately after the first oil crisis. The shipbuilding and textile industries—and other labor-intensive sectors— were severely affected by an increase of wage costs in dollar terms. Thus, while the domestic relative price of oil gradually declined through an increase in producer prices, many labor-intensive sectors faced difficulties because of yen appreciation and the rise in relative wages.

By the fall of 1978, the yen had appreciated rapidly, and the adjustment problem became one of Japan's most important policy concerns. Unlike that of the 1960s, the problem was not limited to a few specific industries, but was spread over many sectors, as described earlier. In response, the government enacted a more broad-based law for adjustment assistance with responsibilities divided among various government ministries.

Table 6.2 displays the performance of fourteen declining industrial sectors specified as "Depressed Industries" and so eligible to receive government assistance: six textile sectors (four synthetic fiber and two natural fiber industries); three chemical industries, including fertilizer; and one each from the electric furnace, aluminum refining, ferro-silicon, cardboard, and shipbuilding industries. The adjustment process varied with the industry, but it can be characterized roughly as follows:

- Operating ratios declined sharply in 1977–78.
- Each sector reduced capacity following its "Basic Stabilization Plan."
- Operating ratios recovered owing to reduction of capacity, although production also recovered in some cases.
- Employment decreased significantly in nearly all industries.
- The behavior of imports varied by sector.
- In the aluminum refining and textile sectors, as well as the ferro-silicon and cardboard industries, imports grew rapidly; but there was no significant change in imports in other sectors.

Most adjustment assistance laws of 1978 were effective for only five years; adjustment problems were considered to be temporary. However, the oil crisis in 1979–80 resulted in a second round of adjustments. The yen exchange rate depreciated from an average of about 210 yen per dollar in 1978 to 249 yen in 1982, which posed problems for petroleum-intensive sectors. The petrochemical industry in particular was hard hit, and the aluminum refining sector continued to shrink. Adjustment to this second rise in relative oil prices triggered yet another contraction of the petroleum-intensive sectors.

Table 6.2
Production, operating and import ratios, and employment in selected declining sectors, 1977–1981

| Industry | Variable | 1977 | 1978 | 1979 | 1980 | 1981 |
|---|---|---|---|---|---|---|
| Open hearth and electric | Production | 9,633 | 11,491 | 14,743 | 12,383 | 11,283 |
| | Operating ratio | 62.7 | 84.5 | 89.8 | 81.0 | 80.0 |
| | Import ratio | 0 | 0 | 0 | 0 | 0 |
| | Employment | 36,400 | 33,900 | 32,600 | 32,000 | 31,300 |
| Aluminum refining | Production | 1,188 | 1,023 | 1,043 | 1,038 | 665 |
| | Operating ratio | 73.0 | 64.4 | 89.9 | 89.9 | 58.5 |
| | Import ratio | 33.5 | 44.1 | 36.7 | 56.7 | 66.0 |
| | Employment | 7,642 | 6,535 | 6,038 | 5,503 | 4,344 |
| Continuous nylon fibers | Production | 287.6 | 284.0 | 292.6 | 286.8 | 270.0 |
| | Operating ratio | 78.9 | 95.7 | 98.6 | 92.9 | 88.5 |
| | Import ratio | 4.1 | 5.9 | 5.6 | 6.7 | 7.2 |
| | Employment | 71,021 | 62,095 | 60,212 | 57,576 | 59,464 |
| Discontinuous acryl fibers | Production | 341.4 | 351.3 | 334.6 | 325.7 | 327.1 |
| | Operating ratio | 80.2 | 96.5 | 91.9 | 87.3 | 92.9 |
| | Import ratio | 6.0 | 22.7 | 21.3 | 14.6 | 13.4 |
| | Employment | 45,270 | 39,607 | 38,793 | 38,475 | 39,408 |
| Continuous polyester | Production | 271.8 | 301.3 | 287.4 | 274.1 | 287.9 |
| | Operating ratio | 76.9 | 96.0 | 89.0 | 81.7 | 86.2 |
| | Import ratio | 8.4 | 15.8 | 10.7 | 16.0 | 19.4 |
| | Employment | 81,330 | 70,690 | 68,899 | 66,695 | 69,317 |

**Table 6.2—continued**

| Industry | Variable | 1977 | 1978 | 1979 | 1980 | 1981 |
|---|---|---|---|---|---|---|
| Discontinuous polyester | Production | 297.4 | 321.5 | 318.2 | 317.8 | 321.1 |
| | Operating ratio | 76.6 | 97.4 | 96.4 | 93.0 | 95.1 |
| | Import ratio | 11.7 | 18.4 | 13.7 | 13.2 | 12.7 |
| | Employment | 66,217 | 56,959 | 55,433 | 53,320 | 55,841 |
| Urea | Production | 1,972 | 2,135 | 2,033 | 1,555 | 1,311 |
| | Operating ratio | 50.1 | 53.6 | 77.4 | 67.1 | 56.5 |
| | Import ratio | 0.1 | 0.3 | 0.3 | 0.5 | 1.2 |
| | Employment | 417 | 355 | 332 | 299 | 300 |
| Ammonia | Production | 2,810 | 2,860 | 2,832 | 2,306 | 2,102 |
| | Operating ratio | 61.7 | 62.9 | 76.5 | 68.4 | 62.4 |
| | Import ratio | 0 | 0 | 0 | 0 | 0 |
| | Employment | 1,057 | 1,002 | 865 | 793 | 790 |
| Hydrous phosphoric acid | Production | 542 | 540 | 593 | 518 | 481 |
| | Operating ratio | 58.0 | 69.1 | 75.8 | 68.1 | 63.6 |
| | Import ratio | 9.8 | 7.9 | 9.4 | 9.4 | 7.2 |
| | Employment | 467 | 434 | 428 | 431 | 422 |
| Cotton spinning, etc. | Production | 883.9 | 982.0 | 1,071.7 | 1,030.0 | 946.4 |
| | Operating ratio | 70.1 | 83.8 | 94.1 | 91.0 | 88.0 |
| | Import ratio | 14.1 | 22.5 | 21.5 | 20.5 | 23.4 |
| | Employment | 71,996 | 67,474 | 65,656 | 61,132 | 61,100 |

**Table 6.2—continued**

| Industry | Variable | 1977 | 1978 | 1979 | 1980 | 1981 |
|---|---|---|---|---|---|---|
| Worsted yarn spinning | Production | 117.1 | 105.2 | 124.0 | 113.4 | 115.0 |
| | Operating ratio | 64.3 | 62.5 | 85.0 | 80.3 | 83.0 |
| | Import ratio | 8.3 | 11.6 | 11.6 | 10.0 | 11.8 |
| | Employment | 22,988 | 20,190 | 18,914 | 16,602 | 15,273 |
| Ferrosilicon | Production | 287 | 270 | 331 | 284 | 220 |
| | Operating ratio | 55.4 | 52.1 | 80.3 | 68.9 | 63.6 |
| | Import ratio | 13.7 | 30.5 | 27.2 | 32.0 | 47.8 |
| | Employment | 1,536 | 1,381 | 1,369 | 1,246 | 1,022 |
| Cardboard | Production | 4,653 | 4,957 | 5,509 | 4,781 | 4,459 |
| | Operating ratio | 62.9 | 65.7 | 88.4 | 75.2 | 68.8 |
| | Import ratio | 1.5 | 2.5 | 2.6 | 4.8 | 5.9 |
| | Employment | 5,828 | 6,059 | 5,836 | 5,810 | 5,960 |
| Shipbuilding | Production | 943 | 492 | 450 | 659 | 862 |
| | Operating ratio | 76.0 | 51.0 | 39.0 | 64.0 | 79.0 |
| | Import ratio | 0 | 0 | 0 | 0 | 0 |
| | Employment | 164,000 | 137,000 | 120,000 | 113,000 | 114,000 |

*Note:* Production in thousands of tons; operating and import ratios in percent.
*Sources:* Sekiguchi and Horiuchi (1988).

**Table 6.3**
**Capacity reduction in specified industries**
**under structural improvement law of 1983**

| Industry | Target Reduction (%)[a] | Target Attained by 1987 (%)[b] | FY 1982 Operating Ratio | FY 1986 Operating Ratio | Notes |
|---|---|---|---|---|---|
| Electric furnace | 3,800 (−14) | 2,380 ( 63) | 75 | 80 | — |
| Aluminum refining | 1,290 (−78) | 1,420 (110) | 40 | 35 | — |
| Viscose fiber continuous | 47.7 (−15) | 31.5 ( 66) | 79 | 84 | — |
| Ammonia | 660 (−20) | 1,120 (170) | 60 | 80 | DL |
| Urea | 830 (−36) | 860 (103) | 47 | 58 | DL |
| Wet phosphoric acid | 130 (−17) | 150 (112) | 65 | 74 | DL |
| Soluble phosphoric fertilizer | 240 (−32) | 210 ( 88) | 47 | 54 | DL |
| Chemical fertilizer | 810 (−13) | 880 (109) | 64 | 71 | M |
| Ferro-silicon | 50 (−14) | 57 (114) | 53 | 40 | — |
| High carbonate ferro-chromium | 57 (−10) | 138 (242) | 47 | 50 | JR&D |
| Ferro-nickel | 51 (−12) | 48 ( 94) | 56 | 68 | — |
| Paper | 950 (−11) | 890 ( 94) | 72 | 91 | M, JR&D |
| Cardboard | 1,540 (−20) | 850 ( 55) | 62 | 86 | DL |
| Ethylene | 2,290 (−36) | 2,020 ( 88) | 56 | 93 | DL |
| Poly-olefine | 990 (−22) | 850 ( 94) | 65 | 98 | JS |

## Table 6.3—continued

| Industry | Target Reduction (%)[a] | Target Attained by 1987 (%)[b] | FY 1982 Operating Ratio | FY 1986 Operating Ratio | Notes |
|---|---|---|---|---|---|
| Polyvinyl chloride resin | 490 (−22) | 450 (92) | 64 | 92 | DL |
| Ethylene oxide | 220 (−27) | 120 (61) | 64 | 80 | DL |
| Styrene | 470 (−26) | 340 (73) | 70 | 98 | DL |
| Hard polyvinyl chloride tube | 116 (−19) | 116 (100) | 62 | 77 | DL |
| Cement | 30,000 (−23) | 31,000 (103) | 62 | 69 | DL, JS |
| Electric wire | 86 (−14) | 86 (100) | 68 | 85 | JI |
| Sugar refining | 1,000 (−26) | 630 (63) | 57 | 65 | DL, JP |

*Notes:*
[a]Ratio of target reduction to existing capacity.
[b]Ratio of scrapped capacity to target reduction.
DL = division of labor; M = merger; JR&D = joint research and development;
JS = joint sales; JI = joint investment; and JP = joint production.

*Source:* MITI, Bureau of Industrial Policy, "Tokutei Sangyo Kogo Kaizen Rinjisotiho no Shikojyokyo" (Policy Implementation under Structural Improvement Law), March 1988.

The Ministry of International Trade and Industry (MITI) enacted the revised law for adjustment assistance in 1983. This time, 22 industrial sectors were designated as eligible to receive assistance (see Table 6.3). Six sectors comprised petrochemical industries; aluminum refining and electric furnace sectors remained on the list, as did fertilizer and some chemical industries. Cement, electric wire, and sugar refining industries were added. To reduce capacity, MITI encouraged a division of labor among firms, mergers, collaborative research and development (R&D), and joint-selling of products. These were added to the policy instruments that MITI had implemented under the preceding law, including joint capacity reduction and the use of credit guarantees for capacity scrapping.

Table 6.4 shows the performance of selected industries during the 1982–87 period. Aluminum refining continued to shrink, with no significant increase in operating ratio, as imports displaced domestic production. Petrochemical industries faced difficulties in 1982, but production and profits

Table 6.4

Performance of selected industries designated by structural improvement law as eligible to receive assistance

| Industry[a] | Fiscal Year | | | | | | Notes |
|---|---|---|---|---|---|---|---|
| | 1982 | 1983 | 1984 | 1985 | 1986 | 1987[b] | |
| *Electric furnace* | | | | | | | |
| Current profits | −2 | −14 | 2 | −10 | −14 | — | 53 companies |
| Prices (1,000 yen/ton) | 57.2 | 55.7 | 57.5 | 51.0 | 35.2 | 58.0 | 21,200 workers |
| Production | 20.2 | 21.2 | 22.3 | 23.1 | 22.2 | — | |
| Exports | 3.6 | 3.0 | 2.6 | 3.0 | 1.6 | 0.1 | |
| Operating ratio | 75.4 | 81.4 | 81.6 | 83.9 | 79.8 | — | |
| *Aluminum refining* | | | | | | | |
| Current profits | −102 | −31 | −32 | −55 | −32 | 4 | 3 companies |
| Prices (1,000 yen/ton) | 318 | 428 | 344 | 275 | 226 | 303 | 1,597 workers |
| Production | 295 | 264 | 278 | 209 | 113 | 27 | |
| Imports | 1,346 | 1,379 | 1,284 | 1,351 | 1,187 | 951 | |
| Exports | 2.0 | 1.4 | 1.3 | 1.4 | 1.2 | 1.0 | |
| Operating ratio | 39.7 | 37.1 | 39.0 | 46.2 | 34.9 | 9.4 | |
| *Fertilizer* | | | | | | | |
| Current profits | −3.0 | −1.0 | −1.1 | −0.2 | 0.7 | — | 48 companies |
| Prices (1,000 yen/ton) | 78.9 | 77.3 | 75.6 | 77.1 | 67.4 | 63.0 | 1,889 workers |
| Production | 3,968 | 4,138 | 4,000 | 3,906 | 3,741 | — | |
| Exports | 105 | 56 | 191 | 167 | 80 | — | |
| Operating ratio | 64 | 71 | 71 | 69 | 71 | — | |

**Table 6.4—continued**

| Industry[a] | Fiscal Year | | | | | | Notes |
|---|---|---|---|---|---|---|---|
| | 1982 | 1983 | 1984 | 1985 | 1986 | 1987[b] | |
| *Paper* | | | | | | | 50 companies |
| Current profits | -2 | 10 | 20 | 12 | 17 | 15 | 38,063 workers |
| Prices (yen/kg) | 160 | 153 | 152 | 149 | 137 | 133 | |
| Production | 6,423 | 6,908 | 7,282 | 7,442 | 7,785 | 4,036 | |
| Imports | 178 | 250 | 261 | 343 | 375 | 162 | |
| Exports | 279 | 280 | 306 | 340 | 299 | 160 | |
| Operating ratio | 72.3 | 77.0 | 82.3 | 84.5 | 91.0 | 94.4 | |
| *Cardboard* | | | | | | | 64 companies |
| Current profits | -10 | -19 | -6 | -41 | -13 | -1 | 13,101 workers |
| Prices (yen/kg) | 128 | 118 | 117 | 90 | 82 | 84 | |
| Production | 4,503 | 4,879 | 5,192 | 5,902 | 6,227 | 3,329 | |
| Imports | 221 | 242 | 207 | 176 | 222 | 105 | |
| Exports | 111 | 191 | 215 | 173 | 310 | 95 | |
| Operating ratio | 62.2 | 62.9 | 68.2 | 82.4 | 85.7 | 91.6 | |
| *Ethylene* | | | | | | | 11 companies |
| Current profits | -19 | 16 | 34 | 28 | 13 | 8 | 1,010 workers |
| Prices (yen/kg) | 160 | 142 | 138 | 125 | 82 | 88 | |
| Production | 3,567 | 3,965 | 4,341 | 4,220 | 4,376 | 2,234 | |
| Imports | 379 | 383 | 415 | 506 | 618 | 318 | |
| Exports | 386 | 424 | 420 | 435 | 617 | 273 | |
| Operating ratio | 56.2 | 63.6 | 80.9 | 97.5 | 93.3 | 95.2 | |

## Table 6.4—continued

| Industry[a] | \_\_\_\_ Fiscal Year \_\_\_\_ | | | | | | Notes |
|---|---|---|---|---|---|---|---|
| | 1982 | 1983 | 1984 | 1985 | 1986 | 1987[b] | |
| *Poly-olefine* | | | | | | | |
| Current profits | -68 | 31 | 100 | -0.04 | 24 | 15 | 20 companies |
| Prices (yen/kg) | 268 | 248 | 250 | 235 | 212 | 215 | 2,537 workers |
| Production | 2,680 | 3,042 | 3,507 | 3,324 | 3,445 | 1,741 | |
| Imports | 59 | 37 | 37 | 87 | 109 | 62 | |
| Exports | 389 | 376 | 378 | 390 | 446 | 201 | |
| Operating ratio | 65.0 | 73.7 | 89.3 | 89.9 | 98.1 | 99.2 | |
| *Cement* | | | | | | | |
| Current profits | -4 | -4 | 24 | 4 | 16 | 14 | 23 companies |
| Prices (1,000 yen/ton) | 14.4 | 13.9 | 14.3 | 14.1 | 13.9 | 13.4 | 14,515 workers |
| Production | 80.1 | 79.4 | 77.4 | 72.2 | 70.4 | 34.1 | |
| Imports | 0.02 | 0.02 | 0.2 | 0.6 | 1.5 | 1.3 | |
| Exports | 12.0 | 13.7 | 10.9 | 8.3 | 4.9 | 2.1 | |
| Operating ratio | 62.5 | 62.0 | 74.4 | 72.9 | 68.7 | 69.5 | |
| *Electric wire* | | | | | | | |
| Current profits | -0.8 | -13 | -11 | -6 | -2 | -0.2 | 47 companies |
| Prices (1,000 yen/ton) | 593 | 566 | 540 | 550 | 499 | 514 | 8,508 workers |
| Production | 478 | 420 | 429 | 442 | 446 | 226 | |
| Exports | 89 | 45 | 43 | 38 | 24 | 0.5 | |
| Operating ratio | 80 | 68 | 70 | 84 | 85 | 86 | |

**Table 6.4—continued**

| Industry[a] | Fiscal Year | | | | | | Notes |
|---|---|---|---|---|---|---|---|
| | 1982 | 1983 | 1984 | 1985 | 1986 | 1987[b] | |
| *Sugar refining* | | | | | | | |
| Current profits | -22 | -6 | 30 | 31 | 23 | 12 | 24 companies |
| Prices (yen/kg) | 178 | 206 | 210 | 203 | 192 | 184 | 2,400 workers |
| Production | 2,102 | 1,974 | 1,999 | 1,976 | 1,972 | 976 | |
| Imports | 1 | — | 1 | 1 | 2 | 1 | |
| Exports | 28 | 30 | 22 | 17 | 15 | 8 | |
| Operating ratio | 57.2 | 54.6 | 66.7 | 65.4 | 65.1 | 64.2 | |

*Notes:*
[a]Profits in billions of yen; production, imports, and exports in millions of tons; operating ratio in percent.
[b]For the first half of FY1987. Industries selected are those with a significant workforce.
*Source:* MITI, "Policy Implementation under Structural Improvement Law," March, 1988.

recovered around 1984, in spite of growing imports. The electric furnace, fertilizer, cement, and sugar-refining industries stagnated, even though import penetration in these industries was relatively low.

When the exchange rate of the yen appreciated sharply after the autumn of 1985, the major factor forcing industrial adjustment changed. Having adjusted to the increased prices of petroleum, Japanese manufacturing industries now had to cope with yen appreciation. Even the steel industry, formerly a leading sector, began to shrink after losing market share abroad and experiencing import pressure from newly industrialized economies (NIEs). Although not apparent in Table 6.4, steel imports from NIEs and other advanced industrial countries increased rapidly after 1987, as Japanese users developed alternative overseas sources for steel.

To deal with this new situation, MITI revised the law of 1983 to specify 18 kinds of equipment to be scrapped: blast furnace, revolving furnace, hot rolling mill, steel pipe maker, spinner, spinning frame, various machines for mining (drilling machine, loader, conveyer, winch, crusher, and ore separator), smelting furnace, electrolytic cell, compressor, air liquidizer and separator, expansion machine, electric furnace, forging machine, and falcination furnace. Under the supervision of the Ministry of Agriculture, silk reeling, cocoon boiler, and cocoon dryer capacity was also targeted for scrapping.

## POLICY RESPONSE AND POLICY INSTRUMENTS

Clearly, government assistance for resource reallocation is not necessary if the factors of production are instantly reallocated in response to price changes. And, even though adjustment costs are incurred in resource reallocations, consumption gains from foreign trade can compensate to some extent for these costs. This picture is complicated, however, when some factor prices are rigid and other factors move out of that sector faster than they might otherwise, causing the unemployment of resources with rigid prices.

The first-best policies to facilitate resource reallocation include removing the barriers to resource reallocation, providing improved information for enterprises and workers to facilitate decision-making, and extending education and retraining so that workers can adapt to new jobs.

Since it is politically difficult to remove the price rigidity of some factors—e.g., wage rates—a set of second-best policies may be warranted. One group of such policies includes restricting imports temporarily under the title of "safeguard mechanisms" to moderate changes in product prices so that producers can buy time to exit; and giving subsidies to maintain production so that unemployment of resources can be minimized (such subsidies must be time-limited so that producers have incentives to exit). These policies, which can be called "defensive adjustment assistance," may reduce short-run unemployment, but they also slow down the adjustment required for attaining efficient production.

Other second-best policies include subsidizing industries that absorb unemployment so that growing sectors can expand rapidly enough to reemploy resources displaced from declining sectors. This "positive adjustment assistance," while promoting adjustment and efficient resource allocation, often has limited effects on employment; also, foregone income may be significant in the short run.[7]

In the area of actual implementation, several problems exist. Who can correctly predict the future competitive position of industries? How are such predictions made? Within an industrial sector, some enterprises prosper and others decline; subsidization of employment sometimes promotes employment reshuffling within the sector, not an interindustry reallocation of labor.

Since 1978, adjustment assistance policies in Japan have been under the control of various ministries:

| Assistance Targeted at: | Ministry in Charge |
|---|---|
| (A) Capital and large firms | MITI |
| (B) Capital and small firms (aid to depressed regions) | Agency for Small- and Medium-Scale Enterprises (under MITI) |
| (C) Workers in troubled industries | Ministry of Labor |
| (D) Workers in depressed regions | Ministry of Labor |

While there were minor changes in the policy framework, the basic structure of adjustment assistance remained the same in 1988.

### Policies During 1978–82

After the first oil crisis, MITI prepared a general law for adjustment assistance. This Industry Stabilization Law, enacted in 1978, became the basic instrument for the other three related laws listed above.[8]

*(A) Assistance to large firms:* The Industry Stabilization Law provided MITI with the following policy instruments: (1) The law (or Ministry Ordinance) specified the industries eligible to receive assistance; (2) MITI could ask manufacturers needing assistance to submit a "Basic Stabilization

Plan," following which producers had to scrap capacity; (3) a Trust Fund for Specified Depressed Industries was created that guaranteed credit from private financial institutions to finance scrapping of capacity; and (4) when it was difficult for producers in the industry to achieve the target capacity reduction by themselves, MITI could recommend that they form a cartel for capacity reduction (*siji karuteru*) to jointly reduce capacity, conditional upon approval from the Fair Trade Commission (FTC) of Japan.

Fourteen industrial sectors, including aluminum refining, shipbuilding, and various categories of synthetic fiber industries, were designated as eligible to receive assistance. Some industries resorted to cartel actions to scrap capacity, but some did not. Some industries made use of the Trust Fund for credit guarantees, while others did not. Table 6.5 shows the target reduction of capacity, the achieved reduction, and such other information as whether cartels and credit guarantees were used. There is no significant difference in the scrapping accomplished by industries that took cartel actions and those that did not. Similarly, industries that did not use the Trust Fund achieved capacity scrapping comparable to that of those using the Fund. If there is a difference, it is that all industries that were recommended to take cartel actions, and did so, made use of the Trust Fund; whereas only the shipbuilding industry resorted to using the Fund among industries not forming cartels.[9]

Credit guarantees were relatively unattractive to the manufacturers in question—they used only 23.2 billion yen of guarantees despite the fact that the Trust Fund was authorized to issue guarantees worth 100 billion yen. The benefit of guarantees may not have been great enough to compensate for the unfavorable effects of being labelled a "declining industry" or "declining enterprise." Because commercial banks did the financing, MITI did not arrange low-interest loans.

As for the safeguard mechanism against imports, there were only a few exceptional increases in import tariff rates: tariffs on unwrought aluminum were reduced in 1983, some tariffs on wrought aluminum were raised.[10] In the case of man-made fiber, the General Agreement on Tariffs and Trade (GATT) concessionary tariff rate was raised from 7.5 percent to 11.3 percent in the same period. Except in these two cases, tariff rates on products in troubled industries were lowered in accordance with the government policy of facilitating market access to foreign products. In this sense, it can be said that the Japanese government seldom resorted to safeguard instruments for assisting industrial adjustment.

*(B) Assistance to small firms and specific regions:* As the sectors listed in Table 6.5 often had many subcontractors—especially in the textile and shipbuilding industries—industries specified by this ordinance largely over-

Table 6.5
**Capacity reduction under the industry stabilization law**
(Thousands of tons per year)

| Industry | Capacity Before Scrapping | Planned Reduction of Capacity | Cumulative Scrapping Through 1981 | Cumulative Credit from Trust Fund |
|---|---|---|---|---|
| A. *Industries with cartel recommendation* | | | | |
| Cont. nylon fiber | 366.7 | 71.5 | 72.9 | |
| Disc. acryl fiber | 430.5 | 73.2 | 95.5 | 3 bil. yen |
| Cont. polyester fiber | 349.8 | 36.8 | 36.6 | |
| Disc. polyester fiber | 397.5 | 67.6 | 70.7 | |
| Urea | 3,985.0 | 1,790.0 | 1,670.0 | 2.7 bil. yen |
| Ammonia | 4,559.0 | 1,190.0 | 1,190.0 | |
| Worsted yarn spinning | 181.7 | 18.3 | 17.6 | 1.2 bil. yen |
| Cardboard | 7,549.0 | 1,147.0 | 1,083.0 | 2.1 bil. yen |
| B. *Industries without cartel recommendation* | | | | |
| Open hearth el. furn | 20,790.0 | 2,850.0 | 2,720.0 | |
| Aluminum refining | 1,642.0 | 530.0 | 899.0 | |
| Shipbuilding (CGRT) | 9,770.0 | 3,420.0 | 3,580.0 | 14.2 bil. yen |
| Ferrosilicon | 487.0 | 100.0 | 100.0 | |
| Hydrous phos. acid | 934.0 | 190.0 | 174.0 | |
| Cotton spinning | 1,204.0 | 67.1 | 52.3 | |

*Notes:* The joint actions were carried out in all industries where recommended. The synthetic fiber industries had a cartel in the initial plan, but one was not recommended in the second plan.
*Source:* Sekiguchi and Horiuchi (1988).

lapped those designated by the Industry Stabilization Law. However, industries such as the fishery and fish processing sectors and plywood manufacturing were also covered by this law.[11] In all, seven sectors and 32 regions designated under this law received the following assistance:

1.  Small firms in the sectors and regions specified received a cumulative 42.7 billion yen in emergency loans at a favorable interest rate of 6.1–6.6 percent per annum (the market rates were 6.0–8.3 percent at this time) by the end of fiscal year 1981. Also, special loans worth 1.7 billion yen for business conversion were extended in the same period. Another governmental financial institution that provided credit guarantees to small firms further expanded the ceiling on guarantees (these guarantees totaled 18.6 billion yen).

2.  Special reduction of corporate and personal income taxes under this law amounted to 2.4 billion yen in the same period. Subsidies given to investments made by outside companies in specified regions amounted to 1.5 billion yen.

3. In addition, repayment of past loans used for modernization of equipment was postponed.

Thus, fiscal assistance under this program was larger than that under the basic law for adjustment assistance. It is difficult, however, to judge the program's effects, for relevant data have not been published.

*(C) Assistance to workers in depressed industries:* This law provided assistance to workers who were to be displaced from industries designated as "depressed" by the Industry Stabilization Law. Industry coverage under this law, however, was broader than that under the other law, as many sectors were affected indirectly. In addition to the industries selected by (A), this law included fishery and fish processing, plywood, silk, and other industries as sectors eligible to receive assistance. In total, the law covered forty industrial sectors. The assistance consisted of a direct subsidy to workers and subsidies to employers.

When a company planned to displace more than a specified number of workers, it had to submit a plan of reemployment to the Ministry of Labor—specifically, to the head of the Public Employment Stabilization Bureau. Once approved, those who were about to be displaced were given Job-Seeker Certificates (JS-Cards). The following assistance was provided to JS-Card holders:

- *To workers:* Two subsidies to promote employment were given directly to workers—one basic subsidy and one training subsidy. These subsidies reportedly provided 101,000 yen per person per month (roughly U.S. $780 at a $1 = 130 yen exchange rate). Subsidies were also given for long-distance job-seeking activities and for relocation to the region of new jobs. In short, assistance to workers with JS-Cards was fairly generous.
- *To new employers:* Employers who offered retraining for newly recruited JS-Card holders were qualified to receive a subsidy worth 16,000 yen per person per month as a training subsidy. Where workers were aged 45–65, new employers were eligible to receive a wage subsidy equivalent to one-fourth of the annual wage bill. If the employer belonged to the category of small- and medium-scale firms, this subsidy was one-third of the wage bill.[12]

*(D) Assistance to workers in depressed regions:* Another dimension of assistance to workers was by region. Forty-four regions—mostly municipalities—were specified as depressed regions by ministry ordinance. Assistance consisted of (1) extended payment of Employment Insurance benefits to those displaced in the specified regions, with preferential treatment given to

older workers; (2) prior allocation of public works projects to these regions; (3) regulations giving seniority privileges to JS-Card holders employed in public works projects; and (4) job mediation activities by the Public Employment Stabilization Bureau.

For fiscal year 1982 alone, the budget for employment assistance amounted to 10.4 billion yen. As it was all direct subsidy, reemployment assistance was much more significant in money terms than the assistance to large firms, which received only credit guarantees. The textile and shipbuilding sectors received the largest portion of this assistance. Through November 1982, a total of 103,200 workers reportedly held the privileged JS-Cards from enactment of these laws.

The public works projects allocated to the priority depressed regions reportedly employed a cumulative 2.58 million man-days by the end of November 1982. As the unemployed numbered about 1.36 million in 1982, the contribution of public works to the reduction of unemployment was less significant. Because the law stated that at least 40 percent of the workers to be employed in public works projects had to be those displaced in specified depressed regions, the employment effects of these public works projects amounted to 2.58 x 0.4 = 1.03 million man-days, assuming that each project attained the preferential employment goal.

### Adjustment Assistance During 1983–87

When the Industry Stabilization Law expired in April 1983, MITI prepared a revised law (*the Structural Improvement Law*) that emphasized the importance of anticipating and preventing crises. This law was also time-limited to be effective for five years.[13] The revised law that local communities enacted in July 1983 provided subsidies for industrial diversification and promotion of research and development (R&D) for new businesses. The two laws providing assistance to workers were combined into one (*the Employment Assistance Law of 1983*) in July 1983. In this law, retraining of workers prior to displacement was encouraged by fairly generous subsidies. Subsidies to enterprises that recruited these unemployed workers were also expanded.[14]

*(A) Assistance to large firms:* The Structural Improvement Law of 1983 revised the policies on cartel actions and credit guarantees for specified industries. The fund was renamed because it was recognized that being labelled "Specified Depressed Industries" made it more difficult for troubled enterprises to raise funds in the financial market. New elements in the policies included: (1) recommendations on mergers and cooperation among firms facing adjustment problems; and (2) incentives for scrapping of

facilities and R&D investment in the exploration of new businesses.[15] The industrial sectors covered by this law were designated either by the law or by ministry ordinance.

Under the new law, MITI designated 21 industrial sectors (11 continued from the preceding designation and 10 newly added) as eligible to receive assistance. The sugar refinery industry, also designated as eligible, was placed under the supervision of the Ministry of Agriculture, for a total of 22 industries (see Table 6.3).

*(B) Assistance to small firms and regions:* The revised law introduced new elements such as subsidies for investment in manpower development and for developing new markets and new technology. These subsidies were provided through the manufacturers' associations of designated industries. If approved, a revitalization program submitted to the prefectural governor was entitled to a subsidy of not more than 10 million yen. The central and local governments each provided one-half of this subsidy. Those small firms designated as eligible were also qualified to receive low-interest loans from the Finance Corporation for Small- and Medium-Scale Enterprises, a government financial institution.[16]

Other policy instruments were similar to those under the previous law. While 30 regions (the same number of municipalities) were designated as eligible under the preceding law, this time the Agency for Small and Medium Enterprise (ASME) specified 53 regions (57 municipalities). Beyond these figures, few quantitative data have been published, making it difficult to assess the role of these programs. A serious flaw in the administration of adjustment assistance to small firms is that the law does not require the government to review policy implementation and its effect. Without such review, it is likely that the number of overlapping laws has increased.[17]

*(C, D) Assistance to workers:* A generous subsidy was provided to employers who retrained workers about to be displaced; two-thirds of the wage bill was subsidized for six months when an employer invested in such retraining. The subsidy was enlarged to three-fourths in the case of small firms. Furthermore, when other employers recruited workers receiving such assistance, they were eligible to receive a wage subsidy worth one-fourth of the wage bill for a year; this subsidy was expanded to one-third in the case of small firms. Direct assistance to workers who received training, sought a new job, and relocated was strengthened. In short, fairly generous subsidies were given both to present and to new employers, as well as to workers themselves—for lay-off compensation, training, recruitment, retraining for new jobs, job search, and other activities.

## Ministry of Labor Policies

Thus far, I have focused on the policies of MITI. I now turn to a more detailed examination of the adjustment assistance policies of the Ministry of Labor (MOL). Under the 1983 Law, "Those who plan to displace more than 30 persons a month, or more than 100 persons in total, must submit an employment adjustment plan to the head of the Public Employment Stabilization Bureau. After authorization by this office, employers and those being displaced are eligible to receive the following subsidies" (from unpublished MOL documents).

*A. Assistance to Employers:*

A-1: Present Employers:

1.  Subsidy for payment of lay-off compensation to workers; 2/3 (3/4 for small firms; same meaning hereinafter).
2.  Subsidy for wage and training expenses for workers to be displaced; 2/3 of wage bill (3/4) plus 1,500 yen per day for training.
3.  Subsidy for wage bill to be shared by the firms that lease workers to other firms (*Shukko system*); 2/3 of shared wage bill (3/4).
4.  Subsidy for training expenses for job conversion; 3/4 of wage bill (4/5).

A-2: New Employers:

1.  Those who recruit the workers displaced by these specified firms are eligible to receive wage subsidy for one year; 1/2 (2/3).
2.  Temporary payment for preparation to work that is borne by the new employer; roughly equivalent to one month's wage bill.
3.  Wage subsidy for new employers who recruit workers of age 35–65; 1/2 for a year (2/3).
4.  Subsidy for training expenses for new jobs; 18,700 yen per worker per month for maximum of six months.

*B. Assistance to Workers:*

Those who hold JS-Cards are eligible to receive the following benefits:

1.  Extension of the period of Employment Insurance Benefit payment; 90 days extension for age not less than 40 and 60 days below 40.

2. Daily payment to those specified unemployed who receive training or are waiting for training provided by the Employment Stabilization Bureau; 2,570–4,740 yen per day depending on the wage they earned before displacement.

3. Subsidy to those who move a long distance for job seeking; total actual expense for transportation and lodging (5,900–6,000 yen per night).

4. Subsidy for moving to and settling down in the place of the new job found by the Employment Stabilization Bureau; total actual cost of transportation and moving cost (46,000–140,000 yen, 1/2 for a single person). A temporary payment of 19,400 yen (1/2 for a single person) for settling down in the new place.

5. Assistance for preparation for new jobs; those who find new jobs within 18 months after displacement and who are aged more than 34 are eligible to receive a one-month equivalent of item 2.

6. Per diem payment to those who receive training assigned by the head of the Employment Stabilization Bureau; this includes per diem, lodging cost, and commuting cost. (Actual average payment in FY 1983 reached 104,770 yen per person per month.)

Tables 6.6 through 6.8 present data about various programs for employment assistance, including direct assistance to workers, to employers, and by industry and region. Table 6.6 shows the number of JS-Cards issued by industry from fiscal year 1983 through the end of November 1987. Over this period, a total of 63,738 workers (summed annual totals) received the JS-Card, with shipbuilding and textile workers making up the majority. The number of recipients increased from FY 1986 onward with the rapid appreciation of the yen.

*Assistance by industries:* Table 6.7 shows various forms of assistance to workers and employers. With regard to assistance for workers, 57,200 persons received JS-Cards from April 1983 through September 1987; of these, 31,945 found new jobs through mediation by the Public Employment Stabilization Bureau. A total of 4.3 billion yen was paid as extended Employment Insurance (EI) benefits. Interestingly, only 5,728 persons received subsidies for training and job preparation, totaling over 0.5 billion yen, and 7,445 persons aged 45–65 were given subsidies worth 2.3 billion yen.

In the same period, subsidies to employers were: for compensation to laid-off workers, 5.7 billion yen; for training, 4.8 billion yen; for leasing of workers to other firms, 1.8 billion yen; and for job mediation, 1.9 billion yen.

**Table 6.6**
**Employment assistance by industry, FY1983 through November 1987: number of programs and JS-cards issued**

| Industry | Number of Programs | | | | | Number of JS Cards | | | | |
|---|---|---|---|---|---|---|---|---|---|---|
| | FY1983 | '84 | '85 | '86 | '87a | FY1983 | '84 | '85 | '86' | '87a |
| Fishery products | 0 | 6 | 2 | 3 | 1 | 0 | 47 | 22 | 0 | 35 |
| Sugar refining | 10 | 2 | 1 | — | — | 106 | 24 | 24 | — | — |
| Silk | 8 | 8 | 11 | 8 | 6 | 57 | 234 | 166 | 159 | 217 |
| Other textiles | 179 | 119 | 74 | 113 | 27 | 1,945 | 760 | 1,027 | 1,616 | 370 |
| Dyeing | 62 | 12 | 8 | 8 | 4 | 492 | 136 | 38 | 44 | 15 |
| Timber and plywood | 100 | 79 | 43 | 54 | 15 | 996 | 1,549 | 878 | 912 | 229 |
| Cardboard | 2 | 4 | 3 | 2 | — | 202 | 28 | 30 | 28 | — |
| Fertilizer | 1 | 2 | 2 | 4 | — | 3 | 0 | 18 | 13 | — |
| Rayon and acetate | — | — | 0 | 8 | 4 | — | — | 0 | 158 | 6 |
| Petrochemical | 0 | 0 | — | — | — | 0 | 1 | — | — | — |
| Synthetic fibers | 4 | 0 | — | — | — | 82 | 79 | — | — | — |
| Oil refining | 1 | 6 | 1 | 2 | 1 | 20 | 64 | 13 | 1 | 12 |
| Cement and bricks | 33 | 3 | 0 | 27 | 15 | 851 | 196 | 11 | 466 | 514 |
| Steel; various | 48 | 13 | 11 | 40 | 77 | 1,446 | 426 | 230 | 1,248 | 1,497 |
| Nonferrous metal | 5 | 2 | — | 12 | 4 | 132 | 4 | — | 437 | 15 |
| Aluminum | 0 | 2 | 0 | 17 | 1 | 54 | 3 | 29 | 119 | 157 |
| Electric wires | — | 1 | — | — | — | — | 1 | — | — | — |
| Shipbuilding | 96 | 56 | 294 | 759 | 173 | 869 | 1,501 | 3,334 | 17,472 | 6,394 |
| Others | 42 | 98 | 35 | 176 | 169 | 902 | 1,857 | 423 | 4,273 | 6,021 |
| TOTAL | 591 | 413 | 485 | 1,233 | 497 | 8,157 | 6,910 | 6,243 | 26,946 | 15,482 |

a To the end of November 1987. *Sources*: Ministry of Labor, unpublished documents.

Table 6.7
Assistance for specified depressed industries

| Items | Fiscal Year | | | | | Cumulative 4/83–9/87 |
|---|---|---|---|---|---|---|
| | 1983 | 1984 | 1985 | 1986 | 1987[a] | |
| **A. *Assistance to Workers*** | | | | | | |
| Number of programs accepted | 434 | 413 | 485 | 1,234 | 394 | 2,960 |
| Number of JS-Cards issued: | 5,686 | 6,833 | 6,191 | 26,741 | 11,749 | 57,200 |
| Number getting jobs | 4,829 | 5,779 | 3,423 | 9,826 | 8,088 | 31,945 |
| Number getting extended EI | 2,553 | 2,105 | 1,164 | 2,695 | 3,731 | 12,248 |
| Payment of extended EI (mil. yen) | 839 | 834 | 436 | 912 | 1,258 | 4,279 |
| | | | | | | |
| Number getting subsidies for training and job preparation | 1,208 | 1,518 | 1,065 | 203 | 1,734 | 5,728 |
| Total subsidies (mil. yen) | 114 | 140 | 98 | 18 | 169 | 539 |
| Job seekers aged 45–65[b] | 1,381 | 2,004 | 1,723 | 1,247 | 1,090 | 7,445 |
| Money assistance (mil. yen) | 378 | 556 | 497 | 381 | 458 | 2,270 |
| | | | | | Payments total: | 7,088 |
| **B. *Assistance to Firms*** | | | | | | |
| Total susbsidies (mil. yen) | 1,881 | 2,054 | 2,035 | 4,585 | 3,702 | 14,257 |
| Subsidy to laid-off workers | | | | | | |
| Thousands of man-days | 224 | 223 | 178 | 402 | 241 | 1,267 |
| Total payment (mil. yen) | 852 | 955 | 773 | 1,877 | 1,256 | 5,713 |

**Table 6.7—continued**

| Items | 1983 | 1984 | 1985 | 1986 | 1987[a] | Cumulative 4/83–9/87 |
|---|---|---|---|---|---|---|
| **Training subsidy** | | | | | | |
| Thousands of man-days | 172 | 76 | 106 | 261 | 157 | 772 |
| Total payment (mil. yen) | 938 | 427 | 641 | 1,653 | 1,147 | 4,806 |
| **Subsidy for loaning workers** | | | | | | |
| Number of loaned-out workers | 313 | 496 | 448 | 2,054 | 2,164 | 5,475 |
| Total payment (mil. yen) | 68 | 142 | 176 | 720 | 686 | 1,793 |
| **Subsidy for job mediation** | | | | | | |
| Number eligible | 40 | 1,485 | 1,043 | 706 | 1,082 | 4,356 |
| Total payment (mil. yen) | 15 | 525 | 441 | 323 | 606 | 1,909 |

[a] through September 1987.
[b] Includes the handicapped.
*Source:* Ministry of Labor, unpublished documents.

Compared with direct assistance to workers, the magnitude of subsidies to employers was significantly larger.[18]

*Assistance by regions:* Panel A of Table 6.8 shows direct assistance to workers in specified depressed regions. Over the FY 1983–86 period, the government gave subsidies totaling 27.1 billion yen: 24.6 billion yen for extended payment of Employment Insurance benefits; 1.5 billion yen for assistance to aged unemployed workers; and only 1.0 billion yen for job conversion. Because the former two categories were not for employment adjustment but for income support programs, direct adjustment assistance was relatively limited. Panel B shows subsidies to firms promoting employment conversion in specified depression regions. During the FY 1983–86 period, the government gave subsidies totaling 9.5 billion yen: 3.3 billion yen for compensation for displaced workers; 5.7 billion yen for retraining and other activities for job conversion; and 0.5 billion yen for the leasing of workers to other firms.

To summarize, the total subsidy to firms in depressed *industries* was 14.3 billion yen during the period FY 1983–September 1987, and that to firms in depressed *regions* was 9.5 billion yen. Thus, employers took a larger share by industry than by region. In contrast, the direct assistance to workers in depressed *industries*—7.1 billion yen (including the extended payment of Employment Insurance benefits)—was much smaller than the corresponding subsidies of 27.1 billion yen to workers in depressed *regions*. This reflects the fact that there were fewer enterprises in depressed regions and the government had to provide income support to workers. As the extended payment of Employment Insurance benefits does not reduce unemployment, it should be distinguished from assistance to employment conversion, where the government emphasized assistance through enterprises. Region-based assistance tended to continue longer where key industrial sectors had been declining for one reason or another. When a specific region stagnates, it is usually not a temporary phenomenon; in such cases, what is needed is not adjustment assistance but policies to promote regional development. In fact, in the most recent period, employment promotion assistance in specified regions has become a policy quite independent of adjustment assistance.

It should be noted that import tariffs were steadily lowered during the 1983–87 period. The government refrained from raising tariff rates, even temporarily, because the economy was accumulating enormous surpluses in overseas accounts and it did not consider import-reducing policy measures to be prudent under these circumstances. The Nakasone administration, in fact, declared that it would pursue structural adjustment through improving access of foreign products to the domestic market. Thus, it became clear to producers in troubled industries that the Japanese government would not resort to import restrictions to facilitate adjustment assistance; although some industries subsequently prepared a lawsuit for imposing an antidumping duty on Korean-made knit products, no safeguard arrangements were actually initiated in the 1983–87 period.

### Adjustment Assistance Policies Since 1988

The sharp appreciation of the yen starting in the fall of 1985 triggered new adjustment problems. Japanese direct foreign investment expanded and switched production from domestic to external bases and original equipment

**Table 6.8**
**Assistance for specified depressed regions**

| Subsidies | Fiscal Year | | | | Cumulative 1983–1986 |
|---|---|---|---|---|---|
| | 1983 | 1984 | 1985 | 1986 | |
| A. *Assistance to Workers* | | | | | |
| Extended EI benefits | | | | | |
| Number of recipients[a] | 6,654 | 6,192 | 5,516 | 5,234 | 23,596 |
| Total payment (mil. yen) | 5,411 | 6,950 | 6,195 | 6,031 | 24,587 |
| Subsidy for reemployment | | | | | |
| Number of recipients | 61 | 3,467 | 4,139 | 2,371 | 10,038 |
| Total payment (mil. yen) | 6 | 355 | 425 | 254 | 1,040 |
| Subsidy to the aged unemployed | | | | | |
| Number of recipients | 1,193 | 1,884 | 1,273 | 916 | 5,266 |
| Total payment (mil. yen) | 344 | 533 | 341 | 236 | 1,454 |
| | | | Payments total | | 27,081 |
| B. *Assistance to Firms* | | | | | |
| Total subsidies (mil. yen) | 1,747 | 1,973 | 1,954 | 3,803 | 9,477 |
| Subsidy to laid-off workers | | | | | |
| Thousands of man-days | 193 | 145 | 140 | 294 | 772 |
| Total payment (mil. yen) | 709 | 598 | 590 | 1,368 | 3,265 |
| Training subsidy | | | | | |
| Thousands of man-days | 170 | 233 | 211 | 344 | 958 |
| Total payment (mil. yen) | 931 | 1,299 | 1,277 | 2,194 | 5,701 |
| Subsidy for loaning workers | | | | | |
| Number of workers | 373 | 240 | 203 | 884 | 1,700 |
| Total payment (mil. yen) | 107 | 76 | 87 | 242 | 512 |

[a]Persons per month.
*Source:* Ministry of Labor, unpublished documents.

manufacturing arrangements increased to import foreign-made manufactured goods to replace domestic ones. All these changes decreased the demand for Japanese workers, raising serious concerns about unemployment, and causing the government to revise the 1983 laws between 1986 and 1988.

MITI revised the 1983 Law in 1988, enacting the *Adjustment Facilitation Law*. In March 1987, the Employment Assistance Law of 1983 was split into the Revised Employment Assistance Law for Depressed Industries and the Law for Promotion of Regional Employment, the former being time-limited, the latter permanent. The Agency for Small- and Medium-Scale Enterprises (ASME) revised the Law for Assistance to Small Firms in December 1986 and enacted a Law for Assistance to Business Conversion of Specified Small Firms.[19]

These laws, and their evolution over time, are summarized in Figure 6.1. The new Adjustment Facilitation Law specified equipment to be scrapped (rather than industries), and provided greater financial incentives than before. Assistance for employment adjustment was again divided into two parts, in recognition of the likelihood that unemployment in a specific region would be a long-lasting phenomenon. In this sense, assistance to regional employment went beyond the scope of adjustment assistance. Assistance to small firms was finally integrated into two laws—one for adjustment assistance by region, including those specialized in specific products, and one for business conversion, initiated as early as 1976. For the first time, the 1988 revision of the Employment Assistance Law covered workers displaced by employers' direct foreign investments.

*(A) Assistance to large firms:* The Adjustment Facilitation Law strengthened financial incentives to promote (1) business conversion, (2) business partnerships for overcoming difficulties, and (3) new investments in specified depressed regions. The main policy instruments consisted of low-interest (5 percent) loans by the Japan Development Bank, in addition to the credit guarantee provided under earlier laws; reduction of taxes on land purchasing and business registration; accelerated depreciation allowances; and more generous carry-over of past losses from capacity scrapping. Emphasis was placed on promoting investments in depressed regions, where the employment impact was likely to be most significant. A controversial issue was the use of financial incentives to promote business partnerships among firms. Although partnerships required prior approval from the FTC, MITI was successful in persuading the Commission to cooperate because of major policy concerns over high unemployment.

The list of equipment to be scrapped covered 18 types of equipment. Reportedly, a major reason that MITI specified equipment to be scrapped,

**Figure 6.1**
**The legal structure of adjustment assistance policies**

| Year | Ministry in Charge | | |
|------|------|------|------|
| | MITI | Ministry of Labor | ASME under MITI |
| | | | Related Laws: |
| 1976 | - - - - - - - - - - - - | - - - - - - - - - - - - - - - - - - - - | - - (A) • Assistance to Small Firms for Business Conversion |
| 1978 | Industry Stabilization Law | Employment Assistance by Region and Industry | • Assistance to Small Firms in Depressed Regions |
| 1979 | - - - - - - - - - - - | - - - - - - - - - - - - - - - - | - - (B) • Assistance to Small Firms in Specialized Regions |
| 1983 | Structural Improvement Law | Integrated Employment Assistance | Revised Assistance to Small Firms in Depressed Regions |
| 1986 | - - - - - - - - - - - | - - - - - - - - - - - - - - - - | The above law was revised and incorporated Law (B). Law (A) was also revised. |
| 1987 | | (C) Employment Assistance by Industry. Promotion of Regional Employment. | |
| 1988 | Adjustment Facilitation Law | (C) Revised to cover adverse effects of investment abroad | |

NOTE:  The dotted horizontal lines denote the year of enactment of laws; The dashed vertical lines indicate the period over which the law is effective.

rather than designating firms eligible to receive assistance, was U.S. government criticism that adjustment assistance to industries might unfairly strengthen the ability of certain firms to compete in the industry in question.[20]

*(B) Assistance to small firms in a specified region:* Assistance to small firms for business conversion was based on a law effective for seven years (the Law of 1986) and a set of policy instruments already implemented in preceding laws. ASME grouped industries to be assisted into two catego-

ries—201 structurally troubled sectors and 151 sectors facing difficulty because of yen appreciation.

The law for adjustment assistance to small firms in specified regions, effective for five years, covered 51 regions containing 216 municipalities. In response to my criticism that the regional distribution of subsidies was politically motivated, an ASME official argued that ASME applied stricter criteria for candidate selection, which resulted in an improved selection of regions to be assisted. ASME provided generous subsidies for municipal government studies to explore new business opportunities. The regions where shipbuilding and textile manufacturing were concentrated tended to be designated as both structurally troubled and affected by yen appreciation. The list of specified regions and industries remained similar to that covered by preceding laws.

*(C, D) Assistance to workers under the laws of 1987 and 1988:* Although the two laws of 1978 were merged in 1983, they were again separated in March 1987 into employment assistance (1) by industry, effective until 1995, and (2) by region. The latter, renamed the Law for Promotion of Regional Employment, became permanent. As rapidly expanding, direct foreign investment by Japanese firms was considered to have reduced employment opportunities in the country, the law on employment assistance by industry was subsequently revised in July 1988 to cover workers displaced by increased investment abroad.

## Summary

Adjustment assistance policies over this period had several important characteristics:

- In both the Adjustment Facilitation Law and the Employment Assistance Law, policy emphasis shifted from short-run assistance to declining industries to longer-run assistance to depressed regions.
- Financial incentives to assist large corporations were strengthened, including low-interest finance and tax reduction for investments in depressed regions. This move resulted from the growing realization that administrative guidance and cartel actions were likely to be ineffective without added financial incentives.
- The FTC softened its position in regard to preventing cartel and other competition-reducing actions, in large part because of concerns over mounting unemployment.
- The present laws appear to benefit firms that create unemployment. By investing abroad and displacing some of its workers, a company

becomes eligible for subsidies to retrain displaced workers; by investing in designated regions with high unemployment rates (to which it
might have contributed), it can further enjoy tax reduction benefits and
various preferential financing programs.

## PROSPECTS AND IMPLICATIONS FOR TRADE

In 1986–87 a sense of crisis grew among many Japanese, as the yen
appreciated rapidly and many industries experienced difficulties switching
to the nontraded goods sector. By the end of 1988, nonetheless, both the
government and industrial circles grew increasingly confident about the
ability of the economy to adapt to the appreciated yen. This optimism, to be
sure, is not universal. Although some argue that Japanese industries can
overcome the competitive disadvantage of currency appreciation through
innovation in their production processes, they ignore the fact that further
success in cost reduction will lead to another round of yen appreciation.[21]

As I have suggested earlier, the yen exchange rate is one of the most important
factors influencing future adjustment tasks in Japan. Let us assume that the
purchasing-power-parity of the yen is a long-run equilibrium rate, and that the
current account records a modest surplus at this exchange rate. Then, a corresponding amount of capital outflow is required to balance the overall account.
As long as demand for the yen expands, and the nation's absorption falls short
of national production, such a situation may last for a decade or so. Although it
is difficult to predict the future performance of the major industrial economies,
one can assume for the moment that no dramatic improvement is likely to occur
over the next decade. It follows that the yen will have to appreciate further to
decrease the present current account surplus, possibly to the 100- to 140-yen-to-
the-dollar range.

Another factor needs to be considered. The invisible trade account of
Japan has had deficits of some $5 to $7 billion per year against some $100
billion surplus in the trade accounts. However, cumulative capital outflow
along with foreign assets held by the Japanese have been increasing rapidly,
and the invisible trade account may turn into a surplus in the near future.
This would also work to appreciate the value of the yen, relative to other
currencies, and lead to a further decline of the traded-goods sector.

Adjustment of the factors of production varies according to their international mobility or immobility. Clearly, the less mobile labor force must find
new employment opportunities within the country. As we have seen, the
domestic adjustment assistance policy has focused primarily on the labor

force. For this reason, MITI's policy has become increasingly oriented toward encouraging investment in regions with high unemployment rates. As the Ministry of Labor is limited in its ability to affect the demand for labor, the policy domain of MITI and the Ministry of Labor must eventually converge in directing adjustment assistance to workers.

However, capital can move more freely across national borders, making adjustment problems potentially more serious. If technological progress speeds up abroad, capital is likely to flow out in search of higher profit opportunities, making it more difficult, in turn, for domestic workers to obtain new jobs paying as well as the jobs from which they were displaced. The same argument applies to invention and the transfer of new technology. A rapid catch-up by the newly industrialized economies (NIEs) and the less developed countries (LDCs) in Asia through technology transfer will increasingly absorb more and more Japanese capital. This, in turn, will aggravate domestic adjustment problems in Japan.

Appreciation of the yen may also promote technology transfer through increased direct foreign investment by firms seeking to survive by relocating production bases abroad. In fact, direct investment by Japanese manufacturers expanded rapidly in the 1986–88 period. Thus, benefits to managerial resources will be great as long as they can exploit overseas opportunities. Reward to technology also stays at a high level, being maintained through an original-equipment-manufacturing (OEM) arrangements by which technology exporters, often manufacturers themselves, procure goods from overseas producers and sell the products under their own brand names.[22]

Generally speaking, the Japanese government has taken a neutral position toward direct foreign investment and technology transfer, although many LDCs as well as NIEs in Asia argue that they should be actively promoted. Since the government generally favors economic cooperation (cooperation for LDCs' industrialization is one of Japan's policy goals), both direct investment and technology transfer are unlikely to be withheld, and Japanese manufacturers are likely to continue overseas production in Asia in the future. All these factors suggest that market forces will work to shift the Japanese industrial structure toward the nontraded goods sector, expanding service and other related activities.

As for the trade consequences of Japanese adjustment assistance policies, the safeguard-free aspects of assistance to declining sectors are sometimes exaggerated. No adjustment assistance policy can be neutral toward foreign trade. Obviously, any policy can be used as a safeguard mechanism against imports, for a subsidy to a declining sector will also reduce imports of the products subsidized. Similarly, a subsidy to a growing sector that absorbs workers displaced by declining sectors may have an impact on reducing imports or increasing exports.

If one takes a sector in two countries and considers the trade consequences of domestic policies toward this industry, it is clear that any policy action made by one country will affect the counterpart sector in the other country. It is almost impossible to accommodate the interests of the four parties involved—the consumers and producers of the two countries—unless the government transfers income among them across national borders.

A more constructive way to solve these problems may be for the government to choose policy instruments that would have less of a trade impact. Article 19 of GATT may be too restrictive, because there is no economic reason for a government that imposes a temporary safeguard to offer compensation to the trading partners. Even though this rule may aim to prevent an abuse of the safeguard mechanism, it is not a meaningful arrangement from an economic standpoint.

Many issues have been discussed and negotiated between the U.S. and Japanese governments. If talks concentrate on the specific problems of particular sectors, such negotiations will invariably end in conflicts and quarrels. In the area of adjustment assistance, a careful comparative study is needed of policies used in the two countries, as well as an exploration of ways to improve adjustment policy. United States policy has depended largely on safeguard mechanisms, while Japanese policy has tended to emphasize sector-specific subsidization of adjustment. The cost of administering Japanese policies is enormous; there is much room for policy simplification and improvement. On the other hand, the U.S. approach, while it may minimize administrative costs, resorts too readily to safeguard arrangements that can impose very high costs on domestic consumers.

---

### NOTES

1. For instance, to protect small firms, the Japanese government sometimes restricts the entry of large corporations into specified industrial sectors. Whether this is done for purely political reasons or as an instrument of economic policy to maintain competition is a controversial issue.
2. This is a sweeping statement if one takes into account monopolistic competition in the international marketplace, where governments can intervene to reduce rents accruing to a foreign monopolist. It is assumed here that economic opportunities, through free trade, increase national welfare under normal circumstances.

3. Although circumstances differ, this point highlights the pitfalls of government intervention in encouraging the growth of aluminum refining in Japan and, ultimately, in encouraging exit from that industry.

4. See Sekiguchi (1976) for a discussion of this industry's problems.

5. These programs were later expanded to cover many other regions and are still effective to this date (with a few revisions).

6. For a more detailed economic analysis of recession cartels, see Sekiguchi (1985).

7. For positive and defensive adjustment, see OECD (1978, 1983).

8. Titles of laws are abbreviated here as follows: the Industry Stabilization Law (*Tokutei Hukyo Sangyo Antei Rinji Sotiho*); the Law on Assistance for Depressed Regions of 1978 (*Tokutei Hukyo Chiiki Chusyokigyo Taisaku Rinjisoti Ho*); and the Law on Assistance to Workers in Damaged Industries and Regions of 1978 (*Tokutei Hukyo Gyosyu Risyokusya Rinji Sotiho* and *Tokutei Hukyo Chiiki Risyokusya Rinji Sotiho,* respectively).

9. The shipbuilding industry had formed a recession cartel for 20 months, which played a role in allocating capacity reduction as well as production restriction.

10. Even in this case, the GATT concessionary rate was reduced from 14.4 percent to 12.6 percent; the rate applicable to non-GATT member exporters was raised to 16 percent (Japan Tariff Association, *Customs Tariff Schedule of Japan,* 1979 and 1983 issues).

11. The fishery and related industries faced difficulties because of the application of 200-mile economic zones by many coastal nations. The plywood industry had been declining for some time because of increased imports from developing countries.

12. I note here, but do not elaborate on, the preferential benefits accorded handicapped workers. This information was culled from unpublished documents provided by the Ministry of Labor.

13. The formal title was the Law on Temporary Measures for Structural Improvement of Specified Industries (*Tokutei Sangyo Kozo Kaizen Rinjisotiho*).

14. The new laws were the Law on Temporary Measures for Small- and Medium-Scale Enterprises in Specified Regions (*Tokutei Hukyogyoshyu kanren Chiiki Taisaku Rinjisotiho*) for small firms, and the Law on Special Measures for Employment Stabilization for Workers in Specified Depressed Industries and Regions (*Tokutei Hukyogyoshyu Hukyo Chiiki kankei Rodosha no Koyo no Antei nikansuru Tokubetsu Sochiho*) for assistance to workers.

15. Preferential tax treatments included the special treatment of carry-over losses for corporate income tax, special depreciation allowances for newly built equipment, and tax reductions for newly established firms. In fiscal year 1983 the subsidy for conversion from oil to coal energy was 2.2 billion yen; for R&D on new energy

technology, 2.3 billion yen; and for R&D investment for "revitalization of industries," 0.46 billion yen.

16. Funds earmarked for this program were expanded from 0.21 billion yen to 0.3 billion yen in fiscal year 1983, and the interest rate was set at 7.1 percent per annum as compared with the ordinary rate of 8.1 percent. This adjusted rate was to be raised to 7.8 percent in the fourth year of the program.

17. In addition to the independent law for assistance to small- and medium-scale enterprises for business conversion mentioned earlier, another adjustment assistance law exists under ASME: assistance for small- and medium-scale firms in regions where producers specialize in specific products, such as the tableware manufacturers in the Tsubame area in Niigata Prefecture. These Temporary Measures for Small- and Medium-Scale Enterprises, enacted in July 1979 to be effective for seven years, designated 198 areas as eligible to receive special assistance. When the law expired in July 1986, the program was integrated into the revised Law on Assistance to Small- and Medium-Scale Enterprises in Specified Regions of 1986, whose major purpose was to assist small firms seriously injured by the appreciation of the yen.

18. As we have seen, most of the direct assistance to workers took the form of extended payment of EI benefits (4.3 billion yen); only a small fraction was allocated to subsidizing job search and job preparation. The total 14.3 billion yen subsidy to employers dominated direct subsidies to workers for reemployment, that is, 2.8 billion yen (0.5 + 2.3 = 2.8 billion yen).

19. For simplicity, "Small- and Medium-Scale Enterprise" is shortened here to "small firms." The formal titles of these laws are: Law on Temporary Measures for Adjustment Facilitation (MITI), Law on Special Measures for Employment Stabilization in Specified Industries (Ministry of Labor), Law on Promotion of Regional Employment (Ministry of Labor), Law on Temporary Measures for Small Firms in Specified Regions (ASME), and Law on Temporary Measures for Business Conversion of Specified Small Firms (ASME). The ministries in charge of policy implementation are shown in parentheses.

20. From an interview by the author with the government officials in charge, summer of 1988.

21. In the autumn and winter of 1988 the exchange rate of the yen fell from 119 yen to 124 yen to the U.S. dollar. The G7 agreement to maintain exchange rate stability through closer macro-policy consultation, and Washington's policy of avoiding further depreciation of the dollar, may have given Japanese manufacturers a sense of relief.

22. According to Sekiguchi et al. (1988), OEM arrangements between the Japanese and Korean and Taiwanese manufacturers have increased in recent years.

## BIBLIOGRAPHY

Komiya, R., M. Okuno, and K. Suzumura (eds.) (1984). *Nihon no Sangyo Seisaku.* Tokyo: University of Tokyo. English edition, 1988, under the title *Industrial Policy of Japan.* New York: Academic Press.

Maekawa Report (1986). "The Report of the Advisory Group on Economic Structural Adjustment for International Harmony." The Advisory Group for Prime Minister Nakasone, Tokyo, April 7.

——— (1987). "The Report of the Economic Council's Special Committee on Economic Restructuring: Action for Economic Restructuring." The Economic Council's Special Committee, Tokyo, April 23.

Organization for Economic Cooperation and Development (1978). *Selected Industrial Policy Instruments: Objectives and Scope.* Paris: OECD.

——— (1983). *Positive Adjustment Policies; Managing Structural Change.* Paris: OECD.

Sekiguchi, Sueo (1976). "Industrial Adjustment Policies in Japan," in OECD, *Adjustment for Trade: Studies in Industrial Adjustment Problems and Policies.* Paris: OECD.

——— (1985). "Hukyo Karuteru no Keizai Bunseki" (Economic Analysis of Recession Cartels). Discussion Paper No. 132, The Institute of Social and Economic Research, Osaka University.

Sekiguchi, Sueo, and T. Horiuchi (1988). "Trade and Adjustment Assistance," in Komiya, Okuno, and Suzumura (eds.), *Industrial Policy of Japan* , pp. 369–393.

Sekiguchi, Sueo, et al. (1988) "Direct Foreign Investment and Technology Transfer" (*Tyokusetsu Toshi to Gijyutu Iten*). Tokyo: Economic Research Institute, Economic Planning Agency, Item 1-88-1, August.

# 7

## An Industry-Level Analysis of Import Relief Petitions Filed by U.S. Manufacturers, 1958–1985

Hong W. Tan and Frank Lichtenberg

### INTRODUCTION

Import-relief petitions constitute one of the most important policy instruments used in the United States to assist troubled industries. Through escape-clause, antidumping, and countervailing-duty complaints, troubled and trade-impacted industries may petition the International Trade Commission (ITC) for protection against injurious imports. If their complaints are determined to have merit, escape-clause petitioners are given temporary import relief through quotas or orderly marketing arrangements; in the case of antidumping or countervailing-duty petitions, affirmative determinations result in offsetting duties being imposed on below-cost sales or unfairly subsidized imports. While there is general agreement that these statutes serve to enhance both free and fair trade[1]—escape-clause action provides temporary relief for trade-impacted industries to adjust, while offsetting duties eliminate the price advantage conferred on imports by unfair trade practices—they have the potential for abuse by domestic industries seeking to protect economic rents (Bhagwati, 1988; Messerlin, 1988; Baldwin, 1984).

The dramatic rise in petitioning by U.S. firms over the past decade has heightened concern about abuses of these laws, and about rising trade protectionism in the United States. Between 1974 and 1979, an average of about 13 antidumping petitions and 37 countervailing-duty petitions were filed each year; from 1980 to 1988, these figures rose to an annual average of 48 and 49 petitions, respectively. Escape-clause petitions also rose, but more moderately—from four petitions per annum between 1963 and 1974, to just under six per annum in the decade from 1975 to 1985.

Three factors may have contributed to this rising trend in petitioning. The first is growing import competition, particularly since the 1970s, when increasing numbers of U.S. industries began losing market share to foreign producers. Second, some scholars have conjectured that increased petitioning may reflect efforts by industries to harass foreign competitors. As evidence, these scholars point to the large proportion of all petitions filed that are withdrawn before a final decision is reached (see Prusa [1988] and Devault [1990] for a dissenting view). Finally, changes in the legal environment may also have contributed to this rising trend. In 1974 and again in 1979, several statutes governing import-relief petitions were modified, making it relatively easier for trade-impacted industries to petition regulatory agencies for relief.

These developments raise numerous policy questions about the use and administration of import-relief petitions. In this chapter, we seek to address these questions by examining the behavior of trade-impacted firms, both between industries and over time, to gain insights into the role of regulatory agencies. We use a unique database assembled from records maintained by the U.S. International Trade Commission (ITC) and the International Trade Administration (ITA) of the Department of Commerce. By linking this petitioning information with time-series industry data, we are able to address several central issues. Which industries petition for import relief? Can we account for interindustry differences in petitioning? What explains the rising patterns of petitioning over time? Are regulatory agencies able to discriminate between "frivolous" petitions and those with merit? What are the consequences of affirmative determinations by the ITC and ITA for the petitioning industry?

We begin with a brief overview of the relevant statutes in U.S. trade law, followed by trends in production, trade, and petitioning activity between 1958 and 1985. We then describe the industry-level data, the hypotheses to explain petitioning behavior, and the results of estimating relatively simple models to explain the timing and intensity of petitions. Subsequently, we compare petitioner-nonpetitioner differences in the time paths of key economic variables, both before and after the petition date. This event analysis, performed by petition type and by outcome, allows us to draw inferences about petitioning behavior, the role of regulatory agencies, and the effects of different outcomes on the postpetition behavior of industries.

## IMPORT RELIEF PETITIONS: AN OVERVIEW

Industries severely hurt by foreign trade have had recourse to import relief under several U.S. trade laws. The most important of these are the escape-clause provisions contained in Section 201 of the 1974 Trade Act and the antidumping and countervailing-duty statutes of the Tariff Act of 1930.

### The Escape Clause

The idea that domestic industries adversely affected by international trade require time to adapt is widely accepted by most countries and is embodied in the safeguard provision (Article XIX) of the General Agreement on Tariffs and Trade (GATT). The U.S. Congress enacted the first escape clause in 1951, requiring the Tariff Commission (later named the International Trade Commission) to initiate an investigation when petitioned and, if an affirmative determination was made, to recommend to the president appropriate remedies to provide import relief. The president had 60 days to implement the recommended remedy, or if he decided that it was not "in the national interest," to advise Congress why he had not done so.

The escape clause underwent several important modifications in 1962 and 1974. As part of the 1962 Trade Expansion Act, the standards used in escape-clause petitions were significantly tightened. Whereas earlier petitions had to demonstrate that imports were an important cause of injury, the 1962 amendments required demonstration that increased imports were causally related "in major part" to trade concessions, and that imports were "the major factor" causing, or threatening to cause, serious injury to the industry. The "major factor" condition meant that rising imports had to be more important than the combined effects of all other factors. The linkage between imports and trade concessions was particularly limiting, because no trade concessions had been made since the last round of tariff negotiations in the 1940s.

The second major change occurred in 1974. In the wake of the severe recession induced by the oil crisis, Congress reversed itself and relaxed the criteria for escape-clause relief. Its intent was to make it easier for trade-impacted industries to seek relief from imports and to defuse support for more protectionist legislation. The 1974 Trade Act removed the requirement that increased imports result from trade concessions and required only that imports be "a substantial cause" of injury. "Substantial" cause is defined as being as important as, but not less important than, any other cause of injury. The relaxed criteria for escape-clause action are generally credited with the rise in escape-clause petitioning (Coughlin, Tezra, and Khalifah, 1989). In this economic environment, and with the relaxed criteria, the ITC made affirmative determinations in a higher proportion of cases (58 percent as compared with 20 percent prior to 1974), and the president approved 42 percent of ITC recommendations as compared with 25 percent previously (Lawrence and Litan, 1986).

### Fair-Trade Statutes

Industries injured (or threatened with injury) by imports may also seek relief under antidumping and countervailing-duty statutes. Broadly speaking, dumping is defined as export sales at prices below those of sales in the home market or, under some circumstances, as transactions where export sales fail to cover a statutory measure of the producer's production costs. In a dumping complaint, import prices are compared with home-market prices or the "fair value" of imports and an antidumping duty equal to the dumping margin is assessed upon evidence of material injury to the relevant U.S. industry. In situations where a foreign nation bestows a subsidy on a producer and imports of this product cause injury to a U.S. industry, countervailing duties set equal to the amount of the subsidy are levied on the product when it enters the country. The rationale is that the levy would offset any unfair advantage gained by the foreign producer because of the government subsidy.

These so-called "Fair Trade Laws" are administered by two agencies. The Department of the Treasury (the Department of Commerce after 1979) investigates complaints of dumping or government subsidization of exports, while the ITC determines whether material injury occurred and whether it resulted from imports. Upon an affirmative finding of *both* unfair trade practices and material injury to the domestic industry, the U.S. Customs imposes a tariff or countervailing duty on the imported items to offset the effect of the unfair trade practice.

Over time, the dumping and countervailing-duty statutes underwent several modifications, first in 1974 and then in 1979. The Trade Act of 1974 broadened the use (in certain circumstances) of a constructed-value criterion in determining dumping. These constructed values probably increased the likelihood of dumping findings during recessions. The major change occurred, however, with modifications to these statutes in the Trade Agreements Act of 1979. In this act, the United States agreed to adopt the higher "material injury" requirements of the 1979 GATT Antidumping and Subsidies Codes negotiated in the Tokyo Round. To enhance the prospects for relief under the stricter injury standard, Congress shortened the time limits for antidumping and countervailing-duty determinations and removed other restrictions on the use of constructed values in dumping cases. The most important change may have been to shift antidumping and countervailing-duty investigations to the Commerce Department, on the grounds that it would be more responsive to industry complaints than the Treasury Department (Borrus and Goldstein, 1987).

## Trends in Imports and Petitions

With the overview of import-relief petitions as background, we now examine the trends in several economic indicators—imports, domestic production, and petitioning intensity. Table 7.1 shows the time-series data on these variables.

The "Industry Mean" column of Table 7.1 shows the ratio of the value of imports to the value of domestically produced output for the U.S. manufacturing sector for the period between 1958 and 1985. The value of this ratio in 1985 was 5.7 times as high as it was in 1958, implying that the average annual growth rate of imports was 6.4 percentage points higher than the growth rate of domestic output. It is possible to partition the 1958–85 period into three distinct subperiods: 1958–63, during which import ratios were essentially constant; 1964–80, during which import ratios increased at a moderate rate (about 6.7 percent per annum); and 1981–85, during which import ratios increased at a high (13.3 percent) annual rate. Thus, not only did imports increase substantially during this period relative to domestic production, they increased at an accelerating rate.

The next two columns of Table 7.1 show the import ratios for all industries that ever petitioned, even once, over this entire period ("petitioning industries") and for industries that never petitioned ("nonpetitioning industries"). In each of the three subperiods, the levels and rates of change in import ratios are always higher in petitioning than in nonpetitioning industries. By 1985, imports reached 18 percent of domestic output in petitioning industries, as compared with 9.6 percent in nonpetitioning industries. The three right-hand columns present data on the number of import-relief petitions filed each year, by type of petition. The series for antidumping (AD) petitions begins in 1958, for countervailing-duty (CV) petitions in 1974, and for escape-clause (EC) petitions in 1961. The column that reports totals for all petition types indicates a rising trend in petitioning over time. Only one part of this rising trend is attributable to the later starting dates for the countervailing-duty and escape-clause series. The antidumping petition series reveals a rising trend, especially after the mid-1970s.

This trend is shown more clearly in Figure 7.1, which plots the total number of petitions filed by type of petition. Furthermore, a close scrutiny of the plots reveals peaks in petitioning in several years—1975, 1978, and 1982—that correspond with economic downturns associated with the two petroleum price-hikes (1975 and 1978), and the severe recession of the 1980s, when unemployment rates peaked (1982).

**Table 7.1**
**Import ratios and number of petitions filed by type**

| Year | Import Ratios[a] | | | Petitions Filed[b,c] | | | |
| | Industry Mean | Ever Petition | Never Petition | All Types | AD | CV | EC |
|---|---|---|---|---|---|---|---|
| 1958 | 2.6 | 3.3 | 1.6 | 35 | 35 | n.a. | n.a. |
| 1959 | 2.9 | 3.7 | 1.7 | 29 | 29 | n.a. | n.a. |
| 1960 | 2.8 | 3.6 | 1.7 | 37 | 37 | n.a. | n.a. |
| 1961 | 2.7 | 3.3 | 1.7 | 21 | 21 | n.a. | 0 |
| 1962 | 2.9 | 3.6 | 1.8 | 32 | 28 | n.a. | 4 |
| 1963 | 2.9 | 3.6 | 1.9 | 28 | 27 | n.a. | 1 |
| 1964 | 3.0 | 3.7 | 1.9 | 35 | 31 | n.a. | 4 |
| 1965 | 3.3 | 4.0 | 2.1 | 12 | 12 | n.a. | 0 |
| 1966 | 3.7 | 4.6 | 2.3 | 14 | 14 | n.a. | 0 |
| 1967 | 3.9 | 4.9 | 2.4 | 19 | 16 | n.a. | 3 |
| 1968 | 4.7 | 5.9 | 2.7 | 17 | 17 | n.a. | 0 |
| 1969 | 4.9 | 6.2 | 2.8 | 27 | 23 | n.a. | 4 |
| 1970 | 5.5 | 7.1 | 3.1 | 10 | 7 | n.a. | 3 |
| 1971 | 6.0 | 7.8 | 3.3 | 23 | 18 | n.a. | 5 |
| 1972 | 6.6 | 8.5 | 3.6 | 36 | 34 | n.a. | 2 |
| 1973 | 6.9 | 8.7 | 3.8 | 35 | 32 | n.a. | 3 |
| 1974 | 7.8 | 9.9 | 4.3 | 16 | 9 | 7 | 0 |
| 1975 | 6.9 | 8.6 | 4.1 | 69 | 21 | 35 | 13 |
| 1976 | 7.4 | 9.2 | 4.4 | 40 | 17 | 16 | 7 |
| 1977 | 7.8 | 9.8 | 4.4 | 44 | 22 | 11 | 11 |
| 1978 | 8.7 | 10.8 | 5.1 | 70 | 33 | 32 | 5 |
| 1979 | 8.8 | 10.7 | 5.3 | 60 | 37 | 20 | 3 |
| 1980 | 9.1 | 11.0 | 5.8 | 44 | 29 | 12 | 3 |
| 1981 | 9.5 | 11.2 | 6.3 | 20 | 14 | 5 | 1 |
| 1982 | 10.0 | 12.0 | 6.5 | 106 | 50 | 52 | 4 |
| 1983 | 10.8 | 13.1 | 6.9 | 64 | 45 | 17 | 2 |
| 1984 | 13.3 | 15.8 | 8.9 | 100 | 52 | 41 | 7 |
| 1985 | 14.8 | 18.0 | 9.6 | 103 | 62 | 37 | 4 |

[a]Import ratio = ratio of imports to domestic output.
[b]n.a.: data not available.
[c]AD = antidumping; CV = countervailing duty; EC = escape clause.

Table 7.2 presents estimates of the cumulative number of petitions filed during 1958–85, by type and disposition of petition. Over two-thirds of the petitions filed were antidumping petitions, and only 7 percent were escape-clause petitions. In Chapter 5 of the present volume, Tan notes that the relative number of different types of petitions filed has changed over time, partly in response to relative changes in the government's criteria for granting relief. Table 7.2 indicates the distribution of each type of petition by disposition. The determination of about 9 percent of the petitions is unknown. Among those where the final outcome is known, no final determination was made by the government in 18 percent of the cases, owing to termination or suspension, usually because the petition was found to be without merit, or was granted relief through extralegal means, such as a "voluntary" restraint agreement. For petitions reaching a final, affirmative-or-negative determination (974 petitions), 40 percent were affirmative in the sense that some form of import relief was granted by the government. The fraction of affirmative final determinations was highest in the case of countervailing-duty (59 percent of 198 petitions), and lowest in the case of antidumping (35 percent of 720 petitions).

**Figure 7.1**
**Trends in petitions for import relief, by type**

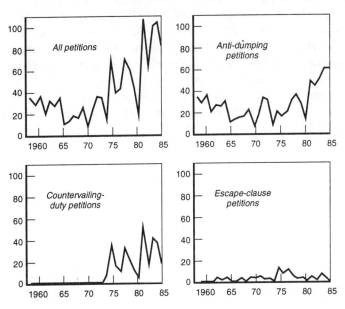

Table 7.2
**Cumulative number of petitions filed by type and disposition, 1958–85**

| Petition Type | Final Determination | | | | | Total Known | Total Petitions |
|---|---|---|---|---|---|---|---|
| | Aff. | Neg. | Ter. | Sus. | Miss. | | |
| Antidumping | 250 | 470 | 110 | 12 | 52 | 842 | 894 |
| Countervailing duty | 117 | 81 | 88 | 5 | 33 | 291 | 324 |
| Escape clause | 23 | 33 | 2 | 0 | 33 | 58 | 91 |
| Total | 390 | 584 | 200 | 17 | 118 | 1,191 | 1,309 |

Aff.  = Affirmative     Sus.  = Suspended
Neg. = Negative        Miss. = Unknown
Ter.  = Terminated

## DETERMINANTS OF AGGREGATE PETITIONING BEHAVIOR

We now turn to a formal analysis of the determinants of petitioning behavior. As noted above, the number of import-relief petitions increased dramatically between 1958 and 1985 and this increase was paralleled by a rise in the ratio of imports to domestic output. Changes over time in the legal criteria used to determine injury and less-than-fair-value pricing—in particular, the modifications to the trade statutes in 1974 and 1979—may also have contributed to this increasing trend. In this section, we shall formally test the hypothesis that import ratios and changes in the legal environment determine the number of petitions filed, as well as alternative hypotheses about factors governing the likelihood and frequency of petitions in each industry.

These analyses are based on pooled, time-series, industry-level data for the period 1962–85. The longitudinal industry data come from two National Bureau of Economic Research (NBER) files—one containing information on trade, the other containing production data derived from the Census of Manufacturing and the Annual Surveys of Manufacturing. Together, these files provide a wealth of four-digit SIC (Standard Industrial Classification) industry information on production, wages, unionization rates, capital stock, productivity growth, and both imports and exports. The data on escape-clause, antidumping, and countervailing-duty petitions were assembled from docket logs, public use files, and other primary data sources at the ITC and ITA (including archival records on petitions filed at the Treasury Department prior to 1980). For each petition, information (incomplete in some years) was collected on the filing date, the product(s) involved, and the outcome—

whether affirmative, negative, terminated, suspended, or missing. Products were assigned four-digit SIC codes, and these codes were used to link the petition data to the NBER industry files. Thus, the unit of analysis is the four-digit SIC industry in a given year.

We shall consider three broad categories of factors in investigating the petition probability and the number of petitions filed in a given year. The first, and most obvious, category includes those variables that reflect the degree of material injury to the industry caused by imports (and other factors). To the extent that these measures coincide with the economic criteria used by the ITC to determine injury (or the threat of injury), industries exhibiting such characteristics might be expected to petition, and to petition more frequently. The second category includes several other variables that shape the industry's petitioning propensity but are factors that ITC is not obliged to consider in determining injury. The final category includes variables representing changes in the legal environment governing the disposition of petitions. Congress and the Administration can affect petitioning by making it easier or more difficult for industries to seek and receive import relief.

The first category includes several economic criteria used by the ITC to determine material injury. They include the levels and rates of change in import penetration, employment and output loss, profits, and capacity utilization rates. We define the following variables as proxies for these criteria. There are two variables for import penetration: the ratio of imports to domestic output in the four-digit industry, and the percentage change in this variable over the past year. Employment loss is simply defined as the percent change in employment over the past year (employment levels are considered below). Output loss (indirectly the rate of capacity utilization) is treated differently. Since the ITC is obliged to weigh the relative importance of competing causes of injury—including imports and business cycle factors—we shall measure output loss relative to changes in total manufacturing output.

Thus, we include the change in manufacturing output to control for business cycle effects and the industry-specific change in output (less the change for all manufacturing) to measure output loss. Profitability, and its change over time, is measured by the price-cost margin of the industry, defined as the ratio of value added less the wage bill to the book value of assets. This variable is widely used in the economics literature as a proxy for the rate of return to capital (for example, see Cowling and Waterson, 1976). In general, we should expect a higher probability of a petition the greater the rise in import ratios and the larger the decline in employment, output, and profits.

The second category includes workforce and industry characteristics that shape the industry's decision to petition but are not considered in ITC injury determinations. Several workforce attributes may be important. For example, one might expect a greater likelihood of petitioning the larger the number of jobs at risk from rising imports. Employment size may also be important if regulatory agencies and politicians are more receptive to complaints from large groups of workers and constituents (Baldwin, 1984; Bhagwati, 1988). The natural logarithm of industry employment is included here as a measure of the number of jobs threatened by import competition. Unions may be better able to organize workers and firms and, through national trade union groups, to lobby Congress and the Administration for import protection (indeed, many petitions are initiated by unions, either acting alone or in concert with employers). Union wage-premiums and a desire to prevent wage erosion and job loss are other reasons that union representatives press for import protection. We attempt to capture these effects by including the unionization rate of the industry.

Several industry characteristics may also determine an industry's propensity to petition. The adjustment costs of responding to increased import competition (e.g., scrapping old plant and equipment) may be relatively greater in capital-intensive industries. We proxy these adjustment costs by the industry's capital intensity, defined as the ratio of the book value of assets to total employment and hypothesize that capital intensity is positively associated with the likelihood of petitioning. Petitioning may be related to market power, as measured by industry concentration, but the relationship is not readily "signed." The prior success of concentrated industries in erecting import barriers would have a negative effect on petitioning, whereas an increase in imports attracted by high industry profits would have a positive effect.[2] Petitioners may also be drawn disproportionately from older, less competitive industries with low rates of productivity growth. We test this proposition using the industry rate of total factor productivity (TFP) growth, the expectation being that petitioners tend to be low TFP industries.[3]

Finally, we include a measure of the industry's product diversification. One hypothesis is that diversified industries are better able to adjust to increases in import competition and are thus less likely to petition for import relief. Faced with import competition in one product line, firms that are already diversified may shift their emphasis into other areas more readily than single-product firms are able to do so (Pugel and Walter, 1985). An alternative hypothesis is that product diversification may dilute the firm's international competitive position by spreading its comparative advantages too thinly over many products (Ghellinck, Geroski, and Jacquemin, 1988). This would tend to make diversified industries more likely to petition. We test these competing hypotheses using the enterprise-based index of product diversification estimated by Gollop and Monahan (1989) for four-digit industries.[4]

The last category comprises variables that capture the effects of changes over time in the legal environment. As noted above, trade statutes were modified twice in the period between 1962 and 1985: first in the Trade Act of 1974 and again in the Trade Agreements Act of 1979. The 1974 legislation relaxed the standards used in ITC decisions regarding escape-clause petitions—eliminating the link between prior trade concessions and injury, and reducing the importance of imports from a "major" to a "substantial" cause of injury. These changes made it more attractive to pursue escape-clause actions. By broadening the use of constructed values, thus loosening the definition of dumping, the 1974 law may also have induced a larger number of fair trade cases. The 1979 legislation shifted the responsibility for less-than-fair-value (LTFV) determinations to the Commerce Department (which was more responsive to industry complaints) and shortened the time limits for disposition of petitions. While somewhat higher injury standards were also adopted, the probable net impact of these changes was to induce greater petitioning under the fair trade statutes.

We define two time-period dummy variables to capture the petitioning effects of these legal changes. The first dummy variable is set equal to one for each year from 1974 to 1979 and zero otherwise; the second dummy variable is similarly defined for the 1980–85 period. These effects will be compared to the reference period, 1962–73, when extremely restrictive import-relief criteria embodied in the 1962 Trade Expansion Act were operative. In addition to these two variables, we use a lagged measure of the approval rates for all petitions filed in a given year. It is possible that legal changes have a delayed impact on the number of petitions filed (some industries respond with a lag) and that these effects vary across years within the periods encompassed by the two dummy variables. To test for these lagged effects, we include the mean of the proportion of petitions approved for all industries in the previous two years (similar variables are computed for each petition type). If firms interpret these as expectations (albeit noisy ones) of a favorable ITC determination, we should expect a higher likelihood of a petition when their expectations rise.

## Empirical Results

Before proceeding to the formal econometric tests, we first examine simple cross-tabulations of some of these variables to gain insights into the data. We partition the data into two groups—industries that have petitioned, even once, during the 1962–85 period, and nonpetitioning industries. Table 7.3 presents the means (and standard deviations) of variables for petitioning and nonpetitioning industries. For reference, Table 7.3 shows the fraction of observations in which one or more petitions of each type were filed, as well as the expectations of an affirmative determination (we discuss these below). Turning to the explanatory variables, we note that they are broadly consistent with the hypotheses described above. Petitioning industries tend, on average, to have higher import ratios (14.2 percent) than do nonpetitioning industries (9.4 percent). They also tend to be more capital intensive, to have higher industry concentration, product diversification, and unionization, and to employ a relatively large workforce. The two groups do not, however, appear different in terms of profitability (as measured by price-cost margins) or rates of total factor productivity growth. Table 7.3 also reports the rates of change (denoted by %$\Delta$) in several variables over the preceding year. The figures for the ever-petition group are difficult to interpret, for they average across both petitioning and nonpetitioning years. With this caveat, the table suggests that the industries that have ever petitioned tend to experience both slower employment growth and larger rates of decline, both in output and profit levels, compared with those that have never petitioned. We investigate the joint effects of these variables more formally below.

The econometric analyses focus on two outcomes: (1) the probability of petitioning in a given year, and (2) the number of petitions filed in a given year. Both outcomes refer initially to all types of petitions combined; in subsequent analyses, we treat each petition type separately. The first outcome is modeled as a (0,1) indicator variable with a value of "1" if the industry filed one or more petitions in a given year and "0" otherwise. This probit model permits probability statements to be made about how each factor affects the likelihood of a petition, all other factors held constant. The second outcome—discrete counts of the number of petitions filed in a year—is modeled as being generated by a Poisson process.[5] Both probit and Poisson models are fit using interactive maximum likelihood methods.[6] Estimated parameters and $t$-statistics are reported in Table 7.4 for all petition types combined. First consider the variables that proxy the economic criteria used in ITC determinations. In general, the results appear to be consistent with their use as indexes of material injury. The industries that petition, and petition more intensively in a given year, are those with high import-ratio levels, those that experience larger percentage losses in employment over the past year, and those whose output has grown less relative to the total manufacturing average. Depressed profit levels in the industry also lead to significantly higher petitioning intensity. Some other results appear counterintuitive, such as the finding that increases in import-ratios over the past year lead to less (not more) petitioning. The inclusion of longer lags in the import-ratio change variable (and other key variables as well) may be needed, especially if petitions are triggered by experience with rising import competition over several years (we take up this issue in the following section). Total manufacturing output growth is also associated with higher (not lower) levels of petitioning. This variable, included to control for business cycle effects, may also be picking up time trends that are positively correlated with the rising petitioning trend.

The view that an industry's petitioning propensity is shaped by worker and industry characteristics receives some empirical support. Consistent with the hypotheses described above, petitioning industries tend to have a larger

**Table 7.3**
**Variable means by petition status**

| Variable | Never Petition | | Ever Petition | |
|---|---|---|---|---|
| | Mean | Standard Deviation | Mean | Standard Deviation |
| Sample size | 6,552 | — | 4,248 | — |
| Any petition in year | — | — | .122 | — |
| AD petition in year[a] | — | — | .084 | — |
| CV petition in year | — | — | .063 | — |
| EC petition in year | — | — | .020 | — |
| E(affirmative)—any[b] | .354 | .189 | .354 | .189 |
| E(affirmative)—AD | .338 | .172 | .338 | .172 |
| E(affirmative)—CV | .493 | .191 | .493 | .191 |
| E(affirmative)—EC | .234 | .225 | .234 | .225 |
| Import ratio | .094 | .416 | .142 | .391 |
| %$\Delta$ import ratio[c] | 16.7 | 131.3 | 13.2 | 51.8 |
| Capital-labor ratio | 17.8 | 18.9 | 25.1 | 37.5 |
| Concentration ratio | 37.9 | 21.1 | 39.5 | 20.2 |
| Diversification index | .289 | .178 | .342 | .181 |
| Unionization rate | 32.5 | 11.8 | 36.1 | 13.6 |
| Log (employment) | 2.93 | .977 | 3.42 | 1.09 |
| TFP growth rate[d] | .007 | .066 | .006 | .065 |
| %$\Delta$ manufacturing output | 4.64 | 5.32 | 4.64 | 5.32 |
| %$\Delta$ industry output | −1.11 | 12.8 | −1.44 | 11.7 |
| %$\Delta$ employment levels | .715 | 11.4 | .162 | 9.85 |
| Profit rate | 26.6 | 8.41 | 26.9 | 8.76 |
| %$\Delta$ profit rate | 1.71 | 49.8 | −8.02 | 474.9 |

[a] AD, CV, and EC refer to antidumping, countervailing-duty, and escape-clause petitions, respectively.
[b] E(affirmative) is the expected probability of an affirmative determination in year $t$.
[c] %$\Delta$ refers to the percentage change in the variable from year $t - 1$ to year $t$.
[d] TFP stands for total factor productivity.

workforce and to be more highly unionized and capital-intensive. These findings reflect the larger number of jobs at risk, a greater ability to organize support for petitions, and higher adjustment costs in these industries. We found no support for the hypothesis that highly diversified industries are less likely to petition because of the risk-pooling aspect of diversification. Indeed, Table 7.4 suggests that diversified industries petition more, a result more in line with the view that diversification dilutes the competitive position of firms relative to their competitors. Finally, for reasons that are unclear, the industries that petition more intensively appear to be those that have higher rates of total factor productivity growth.

In the last rows of Table 7.4, we investigate the effects of changes in the legal environment on the level of petitioning activity. Compared with the 1962–73 reference period, the likelihood of one or more petitions being filed

**Table 7.4**
**Determinants of petition timing and intensity**

| Explanatory Variable | Probit Petition That Year | | Poisson Number of Petitions | |
|---|---|---|---|---|
| | Coef. | $t$-stat. | Coef. | $t$-stat. |
| Constant | −3.3087 | −23.38 | −6.5924 | −32.00 |
| Import ratio | .1933 | 5.33 | .2479 | 7.16 |
| %Δ import ratio[a] | − .0010 | − 1.76 | − .0019 | − 2.02 |
| %Δ employment | − .0074 | − 1.97 | − .0079 | − 1.42 |
| Profit rate | .0030 | 1.11 | − .0136 | − 3.37 |
| %Δ profit rate | .0001 | 0.33 | .0002 | 0.84 |
| %Δ manufacturing output | .0099 | 1.81 | .0148 | 2.02 |
| %Δ industry growth | − .0004 | − 0.08 | − .0389 | − 6.34 |
| Log (employment) | .2552 | 10.41 | .5541 | 17.47 |
| Unionization rate | .0107 | 6.06 | .0381 | 16.15 |
| Concentration ratio | .0003 | 0.20 | − .0049 | − 2.74 |
| Diversification index | .0957 | 0.62 | 1.1270 | 4.92 |
| Capital-labor ratio | .0043 | 7.10 | .0066 | 14.45 |
| TFP growth rate[b] | .3050 | 0.54 | 4.4678 | 5.63 |
| Dummy 1974–79 | .1807 | 2.32 | .6189 | 4.92 |
| Dummy 1980–85 | .0487 | 0.59 | .9297 | 7.42 |
| E(affirmative)—any[c] | .1855 | 0.93 | .2906 | 0.87 |
| Sample size | 10,329 | | 10,329 | |
| Mean of dependent variable | .0492 | | .0948 | |
| Log-likelihood | −1,867.6 | | −3,330.8 | |

[a]%Δ refers to the percentage change in the variable from year $t − 1$ to year $t$.
[b]TFP stands for total factor productivity.
[c]E(affirmative) is the expected probability of an affirmative determination in year $t$ for all petition types.

in a given year rose 18 percentage points in the 1974–79 period and about 5 percentage points in the 1980–85 period (however, the latter increase is not statistically significant). When we consider the second outcome—the number of petitions filed in a given year—the two period dummy variables reveal a secularly increasing time trend in petitioning intensity. They suggest that industries filed, on average, about 62 percent more petitions in the 1974–79 period, and 93 percent more petitions in the 1980s, controlling for the effects of other variables. In these models, lagged-expectations variables were never statistically significant. Together, these results suggest that changes to the trade statutes in 1974 and 1979 contributed significantly not only to the likelihood of petitioning, but also to petitioning intensity over time.[7]

Thus far, the analyses have treated all types of petitions as being similar. In Table 7.5, we report the results of estimating count models for each type of petition, using only years in which data on that petition type are available. The outcome in each case is the number of petitions filed in a given year. The model specification is identical across petition types, with two exceptions. In the countervailing-duty petition model, we drop the 1974–79 dummy variable, because the sample period begins in 1974. Thus, the reference period for the 1980–85 period dummy is the preceding 1974–79 period. A second change is the use in each model of affirmative expectation measures calculated for the specific petition type.

Overall, the results by petition type add little to our understanding of petitioning behavior. Although the magnitude of parameter estimates varies across petition types, in general, they have the same signs and are of comparable size to those reported above for all types of petitions combined. The exceptions lie in the time effects estimated for each petition type. The number of escape-clause petitions rose dramatically (93 percent) in the period 1974–79, but less so in the 1980s (14 percent). These findings are not surprising, for changes embodied in the 1974 Trade Act were most relevant to escape-clause actions. In contrast, the 1979 Trade Agreements Act affected fair trade statutes more directly. As evidence, note that the number of antidumping petitions filed rose moderately (8 percent) between 1974 and 1979 as compared with the 1962–73 reference period, while it increased sharply, by 67 percent, after 1979. In the case of countervailing-duty petitions, the 1980s period effect is not different from that of the 1974–79 reference period. The expectations variable is positive and significant, suggesting that, over this period, industries filed more subsidy cases because of the greater likelihood of an affirmative ITC determination.

To summarize, we have investigated and found some support for several hypotheses about the determinants of both petitioning behavior and the intensity of petitioning over time. The most important determinants include

**Table 7.5**
**Determinants of petitioning intensity[a]**

| Explanatory Variable | Anti-dumping[b] | Countervailing Duty[b] | Escape Clause[b] |
|---|---|---|---|
| Constant | −7.3226[c] | −6.5235[c] | −7.4210[c] |
| Import ratio | .2590[c] | .2113[c] | .2982[c] |
| %Δ import ratio | −.0038[c] | −.0004 | .0002 |
| %Δ employment | −.0095 | −.0076 | −.0105 |
| Profit rate | .0017 | −.0487[c] | −.0166 |
| %Δ profit rate | .0002 | .0010 | .0001 |
| %Δ manufacturing output | .0369[c] | −.0285 | .0011 |
| %Δ industry growth | −.0254[c] | −.0668[c] | −.0260 |
| Log (employment) | .5508[c] | .6404[c] | .4304[c] |
| Unionization rate | .0425[c] | .0281[c] | .0286[c] |
| Concentration ratio | −.0034 | −.0121[c] | .0006 |
| Diversification index | 1.1323[c] | 1.7981[c] | −.6038 |
| Capital-labor ratio | .0073[c] | .0038[c] | .0047 |
| TFP growth rate[d] | 3.3541[c] | 6.0975[c] | 3.8084 |
| Dummy 1974–79 | .0851 | — | .9268[c] |
| Dummy 1980–85 | .6663[c] | −.0206[c] | .1398 |
| E(affirmative) | −.1385 | 1.7345[c] | .6581 |
| Sample size | 10,329 | 5,400 | 10,329 |
| Mean of dependent variable | .0602 | .0528 | .0082 |
| Log-likelihood | −2,308.0 | −1,046.8 | −480.5 |

[a]Petition counts estimated using Poisson model.
[b]1962–85 for antidumping and escape-clause petitions, and 1974–85 for countervailing-duty petitions.
[c]Statistically significant at the 1 percent level.
[d]TFP stands for total factor productivity.

measures of material injury to the industry, workforce and industry characteristics, and changes in the legal environment. We have, thus far, not
explored the factors that actually determine whether petitions are approved
or denied, and what effects these outcomes have on industry behavior. Some
of these issues are addressed below.

## LONGITUDINAL ANALYSIS OF PETITIONING INDUSTRIES

In this section, we exploit the longitudinal nature of the dataset to investigate
patterns of change over time in several key economic variables, comparing
petitioning and nonpetitioning industries. These variables include measures
of import penetration, output, employment, wages, and profitability. The
analysis is motivated by several research questions: How effective are

petitions in reducing imports that injure (or threaten to injure) domestic industries? Are imports slowed only by affirmative determinations, or is the outcome independent of whether petitions are approved, as might be expected if the filing of petitions has a "threat effect" for foreign producers Prusa, 1988)? Do troubled industries use this temporary respite to adjust—to shed redundant labor and reduce wage levels—and are these (and other) adjustments reflected in improved profitability over time? Does petitioner behavior vary with the type of petition filed (escape-clause or fair-trade petitions) and its outcome, whether approved or denied by the ITC?

We use event analysis to investigate these questions. Again, we shall first classify observations (industries by year) as "petitioners" or "nonpetitioners" on the basis of whether the industry filed at least one petition in a given year the "event"); then we shall examine differences in behavior between these two groups in the years before and after the filing of the petition. Subsequently, we shall pursue this event analysis at a finer level of disaggregation, first comparing the behavior of petitioners by whether petitions filed are approved or denied, then, by petition type and outcome.

To compute these differences, we shall estimate regressions of the following form:

$$X_{i,t+k} = \alpha_{t+k}P_{it} + \beta_{t+k}T_{t+k} + e_{i,t+k} \ (k = -4, \ldots, 4)$$

where $X_{i,t+k}$ denotes the value of variable X in industry i in year t+k; k varies from minus 4 to plus 4, so that t+k spans the eight years before and after the event in year t; $P_{i,t}$ has a value of 1 if industry i filed at least one petition in year t, and otherwise equals zero; $T_{t+k}$ is a vector of time dummy variables; $e_{i,t+k}$ is a disturbance term; and $\alpha$ and $\beta$ are parameters to be estimated in the model. The $\alpha_{t+k}$ parameters are interpreted as the difference between the mean values of X in years t+k for industries filing petitions in year t and those not filing petitions, while the $\beta_{t+k}$ parameters may be interpreted as "fixed effects" for years t+k. Table 7.6 presents estimates of the $\alpha$ parameters corresponding to five definitions of the variable X: (1) import ratio, the ratio of imports to domestic production; (2) output, the percentage change in the value of shipments from the previous year; (3) employment, the percentage change in the size of the workforce from the previous year; (4) wages, the natural logarithm of the production workers' hourly wage rate; and (5) profitability, as measured by the price-cost margin (in percent). In each row, the table reports the difference in the value of X between petitioners and nonpetitioners from t – 4 to t + 4 years.

For each X, the table also reports the corresponding differences in X estimated for three mutually exclusive petition outcomes. The outcomes are: (1) "negative," where all petitions filed in a given year receive negative determinations; (2) "positive," where one or more petitions filed receive an affirmative determination; and (3) "other," where all petitions filed are either suspended or terminated subsequently, or the outcomes are unknown (at least to the analyst). These parameters are estimated from a regression model in which the petition variable P is replaced by indicator variables for each of the three outcomes j. Thus, if petition outcomes are represented by $P_{ij,t}$, the estimated parameters $a_{j,t+k}$ measure the petitioner-nonpetitioner differences in X for groups with negative, positive, and other outcomes.

The first row (Panel A) of Table 7.6 shows the import-ratio estimates. As one would expect, they indicate that petitioners have significantly higher ratios of imports to output than nonpetitioners in every year from four years before to four years after the year of the petition. The petitioner-versus-non-petitioner difference in import ratios not only is positive, but it increases every year, from 4.9 percent in year $t - 4$ to 8.9 percent in $t + 4$. There is evidence of acceleration in the import-ratio difference just before year t, when it jumps from 5.5 to 6.7 percent between $t - 1$ and t, suggesting that a sharp rise in imports tends to elicit a petitioning response from affected industries. This difference continues to grow, but it begins to taper off after year $t + 3$ and is virtually unchanged by $t + 4$. Thus, on average, petitions appear to arrest increases in imports with a lag of several years.

Do patterns of change in import ratios vary by petition outcomes? The next three rows of Panel A demonstrate that petition outcomes are important. For the group in which all petitions are denied, import-ratio differences at time t are roughly similar to those prevailing four years earlier (3.9 percent); while this figure rises slightly to 4.4 percent in the year after the petition, it remains at that approximate level over the next three years. For petitioners with one or more affirmative determinations, the initial import-ratio difference is actually lower than that of the first group (3.1 versus 3.9 percent); subsequently, it accelerates and reaches a peak of 10.9 percent two years after the petition date, before declining to the 9.6 percent range. The final group—petitioners with terminated, suspended, or missing outcomes—exhibits both a relatively high initial level and a continuously rising time trend in import-ratio differences over the entire period.

Panels B and C of Table 7.6 report the estimated differences in annual growth of output and employment between petitioning and nonpetitioning industries, and among the three outcome groups. In general, these differences are a mirror image of patterns of changes reported for import ratios. With

**Table 7.6**

**Percentage differences in key variables between petitioning and nonpetitioning industries**

| | Years Before and After Petitioning | | | | | | | | |
|---|---|---|---|---|---|---|---|---|---|
| | $t-4$ | $t-3$ | $t-2$ | $t-1$ | $t$ | $t+1$ | $t+2$ | $t+3$ | $t+4$ |
| A. Import ratio | 4.9[a] | 5.1[a] | 5.4[a] | 5.5[a] | 6.7[a] | 7.7[a] | 8.5[a] | 8.8[a] | 8.9[a] |
| Determination: | | | | | | | | | |
| Negative | 3.9[a] | 3.7[a] | 3.3 | 2.7 | 3.8 | 4.4 | 4.2 | 4.2 | 4.2 |
| Positive | 3.1 | 3.7 | 4.8 | 6.5[a] | 8.3[a] | 9.0[a] | 10.9[a] | 9.6[a] | 9.8[a] |
| Other | 7.6[a] | 7.9[a] | 8.9[a] | 9.2[a] | 10.4[a] | 12.6[a] | 14.6[a] | 16.7[a] | 17.1[a] |
| B. Shipments | -1.2[a] | -0.9 | -1.5[a] | -0.8 | -0.9 | 0.2 | -1.4[a] | -1.6[a] | -0.9 |
| Determination: | | | | | | | | | |
| Negative | 0.6 | 0.3 | 0.5 | 0.2 | -0.1 | 2.3[a] | -0.1 | -0.2 | 0.8 |
| Positive | -1.5 | -2.2 | -2.8[a] | -2.9[a] | -0.5 | -1.9 | -1.7 | -1.7 | -1.6 |
| Other | -3.2[a] | -1.6 | -3.3[a] | -0.9 | -2.4[a] | -2.0[a] | -3.6[a] | -4.0[a] | -3.5[a] |
| C. Employment | -0.6 | -0.7 | -1.1[a] | -0.9[a] | -1.2[a] | -0.4 | -1.1[a] | -1.0[a] | -1.5[a] |
| Determination: | | | | | | | | | |
| Negative | 0.9 | -0.0 | -0.1 | -0.3 | -0.2 | 0.6 | -0.3 | 0.3 | 0.4 |
| Positive | -1.7 | -1.9[a] | -2.1[a] | -2.3[a] | -1.0 | -1.3 | -1.0 | -1.5 | -2.1 |
| Other | -1.6[a] | -0.7 | -1.9[a] | -1.0 | -2.7[a] | -1.7[a] | -2.4[a] | -3.0[a] | -4.5[a] |

**Table 7.6—continued**

| Key Variable/ Petition Outcome | Years Before and After Petitioning | | | | | | | | |
|---|---|---|---|---|---|---|---|---|---|
| | $t-4$ | $t-3$ | $t-2$ | $t-1$ | $t$ | $t+1$ | $t+2$ | $t+3$ | $t+4$ |
| D. Log (Wages) | 10.5[a] | 10.4[a] | 10.2[a] | 10.4[a] | 10.4[a] | 9.9[a] | 9.7[a] | 9.1[a] | 8.5[a] |
| Determination: | | | | | | | | | |
| Negative | 5.0[a] | 4.8[a] | 4.6[a] | 5.2[a] | 5.1[a] | 5.6[a] | 5.6[a] | 5.4[a] | 5.3[a] |
| Positive | 10.5[a] | 10.5[a] | 10.7[a] | 10.5[a] | 11.4[a] | 9.9[a] | 11.1[a] | 9.5[a] | 9.5[a] |
| Other | 17.8[a] | 18.1[a] | 18.1[a] | 18.2[a] | 18.3[a] | 17.0[a] | 15.9[a] | 15.2[a] | 14.0[a] |
| E. Profits | 0.8[a] | 0.8[a] | 0.7 | 0.6 | 0.5 | 0.7 | 0.7[a] | 0.2 | 0.3 |
| Determination: | | | | | | | | | |
| Negative | 0.6 | 0.6 | 0.4 | 0.3 | 0.5 | 0.4 | 0.3 | 0.0 | 0.2 |
| Positive | 0.8 | 0.8 | 0.6 | 0.7 | 0.2 | 0.8 | 1.0 | 1.0 | 0.5 |
| Other | 1.2[a] | 1.1 | 1.1 | 0.9 | 0.6 | 1.1 | 1.3[a] | 0.1 | 0.3 |

Negative = all petitions in that year given negative determination.
Positive = one or more petitions in that year approved.
Other = all petitions terminated, suspended or missing outcome.
[a]Denotes statistical significance at the 5 percent level.

one exception, the aggregate estimates are all negative, indicating that petitioners on average experience both slower output and employment growth in nearly every year relative to nonpetitioners. Like those in Panel A, the three groups of petitioners (by outcome), had very different experiences. The first group—those denied relief—had growth rates of output and employment similar to those of nonpetitioners both before and after the filing of petitions. The second group experienced sharp declines in output and employment growth before filing petitions, declines that were moderated after receiving an affirmative determination. The final group also experienced large declines in output and employment growth, but both measures continued to worsen after the petitions were withdrawn (or the outcomes were unknown).

The final two panels of Table 7.6 show petitioner versus nonpetitioner differences in the logarithm of production worker hourly wage rates and profitability (price-cost margins). Panel D suggests that petitioners tend to be concentrated among high-wage industries (not surprising, for these tend also to have above-average unionization rates). In year $t - 4$, their average wage is 10.5 percent higher than that of nonpetitioners. This wage differential remains relatively constant in the years leading up to the petition, but begins to decline by half a percentage point each year after that. Wage rates also differ across outcome groups. Industries denied relief have the smallest wage premium (about 5.5 percent); these remain virtually unchanged over the entire period. The affirmative and "other" outcome petitioner groups pay higher wage premiums—10.5 and 17.8 percent in $t - 4$, respectively—which are partially eroded after the petition date, especially in the third group of industries. Similarly, Panel E shows that profitability in petitioning industries tends to be higher (by three-quarters of a percentage point) than the nonpetitioner average, but that these "rents" are gradually eroded, especially after the petition year. With positive or "other" petition outcomes, profits tend to recover from levels prevailing in time t, but only temporarily.

Thus far, we have assumed implicitly that all types of petitions are identical. We now relax this assumption and estimate models that characterize different petitioner groups both by the types of petitions filed and by their outcomes. To accommodate multiple filings under the different trade statutes, we define three petition types: (1) escape-clause petitions, (2) fair-trade (antidumping or countervailing-duty) petitions, and (3) a mix of escape-clause and fair-trade petitions (termed "mixed"). An expanded regression model was estimated with nine indicator variables $P_{jk}$, representing all possible combinations of the three petition outcomes j and three petition types m, for a total of nine sets of estimated parameters $\alpha_{jk,t+k}$ for each X variable.

We present the results graphically in Figure 7.2, focusing on the parameters estimated for the import-ratio variable.[8] Shown separately are the time paths of import ratios for each petition type and outcome. Import ratios are displayed on the vertical axis (in percent), time on the horizontal axis (for clarity, a vertical line at $t = 0$ indicates the petition year). Import ratios associated with each outcome are compared with each other and with those for nonpetitioners, and their time paths drawn by fitting cubic splines through these points. Three graphs are used to show the import experiences of the three petition types—escape clause in the top panel, fair trade in the middle panel, and mixed petitions in the bottom panel.[9]

A comparison of the three panels reveals some similarities to the results reported in Table 7.6, as well as some distinct differences in behavior across petition types. For example, like the earlier results, Figure 7.2 shows that affirmative determinations are made only for those able to demonstrate a rapid rise in imports, as is evident from a comparison of prepetition changes in the rate of growth of import ratios for positive and negative petitions in each petition category. While positive outcomes also appear to arrest postpetition increases in imports, Figure 7.2 reveals that the timing and magnitude of these effects vary considerably across petition types. For escape-clause petitions (top panel), affirmative ITC determinations result in a dramatic decline in import ratios (from 35 to 25 percent) in the first year after the petition date. For fair-trade petitions (middle panel), this effect is not apparent until after year $t + 2$. This delayed effect may be inherent in the nature of fair-trade petitions; because they target limited numbers of foreign producers, affirmative determinations in such cases can act only to restrict imports from targeted countries.[10] When petitions are filed under a variety of trade statutes (the bottom panel), the effects occur in the year the petitions are filed. For petitions denied import relief or withdrawn before a determination, import penetration ratios usually continue to rise unabated over time.

These patterns of change over time are suggestive. First, they indicate that regulatory agencies are able to discriminate between industries that deserve assistance—those experiencing rapid increases in imports and corresponding sharp declines in output and employment growth—and industries that do not—those facing gradual (and thus less injurious) increases in imports. Second, affirmative determinations appear to be effective in arresting the subsequent rise in import ratios, although the timing of these effects appears to vary by petition type. In general, the reduction in import competition appears to have moderated output and employment losses for this group of petitioners. Third, petitioners denied relief do not appear to be particularly disadvantaged by this decision. Following negative ITC determinations, import ratios rise, but only marginally,

**Figure 7.2**
**Import ratios, petition types, and outcomes**

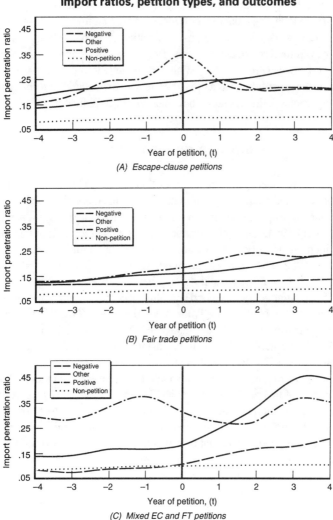

(A)  Escape-clause petitions

(B)  Fair trade petitions

(C)  Mixed EC and FT petitions

and both output and employment growth are virtually indistinguishable from those of nonpetitioners. Fourth, petitioners as a whole tend to be industries with relatively high profitability levels and wage rates, a point noted above. Here, the evidence suggests that above-average factor rewards (which may represent economic rents) are partially eroded over time by import competition, especially for petitioner groups with the highest wage and profitability differentials.

Finally, the petitioners with "other" outcomes appear to be the most severely trade-impacted. Many petitions are suspended or terminated because petitioners are successful in lobbying Congress or the Administration for special assistance outside the framework of these import-relief statutes,[11] or possibly in winning agreements from foreign governments and from producers to remove subsidies or raise export prices (Prusa, 1988). While profits tend to recover, at least for several years, these petitioners as a group continue to experience high and rising levels of import competition, output loss, and workforce reductions.

## CONCLUDING REMARKS

In the 1970s, the number of import-relief petitions filed by U.S. manufacturing firms began to increase at a fairly high rate. Part of this increase in petitioning is attributable to import penetration of a growing number of industries. Beginning about 1964, the ratio of imports to U.S. manufacturing output also began to increase rapidly—at almost 7 percent per annum—and actually doubled after 1982. This increase in imports relative to domestic production stimulated a substantial increase in the number of petitions for import relief filed by U.S. manufacturers. A second stimulus came from changes in the legal environment, notably by the 1974 Trade Act and the 1979 Trade Agreements Act. By making it easier for trade-impacted industries to seek and receive import relief, these acts may have induced increased petitioning under the escape clause after 1974, and under the fair-trade statutes after 1979.

We have used a rich industry-level database to test several hypotheses about the determinants of this petitioning behavior. The empirical results suggest that the propensity to petition is shaped by three broad groups of factors. The first includes variables used by the ITC to determine material injury: high import-ratio levels, large employment and output loss over the previous year, and depressed profitability—all are associated with increased petitioning intensity. The second category includes factors that are not considered in ITC determinations, but that nonetheless are important determinants of petitioning. As might be expected, industries with a large and heavily unionized workforce tend to petition more frequently, as do capital-intensive industries facing heavier costs of adjusting to import competition. Other, less intuitively obvious, correlates of increased petitioning are product diversification, low market concentration, and productivity growth in the industry. The last category includes changes in trade laws, and the expectation of positive findings by the ITC and ITA. The timing of the effects of these changes is consistent not only with the dates when laws were implemented, but also with the specific petition statutes modified. Thus, the 1974

Trade Act had a larger impact on escape-clause actions after 1974, while the 1979 Trade Agreements Act had a larger impact on fair-trade petitions. These results are the basis for our earlier assertion about the role of changes in the legal environment.

The time paths of several economic indicators for petitioning and non-petitioning industries were compared, both before and after the filing of petitions. These event analyses led to several conclusions. First, they indicated that the ITC discriminates fairly well between petitions that deserve assistance and those that do not. Second, affirmative ITC determinations appear to arrest further increases in import ratios, although the timing of these effects varies by petition type. Third, the economic conditions facing petitioners denied import relief are typically little different from those facing nonpetitioners, suggesting that their petitions were of little merit. Fourth, as a whole, petitioners tend to enjoy economic rents, but these above-average factor rewards (wages and profits) are usually eroded, at least in part, over time. Finally, it appears that the most disadvantaged group are those industries that withdraw petitions prior to a final ITC decision. Many may ultimately receive special assistance outside the framework of these statutes, but as a group they do not appear to recover over time.

Import relief petitions are an important component in U.S. policies toward troubled and trade-impacted industries. The findings reported in this paper provide some initial insights into petitioning behavior and the role of the International Trade Commission in regulating the use (and potential abuses) of these trade statutes. Further research using better-specified models and advanced econometric methods is needed to derive other conclusions useful to policymakers.

---

## NOTES

1. These statutes are also embodied in the General Agreement on Tariffs and Trade (GATT) and in the 1979 GATT Antidumping and Subsidies Code.
2. For example, see Ghellinck, Geroski, and Jacquemin (1988) and Clark, Kaserman, and Mayo (1990).
3. The industry-year TFP growth rates are computed using the NBER productivity database. This measure is the residual productivity growth from a five-factor production function with production and nonproduction workers, materials, energy, and capital as inputs.
4. The Gollop-Monahan diversification index is a composite of three separate indexes measuring (1) the number of five-digit products produced by the enter-

prise, (2) the relative share of each in total shipments, and (3) the extent to which products are similar in their use of inputs. These indexes, calculated for each enterprise, are reported as industry averages for five Manufacturing Census years spanning the period 1963–1983. We gratefully acknowledge the generosity of Gollop and Monahan in making these data available to us.

5. Poisson models are a natural way to model count data. See Hausman, Hall, and Griliches (1984) for an application to count data on technology patents filed; and Coughlin, Tezra, and Khalifah (1989) for an application to counts of escape-clause petitions filed over time in the United States.

6. In these models, each industry-year is treated as being independent, even though we have repeated observations on each industry over time. In future research, we will incorporate fixed effects for each industry into the models using recently available, but computationally difficult, panel data methods.

7. Coughlin, Tezra, and Khalifah (1989) report similar kinds of results in their study of aggregate trends in escape-clause petitioning.

8. Results for the other X variables—employment and output growth, wages, and profits—are available, on request, from the authors. In general, they tend to resemble the aggregate results reported in Table 7.6. However, some important level differences by petition type are concealed by aggregation. For example, industries filing fair-trade petitions tend to have profit and wage rates consistently above those of nonpetitioners; in pure escape-clause petitions or mixed petitions, these tend to be more variable, with some petitioner groups above the nonpetitioner average and others below it.

9. To facilitate comparison, these graphs show the import-ratio levels rather than the differentials. We do this by simply adding the "fixed effects" of nonpetitioners (represented by the solid line) to the import ratio differentials estimated for each petitioner group.

10. Import ratios in fair-trade cases also may not fall immediately because other foreign producers—those not named in these fair-trade petitions—step up their imports to meet demand. On the other hand, affirmative determinations in escape-clause cases have an immediate impact, because import-relief measures apply broadly to imports from all sources.

11. Industries that make up this petition group include producers of specialty steel, iron and steel products, and television sets.

### BIBLIOGRAPHY

Baldwin, Robert (1984). "Rent Seeking and Trade Policy: An Industry Approach," *Weltwirtschaftliches Archiv* (Review of World Economics), 120.
——— (1985). *The Political Economy of U. S. Import Policy.* Cambridge, Mass.: MIT Press.

———— (1988). *Trade Policy in a Changing World Economy.* Chicago: University of Chicago Press.

Bhagwati, J. (1988). *Protectionism.* Cambridge, Mass.: MIT Press.

Borrus, Michael, and Judith Goldstein (1987). "U.S. Trade Protectionism: Institutions, Norms, and Practices." *Northwestern Journal of International Law and Business,* vol. 8, no. 2, 328–364.

Clark, Don, David Kaserman, and John Mayo (1990). "Barriers to Trade and the Import Vulnerability of U.S. Manufacturing Industries." *Journal of Industrial Economics,* vol. 38, June, 433–447.

Coughlin, Cletus, Joseph Tezra, and Noor Aini Khalifah (1989). "The Determinants of Escape Clause Petitions." *Review of Economics and Statistics,* vol. 71, no. 2, May, 341–347.

Cowling, Keith, and Michael Waterson (1976). "Price-Cost Margins and Market Structure." *Economica,* vol. 43, August, 267–274.

Devault, James (1990). "The Administration of U. S. Antidumping Duties: Some Empirical Observations." *World Economy,* March, 75–88.

Finger, John, Keith Hall, and Douglas Nelson (1982). "The Political Economy of Administered Protection." *American Economic Review,* vol. 72, June, 452–466.

Ghellinck, Elizabeth, Paul Geroski, and Alexis Jacquemin (1988). "Inter-Industry Variations in the Effect of Trade on Industry Performance." *Journal of Industrial Economics,* vol. 37, September, 1–19.

Gollop, Frank, and James Monahan (1989). *From Homogeneity to Heterogeneity: An Index of Diversification.* U.S. Bureau of the Census, Technical Paper 60, February.

Hausman, Jerry, Bronwyn Hall, and Zvi Griliches (1984). "Econometric Models for Count Data with an Application to the Patents-R&D Relationship." *Econometrica,* vol. 52, July, 909–938.

Huffbauer, Gary, Diane Berliner, and Kimberly Elliott (1986). *Trade Protection in the United States: 31 Case Studies.* Washington, D.C.: Institute for International Economics.

Lawrence, Robert, and Robert Litan (1986). *Saving Free Trade: A Pragmatic Approach.* Washington, D.C.: The Brookings Institution.

Messerlin, Patrick (1988). "The EC Antidumping Regulations: A First Economic Appraisal: 1980–1985." Working paper. Washington, D.C. : The World Bank.

Mussa, M. (1974). "Tariffs and the Distribution of Income: The Importance of Factor Specificity, Substitutability, and Intensity in the Short and Long Run." *Journal of Political Economy,* vol. 82, December, 1191–1204.

Prusa, Thomas (1988). "Why Are So Many Antidumping Petitions Withdrawn?" Paper presented at a conference on Designing Policies to Open Trade, University of California, Davis.

Pugel, Thomas, and Ingo Walter (1985). "U. S. Corporate Interests and the Political Economy of Trade." *Review of Economics and Statistics,* vol. 67, no. 2, August, 465–473.

Tan, Hong W. (1994). "Policies toward Troubled Industries in the United States: An Overview," Ch. 5 in this volume.

# 8

# Industrial Adjustment and Cartel Actions in Japan

Sueo Sekiguchi

## INTRODUCTION

**D**eciding whether an industry faces a short-run difficulty or a long-run decline is not easy, yet such a determination becomes even more difficult in several cases. For example, when exchange rates fluctuate wildly, an industry may expand at one exchange rate but have to contract at another. Another issue concerns integration of domestic and international markets: when the domestic market is insulated from the external market, matching domestic supply and demand may be more easily achieved with domestic policies; when the domestic market is integrated into the world market, foreign supply can easily replace domestic supply.

Japanese policies toward troubled and/or declining industries include two legal exceptions to the general prohibition on cartels: the recession cartel (*hukyo karuteru*) and the designated cartel (*shiji karuteru*). The former, legalized for jointly reducing production when the Anti-Trust Law was revised in 1953 as the government struggled for economic restoration,[1] aimed to reduce a cyclical or temporary overproduction vis-à-vis current demand. The designated cartel, legalized in the adjustment assistance laws of 1978 and 1983 in order to jointly decrease existing overcapacity, aimed to smooth the reduction of capacity or the exit of firms from an industry predicted to decline in the long run.

In this chapter, I will discuss the effectiveness of these joint actions, their allocative consequences, and the political economy behind them—with particular emphasis on short-run stability and the way producers can share the burden of adjustment.

First, I will discuss recession cartels—their economic background, legal framework, and international environment—and present a case study from the import-competing paper industry. Next, I will review designated cartels, their economic background, legal bases, and roles in adjustment assistance policies. In another case study, I will describe how a shipbuilding industry virtually adopted such a designated-cartel approach but later formed a recession cartel. Then, I will examine several theoretical problems from the viewpoint of allocative and technical efficiency, criticizing the efforts of some economists to justify cartel actions as a means of overcoming the prisoner's dilemma in oligopolistic competition. Finally, I will look at the political economy of the cartel approach to industrial adjustment.

## RECESSION CARTELS FOR SHORT-RUN ADJUSTMENT

Although the Japanese government, shortly after World War II, enacted the Anti-Trust Law (*shiteki dokusen no kinshi to koseitorihiki no kakuho nikansuru horitsu*) along the lines of the American model, policymakers recognized that strictly prohibiting joint actions would not help Japanese industries in a war-damaged and high-unemployment economy. Thus, the recession cartel was one of two legal exceptions introduced when the law was revised in 1953. As the domestic market was insulated from the external market by quantitative import restraints and allocation of foreign exchange, a joint reduction of production effectively raised domestic prices, which had fallen sharply because of cyclical overproduction relative to demand.

### Legal Structure of Recession Cartels

The revised Anti-Trust Law of 1953 legalized a recession cartel under the following conditions (Article 24–3).

*Preconditions:* The Fair Trade Commission (FTC) *(kosei torihiki iinkai)* can allow producers to form a cartel when (1) a number of producers face the possibility of bankruptcy as prices of products stay below the average cost to the industry as a whole; and (2) the efforts of individual producers cannot resolve the crisis.

*Contents of joint actions:* A thus-formed recession cartel is allowed to take such joint actions as (1) restricting production, amount of sale, and/or use of existing capacity; and (2), when production control is difficult for technical reasons, permitting the members to control the pricing of products.

*Qualifications:* A recession cartel cannot (1) go beyond the scope set by the original plan; (2) unduly harm the interests of consumers and other related parties; (3) unduly discriminate against some producers; or (4) unduly restrict the movement of producers in and out of the cartel. If there are objections against cartel formation, the FTC must hold an open hearing and consult with the minister in charge.

Although these detailed regulations seem to indicate that a recession cartel can be created without harm from a legal point of view, its economic effectiveness remains dubious. First of all, it is impossible to form a cartel to raise prices without reducing consumers' welfare. Second, a cartel means nothing if free participation and exit are allowed.

### Economic Background of Recession Cartels

When the recession cartel was first legalized, domestic markets were relatively insulated from external markets so that coordinated output reductions by domestic producers were effective in raising prices. As the competitiveness of Japanese manufacturing industries was weak in the early postwar years, exports were subsidized and prices of domestic goods fell substantially during world recessions, while the prices of imported goods were raised by tariffs and other import barriers. Recession cartels that reduced production could, therefore, act to increase domestic prices, so long as they remained below the artificially increased import prices. Cyclical price fluctuations still occurred, as domestic production exceeded domestic demand. This motivated manufacturers to form recession cartels in the 1950s and 1960s.

As the domestic market became more integrated into the international market, the effectiveness of recession cartels declined. In 1960, the cabinet announced a declaration to liberalize imports and foreign exchange, which meant a shift from restricting the quantity of imports to freer imports under import tariffs. A significant reduction in tariffs came after the Kennedy Round of tariff negotiations. Obviously, if an industry's share in the world market is small, a joint reduction of production under free trade results only in a reduced market share. If its market share is large, then cartel actions can raise international prices to some extent, depending on the slope of the foreign supply curve. In the 1950s and 1960s, however, the market share of Japanese imports of manufactured goods was generally small.[2]

**Table 8.1**
**Number of registered Japanese recession cartels**
**at the end of March, each calendar year**
(End of the preceeding fiscal year)

| Year | Cartels | Year | Cartels | Year | Cartels | Year | Cartels | Year | Cartels |
|------|---------|------|---------|------|---------|------|---------|------|---------|
| 1954 | 0 | 1962 | 0 | 1970 | 0 | 1978 | 6 | 1986 | 0 |
| 1955 | 0 | 1963 | 1 | 1971 | 0 | 1979 | 4 | 1987 | 0 |
| 1956 | 0 | 1964 | 2 | 1972 | 9 | 1980 | 1 | 1988 | 2 |
| 1957 | 1 | 1965 | 2 | 1973 | 2 | 1981 | 1 | 1989 | 2 |
| 1958 | 1 | 1966 | 16 | 1974 | 0 | 1982 | 3 | | |
| 1959 | 5 | 1967 | 1 | 1975 | 2 | 1983 | 2 | | |
| 1960 | 4 | 1968 | 0 | 1976 | 1 | 1984 | 0 | | |
| 1961 | 3 | 1969 | 0 | 1977 | 1 | 1985 | 0 | | |

*Note*: This table understates the use of cartels, for many were formed and dissolved before the end of the fiscal year.

*Source*: Annual Report of FTC of Japan, fiscal year 1988.

## Overall Review of Recession Cartels

As Table 8.1 demonstrates, recession cartels were quite frequent in the 1950s and 1960s, especially during recessions. As time went on, however, their number decreased significantly and they became less and less effective. The year 1972 shows an increase that may indicate overreaction to the rapid appreciation of the yen's exchange rate after the Smithsonian realignment. In fact, the real difficulty arose after the first oil crisis and the number of recession cartels grew after each of the two oil crises.

Table 8.2 lists the recession cartels formed during the 1981–82 recession. Although Table 8.1 indicates only five recession cartels in existence at the end of March 1982 and 1983, Table 8.2 shows that 21 cartels were formed and dissolved during the 1981–82 period. The vinyl chloride, high-quality paper, coated paper, craft paper, and polyethylene industries formed recession cartels three times in this period. Although each cartel existed only briefly (two to three months), their total lifetime was often nine months, which again points to the ineffectiveness of recession cartels.

Finally, some industry-specific laws exist concerning adjustment assistance and regulation of competition. The annual report by the FTC gives such examples as the Industry Association of Small- and Medium-Scale Firms, and cartel actions by chemical fertilizer producers and sugar refiners; thus, other cartels than recession cartels also existed based on industry-specific laws.

**Table 8.2**

**Recession cartels formed in Japan during 1981–1982**

| Industry | Number of Firms | Type of Joint Action | Period of Existence | Total Length of Cartels (months) |
|---|---|---|---|---|
| Vinyl chloride | 20 | Production cut | 5/1/81-8/31/81 | 9 |
| | 20 | & scaling of machines | 9/1/81-10/31/81 | |
| | 20 | Same as above | 11/28/81-2/28/82 | |
| Discontinuous fiber yarn | 79 | Scaling of machines | 5/1/81-6/30/81 | 5 |
| | 79 | Same as above | 7/1/81-9/30/81 | |
| High-quality paper | 13 | Operation cut | 6/21/81-8/31/81 | 8 |
| | 13 | Scaling of machines | 9/6/81-11/30/81 | |
| | 13 | Same as above | 12/15/81-2/15/82 | |
| Coated paper | 11 | Same as above | 12/15/81-2/15/82 | 8 |
| Craft paper | 8 | Same as above | 6/6/81-8/31/81 | 7 |
| | 9 | Same as above | 9/6/81-9/30/81 | |
| | 9 | Same as above | 11/8/81-12/31/81 | |
| Polyethylene | 13 | Production cut | 8/1/81-10/31/81 | 7 |
| | 13 | Same as above | 11/8/81-1/31/82 | |
| | 13 | Same as above | 2/1/82-3/31/82 | |
| Glass board (discontinuous fiber) | 11 | Same as above | 8/15/81-10/31/81 | 3 |
| Discontinuous fiber products | 9 | Same as above | 12/25/81-3/31/82 | 3 |
| Ethylene | 12 | Same as above | 10/16/82-3/31/83 | 6 |
| Abestine slate | 26 | Same as above | 11/1/82-1/31/83 | 3 |

*Source:* FTC Group for the Study of the Economy, "Industrial Adjustment and Competition Promotion Policies Under Slow Growth," Unpublished Paper, November 1982, Tokyo.

## Recession Cartel of the Craft Paper Industry

What a cartel accomplished, and the performance of the industry after such joint actions were taken, can be seen in a case study of the craft paper industry. As an import-competing sector, this industry's share in the world market is small. The industry imports chips of needle-leaf trees and from them produces sacks for heavy materials (such as cereals, fertilizer, and cement), as well as lightweight sacks used for envelopes. Ethylene bags and other modes of carrying material, such as pipelines, have replaced the demand for craft paper bags. As demand waned and foreign competition flourished, craft paper manufacturers often formed recession cartels to jointly reduce domestic production, hoping for a price recovery.

*Market structure:* In 1980, 12 firms produced craft paper. Production totaled roughly 690,000 tons, 75 percent of which came from the top five manufacturers. Japan was a net importer country of craft paper, and Japanese imports comprised 3.9 percent of the world trade in 1981, a relatively small market share. Of the total imports of craft paper, some 72 percent came from Canada, 25 percent from the United States, and the rest from Northern Europe and Chile.

The ranking of market shares among domestic producers was fairly stable, although minor changes occurred in the third through eighth positions. The top ten manufacturers were responsible for almost 98 percent of total domestic production. Here, I focus on two recession cartels in the craft paper industry: one for the period November 1978 though April 1979 (the "first recession cartel," following the Association of Paper Industry); the other for the period June through December 1981 (the "second recession cartel").

*First recession cartel:* When the international price of craft paper fell sharply, the top ten manufacturers applied for permission to set up a recession cartel to reduce utilization of existing capacity. They classified the paper-making machines (*shoshiki*), which manufacture paper from liquidized fiber, into two classes: those with a production capacity larger than or equal to 100 tons per day, and those with a capacity less than 100 tons. Small-capacity machines were to operate between 17 and 21 days per month and larger-capacity machines between 16 and 20 days. The cartel participants formed a cartel committee that decided on the details of capacity use and sealed the machines that were not to be used.[3] The committee established rules for production reduction, as some unregulated machines could be used to bypass the cartel control.

It is evident from Figure 8.1, which shows imports and prices of craft paper, that prices had already hit bottom before the cartel cut production.

**Figure 8.1**
**Imports and prices of craft paper**

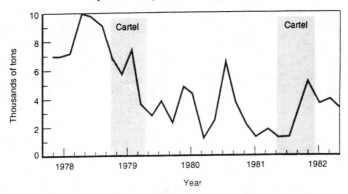

*(A) Imports of craft paper: heavy and light*

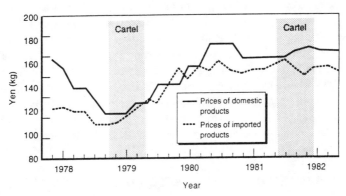

*(B) Prices of domestic and imported craft paper products
for bags for heavy material*

NOTE:  Following expert's suggestions, the price of imported paper is estimated as
FOB + tariff + costs + margin. The last two items add roughly 25 yen/kg.
The price of light paper moved similarly.

SOURCE:  Sueo Sekiguchi (1985).

The price of imported goods was brought into line with the price of domestic products by adding costs of 25 yen/kg.[4] As the import price rose rapidly and the domestic price declined, the gap between the two prices began to narrow, and the quantity of imports declined sharply.

Did cartel actions cause prices to recover? One cannot be sure, because the domestic price merely followed the movement of import prices.

*Second recession cartel:* Although domestic prices remained higher than comparable import prices during 1980, they declined substantially in absolute terms. Therefore, the large producers applied for a second cartel. As Otake Seisi Co., the tenth largest manufacturer, went into bankruptcy in November 1981, and Toyo Pulp Co., the third largest, did not join the cartel, there were only eight participants in this second cartel.[5]

Prices of related paper products also fell sharply, making it necessary to apply production cuts to a broader spectrum of product lines. Thus, conversion of the use of machines was limited, and their operation had to be restricted further. Larger-capacity machines (more than or equal to 100 tons per day) could operate only between 13.5 and 16 days per month; lower-capacity machines (below 100 tons per day), 13.5 to 18 days per month.

The average operating ratio of the ten largest companies fell from 86.4 percent in March 1980 to 64.3 percent in March 1981. The current-account profit of the craft paper department in all these companies was reportedly negative.

Figure 8.1 shows that craft paper imports increased sharply as the domestic price rose and the import price fell following the summer of 1981. This discrepancy may reflect a quality difference, or it may be that importers simply refrained from aggressive importation as most traders, as well as manufacturers, joined the Paper Import Association.[6]

In 1983, when the revised adjustment assistance laws were enacted, the paper industry was designated as a sector that should reduce overcapacity by scrapping existing capacity. In response to this move, a "designated cartel" was formed during November 1983–September 1986 to adjust to long-run decline.

## DESIGNATED CARTELS FOR CAPACITY REDUCTION

Recession cartels, as we have seen, were legalized in Japan to counter cyclical or short-run overproduction. Designated cartels, to which I now turn, were legalized to reduce overcapacity through joint action and to smooth the phasing out altogether of certain declining industries over the long run.

What *is* a declining industry? The answer is a judgment call, but an industry is thought to face long-run decline when the majority of manufacturers cannot produce the good in question at an average cost equal to or less than the international price. This decision is influenced heavily by an industry subcommittee of the Industry Structure Council, consisting of representatives from related industries, labor unions, consumers, and supposedly neutral opinion leaders. Banking sectors are said to influence the decision as well, for they stand to lose heavily if manufacturers are about to default.

## The Designated Cartel in Adjustment Assistance Policy

For several years after the first oil crisis, many industries—among them aluminum refineries, the textile industry, and some chemical industries—were in trouble because of higher energy costs and the appreciation of the yen. Recognizing this, the Ministry of International Trade and Industry (MITI) enacted a basic law for adjustment assistance called the Law on Temporary Measures for Specified Depressed Industries (hereinafter called the Law of 1978). At the same time, the Ministry of Labor enacted two counterpart laws for employment adjustment, by industry and by region; the Agency for Small- and Medium-Size Enterprises also enacted adjustment laws for small firms.[7]

Since most laws were time limited—five years in the case of the MITI law, for instance—they were revised around 1983. MITI altered the Law of 1978 into the Law on Temporary Measures for Structural Improvement for Specified Industries (Law of 1983 hereinafter), and other ministries followed this change. Another step was taken in 1988 when MITI revised the Law of 1983 into the Law on Facilitation of Transformation of Industry Structure (Law of 1988). Corresponding to these changes, the institutional arrangement of "designated cartel" established by the Law of 1978 was modified by the Law of 1983, and then abolished by the Law of 1988.

The Law of 1978, or ministry ordinance, specified the depressed industries that had to scrap capacity, and producers who wanted assistance had to submit a Basic Plan of Stabilization to the minister in charge. Qualified applicants received a credit guarantee from a special fund—the Credit Fund for Specified Depressed Industries—established for adjustment assistance. Industries that scrapped capacity according to the plan received a credit guarantee when they borrowed funds from commercial banks.[8]

When the minister in charge judged that the stabilization plan could not be achieved by individual producers' efforts alone, it could be recommended that the producers form a "designated cartel" in order to jointly reduce capacity. As the Anti-Trust Law was not revised to include this cartel, the minister in charge had to obtain an agreement from the FTC. Although the designated cartel was a controversial issue, this policy instrument was retained by the Law of 1983 and remained effective until the Law of 1988 was implemented.

## Designated Cartels: An Overview

Under the Law of 1978, 14 sectors were specified as depressed industries. Eight formed designated cartels: four in synthetic fiber, two in chemical industries (urea and ammonia), one in worsted yarn spinning, and one in cardboard

Table 8.3
Industries that formed designated cartels
under the law of 1983

| Industry | Capacity Reduction Rate (%) | | Operating Ratio (%) | | Period of Cartel Existence | Other Consolidation Activities |
|---|---|---|---|---|---|---|
| | Target[a] | Actual[b] | FY '82 | FY '86 | | |
| Chemical fertilizer | 13 | 109 | 64 | 71 | 9/83– | M |
| Paper | 11 | 94 | 72 | 91 | 11/83–9/86 | M, JR&D |
| Cardboard | 20 | 55 | 62 | 86 | 6/84– | DL |
| Ethylene | 36 | 88 | 56 | 93 | 9/83–3/86 | DL |
| Polyolefine | 22 | 94 | 65 | 98 | 9/83–9/87 | J. Sales |
| Polyvinyl chloride resin | 21 | 92 | 64 | 92 | 9/83–9/87 | DL |
| Cement | 23 | 103 | 62 | 69 | 1/85– | DL, J. Sales |

[a]Ratio of target reduction to existing capacity.
[b]Ratio of actual reduction to target reduction.
M = merger; JR&D = joint research and development; DL = division of labor; J. Sales = joint sales.
Source: Sekiguchi (1989); original data from documents of MITI and FTC of Japan.

industries. The other six industries—including open hearth and electric fur-
naces, aluminum refineries, shipbuilding, ferrosilicon, hydrous phosphoric
acid, and cotton spinning—did not form cartels. The shipbuilding industry,
however, virtually resorted to a cartel action under a special law for that
industry. Although producers in this sector apparently formed a "recession
cartel," they jointly reduced their capacity, as we shall see in the next section.[9]

Under the Law of 1983, 22 sectors (excluding shipbuilding, which was,
as noted, covered by a special law) were specified as industries to receive
adjustment assistance. Only seven of these sectors formed designated cartels
(see Tables 8.3 and 8.4). According to Sekiguchi and Horiuchi (1984), there
was no significant difference in capacity reduction between industries that
formed a cartel and those that did not. Among industries that formed cartels,
some subsectors of petrochemical industries tried to reduce capacity significantly, but they gave up these capacity-reduction targets as prices in the
international market recovered. Chemical fertilizer, paper, and cement industries used designated cartels, but the operating ratio remained low in the
cement and fertilizer sectors.

The Law of 1983 represented a major change in policy because it
encouraged merger and business tie-ups among producers, thus facilitating
division of labor and joint R&D efforts. Consequently, it built a climate

**Table 8.4**
**Industries that  did not form designated cartels**
**under the law of 1983**

| Industry | Capacity Reduction Rate (%) | | Operating Ratio (%) | | Additional Consolidation Activities |
|---|---|---|---|---|---|
| | Target[a] | Actual[b] | FY '82 | FY '86 | |
| Electric and open furnaces | 14 | 63 | 75 | 80 | — |
| Aluminum refinery | 78 | 110 | 40 | 35 | — |
| Continuous vicose fiber | 15 | 66 | 79 | 84 | — |
| Ammonia | 20 | 170 | 60 | 80 | DL |
| Urea | 36 | 103 | 47 | 58 | DL |
| Wet phosphoric acid | 17 | 112 | 65 | 74 | DL |
| Soluble phosphoric fertilizer | 32 | 88 | 47 | 54 | DL |
| Ferrosilicon | 14 | 114 | 53 | 40 | — |
| High carbonate ferrochromium | 10 | 242 | 47 | 50 | JR&D |
| Ferronickel | 12 | 94 | 56 | 68 | — |
| Ethylene oxide | 27 | 61 | 64 | 80 | DL |
| Styrene | 26 | 73 | 70 | 98 | DL |
| Hard polyvinyl chloride tube | 19 | 100 | 62 | 77 | DL |
| Electric wire | 14 | 100 | 68 | 85 | J. Investment |
| Sugar refinery | 26 | 63 | 57 | 65 | DL, J. Prod |

[a]Ratio of target reduction to existing capacity.
[b]Ratio of actual reduction to target reduction.
*Notes:* DL = division of labor; JR&D = joint research & development; J. Investment = joint investment; J. Prod = joint production.
*Source:* Sekiguchi (1989); original data from documents of MITI and FTC of Japan.

where cooperation within business groups was promoted; collusion, although limited, may have occurred among some producers. One important motivation for the Law of 1983 may have been the rescue of petrochemical industries by means of merger and joint selling efforts.

To evaluate the performance of cartel actions requires data on the actual allocation of capacity reduction among producers. As the government has not published these data, a final evaluation cannot be made. However, it may be that capacity reduction was allocated not on efficiency criteria but on equity and sometimes on actual market-share criteria.[10] The government often adopted the actual market-share principle in allocating fixed investment when it actively intervened in the market in the 1950s and 1960s.

One might guess that the cartel approach was adopted by oligopolistic industries, for such industries tend to fall into the prisoner's dilemma in decision-making. In reality, however, the number of firms entering industries where the producers formed cartels was larger than in other sectors: 48 companies in the chemical fertilizer sector, 50 in the paper industry, 64 in cardboard, 11 in ethylene, 20 in poly-olefin, 15 in polyvinyl chloride resin, and 23 in cement.[11] These numbers were large relative to industries that did not form cartels.

## Joint Capacity Reduction in the Shipbuilding Industry

As mentioned earlier, shipbuilding industries had developed under various government interventions in the 1950s, and by 1970 Japan had become the world's largest ship exporter. After the first oil crisis, however, the demand for ships dropped; many Organization for Economic Cooperation and Development (OECD) countries asked Japan to reduce its market share, as their shipbuilders faced serious difficulties. The Japanese government advised shipbuilders not to accept low-price orders and the Ministry of Transportation (MOT) implemented administrative guidelines for the industry. Because governmental financial institutions offer preferential financing, the government could use this leverage to force manufacturers to follow its guidance.[12]

Although MOT occasionally made so-called "recommended production cuts" (*Kankoku Sotan*) in shipbuilding at times of business downturn, the effectiveness of such cuts was dubious in many cases. Large shipbuilders, to be sure, had already diversified their activities by shifting into machine industries and the importance of shipbuilding had declined significantly by the mid-1970s.

The FTC warned in 1978 that administrative guidance could be a violation of the Anti-Trust Law. Consequently, when MOT enacted a new law in October 1978 for assisting the shipbuilding industry, it changed the policy instrument into a recession cartel for production cuts, specifying that the industry was depressed. From August 1979 to March 1981, the shipbuilding industry reduced production with a cartel action in which 40 large companies joined. Shipbuilders were classified into four groups.

- *Category A:* those with the capacity to build a ship of 10,000 gross tons or greater; they consisted of the seven largest builders, with production of one million gross tons or more per year.

- *Category B:* 17 companies, those that annually produced less than one million tons but at least 100,000 tons.
- *Category C:* 16 companies whose annual construction was 10,000 to 100,000 tons.
- *Category D:* the rest, i.e., those with dock capacity to build a ship of less than 10,000 tons.

The recession cartel of 1979–81, in which all 40 companies in categories A, B, and C participated, allocated output reduction targets by category. Setting the peak of production during 1973–75 at 100, categories A, B, and C had to reduce operation to 34 percent, 45 percent, and 49 percent of previous output, respectively; the larger the company, the heavier the reduction allocated. Virtually all producers with the capacity to build large ships joined the cartel.

During the 1978–80 period, shipbuilders made joint reductions of capacity while they cut operating ratios under the recession cartel. As Table 8.5 shows, they set the target reduction of capacity for categories A, B, C, and D at 40 percent, 30 percent, 27 percent, and 15 percent, respectively. Medium-scale builders—i.e., categories B and C—overshot their targets; they tried to accelerate business conversion because the long-run prospects did not appear promising. Small-scale builders did not meet their target, possibly because they found it more difficult to diversify their activities. Larger builders had already diversified their product lines toward machine industries and they may have judged that existing equipment was competitive enough for the present. Shipbuilding once again became profitable in 1989 as world demand recovered.

One can question whether this rapid reduction of capacity in the shipbuilding industry resulted from cartel action, or whether other policy instruments supported such a reduction. For example, under the special Law of 1978 for this industry, the Stabilization Association bought land and equipment generously. Assistance for employment adjustment, provided by the Ministry of Labor, also supported such a rapid change.

## EFFECT OF CARTEL ACTIONS ON EFFICIENCY

Generally speaking, a reduction in the number of firms in an industry reduces allocative efficiency because prices are raised above marginal cost as the market structure becomes more oligopolistic. In reality, however, import competition makes the mere number of firms in the domestic market less meaningful. In fact, pricing is affected significantly by foreign competition.

## Table 8.5
## Allocation of capacity reduction in the shipbuilding industry during 1978–1983: Targets and actual performance

|  | Basic Plan | | | Actual Reduction | | |
|---|---|---|---|---|---|---|
| Group | Existing Capacity (10,000 CGRT) | Target Reduction (10,000 CGRT) | Reduction Rate (%) | Capacity (10,000 CGRT) | Achieved Reduction Rate (%) | Capacity after Scrapping (10,000 CGRT) |
|  | (1) | (2) | (3) | (4) | (4)/(2) |  |
| Category A | 569 | 228 | 40.1 | 225 | 99 | 343 |
| Category B | 289 | 87 | 30.1 | 103 | 119 | 205 |
| Category C | 79 | 21 | 26.6 | 25 | 119 | 45 |
| Category D | 40 | 6 | 15.0 | 5 | 81 | 26 |
| Average or total | 977 | 342 | 35.0 | 358 | 105 | 619 |

CGRT = gross tons.
*Source*: Yonezawa (1984), simplified by the present author.

## Allocative Efficiency

Within a market structure, it is technically more efficient for production to be concentrated among the lowest-cost producers. In other words, it is technically more efficient for a single decisionmaker to allocate production between two factories than for duopolists to decide their own production in Cournot competition, although allocative efficiency deteriorates because of monopoly pricing.[13] If a cartel action can allocate production in a way that improves technical efficiency, and if it can maintain allocative efficiency under a given market structure, such a cartel can be justified.

Some Japanese economists have pointed out another possibility: a cartel action can solve the prisoner's dilemma of oligopolists with regard to reducing production as well as capacity.[14] Table 8.6 illustrates this case with the pay-off matrix of a duopoly game. If the duopolists play their dominant strategies, competition leads to no change in production. Then profits are at (–2, –4), as shown in the upper-left cell, leading to a social loss of six. It is argued that the social surplus can be maximized if the government can provide administrative guidance, or if the cartel can allocate production reduction so as to reach the middle-right cell in the matrix. In this case company A can realize profits of seven units, whereas company B loses five. If there is some compensation from A to B, such an arrangement is feasible. This is the rationale for a recession cartel. If we replace "output reduction" with "capacity reduction" in Table 8.6, the same argument can apply to designated cartels.

## Relevance of Arguments

In reality, a large gap exists between the cartels discussed above and the matrix in Table 8.6. First of all, if import competition is taken into account, there are few cases where a meaningful pay-off matrix can be constructed. Shipbuilding may be a rare case where actions by domestic producers affect the international price; some high-technology industries where entry into the international market is limited may also be an exception.

Second, although it is difficult to generalize—because data concerning the allocation of output reductions and capacity reductions are not published—the above two case studies show that reductions were not allocated based on efficiency criteria. If the optimal allocation had been pursued, less efficient producers would have exited earlier. The actual cartel did not pool and share profits; decisions were made individually within a range of output and capacity reductions, and some entry occurred in each industry. In this

## Table 8.6
## An illustration of the prisoner's dilemma in output reduction

| | Shipbuilder B's Strategy | | |
|---|---|---|---|
| Shipbuilder A's Strategy | No Change | 20% Reduction | 40% Reduction |
| No change | −2, −4 | 3, −5 | 7, −7 |
| 20% reduction | −6, −3 | 1, −4 | 7, −5 |
| 40% reduction | −8, 2 | −3, −1 | −2, −4 |

*Note:* Minus sign indicates net loss.

context, allocative efficiency might not be seriously damaged. Technical efficiency, however, may have deteriorated because of burden sharing to "protect the weaker."

Even those who have tried to justify some joint actions have had reservations about evaluating the actual cartels, and I suspect that cartel actions have not resulted in the maximum social surplus, but have hindered achieving it. As suggested earlier, a merger could have achieved this target better than administrative guidance and cartels, as maximizing total profit would be more likely to result in social surplus.

Yonezawa (1984) has argued that it was unfair for the survivors to absorb the losses of those who exited by subscribing funds to buy up their land and equipment. From the viewpoint of allocating resources on the basis of technical efficiency, however, it seems reasonable for the survivors to compensate those who exit. If the land and equipment can be sold at higher prices than the prices at which the cartel bought them, the survivors do not bear an undue burden (data concerning these details, however, are not available). However, as we have seen in the preceding sections, actual cartels appear to have allocated reductions of output and capacity in a manner to "protect the weaker at the cost of the stronger," thus lowering overall technical efficiency.

## POLITICAL ECONOMY AND CONCLUDING REMARKS

One may question why designated and recession cartels have existed as institutions for so many years despite the fact that they have lowered technical efficiency. One reason is that the government may place greater importance on short-run stability than on efficiency improvement. Along these lines, one social factor deserves notice: employees who are displaced from larger corporations can find another job more easily than those displaced from smaller firms; the larger enterprises have more affiliates and are more strongly committed to securing new jobs for their displaced employees. Although the Public Employment Stabilization Bureau (*Kokyo Shokugyo Anteisho*) is the official agency for job mediation, personnel departments of large corporations play even greater roles in seeking jobs for their displaced employees.[15] Indeed, this is one reason why frictional unemployment in Japan is low compared with that of other industrial countries. Thus, cartel actions seem to have helped reduce frictional unemployment by protecting the weaker.

Why, then, must larger corporations undertake a larger share of the adjustment burden? One possible answer is this: most industries have their own associations that provide members with information, public relation activities, and other services. Their other important function is lobbying. Larger corporations are usually leaders in such activities and must often make concessions to other members to gain political support for themselves. Thus, political considerations motivate them to undertake disproportionately larger reductions of output and capacity than other smaller firms.

But what about the government's position? Small-scale firms and their employees are influential in terms of their number of votes. It would therefore be politically unpopular for their government to promote the phasing-out of industries or to induce them to reduce production. Making the cartels undertake these unpopular tasks appears to be a preferred option for the government. Although the votes of employees in larger corporations are not negligible, their voting behavior appears to be less sensitive to government policies than that of workers in small-scale firms. The workers of organized unions have tended to vote for the opposition parties. The political gains from obtaining more support from workers at larger corporations appear to be less than the costs of losing support from those at small-scale firms. Furthermore, the one-way pattern of employment adjustment—i.e., it is easy for workers to move from large- to small-scale firms, but extremely difficult the other way around—is another reason that the government is more inclined to assist the weaker firms.[16]

In this chapter, I have discussed Japan's experiences with both recession and designated cartels and reviewed the economic and political justifications for their use in assisting troubled industries. It is clear that these policy instruments have been politically convenient and that cartels have reduced technical efficiency through their support of less efficient producers. Furthermore, the cartel actions examined in this chapter have been both short- and narrow-sighted; they are short-sighted because they emphasize short-run stabilities and narrow-sighted because they ignore import competition.

## NOTES

1. Another exception was legalized at that time: the rationalization cartel (*gorika karuteru*) to allow joint actions to perform R&D and facilitate division of labor in production, and to reduce costs through exchange of specialized products. In this chapter, however, I focus on recession cartels for production cuts.

2. It is true that Japanese imports of some industrial materials became significant, but in general the share of manufactured imports was low. As for Japanese export industries, only textiles had a large share of the world market. Since the late 1960s, shipbuilding and steel have become large export sectors.

3. See Kamakura (1981) for details. Machines were sealed because some producers chose to use fewer machines for more days instead of reducing the operating days of all machines proportionately.

4. Industry experts say that this is equivalent to other import costs and to the margin of traders.

5. The reason why Toyo Pulp did not join the second cartel is unknown. The company fell into a crisis in the spring of 1984, and Oji Seishi Co., the top producer, reportedly sent some executives with financial support to help restructure the management of Toyo Pulp. See *Nihon Keizai Shimbun,* March 24, 1984.

6. For a discussion of import and export associations, see Sekiguchi and Matsumura (1985). While these associations seek to provide collective goods such as information and overseas advertisement, they also make it easier for members to take collusive action, such as threatening retaliation against aggressive importation by distributors.

7. For more details, see Sekiguchi and Horiuchi (1984) for the period 1978–83 and Sekiguchi (1989) for 1978–88.

8. This credit guarantee was not used often, as the interest-lowering effect was canceled by the negative effect of the words "depressed industries."

9. In addition to various existing industry-specific laws, a new law called the Law on the Association for Stabilization of Specified Shipbuilding Industries (*Tokutei senpaku seizogyo antei jigyoukyoukai ho*) was enacted in October 1978. This industry has been subject to strong intervention by the Ministry of Transportation.

10. By equity, I mean that stronger enterprises share a heavier burden in order to save the weaker.

11. See Sekiguchi (1989) for detailed data on entry and number of employees.

12. For details of the industry's evolution and government policies, see Yonezawa (1984) and Sekiguchi (1985).

13. This can be easily shown by a simple model with linear demand and duopolists with quadratic cost functions.

14. See Ito and others (1984). They also applied their arguments to actual cartels, but with reservations.
15. For details of adjustment assistance for employment, see Sekiguchi (1989).
16. The laws on adjustment assistance to small-scale firms by industry and by region have been interpreted as efforts by the government to demonstrate support for small-scale firms (see Sekiguchi, 1989).

## BIBLIOGRAPHY

Ito, M., M. Okuno, K. Kiyono, and K. Suzumura (1984). "Market Failure and Supplementary Industrial Policy (*Shijyo no shippai to Hosei teki sangyo seisaku*)." in R. Komiya, M. Okuno, and K. Suzumura (eds.), *Industrial Policy of Japan,* Ch. 8. New York: Academic Press.

Kamakura, Morio (1981). "On Recession Cartel of Craft Paper Industry Based on Anti-Trust Law (*Ryozara kurafutoshi no Dokkinhojyo no hukyo karuteru nitsuite*)." *Fair Trade (Kosei Torihiki),* Tokyo, August.

Komiya, R., M. Okuno, and K. Suzumura (eds.) (1984). *Industrial Policy of Japan (Nihon no Sangyo Seisaku),* Tokyo Daigaku Shuppankai, Tokyo.

*Nihon Keizai Shimbun* (1984), Tokyo, March 24.

Sekiguchi, Sueo (1985). "Economic Analysis of Recession Cartels." Discussion Paper No.132, The Institute of Social and Economic Research, Osaka University.

———— (1989). "Industrial Adjustment: Problems and Policy Response in Japan." Discussion Paper No. 18, The Economic Society, Seikei University, Tokyo.

Sekiguchi, Sueo, and Toshihiro Horiuchi (1984). "Trade and Adjustment Assistance (*Boeki to Choseienjyo*)." in R. Komiya, M. Okuno, and K. Suzumura (eds.), *Industrial Policy of Japan,* Ch. 13. New York: Academic Press.

Sekiguchi, Sueo, and A. Matsumura (1985). "Cartel Actions in Exports and Imports" (*Yushutsunyu ni kakaru Kyodokoi—Yunyu Kumiai to Yushutsu Kumiai*). Institute of Social and Economic Research Discussion Paper No. 134, Osaka University, June.

Yonezawa, Yoshie (1984). "Shipbuilding Industry (*Zosengyo*)," in R. Komiya, M. Okuno, and K. Suzumura (eds.), *Industrial Policy of Japan,* Ch. 15. New York: Academic Press.

**IV**

**Private Sector Responses**

# 9

## Labor Fixity and Labor Market Adjustments in Japan and the United States

Atsushi Seike and Hong W. Tan

### INTRODUCTION

**O**ver the last two decades, the manufacturing sectors of the United States and Japan have been subjected to a number of demand shocks, rising international competition, and technological change. Many employers, especially those facing declining product demand, have responded by closing obsolete plants, downsizing, diversifying into new product lines, or exiting the industry. U.S. and Japanese firms appear to have responded very differently in the adjustment strategies used, in the way they have managed workforce reductions, and in the speed at which these adjustments have been implemented. Shimada, Orr, and Seike (1985) found that U.S. employers were more likely to respond to decreasing demand by laying off workers and shutting down inefficient plants, and by reallocating capital to other plants elsewhere in the United States or abroad. In contrast, Japanese firms were more likely to initially cut labor costs through reductions in overtime, wages, and bonuses, followed by reallocation of workers to other operations within the firm or to related firms through "worker loan" schemes, before finally resorting to worker layoffs.

The higher degree of job security afforded workers in Japan is widely believed to be the main reason for these differences in workforce adjustment patterns. If job security guarantees are important, in the short-run, employers are more likely to respond to output changes by varying wages and hours of work rather than employment levels. The findings of several recent U.S.-Japan comparisons of labor market adjustments are consistent with a greater degree of job security in Japan than in the United States (Abraham and Houseman, 1989; Hashimoto and Raisian, 1989; and Tachibanaki, 1987). They found that output changes in Japan give rise to relatively smaller changes in employment levels and larger reductions in wages and hours of work. In the long-run, job security results in a high proportion of workers with long job tenure with the firm. According to Hashimoto and Raisian (1989), approximately 48 percent of Japanese male employees in 1979 will have completed job spells in excess of 20 years; in the United States, less than 31 percent of males will have completed this level of job tenure in 1980. Thus, while long-term jobs are not uncommon in the United States, they are clearly more prevalent in Japan.

In this chapter, we seek to gain insights into these employment practices, their determinants, and their consequences for patterns of workforce adjustment and long-term jobs in the two countries. We are motivated by two main reasons. First, these employment practices have implications for the party that bears the cost of workforce adjustment. In Japan, employers are more willing to retain excess workers during a downturn and share in the costs of employment adjustment because of the practice of lifetime employment. In the United States, where the common law employment-at-will doctrine provides employers with greater flexibility in terminating employment relationships, the adjustment burden falls more heavily on workers who become unemployed through layoffs and plant closings. Second, interest in emulating Japanese-type employment practices has grown in the United States, as evidenced by widely-publicized union efforts to negotiate employment guarantees in return for wage concessions, and by recent legal challenges to the employment-at-will doctrine in state courts (Dertouzos and Karoly, 1991; Hamermesh, 1990). This trend raises a number of questions. Are lifetime employment practices somehow idiosyncratic to Japan, as some have argued, or are they economically rational practices and thus potentially transferable to other labor markets? Even if they were transferable, how desirable would it be for U.S. employers to adopt these employment practices more widely? Increased job security would give them greater incentives to invest in their workers' training and productivity, but it would reduce their flexibility in responding to short-run demand changes.

We approach these issues by assembling and presenting broadly comparable industry-level data for the two countries on several key variables—the speed of employment adjustment, the distribution of long-term jobs, and the use of deferred compensation schemes. Our focus on industry-level data yield insights not possible with more aggregated, economy-wide studies. We find aggregate cross-national differences, but also striking similarities across countries in the interindustry distributions of these variables. These similarities call into question culturally based explanations of Japanese lifetime employment practices. They suggest that job security, lifetime employment, and observed patterns of employment adjustment are shaped by technological factors common to industries in both countries. We hypothesize that skill requirements, firm-specific training in particular, are technologically determined. When skill requirements demand it, employers in both countries are more likely to adopt these employment practices to bond workers to the firm and thus, facilitate investments in specific training.

In the following section, we briefly summarize the analytic framework that guides our analysis. Then, we present estimates of the speed of employment adjustment in U.S. and Japanese manufacturing industries, and show how they are related; we report distribution of long-term jobs for the two countries estimated using panel data on workers (Japan) and establishments (United States). This is followed by a comparison of coverage rates by private pension plans in the United States and by severance pay schemes in Japan. We also present the findings of an econometric model of job turnover that suggest that, like pensions in the United States, severance pay schemes in Japan are effective in inhibiting labor turnover. In the final section, we assess these different pieces of evidence and suggest possible explanations for why these employment practices are generally more widespread in Japan than in the United States.

## ANALYTIC FRAMEWORK

The thesis of our chapter is that job security and other employment practices are rational devices used by employers to motivate investments in firm-specific skills and to retain trained workers. Because specific skill requirements are thought to be technologically determined, yet vary across industries, employer incentives to train workers and bond them to firms should also vary systematically across industries in the two countries.

The distinction between general (transferable) skills and firm-specific skills is central to our argument. As Becker (1974) shows, workers must pay for the costs of general training themselves, directly, or indirectly through lower initial wages. Generally trained workers are able to recoup training costs through higher future wages either in the training firm or with another employer. As such, workers with general training are quite mobile. When skills are firm-specific, on the other hand, training only occurs if workers and the employer share training costs and future returns to training. This gives both parties a vested interest in preserving the job match: workers are less likely to quit unless alternative wage offers are sufficient to offset their share of training investments, and employers are less likely to lay off workers when demand declines are small or of brief duration, so as to preserve their share of training investments (Hashimoto and Raisian, 1985). Thus, job security practices are likely to be most common when firm-specific training requirements are high.

Tests of our hypothesis require information on the distributions of job security practices and firm-specific skill requirements. Neither are readily measured. The empirical strategy we will adopt in this paper is to use proxies for job security and compare these employment practices in comparable industries in the two countries. As proxies for job security practices, we will rely on three sets of variables: the speed of employment adjustment, the distribution of lifetime jobs, and the use of deferred compensation schemes. First, the speed of employment adjustment is likely to be slower when job security practices are important, since employers have a vested interest in hoarding specifically trained labor through downturns in economic activity (Oi, 1983). Second, long-term jobs are the realization of job security practices; as such, we would expect to find a higher proportion of workers in lifetime jobs when such practices are important. Finally, employers are more likely to introduce deferred compensation schemes to bond workers to the firm and motivate them to invest in firm-specific training. Several studies conclude that pension plans are an effective instrument for inhibiting labor turnover (Schiller and Weiss, 1979; Clark and McDermed, 1988).

We will compare industries in the two countries as a crude proxy for investments in firm-specific training. This approach may be justified if industries in both countries share common technological constraints—differences in the rate of technological change, output growth, minimum optimal scale of operation, or capital intensity—that shape skill requirements. Employers in high-tech industries are more likely to provide in-house (and more firm-specific) training since few of the skills needed to operate new technologies are readily available outside the firm (Tan, 1980). Rapidly growing industries face the same constraints: employers must provide more of the training in-house because growing demand outstrips the available supply of skilled workers in the open market (Tan, 1991). Incentives to invest in firm-specific training are higher in larger firms than in small firms because company failure rates are lower in larger firms (Dunne and Roberts, 1990). Finally, because human capital (skills) and physical capital are thought to be complementary inputs in production, we might expect the intensity of training to rise in more capital-intensive industries (Bartel and Lichtenberg, 1987).

There is some empirical support for these assertions. Several recent studies have sought to estimate firm-specific training investments in the United States and Japan from the steepness of tenure-wage profiles (Mincer and Higuchi, 1988; Tan, 1991). Both studies find steeper tenure-wage profiles in Japan than in the United States, suggesting that Japanese employers invest more in the firm-specific skills of their employees. A more important finding of both studies is that tenure-wage profiles are steeper, and therefore presumably greater firm-specific training investments are made, in U.S. and Japanese industries experiencing high rates of technological change. There is also evidence, based on self-reported measures of training, that workers tend to get more company-based training and less training from outside sources when the rate of technological change in the industry is high (Lillard and Tan, 1986).

In the following sections, we will compare industry distributions of these employment practices in the two countries. In general, we would expect slower speeds of employment adjustment, more long-term jobs, and greater use of pension plans in Japan than in the United States. Such a finding would be consistent with the large body of literature cited earlier. The more interesting question, from our perspective, is whether the *relative* industry rankings of these variables are similar in the two countries. An affirmative finding would provide support for our hypothesis that these employment practices are determined largely by technological factors common to both countries. It would also call into question more institutional explanations for the cross-national differences in employment practices, especially those that argue that lifetime employment practices are culturally based and idiosyncratic to Japan.

## SPEED OF EMPLOYMENT ADJUSTMENT

We begin the empirical analysis by comparing the speed of employment adjustment in comparable manufacturing industries in the two countries. If the practice of employment security is more pervasive in Japan, as is suggested by the studies cited earlier, we would expect the overall speed of employment adjustment to be slower in Japan than in the United States. The more interesting question, one about which relatively little is known, is how within-country rankings of industries by adjustment speed compare across the two countries. A high correlation in rankings indicates that the practice of job security is distributed very similarly across industries in the two countries. This would suggest that technological factors common to both countries constrain the flexibility employers have to adjust employment in response to output changes.

This comparative exercise draws upon Seike's (1985) study of employment adjustment in the United States and Japan from 1969 to 1979. Though limited to the period before the 1980s, the data cover two major recessions (1974 and 1978) when OPEC oil price hikes induced substantial industrial restructuring and workforce reductions in both countries. Unlike other extant studies, which usually rely on annual data, the analysis in this study was based upon monthly data for the two countries.

## A Model of Short-Run Employment Adjustment

The econometric analysis is based on the short-run labor demand model developed by Fair (1969). The model has the following form:

$$\ln M_t - \ln M_{t-1} = v(\ln M_{t-1} - \ln M_{t-1}^d) + \sum_i^N b_i (\ln X_{t+i}^e - \ln X_{t+i-1}^e)$$

$$+ \sum_j^m c_j (\ln X_{t-j} - \ln X_{t-j-1})$$

where M is the actual level of employment, $M^d$ is the optimal employment level, X is the actual level of output, $X^e$ is expected output, and v, b, and c are parameters to be estimated, and subscript t refers to the month in question.

For a representative employer, this equation shows that the extent of employment adjustment from month $t-1$ to month t is related to three factors: the amount of excess labor in the past period (the first term), changes in expected or future output forecast over the next N months (the second term), and changes in output over m months (the third term), which proxy the amounts of excess labor short falls accumulated over past periods. In general, we would expect the parameter v to be negative, since firms with excess labor would attempt to reduce the size of the workforce and to increase it if there were labor shortages. This parameter v is of central interest here since it reflects the extent to which employers are able, or willing, to adjust the size of the workforce over a month in response to output changes. Thus, the larger the absolute value of v, the lower the employment security afforded workers in times of declining product demand. The two other parameters, b and c, are expected to be positive since firms are likely to increase their employment levels in anticipation of future output increases or because of accumulated past labor shortages.

As shown, this model is not estimable since information is required on desired levels of employment, $M^d$, and expected future output, $X^e$. To make the model empirically tractable, Seike made the following assumptions. First, output is assumed to be produced by a production function with just one input, nonidle man-hours. Second, if cost minimizing hours of work per worker is proportional to the standard hours of work, H, then the optimal level of employment $M^d$ is simply derived as output X divided by H. Finally, adaptive expectations in forecasting future output is assumed in order to express expected output, $X^e$, as a function of past output. With these assumptions, the employment adjustment model can be estimated with time-series data on employment, output, total hours of work, and overtime hours.

For data on employment levels and hours of work, Seike relied on the Ministry of Labor's *Monthly Employment and Earnings Survey* for Japan and the Department of Labor's *Employment and Earnings* for the United States. Indices of manufacturing output were taken from the *Industrial Statistics Monthly* published by the Ministry of International Trade and Industry, and *Industrial Production Statistics* published by the Federal Reserve Board. Monthly data on these variables spanning the 1969 to 1979 period were collected separately for 16 (roughly comparable) two-digit industries in the two countries.

Estimates of the v parameters for U.S. and Japanese industries are reported in Table 9.1. Parameter estimates that are not statistically significant at the 5 percent level are omitted from the table. With these exceptions, the v estimates are all negative, as suggested by theory. As noted before, the absolute value of v shows the fraction of redundant labor that is eliminated in the period. Thus, a high value of v suggests that workforce adjustment is effected relatively quickly and that employment security is low; conversely, a low value of v indicates slow adjustment and strong job security. With the exception of three industries—textile mill, petroleum and coal, and leather products—v is estimated to be smaller for Japan than for the United States. This finding indicates that, on average, the speed of employment adjustment is faster in the United States than in Japan. In other words, workers in Japan enjoy a much higher level of employment security than their American counterparts, a finding that confirms much of the other evidence in the literature.

**Table 9.1**
**Speed of employment adjustment in**
**the United States and Japan**

| Two-Digit Manufacturing Industry | Parameter Estimate $v$ | |
| --- | --- | --- |
| | Japan | United States |
| Food and kindred products | n.a. | −.186 |
| Textile mill products | −.143 | −.091 |
| Lumber and wood products | −.111 | −.115 |
| Paper and allied products | −.068 | −.115 |
| Chemicals and allied products | −.042 | −.061 |
| Petroleum and coal products | −.120 | −.082 |
| Rubber and miscellaneous plastics | −.108 | −.124 |
| Leather and leather products | −.145 | −.094 |
| Stone, clay, and glass products | −.071 | −.187 |
| Steel industries | −.036 | −.066 |
| Nonferrous metals (steel in the U.S.) | −.040 | −.066 |
| Primary metal industries | −.085 | −.147 |
| Fabricated metal products | −.054 | −.084 |
| Machinery, except electrical | −.102 | n.a. |
| Transportation equipment | −.081 | n.a. |
| Instruments and related products | −.065 | −.120 |

*Note*: n. a. = statistically insignificant and not reported.
*Source*: Seike (1985).

Figure 9.1 graphs the relationship between the v estimates in the two countries by industry. The vertical axis measures the speed of employment adjustment for Japanese industries and the horizontal axis that for U.S. industries. Each point maps the relative magnitude of v for the same industry in the two countries; the 45-degree line represents identical v's for each country. Most U.S. industries lie below this 45-degree line, which is to be expected since their v's are generally larger than those estimated for their Japanese counterparts. The more interesting result is that v's are highly correlated across countries. A positive relationship emerges from the scatter plot. The correlation coefficient for the two sets of parameters is 0.447. The correlation is even higher (0.768) when the three Japanese outliers with large estimated v's are excluded; each experienced large secular declines in employment and output over much of this period.

These similarities in employment adjustment by industry point to the potentially important role of technological factors common to both countries. In both countries, large values of v tend to be associated with light industries and small v's with heavy industries. In light industries, low minimum efficient scale of production may make the guarantee of job security im-

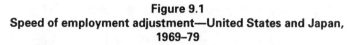

Figure 9.1
Speed of employment adjustment—United States and Japan,
1969–79

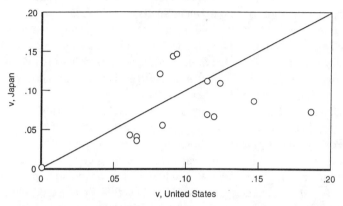

practical because of greater risk of firm failure among small firms (Abrahams and Houseman, 1989). This is less of an issue for heavy industries, which tend to be dominated by larger firms. Heavy, capital-intensive industries may also have greater skill requirements. Because human and physical capital are widely thought to be complementary inputs in production, employers in heavy industries have greater incentives to motivate workers to invest in training by offering them job security.

## DISTRIBUTION OF LONG-TERM JOBS

Long-term jobs are, in principle, the realization of employment security practices. In practice, job separations may occur even in the presence of job security guarantees because of voluntary quits or firm failure. On average, however, job security should be associated with a higher probability of long completed employment spells with one employer. In this section, we compare the distributions of long-term jobs—defined as jobs lasting 20 or more years—by industry in the two countries. Given the previous results, we should also anticipate finding strong similarities across countries in the inter-industry rankings of the prevalence of long-term jobs.

Several studies have made economy-wide estimates of the duration of completed job spells in the two countries (Hall, 1982; Hashimoto and Raisian, 1985), but not at the industry detail needed for our cross-national comparison. One method of calculating completed job spells is to apply the "doubling rule" suggested by Salant (1977) to the distribution of job tenure in progress in a given year. Briefly, under certain steady-state (static) assumptions, the distribution of completed job spells may be calculated by doubling the duration of employment spells in progress. However, these assumptions are unlikely to hold in a dynamically changing economy, especially given the industrial restructuring that has characterized the manufacturing sectors of the United States and Japan over the past two decades. An alternative, and more data-intensive, approach is to use panel information to estimate distributions of long-term jobs in both countries.

For Japan, we will rely on panel data developed by Tan (1990) from the Ministry of Labor's "Wage Census" in four years—1971, 1976, 1981, and 1986. For each industry and education group, the survey reports numbers of workers and their mean monthly wages in cells cross-classified by age and seniority intervals. These data are used to track the job retention patterns of synthetic cohorts of workers over the 1971–86 period. To illustrate, consider the 1971 cohort of high-school graduates in the steel industry who are age 20–24 with 0–4 years of seniority in the current firm. Let the size of this cohort be N(t). Five years later, in 1976, members of this cohort should be age 25–29 and have 5–9 years of seniority if they remain with the same employer. If N(t + 5) is the number that remain by 1976, the five-year job retention rate may be approximated (with some error) by the ratio N(t + 5) / N(t). This methodology was used to calculate job retention rates for each age-seniority cohort by industry and time period (for this exercise, we aggregate across levels of education).

These five-year job retention rates are used to estimate the distribution of completed employment spells in Japan. Starting with the existing distribution of job tenures in 1971, N, the issue here is how to project the remaining length of time jobs are expected to last. For each industry, we compute the cumulative probability P of job retention between 1971 and 1986 (the product of 1971–76, 1976–81, and 1981–86 job retention rates) for each age-tenure group, ending this process at age 60, when mandatory retirement is assumed to occur. Those reaching mandatory retirement age after 1986 (when our data end) are given the job retention rates of similar worker groups in 1986. The product of N and P gives the distribution of completed job spells from which the proportion of jobs lasting 20 or more years is readily calculated for each industry.

Similar kinds of worker surveys exist for the United States, but not in the industry detail or years needed to duplicate the Japanese data exercise. The closest estimates that exist for the United States are those of Dunne and Roberts (1990) based on plant-level data. Using panel information on individual U.S. manufacturing plants at the Census Bureau, they track expansions, contractions, and exits of plants to assess the durability of employment positions in these plants over the 1963–82 period. They estimate a model where plant-level employment survival rates are regressed on several variables—plant cohorts, plant size, region, time period, and industry—and use the regression results to estimate the duration distribution of completed job positions. To the extent that a given job position may be held by more than one worker over its life, these estimates overstate the length of jobs held by individual workers. Nonetheless, while the levels are not comparable to the Japanese figures, the Dunne-Roberts estimates provide useful information about the relative importance of lifetime jobs across U.S. industries.

Table 9.2 reports industry-level estimates of long-term jobs in Japan and job positions in the United States. Column one shows, for each two-digit manufacturing industry in Japan, the proportion of jobs in progress in 1971 that will eventually last 20 or more years. It suggests that just over half of

**Table 9.2**
**Distribution of long-term jobs and job positions:**
**United States and Japan**

| Industry | Japan[a] | United States[b] |
|---|---|---|
| Food products | .504 | .537 |
| Textiles | .442 | .606 |
| Apparel products | .302 | .398 |
| Wood products | .325 | .349 |
| Furniture | .342 | .488 |
| Paper products | .525 | .708 |
| Publishing | .535 | .518 |
| Chemicals | .659 | .654 |
| Petroleum products | .583 | .739 |
| Rubber products | .568 | .486 |
| Ceramics and clay products | .474 | .550 |
| Steel products | .657 | .735 |
| Nonferrous metal products | .637 | .735 |
| General machinery | .530 | .510 |
| Electrical machinery | .574 | .529 |
| Transportation equipment | .572 | .647 |
| Precision equipment | .556 | .518 |
| Miscellaneous manufacturing | .391 | .444 |
| Unweighted average | .509 | .562 |

[a]Japan: proportion of completed employment spells lasting 20 or more years among 1971 worker cohort.
[b]United States: proportion of job positions in progress in 1982 lasting 20 or more years.
*Sources*: Japan Wage Census, various years: Dunne and Roberts (1990).

all manufacturing jobs in Japan are long-term in nature, though this figure varies from a low of about 30 percent in apparel products to a high of 66 percent in chemicals. Column two reproduces, for the United States, by the same industries, the Dunne-Roberts estimates of the proportion of job positions in progress in 1982 that will eventually last 20 or more years. They suggest that 56 percent of job positions existing in U.S. manufacturing are long-term ones. These figures overstate the prevalence of long-term jobs that individuals hold; the 31 percent figure computed using the doubling rule (Hashimoto and Raisian, 1985) may be a more reasonable estimate. Like Japan, the Dunne-Roberts estimates of long-term job positions vary widely across industries, ranging from a low of 35 percent in wood products to a high of 74 percent in petroleum products.

Are distributions of long-term jobs across industries similar in the two countries, as hypothesized? A casual comparison of the ranking of industries by prevalence of long-term jobs suggests that they are very similar. In both countries, the industries with few long-term jobs or job positions are found in textiles, apparel, and wood products; those where long-term jobs are more prevalent are found in metal products, chemicals, and machinery. Figure 9.2 depicts this relationship graphically by plotting the fraction of long-term jobs in Japan (on the X-axis) against the Dunne-Roberts estimates for the United States (on the Y-axis). It is clear that the two variables are positively related; the correlation coefficient between them is 0.766.

Finally, we note that within each country, industry-level estimates of the speed of employment adjustment and long-term jobs are intimately linked. The correlation coefficient between the absolute values of v, the speed of

**Figure 9.2**
**Industry distribution of long-term jobs (held 20 years or more)**

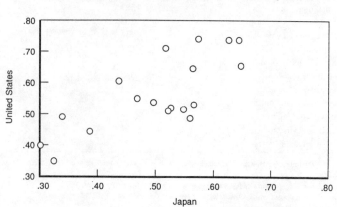

employment adjustment parameter, and the prevalence of long-term jobs is
−0.653 for Japan and −0.552 for the United States. In other words, a large
value of v (greater employment flexibility) is associated with a lower
proportion of jobs that will last 20 years or more. These results provide
corroborating evidence that common technological factors play a critical role
in determining the incidence of job security and lifetime employment practices in the two countries.

## PENSIONS AND LABOR TURNOVER

Thus far, we have focused on documenting patterns of employment adjustment and long-term jobs as outcomes of job security practices. In this section,
we turn to a discussion of a choice variable closely associated with the
practice of job security, namely pension plans. We will compare the distributions of pension coverage rates in the two countries, and ask whether the
use of pension plans by employers are important in explaining industry
patterns of employment adjustment and long-term jobs in the two countries.
We also report the results of estimating a job turnover model for Japan to
study the effects of private pension plans.

To motivate this discussion, recall that employment security represents a
commitment by the employer to retain workers during periods of output
declines. However, it does not preclude workers themselves from leaving the
firm for improved job opportunities elsewhere. If employment security is
designed to induce workers to train, as some have argued (Tan, 1980;
Hashimoto and Raisian, 1985), it is in the firm's interest to reduce job turnover
in order to secure its investments in workers' training. Firms may do this
through a variety of deferred compensation schemes—such as a steeply-
inclined seniority wage system or a company pension plan—based on an implicit
performance bond that workers forfeit when they leave the firm prematurely
(Lazear 1981, 1983). The empirical evidence for the United States suggests
that private pension plans can be effective in inhibiting job turnover (Schiller
and Weiss 1979, Clark and McDermed 1988). In contrast, virtually nothing is
known about private pension plans in Japan or their impact on job turnover.

### Pension Plans in the United States and Japan

Why do pensions reduce job turnover? Most pension plans tie retirement
benefit amounts to both final-year earnings and years of service in the firm.
Benefits and years-of-service credits are also rarely portable across firms.

Together, these features of pension plans produce strong incentives for workers to remain with the current employer because of the potential loss of benefits associated with job change. Defined benefit plans, the most common form of pension plan in the United States, have these features. In Japan, retirement benefits may come from several sources—*taishokukin* or severance pay, *nenkin* or a fixed-term pension plan, or a combination of the two schemes. We will collectively refer to these retirement benefit schemes as pension plans. Note, however, that these benefits are not paid as an annuity (as is the case in the United States) but rather as a lump-sum payment at job separation or mandatory retirement, typically at age 55 or 60. These differences aside, the pension benefit formulas in Japan are structured much like those in the United States in linking separation benefits to final year's pay and years of seniority.

One summary measure of the bonding incentives implicit in the structure of pension plans is the income replacement rate. The income replacement rate is the ratio of the discounted present value of retirement benefits to final year's pay. Estimates of the present value of lump-sum severance pay in Japan are available from a 1981 *Survey of Severance Pay* conducted by the Ministry of Labor. The corresponding figures for the United States are calculated from the average 1980 pension annuity payments reported by Kotlikoff and Smith (1983). The present value of the annuity at retirement age can be computed using an interest rate of 5 percent to discount the annuity stream from retirement to age 80, the assumed age of death when pension payments cease.

Table 9.3 reports income replacement rates for the average male worker covered by a pension plan and retiring with different levels of job seniority. The table shows that pension plans in both countries provide roughly the same income replacement, about two times final year earnings. Of greater interest is the rapid rise in income replacement rates with the length of seniority at retirement in both countries, especially in Japan. In Japan, they rise from 0.4 for retirees with 6–10 years of seniority to 4.6 for those with over 35 years of seniority. This translates into a tenfold increase in replacement rates between low and high seniority workers. In the United States the corresponding figures are 0.9 and 3.4, or about a fourfold increase. Thus, while pension plans in both countries provide incentives for workers to develop long-term job attachments, those in Japan provide significantly stronger financial incentives to remain with the employer until retirement.

The overall impact of pension plans on labor mobility in a country depends not only on how pension benefits are structured, but also on the proportion of the workforce covered by a pension plan. Table 9.4 presents estimates of pension coverage among male workers in the two countries,

**Table 9.3**
**Income replacement rates in the United States and Japan**

| Seniority Categories (No. of years) | Japan[a] | | United States[b] | |
|---|---|---|---|---|
| | Final Earnings | Replacement Rate | Final Earnings | Replacement Rate |
| 1– 5 years | 2.107 | .19 | 16,145 | .46 |
| 6–10 years | 2.076 | .43 | 16,149 | .94 |
| 11–15 years | 2.224 | .78 | 17,196 | 1.25 |
| 16–20 years | 2.537 | 1.56 | 16,985 | 1.70 |
| 21–25 years | 2.942 | 2.28 | 19,458 | 2.15 |
| 26–30 years | 3.372 | 3.08 | 21,018 | 2.79 |
| 31–35 years | 3.389 | 3.97 | 21,654 | 3.16 |
| Over 35 years | 3.554 | 4.60 | 22,839 | 3.41 |
| Average | 2.749 | 2.05 | 19,952 | 2.28 |

[a]Japanese earnings in constant 1981 1.000 yen.
[b]U.S. earnings in constant 1980 dollars.
*Sources*: Kotlikoff and Smith (1983). Table 9.3.8.7. Japan. Ministry of Labor (1983).

with additional breakdowns of these data by two-digit industries. The U.S. estimates were developed by Kotlikoff and Smith (1983) from individual worker responses to a question about pension coverage in the Current Population Survey. Estimates of pension coverage in Japan were developed by one of the authors (Tan, 1990) from the Ministry of Labor's 1981 *Severance Pay Survey* of approximately 6,000 firms. Survey weights reported in the survey were used to adjust for the oversampling of large firms (which usually have a pension plan) and firm-size differences across industries in the distribution of male regular workers (workers on temporary contracts are not covered by pension plans).

Table 9.4 clearly demonstrates that pension coverage is much more widespread in Japan than in the United States—over 90 percent of male regular workers in Japan are covered as compared to just under 50 percent in the United States. We should not be surprised, therefore, if job turnover rates are much lower in Japan than in the United States.

Level differences aside, Table 9.4 also points to strong similarities in distributions of pension coverage across industries. In both countries, industries with low pension coverage rates are concentrated in retail, services, lumber and wood, and apparel products while the industries with high coverage rates are found primarily in chemicals, metals, petroleum refining, and transportation equipment. The Spearman rank correlation coefficient of 0.803 suggests that rankings of industries by coverage are highly correlated in the two countries. Figure 9.3 shows this relationship more graphically. It

Table 9.4
Proportion of male workers covered by a pension plan by
two-digit industry in the United States and Japan

| Industry | United States | | Japan | |
|---|---|---|---|---|
| | Rank | Coverage | Rank | Coverage |
| Retail | 1 | 27.40 | 2 | 86.88 |
| Services | 2 | 32.05 | 3 | 87.53 |
| Lumber & wood | 3 | 40.25 | 6 | 89.44 |
| Apparel | 4 | 40.48 | 1 | 80.06 |
| Construction | 5 | 40.93 | 7 | 90.27 |
| Wholesale | 6 | 51.88 | 15 | 95.59 |
| Publishing & printing | 7 | 51.89 | 11 | 91.49 |
| Finance & insurance | 8 | 52.18 | 17 | 95.97 |
| Furniture | 9 | 52.42 | 12 | 92.62 |
| Miscellaneous manufacturing | 10 | 60.26 | 8 | 90.81 |
| Rubber & plastics | 11 | 62.31 | 13 | 93.41 |
| Textile products | 12 | 63.14 | 5 | 89.28 |
| Transport & communication | 13 | 64.55 | 18 | 96.02 |
| Metal products | 14 | 69.34 | 14 | 94.54 |
| Machinery | 15 | 69.81 | 20 | 97.34 |
| Precision instruments | 16 | 70.54 | 9 | 91.31 |
| Elec. machinery | 17 | 71.74 | 10 | 91.36 |
| Food products | 18 | 71.97 | 4 | 89.18 |
| Mining | 19 | 72.60 | 16 | 95.83 |
| Stone & clay products | 20 | 77.36 | 19 | 96.57 |
| Paper products | 21 | 78.49 | 21 | 98.03 |
| Chemicals | 22 | 82.94 | 26 | 99.18 |
| Transport equipment | 23 | 83.00 | 22 | 98.16 |
| Steel | 24 | 86.17 | 25 | 98.85 |
| Nonferrous metals | 25 | 86.17 | 23 | 98.72 |
| Utilities | 26 | 86.93 | 24 | 98.84 |
| Petroleum products | 27 | 87.46 | 27 | 99.71 |
| Average | | 48.79 | | 92.73 |

*Sources:* Kotlikoff and Smith (1983), Table 9.3.2.10. Japan, Ministry of Labor (1981).

plots U.S. pension coverage rates (on the Y-axis) against pension coverage rates in Japan (on the X-axis). While levels are higher in Japan, Figure 9.3 makes clear the strong positive relationship that exists between industry pension coverage rates in the two countries.

Do pensions help explain differential speeds of short-run employment adjustment and long-term jobs across industries in the two countries? The simple correlations between pension coverage and the absolute value of v, the employment adjustment parameter, are revealing. For Japan, the correlation coefficient is –0.612, suggesting that speeds of employment adjustment are slower the

**Figure 9.3**
**Pension coverage rates, United States and Japan**

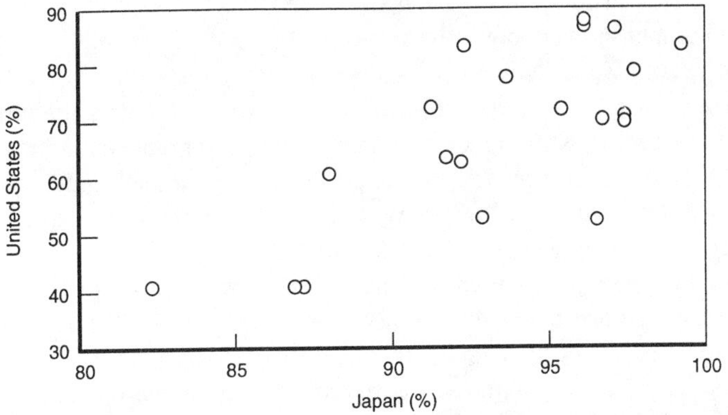

higher are pension coverage rates in the industry. For the United States, this figure is also negative (−0.308) but the relationship between employment adjustment speed and pension coverage is not very strong. The relationships between pension coverage and the prevalence of long-term jobs are also striking. The correlation coefficient is −0.647 for Japan and a very high −0.904 for the United States. Apparently employers can shape patterns of job turnover and job attachment through deliberate use of deferred compensation schemes such as pension plans. Given similarities in these variables across countries, it is clear that these employment practices are adopted only when warranted by the technological characteristics of the industry.

## Pensions and Job Mobility in Japan

Do pension plans inhibit job mobility in Japan? In the United States, a large body of empirical evidence suggests that this is the case. No comparable literature exists for Japan, with the exception of a study by one of the authors. Tan (1990) investigates the pension-turnover issue using panel data on male workers linked by industry to pension information contained in the 1981 *Survey of Severance Pay*. The panel dataset was described earlier. In this analysis, the focus shifts to investigating the impact of pension plan coverage and benefits on five-year job turnover rates, measured as one minus the five-year job retention rate defined previously. This five-year prospective job turnover rate was calculated for each industry, education, and age-tenure group in each of the census years.

An econometric model was estimated to test this relationship. The five-year job turnover rate was regressed on several key variables—pension coverage rates in the industry, and the present values of both wage and pension compensation opportunities from staying with the current employer until retirement versus leaving in the current period—as well as a vector of control variables for age, years of seniority, level of schooling attainment, and time period. Present values of expected wages for stayers and leavers were computed from a model, estimated separately for each industry and education group, where the logarithm of wages was regressed on a quadratic specification of age and tenure. For stayers, this is the industry- and education-specific wage stream of continuing with the current employer until age 60, the assumed age of mandatory retirement. For leavers, the alternative wage stream is that of the average job changer (with no years of seniority) who is assumed to stay with the future employer until age 60. The corresponding pension benefits variables were based upon the 1981 *Survey of Severance Pay,* which reports benefit formulas as a multiple of wages by years of seniority, education, and industry. For both stayers and leavers, the present value of pension benefits was calculated for the level of seniority and pay prevailing at mandatory retirement age. When seniority is an important determination of compensation, loss of seniority can mean substantially reduced wage and pension payments for potential job changers with long tenure with the firm.

Table 9.5 reports the parameter estimates for several specifications of this job turnover model. The first is a fairly conventional job turnover model with worker attributes and alternative wages as explanatory variables; the second augments this model with information on pension coverage and alternative pension benefit payments. These two models are estimated by maximum likelihood grouped probit methods. In general, the results are very similar to those reported in the U.S. literature: compared with the omitted worker group (college graduates with over 20 years of schooling in 1986), younger, less-educated workers with low levels of seniority are more likely to turn over.

In the first specification, the estimated effects of both wage variables are statistically significant and consistent with the predictions of theory. Other things being equal, turnover rates are higher the larger are wage alternatives outside the firm; in contrast, turnover rates fall as wages rise in the firm. In the second specification, inclusion of the pension variables reduces both the magnitude and statistical significance of these wage effects. Pension coverage has a large negative impact on job turnover rates, as predicted by theory. Like the wage effects above, turnover rates rise with the generosity of pension benefits available in other manufacturing jobs, but decline with the generosity of benefits offered in the current job. The effects of the latter, however, are not measured very precisely.

The third specification is from a structural model where pension coverage and job turnover rates are jointly determined. While pensions may affect job turnover, turnover itself may determine pension coverage, especially if employers adopt pension plans to reduce (historically) high rates of job turnover in the industry. To address this possibility, a two-equation structural model of job turnover and pension coverage was estimated by two-stage methods (Barnow, Cain, and Goldberger, 1981). If pension adoption is a response to high job turnover rates, models that ignore this reverse causal effect (such as specification 2) potentially underestimate the job turnover effects of pension plans. This prediction is confirmed by the larger parameter estimate of pension coverage in specification 3 (–2.135), as compared to specification 2 (–1.822).

**Table 9.5**
**Parameter estimates of a labor turnover model with pensions**

| Explanatory Variables | Probit Model | | Structural Model (Predicted Coverage) |
|---|---|---|---|
| | (1) | (2) | |
| Constant | –2.527 | 1.846[a] | 2.298 |
| 1971 year dummy | .167[a] | .176[a] | .176[a] |
| 1976 year dummy | .093[b] | .097[b] | .097[b] |
| Junior high school | .395[a] | .203 | .207 |
| High school | .202[a] | .064 | .064 |
| 0–4 years seniority | .018 | .031 | .066 |
| 5–9 years seniority | –.149 | –.141 | –.114 |
| 10–14 years seniority | –.211 | –.207 | –.189 |
| 15–19 years seniority | –.238[a] | –.238[a] | –.229[b] |
| Age | –.075[a] | –.067[a] | –.064[b] |
| Age-squared | .001[a] | .001[a] | .001[b] |
| Age 50 and over | .449[a] | .491[a] | .469[a] |
| Mandatory retirement < 60 | –.164 | .104 | .130 |
| Log (alternative wages) | 1.778[a] | .954 | .931 |
| Log (wages of stayers) | –1.516[a] | –.846 | –.874 |
| Pension coverage | | –1.822[a] | –2.135[a] |
| Log (alternative benefits) | | .082[a] | .077[a] |
| Log (benefits of stayers) | | – .209 | – .166 |
| Log-likelihood ratio | –2404.8 | –2394.5 | –2394.9 |

*Notes:*
[a]Denotes statistical significance at the 1 percent level.
[b]Denotes statistical significance at the 5 percent level.
Pension coverage and labor turnover are jointly determined in the structural model. Two-stage procedures are used to estimate this model and predict pension coverage.
*Source:* Tan (1990).

The results of the pension-coverage equation, though not reported here, indicate that coverage is higher in industries with high rates of technological change, a high proportion of large firms, and low output variability over the business cycle. These results are consistent with a firm-specific training interpretation. In both the United States and Japan, there is empirical evidence of increased investments in firm-specific training in large firms and in industries characterized by rapid technological change (Mincer and Higuchi, 1988; Tan, 1991; Lillard and Tan, 1986). Greater output variability over the business cycle increases the cost to employers of hoarding redundant labor during downturns, and lowers the likelihood of their introducing job security and other employment practices to bond workers to the firm.

How high would job turnover rates in Japanese manufacturing be if industry pension coverage rates were similar to those prevailing in the United States? We address this question through simulations using the parameters estimated for model specification 2 and U.S. pension-coverage rates reported in Kotlikoff and Smith (1984). These simulations suggest that mean labor turnover rates in Japan rise to 35.7 percent with lower U.S. pension-coverage rates, up from the mean of 22.6 percent. Since U.S. job turnover rates are about twice as high as those in Japan, these simulations suggest that over half of the differences in U.S.-Japan labor-turnover rates are attributable simply to differences in pension-coverage rates. The remaining gap may be the result of cross-national differences in early career job-shopping (higher in the United States), pension benefit formulas (they reward long tenure more in Japan), and firm failure rates, as well as other economic and institutional factors for which we have not accounted.

To summarize, the results indicate that, like the United States, pension plans in Japan have a strong inhibiting effect on labor turnover. Furthermore, they suggest that the role of wages—the focus of most comparative labor turnover studies (see Mincer and Higuchi, 1988)—is less important once the effects of pension plans are taken into account. Finally, it appears that a large part (about half) of the U.S.-Japan difference in labor turnover is attributable simply to differential rates of adoption of pension plans by employers in the two countries.

## CONCLUDING REMARKS

Economy-wide comparisons of the United States and Japan reveal such marked differences in employment practices that many are tempted to explain them in sociocultural terms. Our chapter sought to provide a more balanced view of these employment practices, arguing that they are economically rational practices designed to bond workers to the firm and to motivate investments in firm-specific training. While these employment practices are generally more prevalent in Japan than in the United States, employers in both countries face a common set of economic forces, and they appear to respond rationally in their decisions to adopt these practices.

We presented estimates of the speed of employment adjustment, the prevalence of lifetime jobs, and the use of pension plans for comparable two-digit manufacturing industries in the two countries. These estimates, many of which are novel in the literature, revealed striking similarities in the distributions of these employment practices across industries in the two countries. We interpreted these results as outcomes of employer responses to different skill requirements; these vary systematically across industries in both countries because training requirements are largely technologically determined. In both countries, job security and lifetime employment practices are more prevalent in heavy, capital-intensive industries that tend to be dominated by large firms. In Japan, pension plans are more prevalent in those industries with high rates of technological change, a high proportion of large firms, and low output variability. There is evidence that these industry characteristics are associated with increased firm-specific training.

The question that remains is how to explain the greater overall levels of long-term employment practices in Japan than in the United States. Part of the answer may lie in the roles of technological change and output growth in raising training requirements (and hence the use of employment practices) of industries in the two countries (Tan, 1991; Lillard and Tan, 1986). By extension, the greater use of long-term employment practices in Japan is the logical outcome of more rapid technological change and output growth in Japan than in the United States over much of the postwar period (see Jorgenson, Kuroda, and Nishimizu, 1991). Perhaps not surprisingly, these employment practices in Japan did not become widespread until the onset of rapid economic growth in the postwar period (Taira, 1970). Other factors— such as cross-national differences in the organization of firms and interfirm links (Aoki, 1984), firm failure rates (Curme and Kahn, 1990), and government policies regulating industry and labor markets—may also have contributed, but less is known about their impacts upon worker training and employment practices in the two countries.

## BIBLIOGRAPHY

Abraham, Katharine, and Susan Houseman (1989). "Job Security and Workforce Adjustment: How Different are U.S. and Japanese Practice?" *Journal of the Japanese and International Economies,* vol. 3 (4), December, 500–521.

Allen, S., R. Clark, and A. McDermed (1988). "Why Do Pensions Reduce Mobility?" NBER Working Paper, No 2509.

Aoki, M. (1984). "Aspects of the Japanese Firm," in *The Economic Analysis of the Japanese Firm,* M. Aoki (ed.), New York, London, Amsterdam: North-Holland, 3–43.

Bartel, Ann, and Frank Lichtenberg (1987). "The Comparative Advantage of Educated Workers in Implementing New Technologies." *Review of Economics and Statistics,* vol. 69 (1), February, 1–11.

Becker, Gary, (1975). *Human Capital,* 2nd edition. New York: Columbia University Press.

Clark, Robert, and Ann McDermed (1988). "Pension Wealth and Job Changes: The Effects of Vesting, Portability, and Lump-sum Distributions." *The Gerontologist,* vol. 28, August, 524–532.

Curme, Michael, and Lawrence Kahn (1990). "The Impact of the Threat of Bankruptcy on the Structure of Compensation." *Journal of Labor Economics,* vol. 8, 419–447.

Dertouzos, James, and Lynn Karoly (1991). "The Impact of Wrongful Termination Doctrines on U.S. Employment." RAND Working Paper, June.

Dunne, Timothy, and Mark Roberts (1990). "The Duration of Employment Opportunities in U.S. Manufacturing." Center for Economic Studies Working Paper, U.S. Census Bureau.

Fair, Ray C. (1969). *The Short-Run Demand for Workers and Hours.* New York, London, Amsterdam: North-Holland.

Hall, Robert (1982). "The Importance of Lifetime Jobs in the U.S. Economy." *American Economic Review,* vol. 72, September, 716–724.

Hamermesh, Daniel (1990). "Aggregate Employment Dynamics and Lumpy Adjustment Costs." Carnegie-Rochester Conference Series on Public Policy.

Hashimoto, Masanori, and John Raisian (1985). "Employment Tenure and Earnings Profiles in Japan and the United States." *American Economic Review,* vol. 75, September, 721–735.

Hashimoto, Masanori, and John Raisian (1989). "Investments in Employer-Employee Attachment by Japanese and U.S. Workers in Firms of Varying Sizes." *Journal of the Japanese and International Economies,* vol. 3, 31–48.

Jorgenson, Dale, Masahiro Kuroda, and Mieko Nishimizu (1991). "Japan-U.S. Industry Level Productivity Comparison, 1960–1979," in C. Hulten (ed.),

*Productivity Growth in Japan and the United States.* NBER Income and Wealth Conference Volume.

Kotlikoff, L., and D. Smith (1983). *Pensions in the U.S. Economy.* Chicago: University of Chicago Press.

Lazear, Edward (1983). "Pensions as Severance Pay," in Brodie and Shoven (eds.), *Financial Aspects of the U.S. Pension System.* Chicago: University of Chicago Press.

Lillard, Lee, and Hong Tan (1992). "Private Sector Training: Who Gets It and Why," R. Ehrenberg (ed.), *Research in Labor Economics,* vol. 13, 1–62.

Oi, Walter (1983). "The Fixed Employment Cost of Specialized Labor," in J. Triplett (ed.) *The Measurement of Labor Cost.* Chicago: University of Chicago Press.

Salant, Stephen (1985). "Search Theory and Duration Data: A Theory of Sorts." *Quarterly Journal of Economics,* vol. 91, 39–57.

Schiller, B., and R. Weiss (1979). "The Impact of Private Pensions on Firm Attachment." *Review of Economics and Statistics,* vol. 61, August, 369–380.

Seike, Atsushi (1985). "Employment Adjustment in Japanese Manufacturing Industries in the 1970s." *Keio Business Review,* vol. 22, 25–57.

Shimada, Haruo, James Orr, and Atsushi Seike (1985). "U.S.-Japan Comparative Study of Employment Adjustment." U.S. Department of Labor and Japanese Ministry of Labor.

Tachibanaki, Toshiaki (1987). "Labor Market Flexibility in Japan in Comparison with Europe and the U.S." *European Economic Review,* vol. 31, 647–684.

Taira, Koji (1970). *Economic Development and the Labor Market in Japan.* New York: Columbia University Press.

Tan, Hong (1990). "Pensions and Labor Turnover in Japan." RAND Working Paper, November.

Tan, Hong (1991). "Technical Change and Human Capital Investments in the United States and Japan," in C. Hulten (ed.), *Productivity Growth in Japan and the United States.* NBER Income and Wealth Conference Volume.

# 10

## The Responsiveness of Factor Proportions to Changing Factor Prices: A Comparison of U.S. and Japanese Manufacturing

Yoshie Yonezawa

### INTRODUCTION

International competitiveness depends upon numerous factors, including management and industrial relations systems, education and the quality of the workforce, and industrial policy.[1] Another factor—the subject of this chapter—is the responsiveness of industries to changing prices for the two principal factors of production—capital and labor. Firms and industries that do not adjust their factor proportions in response to these price signals stand to lose competitiveness in the long run.

In this chapter, I will investigate the adjustment responsiveness of U.S. and Japanese manufacturing industries to changing wage and rate-of-return signals. Specifically, I will compare the ratios of capital and labor for 38 manufacturing industries in the two countries between 1967 and 1986 and relate them to changes in the relative prices of capital and labor. (To anticipate the results of this comparative analysis, I find that the adjustment responses of U.S. manufacturers are generally less sensitive to changing price signals than those of Japanese manufacturers.) Furthermore, Japanese large companies appear to enjoy greater access to factor markets than their U.S. counterparts, which may in turn influence their adjustment responses.

The following section describes the model framework and assumptions used in the analysis reported in this paper. Quantitative aspects of the adjustment patterns of U.S. and Japanese manufacturing industries are then discussed and hypotheses are tested by means of regression analysis. The final section presents qualifying comments and conclusions.

## ANALYTIC FRAMEWORK

### A Model of Production

The framework for analysis is based on a simple, neoclassical model of production. In this model, profit-maximizing producers are induced to change the proportion of capital and labor factors in response to changes in the wage rate and the rental rate. Figure 10.1 shows the optimal capital-labor ratios that would be realized by rational firms with well-behaved production functions in a freely competitive market environment. In Figure 10.1, for a given production technology $f_0(k)$, the curve $R_0$ traces out the optimal capital-labor ratio at different wage-rental ratios. Thus, the optimal capital-labor ratio (i.e., capital intensity) is raised from $k_0$ to $k_1$ when the wage-rental ratio (the ratio of factor rewards) increases from $(w/r)_0$ to $(w/r)_1$.

Figure 10.1 also demonstrates that, even if the ratio of factor rewards were constant, a change in the production function from $f_0(k)$ to $f_1(k)$, corresponding to a shift from $R_0$ to $R_1$, would change the relationship between the optimal capital intensity and the ratio of factor rewards. Therefore, assuming that the ratio of factor rewards is constant at $(w/r)_0$, the capital intensity will rise from $k_0$ to $k_{10}$. This change in production technology corresponds to the capital-deepening process induced by technological progress in manufacturing. Further, one can derive quite interesting relations between capital intensity and the ratio of factor rewards. (See the stepwise functions $R'_0$ and $R'_1$ in Figure 10.1.) These cases occur when the producer seeks profit-maximization under a kinked, "non-well-behaved" production function. For example, assuming that the production technology $f'_0(k)$ is kinked at $k_0$ and $k_1$, it will be economically rational for the producer to maintain capital intensity at $k_0$, at least until the ratio of factor rewards moves from $(w/r)_0$ to $(w/r)_1$.

Theoretically, the gradient of curve R in Figure 10.1 denotes the elasticity of substitution between capital and labor for a given production function. But note the movement of this elasticity of substitution as the ratio of factor rewards changes. On smooth curves like $R_0$ and $R_1$, corresponding to well-behaved production technologies, the elasticity of substitution of factors of production takes on finite values without any discontinuities. By contrast, the elasticity of substitution on the stepwise functions $R'_0$ and $R'_1$ takes on only one of two values, zero or infinity. In other words, producers using a well-behaved production function can quickly adjust their capital intensity whenever the ratio of factor rewards changes. Rigidities exist, however, in the reallocation of capital and labor if producers operate with non-well-behaved production technologies with kinks.

## Industry Characteristics

This model can be extended to investigate the characteristics of each industry that may affect its adjustment process. These characteristics include the firm's size and market power in factor markets and the technology peculiar to the specific industry.

A firm's relative position in the market for factors of production depends strongly on company size. Generally, large firms face fewer risks of bankruptcy than small- to medium-sized ones. Therefore, large firms have improved access to capital markets, are able to raise funds for investment at a lower cost than small firms, and can operate profitably at a lower rate of return to capital. Because of lower capital costs, large firms can also offer higher wages than smaller firms and attract highly talented employees from the labor market.

**Figure 10.1**
**Capital intensity, factor rewards, and the elasticity of substitution**

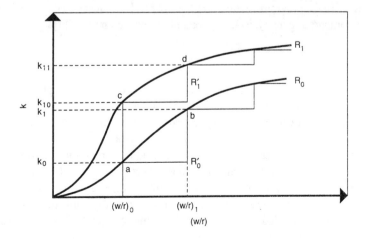

Another factor that shapes the adjustment process is the production technology specific to different industries. Generally, the technologies characteristic of light industries are labor-intensive, while those of heavy industries are capital-intensive. These technological factors constrain the range of adjustments possible in different industries.

Figure 10.2 illustrates these two cases. $R_1$ and $R_2$ in this figure show optimal capital intensities of light industry and heavy industry, respectively. Now, if small- to medium-sized firms, along with large firms, are assumed to face different labor and capital markets as explained above, the ratio of factor rewards for the former is $(w/r)_S$ and the ratio of factor rewards for the latter is $(w/r)_L$. This results in large companies becoming more capital-intensive than smaller companies in every industry. Moreover, the differences in capital intensity between firms of the same size, across industries, will depend on differences in the industrial technologies used.

However, it is difficult for small- to medium-sized firms to enter into capital-intensive industries, for the set-up costs of heavy equipment are often beyond their procurement capacities in the capital markets. Therefore, in Figure 10.2, point a, identifying labor-intensive industries, would correspond to small- to medium-sized firms, and point d, identifying capital-intensive industries, would correspond to large firms.

## DATA AND ANALYSIS

In this section, I compare the adjustment processes of manufacturing industries in Japan and in the United States from the perspective of the model discussed in the previous section. First, however, I will describe the data used in the comparative analysis and comment on their comparability.

### Data

The primary data source for this study is the United Nations publication *Industrial Statistics Yearbook,* which adopts the U.N. International Standard Industrial Classification (ISIC) system. For both the United States and Japan, this yearbook provides time-series, ISIC-level data on average number of employees, wage and salary payments, value added, and gross fixed capital formation (or investment). Data on number of establishments, for Japan, are included as well; comparable data for the United States are found in the U.S. Department of Commerce's *Census of Manufactures.* Unfortunately, no information is provided on the gross book value of capital assets. For these data, I draw upon the Japanese Ministry of International Trade and Industry's (MITI's) *Census of Manufactures* and the U.S. Department of Commerce's *Annual Survey of Manufactures*. Finally, I use the capital goods price indexes reported in the Bank of Japan's *Economic Statistics Annual* for Japan, and its companion publication, *Foreign Economic Statistics Annual* for the United States.

Key variables included in this analysis are the capital-stock variable and the wage-rental ratio. The capital-stock variable is measured as the sum of gross fixed assets in 1967 (the benchmark year) and annual capital formation, as expressed in 1980 currency units, after adjusting for inflation. Dividing this capital stock variable by total employment yields the capital-labor ratio, KL. The second key variable is the wage-rental ratio. The wage rate per worker is defined as wages and salaries divided by total employment. The corresponding factor price for capital is the rate of return to capital. This is approximated by the residual payments to capital (value added minus wages and salaries) divided by the capital stock. The wage-rental variable, WR, is defined as the ratio of these two factor prices. Finally, I use these data to define two size measures to characterize the industry—the number of workers per establishment, LF, and the mean capital intensity of establishments, KF.

The final dataset includes observations for 38 manufacturing industries in the two countries for the 20-year period, 1967–86. Before turning to the analysis, I must sound a cautionary note about these data. The capital stock data from MITI and the U.S. Department of Commerce may introduce some

**Figure 10.2**
**Market structure and industry-specific technology**

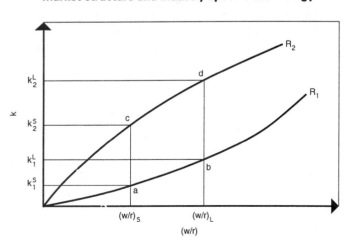

measurement error into the analysis because the correspondence between the U.N. ISIC and the Standard Industrial Classification (SIC) of the United States is not as good as that between the ISIC and the Japanese classification system (JSIC). Thus, the model parameters estimated for the United States may be less reliable than those for Japan.

## Overview

Figure 10.3 plots means of the two principal variables, capital intensity and the ratio of factor rewards, for 38 manufacturing industries of Japan and the United States over this period. Generally, movements over time in the two variables appear to be positively related, as predicted by the simple production model. On closer examination, one can identify a phase where capital intensity in U.S. industry did not change in response to the rising ratio of factor rewards. Comparison of within-industry patterns of change (not shown here) reveals a larger number of industries with inflexible patterns of responses in the United States than in Japan. Japanese industries with abnormal patterns include such troubled industries as spinning and weaving, iron and steel, and motor vehicles—which fall under the so-called voluntary export restraints imposed by the United States on Japan.

To what extent are these systematic differences among industries in the structure of the ratios of factor rewards attributable to industry characteristics? To address this issue, I express the ratio of factor rewards in each industry as a deviation from the mean factor-rewards ratio of all manufacturing industries. These differences are calculated for each five-year interval beginning in 1967. Overall, the interindustry structure of these factor rewards appears to be very similar between the two countries. The correlation coefficients between the ratios of factor rewards by industry in Japan and in the United States are as follows: 0.71 in 1967, 0.81 in 1972, 0.62 in 1977, and 0.58 in 1982.

In Japan, the ratios of factor rewards are high for such industries as pulp and paper, industrial chemicals, basic fertilizers, synthetic resins, petroleum refining, coal products, iron and steel, and nonferrous metals. In the United States, the factor-rewards ratios of these industries are similar, although the motor vehicle industry exhibited a sharp rise in the ratio of factor rewards between 1977 and 1982. The industries named are typically "heavy" industries and are dominated by large establishments. As discussed above, large firms tend to dominate such industries (see point d in Figure 10.2) because they can exploit their advantages in the factor markets and can enter easily into capital-intensive lines of production.

## Analysis

I now turn to a more formal analysis of these simple relationships. I focus on the elasticity of substitution, a measure of the responsiveness of adjustments of factor proportions to relative factor prices. The assertion that Japanese manufacturing industries are relatively more responsive to changing price signals is supported if larger elasticity estimates are found for them than for their U.S. counterparts.

Estimates of the elasticity of substitution are obtained by estimating the following log-linear model:

$$\log(KL) = a_0 + a_1 \log(WR) + a_2 T + a_3 OIL \tag{1}$$

where KL is the capital-labor ratio, WR is the ratio of wages to the rate of return to capital, T is a time trend, OIL is a dummy variable for the oil crisis (OIL takes a value of zero prior to 1974 and one thereafter), and the a's are parameters to be estimated.

This model specification addresses several issues. First, it allows us to distinguish between movements along the production function (from point a to point b in Figure 10.1) as opposed to shifts in the function itself (from point a to point c). This identification is achieved by including a time-trend variable, T, to capture the effects of secularly increasing capital-intensity due to technological changes. Controlling for T, movements along the production function are captured by the coefficient of log (WR), $a_1$, which I shall term the elasticity of substitution. Second, the OIL dummy variable is included to control for the impact on manufacturing of the oil crises in the late 1970s.

For each country, the model is estimated separately by industry using time-series data for the 1967 to 1986 period. The generalized-least-squares regression method is used. The elasticity-of-substitution estimates for the two countries are reported in Table 10.1 (full results are available from the author).

Judging by such statistical indicators as the t-value, the coefficient of determination, the Durbin-Watson ratio, and the expected signs of the parameters, one finds that the response patterns of most Japanese manufacturers were well-behaved during the period observed (1967–86). In most of the U.S. cases, however, the estimated elasticities were not statistically significant, and the directions of their signs were mixed; only the time-trend parameter and the OIL dummy variable were statistically significant. In other words, the factor proportions of U.S. manufacturing industries were relatively unresponsive in this period to changing price signals for the factors of production.

Figure 10.3
Manufacturing-industry capital intensity and the ratio of factor rewards,
Japan and the United States

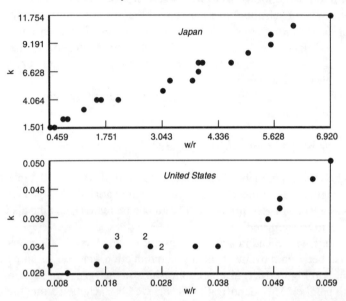

However, there are exceptions to this overall result. In the case of petroleum refineries, for example, the elasticity of factor substitution for both Japan and the United States is statistically insignificant. Furthermore, in the case of iron and steel, the elasticity of factor substitution for Japan is insignificant, while that of the United States remains significant. Additionally, the expected positive elasticity of substitution was obtained for certain U.S. industries, such as beverages, leather products, footwear, wood products, pottery, nonferrous metals, radio and television sets, and motor vehicles.

I now turn to a comparison of U.S.-Japan differences in the ratio of factor rewards. As noted earlier, the structure of factor rewards across manufacturing industries was similar in both the United States and Japan, suggesting the existence of industry-specific technologies common to both countries. Some part of this observed relationship, however, may also be attributable to other characteristics of the industry, such as mean firm size. In the following analysis, I attempt to distinguish between two effects: that associated with technology (movement from point a to point c in Figure 10.2) and that associated with market structure (movement from point a to point b along $R_1$ in Figure 10.2).

**Table 10.1**
**Estimates of the elasticity of substitution of productive factors,**
**U.S. and Japanese manufacturing industries** [a]

| Industry | Japan | United States |
|---|---|---|
| Food products | 0.85[b] | −0.37 |
| Beverages | 0.48[b] | 0.72[b] |
| Tobacco | n.a. | −0.12 |
| Textiles | 0.82[b] | 0.01 |
| Spinning, weaving, etc. | 0.88[b] | 0.12 |
| Wearing apparel | 0.73[b] | 0.18 |
| Leather and products | 0.78[b] | 0.21[b] |
| Footwear | 0.14[b] | 0.19[b] |
| Wood products | 0.27[b] | 0.12[b] |
| Furniture, fixtures | 0.33[b] | 0.14 |
| Paper and products | 0.30[b] | −0.03 |
| Pulp, paper, etc. | 0.24[b] | −0.01 |
| Printing, publishing | 0.75[b] | −0.02 |
| Industrial chemicals | 0.46[b] | −0.04 |
| Basic excl. fertilizers | 0.81[b] | −0.04 |
| Synthetic resins, etc | 0.33[b] | 0.01 |
| Other chemical products | 0.57[b] | −0.08 |
| Drugs and medicines | 0.54[b] | −0.04 |
| Petroleum refineries | 0.08 | 0.09 |
| Petroleum, coal products | 0.41[b] | 0.19 |
| Rubber products | 0.77[b] | 0.09 |
| Plastic products n.e.c. | 0.22[b] | 0.16 |
| Pottery, china, etc. | 0.29[b] | 0.45[b] |
| Glass and products | 0.63[b] | −0.05 |
| Nonmetal products n.e.c. | 0.38[b] | 0.08 |
| Iron and steel | 0.08 | 0.09[b] |
| Nonferrous metals | 0.18[b] | 0.10[b] |
| Metal products | 0.38[b] | −0.01 |
| Machinery n.e.c. | 0.49[b] | 0.08 |
| Office computing, etc. | 0.76[b] | 0.04 |
| Electrical machinery | 0.55[b] | 0.06 |
| Radio, television, etc. | 0.51[b] | 0.67[b] |
| Transport equipment | 0.72[b] | 0.11 |
| Shipbuilding, repair | 0.18[b] | 0.01 |
| Motor vehicles | 0.59[b] | 0.24[b] |
| Professional goods | 0.46[b] | 0.12[b] |
| Other industries | 0.28[b] | 0.04 |
| All manufacturing | 0.74[b] | 0.02 |

[a]See text for a description of the statistical model.
[b]Statistically significant at the 5 percent level.
n.a.: not available    n.e.c.: not elsewhere classified.

The relative importance of these two factors may be gauged from the following model:

$$WR = b_1 + b_2\,KL + b_3\,LF + b_4\,KF \qquad (2)$$

where WR is the wage-rental ratio, KL is the capital-labor ratio, LF is the number of employees per establishment, KF is the real value of tangible fixed assets per establishment, and the b's are parameters to be estimated. All variables are expressed as deviations from the means for aggregate manufacturing. In this model, we are proxying market structure, and firm size in particular, by two variables: (1) the number of employees per establishment ("employment size"), and (2) the fixed tangible assets per establishment ("asset size"). Technological characteristics of the industry are captured by changes in the capital-labor ratio.

The model is estimated separately for each year in which data are available using ordinary-least-squares regression methods. Annual data are available for the Japanese sample. For the United States, data on the number of establishments are available only in four census years—1967, 1972, 1977, and 1982. The U.S. and Japanese results are presented in Table 10.2 and, for comparability, are restricted to these four years.

The first finding is that the coefficients of determination in both countries were relatively low, although the U.S. coefficient was lower than the Japanese coefficient. The lower level of precision of the U.S. estimates may be partly explained by measurement error in the capital-stock variable. In both countries, differences in capital intensity were significantly and positively correlated with the ratio of factor rewards. These observations follow from the technology of the industry. Differences in company size had no statistically significant effect on the wage-rental ratio in the United States except in 1977; but the effect of size was significant in Japan in most years. In Japan, asset size (a proxy variable for company size) had a negative impact on the ratio of factor rewards, which is counterintuitive. Nevertheless, the overall effect of company size in Japan appears to be positive, since the estimated impact of employment size dominates that of asset size. In contrast, the sizes of firms in U.S. manufacturing industries did not appear to significantly affect differences in factor rewards.

This statistical result leads to an interesting interpretation of the nature of the factor markets in the two countries. It implies that, in procurement of the factors of production, company size is not as critical in the United States as it is in Japan.

**Table 10.2**

**Statistical analysis of differences in wage-rental ratios, Japan and the United States**

| Year | Country | Constant | KL | LF | KF | $R^2$ |
|---|---|---|---|---|---|---|
| 1967 | Japan | 0.38 (2.51) | 0.54 (6.01) | 0.09 (2.22) | −0.04 (−3.39) | 0.66 |
| | U.S. | 0.67 (5.87) | 0.23 (2.84) | −0.17 (−0.93) | 0.33 (1.55) | 0.66 |
| 1972 | Japan | 0.23 (1.73) | 0.50 (8.24) | 0.14 (3.87) | −0.03 (−4.14) | 0.75 |
| | U.S. | 0.55 (2.90) | 0.30 (2.29) | 0.01 (0.32) | 0.03 (1.08) | 0.61 |
| 1977 | Japan | 0.21 (1.43) | 0.44 (6.21) | 0.16 (4.16) | −0.03 (−3.18) | 0.74 |
| | U.S. | 0.06 (0.21) | 0.63 (3.22) | 0.30 (2.45) | −0.10 (−2.25) | 0.37 |
| 1982 | Japan | 0.03 (0.15) | 0.51 (5.72) | 0.36 (4.66) | −0.06 (−3.91) | 0.70 |
| | U.S. | 0.45 (0.14) | 1.02 (4.60) | 0.21 (1.53) | −0.17 (−2.89) | 0.48 |

Figures in parentheses are $t$-values; $R^2$ is the coefficient of determination adjusted by the degrees of freedom.
Sample size: Japan, 37; United States, 38.

## CONCLUDING REMARKS

This chapter was motivated by the view that a country's industrial competitiveness is shaped dramatically by the flexibility with which manufacturers reallocate resources in response to changing factor prices. A simple neoclassical production model was used to investigate this hypothesis and to compare the adjustment responses of U.S. and Japanese manufacturing industries.

In general, I find that a higher proportion of U.S. manufacturing, as compared with Japanese manufacturing, exhibits inflexible patterns of adjustment in capital-labor ratios in response to changes in their relative prices. Furthermore, I find some evidence that Japanese industries dominated by large establishments are able to exercise market power in the procurement of labor and capital, a result not found in the United States.

These preliminary findings are subject to the following caveats. First, as is common to such studies, there are problems associated with measurement error (capital stocks in particular) and data comparability across countries. Second, relatively simple, reduced-form models were estimated to gain insights into the economic relationships of interest. More definitive conclusions will require further work to improve data quality and estimation of structural models.

---

### NOTES

1. For example, see the 1989 report of the MIT Commission on Industrial Competitiveness.

### BIBLIOGRAPHY

Arrow, K. J., H. B. Chenery, B. S. Minhas, and R. M. Solow (1961). "Capital-Labor Substitution and Economic Efficiency." *Review of Economic and Statistics,* LXIII, 3, August, 225–250.

Blackaby, F. (ed.) (1979). *De-Industrialization.* New York: Heinemann/National Institute of Economic and Social Research.

Dertouzos, M. L., R. K. Lester, R. M. Solow, and the MIT Commission on Industrial Productivity (1989). *Made in America.* Cambridge, Mass.: MIT Press.

Kemp, M. C. (1969). *The Pure Theory of International Trade and Investment.* Englewood Cliffs, NJ: Prentice-Hall.

Lovell, C. A. K. (1973). "Estimation and Prediction with CES and VES Production Functions." *International Economic Review,* vol. 14, no. 3, October, 676–692.

The MIT Commission on Industrial Productivity (1989). *The Working Papers of the MIT Commission on Industrial Productivity,* I, II. Cambridge, Mass.: MIT Press.

The Organization for Economic Cooperation and Development (1987). *Structural Adjustment and Economic Performance.* Washington D. C.: OECD Publications and Information Centre.

Sato, K. (1975). *Production Functions and Aggregation.* New York, London, Amsterdam: North-Holland.

Williams, K., J. Williams, and D. Thomas (1983). *Why Are the British Bad at Manufacturing?* London: Routledge & Kegan Paul.

Yamawaki, H. (1989). "A Comparative Analysis of Intertemporal Behavior of Profits: Japan and the United States." *Journal of Industrial Economics,* XXXVII, June, 389–410.

# 11

## Comparative Innovation in Japan and the United States

Arthur J. Alexander

### INTRODUCTION

**A**mong the many factors that would explain why industries within a country encounter serious long-term trouble are sharply-lowered prices and the availability of competitive new products from foreign firms. In the 1970s and 1980s in the United States, for example, companies in such industries as steel, automobiles, machine tools, and computer memory chips saw their markets severely challenged by Japanese producers offering more reliable products at lower prices. It gradually became apparent to investigators seeking the sources of the Japanese advantage that it was not simply low labor costs or an undervalued exchange rate or the "dumping" of goods at below-cost prices that allowed these products to compete so successfully in the American market. Rather, the Japanese advantage came from one of the most significant innovations of the twentieth century: the creation of new methods of organizing production and product development.

In Japan, companies producing aircraft, mainframe computers, computer software, and biotechnology products found themselves at a disadvantage vis-à-vis their competitors from the United States. In these cases, a steady stream of new products embodying the most advanced technology seemed to keep Japanese companies in a permanently "troubled" state. As soon as a Japanese firm had mastered one generation of products, a new one appeared with even more advanced features; or, worse, the old product was superseded by a different type of product—as desktop computers and powerful workstations supplanted mainframe computers in many applications.

The evidence reviewed in this chapter suggests that national styles of innovation account for the broad traits of competitive strength, stagnation, and decline alluded to in the examples mentioned above. Style itself, though, is dependent on national circumstances—and these, of course, are subject to change. Sharp national differences in the 1960s and 1970s are becoming blurred in the 1980s and 1990s as learning and diffusion combine with evolving economic conditions and political constraints to soften many of the earlier national distinctions. Nevertheless, as we enter the twenty-first century, certain styles will persist and companies and governments in both countries will continue to confront the challenges of Japanese production efficiency and American product innovation while simultaneously trying to incorporate the others' strengths into their own strategies. Likewise, policy analysts will be struggling to keep up with their understanding of these changes and the shifting conditions that constrain and motivate them.

The subject of this chapter is innovation, defined here as any activity that provides users with new or improved processes or products; innovation generates positive economic value to its immediate beneficiaries. Users or beneficiaries may be producers or final consumers; innovations may be marketed, used directly by the innovator, or made freely available to others.

The discussion focuses on, and addresses several key questions: (1) What are the differences between the United States and Japan in their approaches to innovation? (2) What are the reasons for, and the sources of, these differences? (3) How are these differences and their sources changing? (4) What are the implications for innovation in the future?

To answer these key questions, I sought out previous studies in which comparisons could be drawn between Japan and the United States. Some studies were explicitly comparative; others included both countries as only two points in broader, multinational analyses. Many of the best comparative research efforts were carried out at U.S. business schools, perhaps because of the demands of their main client: American industry. Obviously, something was occurring in Japanese manufacturing that required closer observation and better understanding. This research collected data across samples of observations and analyzed these data according to the fairly rigorous standards of the academic, scientific community; although these standards were often neither as theoretically based nor as empirically rigorous as the more orthodox economics community would have demanded, there is a consistency and a sensibility in the cumulative volume of results that give strength to the main findings. For this analysis, I reviewed approximately 50 comparative studies.

By and large, most of the reviewed literature covers the period from 1950 to the 1980s. It describes the postwar transformation of Japan and the evolutionary change in the U.S. economy. The selection of comparative studies was opportunistic; I would have preferred more cases, for example, in electronics or computers (to note just one deficient area), but found only a few that met the criteria of data-based comparisons. The selection process also tended to favor production innovations rather than science and research and development (R&D); the apparent bias was dictated by the major innovations in postwar Japan, which were in production processes. The focus of the study was on innovation with *direct economic consequences;* therefore, industrial behavior was more thoroughly reviewed than pure research.

## POSTWAR ENVIRONMENTS IN JAPAN AND THE UNITED STATES

### Circumstances and Policies in Japan

From 1945 to 1973, circumstances in Japan established the conditions under which a peculiarly Japanese approach to innovation evolved and flourished. These circumstances began to change around the time of the rapid increase in energy prices and the slowdown of the national economy in 1973.[1] By the mid-1980s, and certainly in the 1990s, these conditions have once again been altered, and new circumstances have arisen in such numbers that Japan is now moving on a new trajectory.

The postwar circumstances were composed of a mixture of environmental factors and policies.[2] First, a broad national consensus for postwar recovery and growth explicitly favored growth over equity, thus avoiding the ideological debates over distribution that engendered serious political disagreements in Europe. Because of this consensus, there was little debate over the policies adopted by the government ministries and the legislature dominated by the Liberal Democratic party.

Second, Japanese industry lagged behind the world leaders in industrial productivity, technology, and science, in no small part because of wartime destruction. This situation provided the opportunity to start anew; the clear incentive was to buy, borrow, and copy technology and all the other knowledge associated with it: products, processes, designs, and market concepts. Although the investment in industrial infrastructure, equipment, and technology required enormous sacrifices in the early postwar period, it created a modern base for subsequent expansion.

A third area of considerable importance was the economic and national security stability that prevailed during much of the period. Until 1973, growth was unaffected by major downturns or the disrupting influence of war. Indeed, both the Korean and Vietnamese wars provided market opportunities for several Japanese industries, including motor vehicles and aviation.

Finally, Japan was lucky in its resources and markets. Internally, the supply of labor never constrained the very rapid growth of investment and output; externally, supplies of materials and energy were abundant and fairly low priced (although the oil price increases after 1973 severely disrupted several important industries and adversely affected productivity growth for a decade). The market-opening policies and economic growth of the United States, Europe, and the rest of the industrialized world also provided export markets for Japan's hugely increased productive capacity.

These generally favorable circumstances, largely independent of Japanese actions, were abetted by central government policies. A major goal of the growth-oriented government was to provide as much capital as possible at the lowest possible cost to firms pushing new technology and expanding capacity.[3] The most important policy involved the encouragement of household saving and the channeling of capital to industry. The Japanese tax system contained numerous breaks for saving. In addition, capital gains received favorable tax treatment, which favored investment. Unlike the situation in the United States, interest paid on housing loans and other consumer loans was not tax deductible. These financial policies, together with an official and widely accepted national norm favoring savings, were important contributors to very high Japanese saving rates.[4] Another important influence on the Japanese saving rate was economic growth itself. Most cross-country analyses find that income growth has a highly significant effect on the private saving rate.

A highly controlled and regulated financial market directed the enormous flow of savings not only to selected firms and industries, but also to industry more generally. Government budgets were largely in balance until 1973, and consumer credit was tightly restricted, thus eliminating two potentially large competitors for funds. Restrictions on international financial flows permitted the Ministry of Finance (MOF) to control the allocation of foreign currencies and the Ministry of International Trade and Industry (MITI) to regulate the importation of goods; most important, capital controls kept domestic savings from flowing abroad.

The control of foreign trade through financial controls was allied with explicit restrictions on selected imports through tariffs, quotas, and other mechanisms, such as the allocation of import licenses. MITI was thus able to protect several industries whose productivity did not match the levels attained by firms in the United States and elsewhere.

Government coordination and ministerial guidance of business behavior were of mixed effectiveness. It is this Japanese approach to targeting, coordination, and guidance that has been most often singled out as representative of Japanese industrial policy. In some cases, such as steel, shipbuilding, and chemicals, government coordination and targeting achieved cartel-like results, especially during periods of weak demand. Overinvestment could be avoided in good times, and excess capacity could be reduced in an orderly manner when demand fell. However, often this approach was ineffective. In several important products, industry did not support the government's strategic plans. Machine tools, automobiles, and microelectronics were cases where government advice often went unheeded.

In automobiles, for example, several government agencies argued against the three major vehicle companies entering the automobile market in 1950, based on government assumptions that domestic productivity and scale of production were too low to be competitive with European and American producers.[5] When companies ignored this advice and began domestic production, MITI curtailed imports to protect the Japanese producers. Subsequently, imports fell from 45 percent of sales in 1951 to 9 percent in 1955, and to only 1 percent in 1960. Under this umbrella, and with access to low-cost public and private financing, eight more firms subsequently entered the motor vehicle market; these firms shared an annual market in 1955 equal to less than a single day's output of the U.S. industry.[6] Several times in the following years, MITI tried to encourage consolidation and mergers of automobile producers, but with no success.[7]

In the automobile case, and in many other products and industries, the most important elements of government policy were the control and channeling of financial resources and the protection from foreign competition during vulnerable periods of industrial growth.

Because of fairly small government budgets and minuscule defense R&D, the Japanese government funded very little science, research, or development. As a percentage of Japanese gross national product (GNP), 1970 public funding of R&D was only 0.55 percent, compared with 1.48 percent in the

United States.[8] In absolute terms, the amounts were tiny—only $3.7 billion in 1970, rising to $7.6 billion in 1985. (U.S. expenditures grew from $35.6 billion to $40.6 billion in this period.) Because of the small involvement of the Japanese government in financing science, and the weak communication among Japanese scientists, the government promoted a research approach quite different from U.S. experience: the encouragement of cooperative industrial research. More than 80 technology research associations were established, mainly under MITI's aegis and coordination; typically these ventures brought together several companies for information exchange and mutual coordination of a small research agenda, financed partly through public funds and favorable tax policy.[9]

### Consequences of Japan's Circumstances and Policies

A large volume of capital was available to industry because of the government's policies of regulated capital markets and high household savings rates. Lending by private and government financial organizations at interest rates that were often below market equilibrium rates encouraged rapid investment and capacity expansion.[10]

Import restrictions supplied a protective umbrella against the onslaughts of more productive foreign competitors. Domestically, however, an inefficient Japanese firm only had to contend with equally inefficient Japanese competitors. With the easy availability of capital, the benefits of protection, and the small scale of production required to meet the demands of a still-recovering domestic market, market entry was easy in many products. By 1960, for example, 11 companies were producing automobiles. Thousands of tiny manufacturing firms produced components and parts for the larger firms in automobiles, machine tools, and other manufacturing industries.[11] These tiny firms were supported by a protected financial sector that specialized in small companies.[12]

In product after product, fierce competition was engendered by the entry of many firms, often fighting over a small domestic market. Later, as Japanese industry became more efficient and competed on a global scale, the same processes continued to operate. For example, 25 Japanese companies are fighting for the facsimile machine market. According to one analysis:

> The bitter competition means no easy profits for any of them. . . . With so many competitors, success today is no guarantee for tomorrow. . . . Newcomers have an edge over entrenched electronics establishments. Their small size gives them the flexibility to produce new models quickly.[13]

A similar story is told in semiconductors:

> The semiconductor industry is so competitive that the production ranking of companies could change any time, industry watchers say. Technological innovation often leads to a dramatic shift in market share and subsequent changes in the leading players. Also, new entrants have become conspicuous recently.[14]

The fierce competition in manufacturing and electronics, in traditional industries and new products, from the 1950s to the 1980s, drove a search for efficiency as a means toward profitability. Since science, technology development, and new product concepts and innovation were occurring elsewhere in the world, Japanese manufacturers had little need to devote their scarce resources and energies to these activities; it was feasible, less costly, and rational to license, copy, or otherwise learn from the technology developments occurring elsewhere. Instead, the domestic competitive environment stimulated a focus on production efficiency. The hallmark of Japanese innovation in much of the postwar period has been the transformation of production processes that has arisen from the competitive demands for efficiency and productivity. Moreover, these productivity gains had to be achieved with production volumes much lower than were typical in the larger American and European markets.

The imperative for cost-reducing innovation, although focused on production, carried over into product development and R&D, which were also harnessed to the crusade for greater efficiency. Product improvement was not neglected in R&D, but much of it was aimed at incremental changes and fast development times to meet competitive challenges.

The combination of circumstances and policies in Japan led to a dynamic production sector that transformed manufacturing, rivaling in scale and importance the earlier revolutions that have been attributed to Eli Whitney and Henry Ford. Of course, more than circumstances and policies were necessary for such a revolution. Energy, genius, and passion were also ingredients. Taiichi Ohno, the chief architect of the Toyota production system, was thus described by the Nissan director for manufacturing: "To devise and implement these techniques required a fanatic, a Taiichi Ohno. Nissan simply did not have one."[15]

### Circumstances and Policies in the United States

*Postwar opportunities.* Circumstances in the United States following World War II had little of the transformational qualities witnessed in Japan. Having come out of the war undamaged and with its economic structure buttressed by large wartime machinery investment in selected industries, the U.S.

economy was the most efficient and productive in the world. However, large sectors of the more traditional American industries were still saddled by investments made in the 1920s, having had little renewal during the Depression-bound 1930s.

With a continent-wide domestic market, the newer U.S. industries were able to combine advanced machinery with well-honed manufacturing management techniques to take advantage of economies of scale in domestic and international markets. The destruction and disruption of the war in Europe and Asia gave the United States an extended period of uncontested foreign sales that extended even to the less well positioned traditional sectors.

*Importance of science.* One of the sources of American productivity advantage was the country's dedication to science, research, and industrial R&D, which produced not only a stream of innovations advancing productivity, but also a flow of new products. This attachment of U.S. business to science was not new; its roots were in the nineteenth century and by 1899, U.S. industry had already established, by one count, 139 industrial laboratories. This figure had increased to 813 by 1928.[16] Along with this growth in industrial R&D came a simultaneous increase in the research activities of universities and the government, as well as a sharp expansion in the numbers of engineers and technically trained workers.[17]

The World War II experience stimulated this historical penchant to apply science to industrial ends. Several technologies that had their origins in the civilian sector had high wartime value for the military, which, with its enormously expanded resources, contributed to their accelerated development. Aviation, electronics, nuclear technologies, communications, computing, certain medical products, and numerous other technologies benefited from this infusion of military R&D as well as from the impetus provided by the military as a ready buyer of many advanced products. U.S. industry subsequently entered the peacetime period with the opportunity to commercialize these new technologies and products.

*Defense expenditures and R&D.* The returns from the military-related developments continued to influence civilian developments for the next several decades. However, the circumstances that created the opportunities for profitable commercial spin-offs from military R&D also created myths about the universality of the phenomenon. With the benefit of a still hazy hindsight, we can now see waves of technology spin-on and spin-off, from civilian to military to civilian use. At the present time, this phase of the cycle appears to emphasize spin-on: the creation of military benefits from civilian efforts in microelectronics, computing, materials, and other technologies. As military requirements, supported by unprecedented defense expenditures, further developed the findings of the civilian sector from the

1930s to the 1950s, military uses diverged from civilian applications in a process of specialization and refinement that reduced the probability of later civilian applications.[18] Unfortunately, governments all over the world interpreted the congruence of military and civilian requirements of the middle part of the twentieth century as a general and usual occurrence and promoted military R&D for its presumed civilian return.

The defense R&D spin-off theory has been countered by another argument that has gained some currency in recent years: Defense expenditures impose a drain on economic resources, thus retarding growth and productivity. It is also asserted that the best engineers and scientists are bid away from the civilian sector to work on exotic and technologically attractive military technology, thus starving civilian activities of the best talent; at a minimum, it is claimed, the demands of defense R&D will raise the salaries of technical people, thereby leading to smaller numbers employed in civilian efforts. Since U.S. expenditures on defense have ranged from about 5 to 8 percent of GNP, whereas the Japanese contribution to defense has been consistently under 1 percent, these arguments imply that defense has adversely affected American growth and productivity.

Several recent review articles have attempted to determine the consistency of research findings that are based on adequate methods and data. One review concluded, "the available evidence suggests that moderate levels of defense spending, while they do have a dampening effect on economic growth, play a marginal role in shaping overall economic performance. . . . The trade-off does not appear to be severe."[19] Defense expenditures will have their major long-term effect on the economy when military spending crowds out civilian investment. This reduction amounts to only a small percentage of annual investment, yet its cumulative effect can be substantial. Although this effect is not found consistently across all countries and time periods, it has been observed in the United States both before and after World War II.[20] In cross-national studies, crowding out is found more often than not.[21] One major review of this literature concludes that "defense spending is not an important determinant of investment, . . . with little historic evidence of any consistent trade-off between defense and investment operating either through the mechanism of the federal budget or through the private market.[22]

The essence of the argument that defense R&D diverts talent and technical resources from private endeavors is that the supply of both research personnel and funds is inelastic. Studies on the supply of engineers and scientists do not support the inelasticity argument for other than the short run of about three to four years.[23] Neither does the evidence support the argument that the best technical people go to defense. A National Research Council survey of university placement officers found that students prize commercial positions over defense because they offer more varied challenges and greater potential for advancement.[24] Moreover, a survey of electrical engineers by the Office of Technology Assessment concluded: "The military engineer is viewed as more risk averse, less creative, and less likely to be interested in advancement. In contrast, the civilian engineer is viewed as more people-oriented, more talented, better able to bring out products, and is more selective."[25] A review of a dozen or so studies on the differential effects of private- versus government-funded R&D in industry (more than 30 percent of which is defense R&D) found that privately funded R&D yields returns to productivity, output, and value-added that are two to three times higher than the returns to investments in plant and equipment. Government-funded R&D, in contrast, produced low, zero, or negative social returns.[26]

*Capital markets.* The growth of new industries in the United States was supported by a well-developed infrastructure of capital markets that was able to supply to both established companies and newcomers the investment funds needed to develop new industries on a massive scale. Market and production uncertainties were often handled by the U.S. venture capital market, which helped to create thousands of new companies attempting to exploit technological and market opportunities. Needless to say, a large proportion of these ventures did not pay off, but out of the maelstrom of market experimentation arose the companies and products that have since become familiar to observers of the American industrial scene.

*Government policies.* Several government policies contributed to this growth, some by commission, others by omission. One important active policy was the support of research by government agencies, both civilian and military. Whether measured by the number of Nobel Prize winners, science literature citations, patents, or technology-licensing revenues, American performance in academia, government laboratories, and industry dominated world science. For several decades, in pursuing its own requirements, defense R&D also contributed to an American strength in the emerging industries.

Another policy—or, one may better say, a pervasive philosophy—was the government's pro-market orientation. Although there were considerable deviations from this approach (nuclear power, for example), it generally restrained government intervention in market choices; such restraint is especially noteworthy in comparison with policies adopted in Japan and many European countries.

*Results on U.S. innovation.* The effects of this set of circumstances and policies on U.S. innovation were as powerful and as pervasive as the forces operating in Japan. First, competition was less intense in the United States than in Japan. U.S. firms did not have to be concerned with foreign competition, and the size of the U.S. internal market allowed companies in many industries to take advantage of economies of scale and to operate profitably and efficiently without having to capture the entire national market.

Second, the innovation focus tended to be devoted to new products, new markets, wholly new production technologies, and new materials. Cost and efficiency of manufacture took second place to coming up with something new. It made little commercial sense for a firm to concentrate its energies on cutting costs when it was struggling to bring out a new product, or when a competitor could come up with a new product that would displace an older model.[27]

Third, the mature, little-regulated, and well-developed financial markets meant that firms paid the market price of capital. Their decisions were dominated by expected rates of return. In the rapidly evolving new industries, venture capitalists could reasonably balance the probabilities of very large gains against the likelihood of many failures. With this access to capital, the new technology start-ups—often located near major universities—became a standard feature of the American industrial scene. However, in contrast to Japanese policy, U.S. tax policy tended to favor consumption over saving: interest, capital gains, and dividends were taxable, and interest payments on mortgages and consumption loans were deductible for tax purposes. For these and other reasons, the rate of flow of household savings into investment was substantially less than in Japan.

Thus, the patterns of development in postwar Japan and America were quite different from each other, having been conditioned by dissimilar circumstances and policies. It is no exaggeration to say that both countries benefited mutually from these diverse developments. Japan's growth and innovation would not have been possible without the technology, science, and markets of the United States; and American welfare would have been diminished without the Japanese pursuit of efficiency, productivity, and skills in product evolution.

## INNOVATION STYLES IN R&D

### Differences in Research Projects

The Japanese emphasis on production begins in R&D. As a general tendency, Japanese industrial R&D has favored projects directed toward manufacturing processes, whereas U.S. projects tend to be aimed at new products.

Professor Edwin Mansfield has conducted several studies of research projects ongoing in 1985 among 50 pairs of firms in the United States and Japan, matched by industry, products, and company size. One of the sharpest intercountry differences in his samples is the percentage of R&D expenditures spent on products and processes. Mansfield finds that U.S. producers outspend their Japanese counterparts by almost two to one in product (rather than process) R&D: 68 percent versus 36 percent. Also, U.S. firms spend almost half (47 percent) of their R&D budget on entirely new products and new processes (rather than product or process improvements), compared with only one-third (32 percent) for the Japanese firms.[28]

Examinations of the distribution of expenditures across R&D phases show that U.S. firms spent 26 percent of their innovation costs, compared with 21 percent for Japanese firms, on the "front end" of the R&D process—in the stages designated as "applied research" and "preparation of product specification."[29] Expenditures on preparation for production—"tooling and manufacturing equipment and facilities"—were emphasized by Japanese firms: 44 percent of their total R&D, versus only 23 percent for the U.S. sample. However, U.S. firms devoted a much larger share of their resources to the marketing portion of innovation and commercialization: 17 percent versus 8 percent.

Many observers have characterized Japanese industrial R&D as low risk and short term, especially when compared with U.S. practice. This observation seemed to have been especially true in the 1970s.[30] Mansfield attempted to test this characterization by questioning 50 matched pairs of companies concerning the percentage of their R&D expenditures on projects with less than a 50 percent estimated chance of success and on projects expected to last longer than five years. Mansfield's data indicate no difference between the companies' R&D expenditures, in the two countries, in their devotion to such long-term or riskier projects in 1985.[31]

The sources of ideas for R&D projects are distinctly different in the United States and Japan and are consistent with the above-noted emphases. Of the sources of projects in Japan, 30 percent come from ultimate users: internal production organizations and customers. The U.S. proportion is only 18 percent. However, U.S. firms are more influenced by their R&D organizations, with 58 percent of the projects emanating from them, against 47 percent in Japan. In the electrical equipment industry, this U.S. tendency is found in exaggerated proportions: 90 percent of the R&D project ideas came from R&D personnel (47 percent in Japan), and a bare 2 percent flowed from production and customers (32 percent in Japan).[32]

The American focus on the front end of the R&D process is illustrated by a study of electronics manufacturing carried out by the U.S. National

Research Council (NRC).[33] A questionnaire was distributed to a worldwide panel of experts specializing in electronics R&D and applications in industry, universities, government research laboratories, and other organizations.[34] Among the questions asked was the relative lead or lag in years of U.S. producers in 11 "critical" technologies (out of an original list of 30) as applied to six R&D functions. The R&D functions spanned the creative process from the conception of a new product to its support once it was marketed: requirements, design, fabrication, assembly, test, and support. In every case, the country with the most advanced capabilities, relative to the United States, was Japan. For analytical purposes, I selected all those technology applications where the U.S. lead or lag exceeded two years.[35] This criterion emphasizes substantial differences in technological competency and eliminates cases where experts' judgments showed considerable dispersion. Table 11.1, which displays these leads and lags, shows that the U.S. strength is in technologies applied to the conceptual development of products (requirements) and to product design. Japanese strengths are devoted to production: fabrication, assembly, and test. The United States is strong again in the final stages of test and support. However, this focus on leads and lags obscures the fact that firms in both countries devote considerable effort across all six R&D functions. Thus, one should not conclude that Japanese companies cannot or will not develop new products, or that U.S. industry ignores costs and productivity. The main emphases in innovation are dissimilar, but considerable overlap remains apparent.

## Differences in Automobile Developments

The distinct sets of forces in each country have also affected the speed, efficiency, and management of the R&D process itself. A driving force in many Japanese markets was the necessity to be profitable with the considerably smaller production runs than were typical in the United States. For smaller production runs to be efficient and profitable, "setup costs" or fixed costs must be reduced as much as possible. This principle played a major role in the development of the Japanese production system; it also led to remarkable innovations in the product-development process itself. Chronic shortages of engineers in postwar Japan reinforced the search for methods to reduce engineering inputs in R&D. Moreover, lower development costs allowed shorter product development cycles and greater flexibility in reacting to technological opportunities and to competitive pressures.

One major study examined 29 automobile development projects in the United States, Japan, and Europe.[36] The cases covered the period from 1980

**Table 11.1**
**Substantial U.S. and Japanese leads in electronics production technology**

| Function | Technologies | | | | | |
|---|---|---|---|---|---|---|
| | Design Automation | Computing | Artificial Intelligence | Database | Process Control | Robotics |
| Requirements | U.S. | | U.S. | | | |
| Design | U.S. | U.S. | U.S. | U.S. | | |
| Fabrication | | | | | Japan | Japan |
| Assembly | | | | | Japan | Japan |
| Test | | U.S. | U.S. | U.S. | Japan | Japan |
| Support | | | U.S. | U.S. | | |

*Source:* N.R.C. (1988), Figure 3-1, p. 26.

to 1987. The average Japanese project required only one-third as many engineering hours as a typical American project (1.155 million hours versus 3.478 million hours).[37] The length of time per project was also considerably smaller in Japan: 42.6 months rather than 61.9 months. (Average European experience was similar to the U.S. figures.) Clark et al. attempted to standardize these raw figures by taking account of such variables as the proportion of parts that were common to other existing models, the ratio of parts carried over from previous models, the ratio of unique parts, the ratio of parts developed entirely by parts suppliers, the number of parts where the auto manufacturer did the basic engineering (but suppliers performed detailed engineering), and the number of so-called "detail-controlled parts": those developed entirely from basic to detailed engineering.

The Japanese projects had fewer common parts and more unique parts, which should increase the engineering tasks; but they also had considerably more design participation by suppliers and many fewer detail-controlled parts, which would reduce the engineering effort. Adjustments to the data were made on the basis of extended analyses and discussions with automotive engineers. The adjusted data describe how many engineering hours would have been required to develop the entire vehicle in-house with no carryover or common parts. This standardization for the origin of parts slightly reduced the Japanese advantage; the estimated hours are 2.701 million for Japanese projects, 4.892 million hours for American, and 6.426 million for European.[38] These adjustments however, did not include the effects of body size, number of body types, or quality (as proxied by price). Regression equations were estimated with the adjusted engineering hours as dependent variable and body size, number of body types, price, and a Japanese dummy variable as independent variables. The point estimate of the dummy variable suggested that the U.S. and European companies use about 2.6 million more engineering hours than the Japanese to complete a standardized project, or about twice as many engineering resources.[39] Equations with the same independent variables were used to estimate a Japanese effect on lead time. Holding body size, body types, price, and percent of in-house designed parts constant, Japanese projects continued to have a time advantage of 12 to 13 months. Much of the unadjusted Japanese lead time advantage appeared to be a result of supplier participation, which itself was largely a Japanese phenomenon—the variable explained little of the variation within region.[40]

## Differences in Project Organization and Management

Additional analysis of the automobile developments suggested that project organization and management style were strongly associated with the standardized Japanese time and cost advantage. The authors defined three types of management structure. (1) "Functional structure," which used to be common in the United States and remains so in Europe, is organized according to specialized departments (e.g., body engineering, controls); coordination is by hierarchy, rules, and procedures. (2) "Lightweight project management" organizes work into functional departments, but a fairly low-status project manager coordinates activities through lower-level liaison workers; most U.S. projects, some European, and a few Japanese projects used such an approach. (3) "Heavyweight project management" places great authority in the manager, who has direct responsibility for all aspects of the project and holds high status within the company; four projects, all Japanese, used heavyweight project management.

Project team size was closely related to the style of management. Heavyweight teams had an average of 333 engineers, lightweight projects used 573, and functional projects had over 1,400 engineers. Project management variables were included in the engineering hours and lead time equations described above. In addition, the dependent variables were adjusted for standard engineering tasks and the independent variables accounted for product size and complexity. Inclusion of the project management variables reduced the size of the Japanese advantage in engineering from 2.6 million to 1.4 million hours and in development time from 12.5 to 9.7 months. The project management variables, therefore, had very important effects, even after the raw data were adjusted and other project characteristics were included. However, the Japanese dummy variable also continued to show a substantial and competitively important advantage in project efficiency and lead time.

Two other features of project management appear to account for at least part of the residual differences among projects. Mansfield and others have shown that overlapping project phases can save time and resources, but only if mistakes and pursuit of poor alternatives do not lead to additional correction work downstream. For an overlapping strategy to work, intense communications are required so that upstream and downstream activities are constantly informed about each other's activities. The Japanese projects were found to have high degrees of overlap among activities and high levels of the required information flows across activities.[41] U.S. projects had medium overlap and low information flows. European projects were low in both dimensions; each project phase occurred in strict sequence upon conclusion of the previous phase. In some U.S. projects, a high degree of overlap was not supported by the necessary information flows, so surprises, confusion, and delays often disrupted later project phases, with disastrous consequences for project performance.[42]

The study of automobile development projects is important in our understanding of innovation differences because its sample size, cross-national selection, and standardization of observations permit statistical analyses not possible in other studies. The findings here, however, support those discovered in more limited case studies. For example, research on five innovative and successful Japanese product developments listed "overlapping development phases" as one of six intrafirm factors that contributed to speedy and flexible development efforts.[43] The authors, however, also list some limitations to overlapping project organization. It may not be applicable to very large or breakthrough projects: extensive communications in face-to-face interactions may be limited by project size; and the scale of the uncertainties may constrain the efficiency of overlapping phases when projects aim at major technological advances. Nevertheless, for a wide range of R&D projects, the organizational methods described in these studies appear to contribute to lower costs, shorter lead times, and greater flexibility.

## Efficiency in Adapting and Developing Technology

The traditional strengths of U.S. firms in pursuing new products and new technologies have been matched by the organizational innovations of many Japanese firms in becoming more efficient at this kind of R&D. Japanese firms' strengths, however, are commonly believed to lie in their ability to copy and adapt technology developed by others, rather than developing it internally. To test this view, Mansfield compared 30 pairs of Japanese and U.S. firms, matched according to industry and size of firm.[44] For roughly comparable projects undertaken from 1975 to 1985, he collected data on the time and money devoted to the development and commercialization of new products. The time and cost of projects based on technologies developed within the firm were not significantly different across the two countries.[45] American firms were also about as efficient at using technology developed externally to the firm as in developing and commercializing their own innovations. Japanese firms, however, were significantly more effective in using external technology than in producing it internally. In Japan, firms spent about 25 percent less time and 50 percent less money in carrying out projects based on external than on internal technologies.[46] In partial agreement with conventional wisdom, Japanese firms have proven to be highly effective imitators, to be skilled at modifying a product and reducing its costs; but, unexpectedly, they were quite as efficient as their American counterparts in developing new technologies.

### Time and Cost Trade-offs

Many studies on R&D demonstrate a trade-off between time and costs: innovation time can often be reduced by measures that increase project costs. Mansfield's data suggest that Japanese firms seem to be willing to devote about twice as many resources to reduce development time as U.S. firms.[47] This behavior is consistent with Japanese firms' belief that profits from innovation decrease rapidly because of project delays.

### A Japanese Approach to R&D: Research Cooperatives

Government promotion of research cooperatives was encouraged by the character of the Japanese research environment: the low mobility of industrial researchers, the weak links between university laboratories and industry, the small amount of government funding of generic research in either industry or universities, and the official willingness to accept the possible anticompetitive results of collaboration among otherwise competitive firms. Reacting to these circumstances, MITI promoted collaborative associations among firms.

Usually, the associations did not actually perform research, which was almost always conducted in the member firms' own facilities by their own personnel. Only a small fraction of the members' R&D was performed in this cooperative context, and the government funds themselves were quite modest. A company official in one such venture commented, "Government funding is typically so small as to be insignificant to our overall research portfolio."[48] In 1980, for example, total funding of six major MITI projects in semiconductors and computers came to approximately $88 million;[49] the number of project participants ranged from 5 to over 100 (in the case of one software automation project).

The very large-scale integration (VLSI) project of the late 1970s and early 1980s was perhaps the best known and most successful cooperative research venture, but in many ways it was highly atypical. Five participants received generous government funding to perform intensive research in a single facility with clear technical goals: development of one-micron device technology, submicron process technology, and 64K-bit dynamic memories. The typical projects were different in all major respects from the VLSI collaboration; they received less support, involved more participants, had broader and more research-oriented goals, and were performed at the sites of the participants.[50]

The VLSI project was one of a series of collaborative ventures promoted by MITI to challenge the U.S. computer industry, particularly IBM. Earlier projects included the "large-scale project system" in 1966–72 to develop a supercapacity computer and the integrated circuit development promotion in 1972–74. The VLSI project sought to develop a domestic computer to compete with the IBM models to follow the 370 series.[51] Despite the earlier collaborative projects, the technology of integrated circuits was moving so fast that Japanese computer firms faced great difficulties in breaking into the market. In mid-1975, MITI and state-owned Nippon Telegraph and Telephone (NTT) agreed to unite parts of their separate R&D programs and to support developments in the components industry.[52]

One particular focus of the VLSI project was production technology. Between one-third and one-half of the funds were used to purchase advanced U.S. equipment, much of which was dismantled and analyzed in an attempt to design Japanese versions with superior performance.[53]

The focus on production was consistent with the general Japanese approach to innovation, in which cost reduction was of central concern. The VLSI project provided an organizational framework such that the device and component firms could work toward a production system that could be constantly improved and refined; because all of the participants in the project possessed a common technology base, this strategy created an incentive for semiconductor producers to seek competitive cost advantage by working closely with their equipment suppliers. Thus, by concentrating on production and costs, and by sharing the fruits of the research among the five participants, the firms were driven even more to find ways to improve their competitive positions.

The actual value of the government contribution to the VLSI project over its lifetime (from 1976 to 1981) has been open to some debate. The subsidy granted through actual contracts was about 30 billion yen, or roughly $132 million.[54] NTT also invested $350 million independently of MITI's VLSI project.[55] Finan and LaMond count up at least $500 million in direct government subsidies and soft loans.[56] The companies also contributed 40 billion yen ($176 million) to the collaborative VLSI project.[57] At a minimum, the government's 30 billion yen direct subsidy was a substantial contribution to R&D at a critical juncture for Japanese manufacturers. The quick introduction of the 64K dynamic random access memory (DRAM) moved the Japanese industry into its first large-scale volume production of integrated circuits. One Japanese academic analyst suspects that "if there had been no subsidy, the joint R&D system would not have materialized and, as a consequence, the technological progress regarding VLSI would not have been generated."[58]

Despite the success of the VLSI project, its analysts warn that this model of R&D management is not one that can be expected to be universally efficient and successful; certain crucial elements of this particular project may not always be present. First, the production technologies at the heart of the VLSI project were applicable throughout semiconductor production processes. Second, the coming together in a single laboratory of the five companies stimulated efficient interfirm transfer of the common technologies.[59] Third, the R&D goals were clearly defined in advance, a time limit was established, and a fixed amount of funds was allocated. These conditions established clear and tight constraints on the participants and helped to focus their efforts. Wakasugi believes that these reasons for success were unique to the project and that "they cannot be a basis for arguing that R&D activities by the technology research cooperative approach are generally rational."[60] To test the validity of this evaluation more broadly, it would be necessary to assess the relative success or failure of a broad sample of collaborative projects and to relate the measure of success to the project characteristics.

## INNOVATION IN PRODUCTION

Innovations in production have had notable effects on the economic and political relations between the United States and Japan. Even more than in science, R&D, and the development of new products, the dramatic advances in production efficiency pioneered in Japan have led to profound changes in relative efficiencies and economic power.

## Innovation in Automobile Production

Despite sharply lower production rates, crude measures of productivity (annual output of vehicles per employee) were higher in Toyota by 1960 than in the American automobile companies. Table 11.2 shows that the second largest Japanese company, Nissan, had higher crude productivity levels than both General Motors and Chrysler, despite production rates that were barely 3 percent of those of General Motors. By 1980, the Japanese companies had improved by 400 percent, whereas the United States experienced about 20 percent increases in two companies and a 30 percent decline in the third.

These figures, though dramatic, hide important differences among the companies: levels of vertical integration, capacity utilization, and labor hours per employee, to name just three. Vertical integration is substantially lower in many Japanese producers than in their U.S. counterparts, as a greater responsibility for production is placed on suppliers. In 1979, the rate of integration stood at 29 percent and 26 percent for Toyota and Nissan, and at 43, 36, and 32 percent for GM, Ford, and Chrysler.[61] Productivity measures based on output per company employee could, therefore, vary by up to 65 percent from vertical integration differences alone.

Capacity utilization rates were also significantly different, with Toyota typically operating at full capacity and Nissan in the 82 to 97 percent range. U.S. factory utilization rates were more variable, falling as low as 60 percent in 1982. Also, Japanese workers put in about 10 percent more hours per year than the U.S. automobile labor force.

**Table 11.2**
**Annual vehicle output**
(Per employee)

| Company | 1960 | 1970 | 1980 |
|---------|------|------|------|
| G.M. | 8 | 8 | 10 |
| Ford | 14 | 12 | 10 |
| Chrysler | 11 | 11 | 13 |
| Nissan | 12 | 30 | 47 |
| Toyota | 15 | 38 | 61 |

*Source:* Cusumano (1985), Table 44, p. 187.

Table 11.3 corrects for vertical integration, capacity utilization, and employee-hours differences. By 1965, Toyota was already 50 percent more productive than the average U.S. company, and Nissan had about the same productivity as the American companies. By 1983, both Japanese companies were about twice as productive as the American "Big Three," Nissan productivity having grown by more than 2.5 times from 1965 to 1983 and Toyota by more than 80 percent; the U.S. companies had managed a bare 20 percent gain over the same period.

Even adjusted labor productivity figures reported in Table 11.3 do not tell the full story. Labor is only one of the inputs into the production process; other input factors such as capital need to be included in estimates of total input factor productivity. Cusumano did not calculate total input factor productivities but did provide measures of fixed assets per vehicle, adjusted for vertical integration and capacity utilization, as shown in Table 11.4. According to these figures, the American manufacturers used more capital per unit output until 1983, so that capital intensities could not account for the large differences in adjusted labor productivity.

One additional point must be considered in evaluation of the productivity gains of the Japanese companies: scale economies. A widely used study in the automobile industry estimates that most economies of scale are exhausted at annual production rates of 200,000 vehicles in an integrated company, with no gains to be expected after one million vehicles.[62] Both Nissan and Toyota had passed the 200,000 mark by 1962; until then, reductions in manufacturing costs per unit output had largely followed general industry experience. Yet both companies continued to achieve remarkable productivity gains, even after reaching the million-vehicle level. According to Cusumano, "much of the twofold productivity differential (over the U.S.

**Table 11.3**
**Vehicle productivity adjusted for vertical integration,
capacity utilization, and labor-hour differences**
(Vehicles per employee)

| FY | U.S. Big 3 | Nissan | Toyota |
|------|-----------|--------|--------|
| 1965 | 4.7 | 4.8 | 6.9 |
| 1970 | 4.6 | 8.8 | 10.9 |
| 1975 | 5.3 | 9.0 | 13.7 |
| 1979 | 5.5 | 11.1 | 15.0 |
| 1983 | 5.7 | 11.0 | 12.7 |

*Source:* Cusumano (1985), Table 49, p. 299.

**Table 11.4**
**Fixed assets per annual output, adjusted for**
**vertical integration and capacity utilization**
(1983 dollar values)

| FY | U.S. Big 3 | Nissan | Toyota |
|----|-----------|--------|--------|
| 1965 | 8,030 | 6,126 | 4,397 |
| 1970 | 9,816 | 4,148 | 5,280 |
| 1975 | 8,055 | 6,405 | 5,270 |
| 1979 | 7,165 | 6,165 | 7,705 |
| 1983 | 10,450 | 10,796 | 11,853 |

*Source:* Cusumano (1985), Table 57, p. 212.

companies) stemmed from the techniques Nissan and Toyota developed, prior to 1970, to manage their technological, capital, and labor resources to raise worker output and lower costs far beyond the levels expected or achieved outside of Japan."[63]

Researchers at MIT sought better productivity measures than those calculated by Cusumano and others in order to analyze the effects of management methods on such output measures as productivity and product quality across a wide range of management styles. To do this, they collected plant level data for similar operations—automobile assembly—standardized to account for differences in such variables as automobile size and number of models produced.

Krafcik's sample of 38 final assembly plants in 13 countries represented 15 major companies and included roughly 25 percent of world automotive assembly capacity.[64] Krafcik adjusted total employee hours by defining a list of "standard" operations based on the most common set of plant activities in the sample of plants. If a plant performed nonstandard activities, the people associated with them were removed from the productivity calculations.[65] He also made adjustments for absenteeism and actual working hours. On the output side, a standard vehicle was defined to adjust for product size, number of welds, and equipment content. Quality measures were based on a J. D. Power and Associates questionnaire to new car buyers in the United States on problems experienced in 12 different areas. However, since not all defects are related to assembly, he purged the raw data of nonassembly defects.[66]

The results of this analysis are shown in Figures 11.1 and 11.2. The average domestically owned plant in North America is almost 40 percent less productive than the average Japanese plant, and the European level is almost 90 percent worse than the Japanese figures. Japanese companies' productivity experience in their North American plants is equal to average Japanese productivity.

The quality levels (shown in Figure 11.2) also vary widely, but there is considerably less overlap than in productivity. The best American and European values are worse than the average Japanese, although the detailed data show that at least one Japanese transplant in the United States produces at the same quality level as its mother plant in Japan.

Several variables were used to investigate alternative explanations for the wide productivity and quality differences among plants. A robotics index, designed to measure the use of high-technology hardware, was completely uncorrelated with plant productivity.[67] Since the number of models and body types was expected to increase the complexity of plant operation and reduce the possibilities of scale economies, a model mix complexity index was constructed. Contrary to expectations, the Japanese plants accommodated a more complex mix of platforms and body types than their North American or European competitors.

Conventional manufacturing analysis asserts that productivity and quality are negatively related: As factories devote more resources to obtain higher-quality output, costs will increase and productivity will decline as a consequence. However, a plot of productivity versus quality (Figure 11.3) shows just the opposite for the cross section of assembly plants. Productivity and quality are *positively* related (the correlation coefficient is 0.60). "Those plants producing high-quality products do so with *substantially less effort* than low-quality plants."[68]

### Innovation in Japanese Production: Just-In-Time

High levels of productivity and quality in the Japanese automobile industry are not associated with capital, high technology, complexity of product mix, or scale effects; neither are productivity and quality negatively related to each other. The explanation for high productivity lies in the organization and management of the production process. Elements of this management approach arose in several Japanese companies in the postwar period, but the system in its most complete form evolved in Toyota under the driving pressure of its manufacturing director Taiichi Ohno. It was then adopted by the other automobile companies and their suppliers and later diffused throughout Japanese industry. In the 1980s, this approach began to spread around the world, as it was adapted to many kinds of products and production processes.

The Japanese production process has been given different labels by analysts: lean, unbuffered, fragile, and high-stress. The "just-in-time" (JIT) method of parts supply has been used as a shorthand designation to describe the entire process; although the Toyota approach encompasses many other interrelated elements, JIT is a convenient tag.

The Japanese automobile management problem was to produce efficiently at low volume, a requirement imposed by a rising number of competitors for a very limited market. Ohno's approach to this problem emphasized several related elements: flexibility; the fullest possible use of equipment, workers, and supplies; and the reduction of in-plant personnel, factory and warehouse space, and in-process and finished goods inventories. JIT, in the narrow parts-supply sense, accomplished many of these goals. JIT accepted the Henry Ford goal of minimizing the elapsed time between beginning and ending production. But, whereas Ford achieved this through high-volume production of standardized products, Toyota found ways to do it in lot sizes of a few hundred parts; when carried as far as possible, lot sizes of a single piece were possible.

As assembly line production based on Ford's approach established its dominance over other methods in the first half of the twentieth century, it gradually evolved and developed rococo variants. In many cases, management focused on the simple goal of keeping the line moving. But to accomplish this, they embellished the original concept by designing a highly buffered system with stocks of parts and assemblies in warehouses and on the shop floor to provide insurance against disruptions anywhere in the process; this approach was also extended to people, as specialists were added to the payroll to expedite production, order supplies, inspect output, and manage warehouses.

**Figure 11.1**
**Productivity levels in world automobile assembly plants**

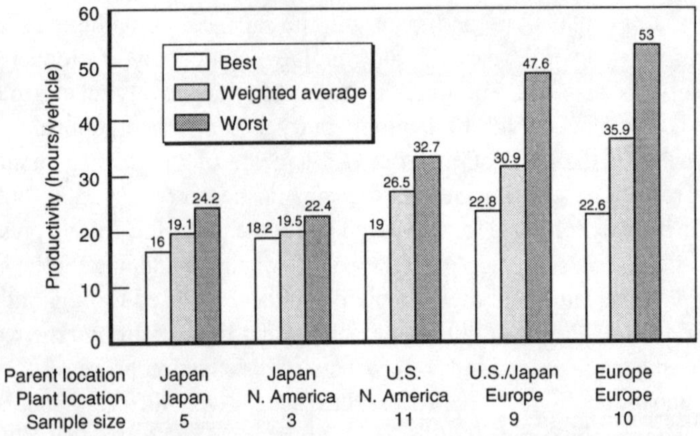

| Parent location | Japan | Japan | U.S. | U.S./Japan | Europe |
|---|---|---|---|---|---|
| Plant location | Japan | N. America | N. America | Europe | Europe |
| Sample size | 5 | 3 | 11 | 9 | 10 |

SOURCE: Krafcik (1988b), Figure 2, p. 46.

**Figure 11.2**
**Quality levels in world automobile assembly plants**

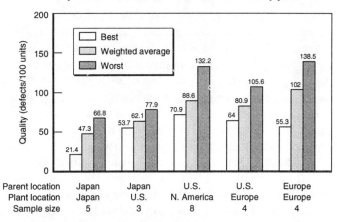

| Parent location | Japan | Japan | U.S. | U.S. | Europe |
|---|---|---|---|---|---|
| Plant location | Japan | U.S. | N. America | Europe | Europe |
| Sample size | 5 | 3 | 8 | 4 | 4 |

SOURCE: Krafcik (1988b), Figure 22, p. 93.

**Figure 11.3**
**Quality and productivity for world automobile plants**

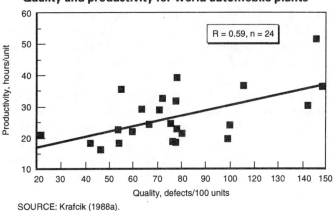

SOURCE: Krafcik (1988a).

The problem with a buffered system is that it absorbs information. A quality problem, a missed delivery, an inefficient worker, or a poorly planned equipment layout does not stop the system; another part is in the bin, a full shelf is in the warehouse, another worker takes up the slack. Over time, the buffered system can hide the sources of inefficiencies and deficiencies; productivity may be low and quality poor, but finding the cause can be extraordinarily difficult. Moreover, if competitors are producing according to the same system, their costs and quality will have suffered in the same way, thereby generating little pressure for improvement.

The drive to reduce inventories is one of the chief elements of the JIT approach. Lower inventories both reduced financial carrying costs and produced several other planned and unintentional consequences. Warehouse and storage space is drastically diminished in JIT plants; the need for bins, conveying devices, forklifts, and stock specialists is lower; equipment can be placed closer together, which enhances direct personal relations among manufacturing operations and eliminates much of the need for in-plant transportation; and through-put time is reduced as work in process moves quickly through sequential operations rather than spending time in storage.

A second element of Ohno's production innovation was the "pull" system of scheduling and moving parts. Instead of the customary practice of building parts for stock, with each successive operation withdrawing stored parts, the pull system initiates an operation only when an operator moves back to the previous station to retrieve work in process, just at the necessary time and in the amount needed for immediate processing.[69] The pull system was gradually extended to virtually all operations, including marketing—production only began with an order for a finished product; such an approach is possible only if the through-put time is less than the desired period from order receipt to product shipment.

To facilitate the pull system, Toyota engineers introduced the so-called *kanban,* or ticket; an operation was authorized only by receipt of a *kanban* from the next station. This ticket would proceed backward as each operation required a part or batch of parts, finally arriving at the raw-materials or purchased-part station. This system was a key element in reducing inventories. Toyota later extended the pull system to suppliers; to do this, the company established tight supplier relationships so that eventually they delivered parts directly to assembly lines, fully integrating them into the in-house parts supply system.

Batch size, or economic order quantity, is typically determined by an optimizing calculation that balances setup time and costs against lost production and inventory costs (interest charges, warehousing expense, and breakage and loss). The greater the setup costs for a batch of parts, the larger will be the economic production quantity. Customarily, setup costs were treated as fixed, and batch size was the result of simple calculations. However, with the goal of reducing inventories, Ohno set to work on reducing setup costs. The examples of this effort are legendary: For example, stamping press changeover time for body part dies was reduced from several hours to 15 minutes by 1962; by 1971, this time was lowered further, to 3 minutes.[70] U.S. automobile manufacturers took as long as half a day or more to change dies and consequently produced in batches of 10 to 30 days' supply. Toyota changed dies three times a day and produced no more than a single day's usage.[71]

Other techniques used in the full JIT system included multiple machine operation by individual workers, worker inspection of output, mixed loading of assembly lines, component production for different automobile models, and line-stop buttons on assembly lines that gave workers authority to halt production if defects or other problems arose.[72]

The combination of the line-stop system, the *kanban* parts pull approach, and the minimal inventories produced a most important and unplanned result. They increased the feedback of information generated in the production process. A defect, an inability to keep up, a missing part, a slow delivery, or an ineffective worker immediately made itself known. The source of a problem was easier to spot because it showed up immediately, and engineers, managers, and shop workers could address it directly. Indeed, the system *compels* attention to problems because they stop production. The lean, unbuffered, fragile system *demands* the energy and creativity of its participants.

This constant attention and problem solving has also earned the Toyota production process the designation of a "high-stress" process. Not only was quality improved by the feedback of information, but efficiency increased as production was quickened with the steady progress in addressing problems. As each problem was dealt with, a faster flow of parts and assembly would stress new areas.[73]

For a standard American or European assembly line, it was considered a cardinal sin to stop the line—thus, the building of buffers. In the Japanese factory, it was recognized (after 20 years of fanatical devotion to the JIT approach) that a stopped line or a problem generated information on which improvements could be based. Instead of the information being absorbed by a well-protected production process, the Japanese factory forced the information to the surface in such a manner that it could not be ignored; employees at all levels could then devote their detailed knowledge to dealing with it.

As is apparent from the above description, the individual worker is a key element in the JIT system. The typical employee is called upon to monitor several different machines or operations, inspect output, constantly evaluate the ongoing production process and stop the line if necessary, contribute to solving problems, and supply a steady stream of suggestions for improving the product or production process. Japanese firms tend to give production workers broad exposure to different manufacturing methods by moving them at regular intervals to new positions. After several years, workers would have gained wide knowledge of plant operations and the relationships among them. They are also called on to make creative contributions to improving the product or the process.[74] It is not an exaggeration to state that in a well-run JIT operation, the worker is paid to accept and promote the goals of the company, and to contribute not only physical labor and manual dexterity, but also emotional commitment and intellectual energy.

In an attempt to determine whether management approach was statistically related to productivity and quality in the 38 auto assembly plants described above, Krafcik estimated regression equations with productivity and quality as dependent variables; the independent variables included a management style index, space use, model mix, product age, and production scale variables.[75] The management style index was based on abstracted models of management tasks in "fragile" and "robust" systems. Management in a fragile system must tend to the skills and motivation of the work force, develop the logistics of a JIT inventory system, and create a "supportive, nonadversarial environment" in which workers contribute actively to the success and improvement of the process.[76] Production management in a robust system revolves around the establishment and maintenance of various safety nets to keep the system running if something goes wrong. To quantify management style, Krafcik collected data on four areas to produce a single index: percentage of floor space dedicated to postprocess repair, evidence of worker awareness and participation in the control of the production process, the degree to which employee interactions were required in all facets of operations, and the average level of unscheduled absenteeism.[77] The management index had the highest statistical significance in both the productivity and quality equations, producing the greatest effect of all the variables.

## The Diffusion of JIT

The dominance of the Toyota production system was clearly recognized by the other Japanese automobile producers. Although most of them were already motivated by similar circumstances to adopt many of the same practices, none had gone as far as Taiichi Ohno; by the 1970s, the process was diffusing throughout the industry. As word of the success of JIT spread, other Japanese companies studied and adopted it; some were pushed in this direction by the auto companies who demanded high quality, low costs, and just-in-time deliveries from their suppliers, while others were driven by their own competitive search for efficiency.

Eventually, the process spread out of Japan to other countries in many different products. For example, the Spanish subsidiary of the accounting and management firm Price Waterhouse made arrangements with Kawasaki

Heavy Industry (KHI) to learn the JIT system from KHI in order to teach the system to clients in Spain. Spanish customers were said to have been particularly receptive to new techniques that would improve productivity because their approaching entry into the European Common Market was about to confront them with more efficient competitors.

JIT is now a frequent subject of the manufacturing press with how-to-do-it features, surveys, and anecdotes. Research on productivity based on world-wide samples of production plants "clearly linked throughput time reduction and several other linchpins of JIT manufacturing to factory productivity gains."[78] Research studies have involved a cross section of 265 U.S. plants in diverse industries, panel data on 26 U.S. plants over a five-year period, and an international sample of 128 plants in 30 countries.[79] Although statistical results varied somewhat in detail from one sample to another, they were consistent overall. The only variables that were always related to productivity gains were those associated with JIT, "specifically throughput time reduction, improved quality, lower inventories, and participative management techniques."[80] Just as interesting is the list of variables *not* related to productivity. Plants with high productivity improvements were not distinguishable by their investment in high-tech equipment.

> In addition, younger plants did no better than older ones, and smaller plants no better than bigger ones. Similarly, there was no distinction between union and nonunion, sunbelt and frostbelt, Asian and non-Asian, and Northern European and Southern European plants. Moreover, the type of industry does not seem to affect the results: process and nonprocess industries do about the same. It appears that management, rather than geography, size, union status, age, or industry holds the key to a factory's productivity gain.[81]

Although the gains from JIT are clear and transferable, the actual adoption of the process can be extraordinarily difficult, as it often requires a transformation of corporate culture, affecting both management and labor. A British study of the worldwide automobile industry noted:

> Despite the significant changes, the process of changing established concepts and practices in the social organization of production is proving to be a difficult and painful process. Although the new best practice can be observed where it exists, diffusing this knowledge through highly structured and complex organizations takes considerably longer than investing in new equipment. . . . *The most successful example of this seems to be in cases where the competitive pressures for survival were intense enough to break down the social resistance to change.*[82]

## Extending JIT

Innovation in production management has not required new investment and high technology. But where technology is appropriately integrated in the JIT framework, the payoff appears to be substantial. The flexible manufacturing system (FMS) is a case in point. FMS joins together several computer-controlled machining centers and other machine tools through a network of conveyors. The entire system is under supervisory control of a central computer that identifies each arriving pallet containing a piece to be worked on and controls the scheduling and movement of the workpiece (whose identity can change from pallet to pallet) through the system. Tool supply, automated inspection, and machine loading and balancing are coordinated and directed from the FMS computer. The advantages of FMS include flexibility, increased machine utilization, reduced number of machines, reduced lead times, more consistent product quality, reduced setup costs, and reduced inventory of tools through standardization.[83]

Since this list of advantages is similar to the goals and advantages of JIT, it is reasonable to expect an especially good fit between FMS and JIT; however, even in a traditional production operation, FMS should also deliver the same qualitative returns. A study of 35 FMSs in the United States and 60 in Japan (more than half the installed systems in both countries) showed something quite different. Although the kinds of products they made were comparable across the two countries in size, complexity, metal-cutting times, precision, and number of tools per part, great disparities were evident in efficiency and flexibility.[84]

The American systems produced only ten parts per system compared with 93 on the Japanese machines (see Table 11.5). The U.S. penchant for long production runs was revealed by high annual volumes per part (consistent with the few types of parts); the U.S. machines turned out an average 1,727 of each part and the Japanese only 258. Japanese flexibility was also demonstrated by their introduction of new parts over the course of the year: 22 versus 1. Flexibility, though, was not achieved at the cost of productivity: 18 Japanese systems went unattended (none in the United States), utilization was 84 percent (52 percent in the United States), and metal-cutting time per day averaged 20.2 hours (8.3 hours in the United States).

By and large, the U.S. companies' investment in expensive FMS is being wasted. Inappropriately used, high-cost equipment actually increases the productivity gap. A stand-alone FMS designed for flexibility but surrounded by a traditional production process forms "at best, a small oasis in a desert of mediocrity."[85]

**Table 11.5**
**Comparison of flexible manufacturing systems**
**in the United States and Japan**

|  | United States | Japan |
|---|---|---|
| System development time (years) | 2.5 to 3 | 1.25 to 1.75 |
| Number of machines per system | 7 | 6 |
| Types of parts produced per system | 10 | 93 |
| Annual volume per part | 1,727 | 258 |
| Number of parts produced per day | 88 | 120 |
| Number of new parts introduced per year | 1 | 22 |
| Number of systems with unattended operations | 0 | 18 |
| Utilization rate (two shifts) | 52% | 84% |
| Average metal-cutting time per day (hours) | 8.3 | 20.2 |

*Source:* Jaikumar (1986), Exhibit 1, p. 70.

There are many explanations for the failure of U.S. manufacturers to make good use of FMS, but manpower use is one of the largest contributors. Software development is critical to this information-intensive manufacturing process and workers' technological literacy is essential. In the Japanese companies, more than 40 percent of the work force was made up of college-educated engineers, and all had been trained on computer-numerical-controlled (CNC) machines. Among the U.S. companies, only 8 percent were engineers, and fewer than 25 percent had CNC training.[86] Also, skill upgrading training was three times longer in Japan. The use of FMS is growing in Japan, with high returns to the users.[87] In the United States, by contrast, FMSs are being withdrawn from many operations because of inadequate returns, high complexity, and insufficient use.

High Japanese productivity in complex manufacturing operations is not confined to traditional metal-cutting jobs. In the production of memory chips, several hundred dies (on which the memory circuits are printed) are produced from a single wafer. The production process requires an extended sequence of complex operations, in the course of which the wafers and dies are tested for defects. The final cost per memory chip is compounded from the cumulative yields and costs of the separate operations. Table 11.6 exhibits 1983 manufacturing cost comparisons of 64K DRAMs. In the first stage of memory chip production, the costs per wafer were 25 percent higher in Japan. However, these higher costs were partly an investment in higher yields at later production phases: for example, the higher Japanese material cost arose, in part, from stricter purity standards and the capital cost component was higher because of an emphasis on automation.[88]

**Table 11.6**
**Cost comparison for U.S. and Japanese 64K DRAM**
(1983)

|  | United States | Japan |
|---|---|---|
| Components of Whole Wafer Cost ($ per wafer) | | |
| Materials | $ 32 | $ 49 |
| Capital (depreciation) | 29 | 37 |
| Labor | 24 | 20 |
| TOTAL | $ 85 | $106 |
| Components of DRAM Cost | | |
| Wafer | $ 85 | $106 |
| Wafer process yield | 80% | 95% |
| Yielded whole wafer cost | $106 | $112 |
| Die size (mil$^2$) | 35,000 | 38,600 |
| Total die/wafer | 313 | 280 |
| Probe yield | 40% | 52% |
| Good die | 125 | 146 |
| Cost per good die | $0.96 | $0.85 |
| Assembly cost | $0.20 | $0.40 |
| Assembly yield | 90% | 95% |
| Yielded assembly cost | $1.40 | $1.32 |
| Final test cost | $0.20 | $0.20 |
| Final test yield | 80% | 80% |
| Factory cost per good die | $2.00 | $1.90 |
| Cumulative yield | 23% | 38% |
| Number of good die | 72 | 106 |
| Gross margin | 45% | 40% |
| Final selling price | $3.64 | $3.17 |
| Total revenue | $262 | $336 |

*Source:* Finan and LaMond (1985), Table 3-5.

The cumulative yield in Japan of 38 percent was 65 percent greater than the U.S. yield, which more than compensated for the higher Japanese wafer cost and fewer dies per wafer. (The Japanese companies accepted a larger die and consequent reduction in available dies per wafer because of the requirements for greater automation.) With the cost structures and yields shown in Table 11.6, Japanese semiconductor producers would enjoy a 13 percent selling price advantage. As Finan and LaMond point out, though, these costs are fairly close to each other, and for a standard device like a 64K DRAM the final selling price would probably be identical; if forced to sell at the lower price, the U.S. gross margin would fall from a preferred 45 percent to a competitive 37 percent.[89] In any event, exchange rate variations could easily swamp these cost differences. However, an important difference would still persist: for comparable plant capacities and utilization rates, Japanese producers would obtain 50 percent greater revenues than U.S. companies because of their higher yields. In other words, U.S. companies would have to make a 40 percent greater investment in capacity to generate the same revenues.

### Culture or Competition

Many people have questioned whether the truly revolutionary nature of the organizational and managerial innovations in Japan, in both development and production, flowed out of features of Japanese culture (and are therefore difficult to transfer to other cultures) or whether they arose as a creative but otherwise random development, having little to do with either culture or economics. The use of worker teams, intense communication among project participants, and nonadversarial worker-management relations are particularly congenial to Japanese culture. However, such an explanation would ignore the very different (and American) approach to management in prewar Japan, the bitter labor-management strife throughout the Japanese economy in the early postwar period, and the extremely hierarchical (even dictatorial) style of management found in most of the higher echelons of Japanese organizations. There is an alternative hypothesis.

Consider the U.S. automobile industry in its early days. Between 1903 and 1926, 181 companies produced automobiles in the U.S. market. At that time, the concept of the automobile was an open issue. Technology was unsettled: Would the powerplant be steam, electric, or an internal combustion engine? Would steering be by a wheel, tiller, or handlebars? How many wheels were adequate—two, three, four, or more? Would the frame be lightweight and flexible like a bicycle or a horse-drawn buggy, rigid like a wagon, or massively based on iron and steel like a locomotive?

The use of automobiles was just as ambiguous as the technology. Would they be used by the rich, by farmers, by commerce and industry? Would there be a road system, a rail system, or would the vehicles move cross-country like tractors? Would they be used for moving people or goods, for business or pleasure, for long or short distances?

Similarly, many methods of production were being evaluated. Some producers turned out automobiles one by one, like locomotives. Others developed batch production systems drawing on bicycle experience.

Each of the almost 200 companies entering this business believed that it had the correct answers to all of these questions. Most of them failed; 20 percent lasted three years or less, and half survived for less than six years.[90] Of the top ten automobile producers in 1903, only two remained in those ranks six years later. But each of these ventures was an experiment—in technology, use, production, and marketing. The large number of trials, combined with the growth of demand and the intensity of the competition, produced a feedback that was rapid and demanded attention. Out of the turmoil of multiple uncertainties and market experimentation, the modern automobile was born and with it the creation of a production system that came to dominate manufacturing worldwide for almost a century.

The analytical question is whether the revolution brought about by Henry Ford arose from his personal genius, the nature of the U.S. economy, or the American cultural character. The full flowering of the automobile and of mass production techniques probably depended on all these contributions and more. I hypothesize that the essential quality was the nature of market experimentation embedded in a competitive framework. The large number of trials increased the probability of coming up with a winner, of identifying genius. The competitive situation provided the incentive to play the game with skill and passion; competition established a method for picking the winners and the requirement to respond to feedback. This process demanded, created, and used ideas and information intensively.

This pattern is not limited to the automobile industry in the United States in 1900 or in Japan in 1960; similar patterns have been observed in aircraft, electronics, computers, and facsimile machines.[91] Innovation in all of these products embodied much more than technology; it included concepts of product use, manufacturing methods, and R&D strategies. Moreover, the results were unpredictable; analysts are just as handicapped in forecasting outcomes as were the hundreds of entrepreneurs in automobiles in 1903 or in biotechnology in 1990. However, to the degree that the hypothesis outlined here accurately depicts a major source of innovative behavior, analysts may be in a better position to specify the conditions that promote industrial innovation: the support of competition and the ability to respond to its demands.

## U.S. AND JAPANESE INNOVATION IN THE 1990s

### The Situation in Japan

*Growth consensus and national savings.* The circumstances that prevailed for several postwar decades are now evaporating. In Japan, the social consensus favoring growth and growth-stimulating policies no longer has the same hold on the population as it once did. Environmental concerns and a nascent consumerism now challenge the traditional growth ethic. The demand for investment in social infrastructure is competing with private investment on the political agenda. The Liberal Democratic party has lost its hold on power, and the political structure is splintering.

Domestic savings rates are falling: a growing proportion of retired people, slower economic growth, and reduced tax advantages contribute to the decline. By the end of the century, Japan's savings are projected to be at about the rate of West Germany's; although Japan will be far from a pauper country, it will not be able to support the volume of domestic and foreign investment that was seen in the past.

*Financial markets.* Japanese financial markets have been gradually deregulated and internationalized since the early 1980s. The government's ability to control financial flows and channel investments to favored industries is, generally, a thing of the past. However, some parts of the financial sector are still fairly immature, especially the venture capital market.

Venture capital in Japan is small in comparison with that in the United States: $2.1 billion versus $30 billion in 1988.[92] The number of venture capitalists are few and most of these are associated with the large banks and securities companies; only 6 out of 86 are independent.[93] One reason for the weakness in venture capital is that Japanese investors seem to prefer larger companies in proven fields. Also impeding the growth of startups is the fact that until the mid-1980s, regulations required a long wait before an initial public offering on the over-the-counter market. In the United States, 42 percent of listed firms are under ten years old; in Japan, such companies account for less than 1 percent of the listings.[94] In fact, even the largest and boldest of the independent venture capital firms has invested in only 25 Japanese companies out of the 200 in its portfolio, the rest being mainly American startups, many in Japan.[95] Large Japanese companies, however, may substitute to some degree for an underdeveloped venture capital market by creating new ventures within the existing company framework.

As in other areas with structural or other impediments to efficient operations, the Japanese government has stepped into the venture capital arena. Between 1985 and 1988, MITI contributed about $250 million to the Japan Key Technology Center, a state agency that invests in research consortia. The government expected that by providing venture funds to research collaborations that come up with their own proposals, the companies would shoulder more of the burden of technology development.[96] According to the views of MITI officials, this represents a radical departure from earlier policies under which the government itself would often identify the new technologies and provide a certain comfort to companies that would have shied away from unbacked new technologies.[97]

*Protectionist policies.* In the early postwar decades, the Japanese government could protect inefficient domestic industry through the imposition of import restrictions. This policy is no longer permitted by the international community and is encountering opposition by domestic interests. Japan's international trading partners are demanding the removal of indirect trade impediments caused by domestic regulation and customary business practices. Consumers and business users of domestic products are now seeking lower prices and greater efficiency from removal of the costly protection of domestic enterprises in finance, communications, transportation, distribution, agriculture, construction, and other protected areas.

*Resource constraints.* Resource constraints are becoming more binding. Where Japan once had an ample supply of labor and energy for many decades, it now faces higher relative costs in both of these critical areas. Energy costs have risen since the 1970s, and the nation's adjustment to the shift in the relative price of energy caused an estimated ten-year decline in productivity growth.[98]

Japanese birth cohorts have been steadily falling, and in the next ten years the number entering the labor market will be the smallest since the early 1930s. Over the next several years, the share of national income flowing to labor may end its long-term decline and begin rising—at the expense of the share going to profits. Firms would then be forced to obtain a greater share of their financing from the market instead of from retained earnings. The increasing marketization of corporate finance will confront managers with the market rate of interest more sharply than when they relied on their own funds. This process, plus higher interest rates because of reduced savings and the internationalization of the flow of funds, may restrain the free-wheeling investment strategies in equipment, R&D, and human capital that were so characteristic of past behavior.

*Technology and R&D.* A large proportion of Japanese postwar productivity growth can be attributed to a convergence phenomenon whereby countries' total factor productivity growth rates are related to their initial distance from the technological leaders. When other factor inputs are accounted for, Japan's growth from productivity "catch-up" came to an end by the 1970s.[99] Japan is no longer lagging in most applied technologies. Its production capabilities are at world levels and the direction of movement is toward leadership in several areas. For example, in a comparison of 20 technologies with military applications (an area of long-time U.S. strength), the United States had a lead in 11, Japan led in 5, and essential parity existed in 4. However, in the 15 technologies with a U.S. lead or parity, Japan was improving its relative position in 6 of these and was expected to become equal or draw ahead within a few years.[100]

Research performed by Japanese companies is strong, and its growth is impressive; in 1988, the company share of total national R&D had risen to about 70 percent, up from 55 percent in 1970. Basic research, though, in the nation as a whole remained a low-priority area with 13 percent of total expenditures, despite government exhortations on the necessity of supporting basic research; the growth rate of basic research was only 3 percent in 1988 compared with 10 percent growth of expenditures on development.[101] The relative weakness of Japanese science compared with that in the United States is indicated by the amount of basic research performed by Japanese universities in 1985, which was only 36 percent of the U.S. figure; company-sponsored basic research was 34 percent of the amount in U.S. industry.[102] Furthermore, much of what is defined as basic research in Japanese industry may be misclassified. A vice-president of the U.S. Bell Laboratories touring Japanese corporate laboratories noted: "Japan's corporations are not doing basic research of real significance. . . . Their success rate is 90–95 percent; what we call basic research at Bell Labs has a success rate of 30–35 percent."[103]

Japan's laboratories lag behind in many basic research areas. One measure of this overall tendency is that Japanese scientists have been awarded only five Nobel Prizes in science since 1901 and two of the recent awards were for work done outside of Japan. A Japanese government survey of international comparisons of basic research levels supports this broad view; in the 20 reviewed areas, Japanese research achieved parity with the United States only in materials based on crystal structure.[104] Another survey conducted by the leading business newspaper of more than 300 scholars of the Science Council of Japan concluded that Japan leads the United States in only two of 47 major basic research technologies—robotics and ferromagnetic materials.[105]

The relative weakness of Japanese science has been attributed to poor funding and to rigid, hierarchical, conservative research organization and management, especially in universities. Widespread concern over the state of science has emerged in recent years as Japanese policymakers see Japan as having reached a stage of development where it must base more of its economic developments on its own research foundations.[106] Reform of university research is under discussion, and MITI and other government agencies are urging that universities and industry form new partnerships with each other and push creativity into new areas. But many of the government efforts are enmeshed in interagency turf battles that are combined with a general decline in the high level of consensus and consistency that characterized Japanese science and technology in the past.[107] In the meantime, many firms are reorganizing their R&D and creating new laboratories, especially overseas.[108]

## The Situation in the United States

*The competitive situation.* Unlike the situation in the first decades after World War II, the United States today faces intense competition from both developed and developing countries. High productivity levels and advanced technologies have spread throughout the industrial world. Countries with the lowest productivity in the past (among them, Japan) have tended to show the greatest gains. Total factor productivity convergence has been operating for all except the poorest non–Organization for Economic Cooperation and Development (OECD) countries, at a rate similar to the convergence observed within the OECD group.[109] In the past, Europe, Japan, and the other Asian newly industrializing countries were the chief competitors of the United States. In the future, the breadth of competition is certain to expand. The large, continental American markets are no longer locked up by American producers.

*Science, R&D, and investment.* The United States outspends Japan in science and R&D in industry, government, and higher education, even when the military-sponsored effort is eliminated from the comparison. However, several important ratios suggest that trends favor Japan: the ratios of R&D to GNP, R&D per capita, and company-sponsored industrial R&D to sales are all higher in Japan.

R&D is one form of investment in innovation and productivity improvements; it is highly complementary to capital investment in equipment, mainly because new capital is the primary means of embodying technical change.[110] Human capital investment is also complementary to both R&D and equipment investment in productivity growth.[111] The United States produces five times the number of doctorate-level specialists in the natural sciences and engineering as Japan, and ten times the number of first-degree specialists in science. However, the number of graduating engineers at the first-degree level is now about equal in the two countries.[112] Education at the high school level is a different story, with accumulating evidence that Japanese students outperform Americans both in quality and, increasingly, in the numbers of students completing high school. However, the relationship between high school level education and innovation is not clear, although hypotheses abound on such matters as the flexibility of workers and their ability to handle complex tasks.

The complementarities among R&D, capital investment, and educational attainments are important because increases in any one of these raises the marginal product of the others. Nelson suggests that forces leading to the growth of one are likely to stimulate an increase in the others.[113]

Several studies of the determinants of the structure of trade have concluded that R&D has been an important factor in the comparative advantage of U.S. industries. A study of U.S. and Japanese trade structure based on 168 industries from 1967 to 1983 indicated that R&D "is highly significant statistically and shows the continued comparative advantage of the United States in R&D intensive products."[114] Over this period, Japan moved from a position of comparative advantage in unskilled-labor-intensive manufactured goods and disadvantage in human-capital-intensive products to a new position of comparative advantage in human capital; its position, in regard to physical capital, was roughly the same over the years.[115] Until the mid-1970s, Japan was also at a comparative disadvantage in R&D-intensive industries, but this had shifted sharply by 1975. Among high-tech products (those with a ratio of R&D to sales greater than 3.5 percent), the importance of R&D to both countries has increased monotonically over the years, but its absolute importance to the United States has been and remains greater than for Japan.[116]

Although the United States has been weaker than Japan in equipment investment, the situation in venture capital and the financing of new firms is quite different. As suggested above, the financial structure for the support of new products, new firms, and even wholly new industries is well developed and oriented toward risky investments. The venture capital market is characterized by hundreds of participants with access to capital from such sources as individuals, pension funds, and insurance; the actual investment volume exceeds that in Japan by an order of magnitude.

In summary, the situation in the United States with respect to R&D and investment is complex. Science is strong, government contributions to nonmilitary R&D are large, and university research is the best in the world. Industrial R&D is also strong, but the trend relative to Japan is declining. Overall investment is weak, but venture capital has been the engine driving many important innovations. Education is mixed, with world-class education at the college and graduate levels, but with a poorer distribution of educational investments at the lower grades. This mix of strengths and weaknesses creates a kaleidoscopic array of implications for future innovation.

### Biotechnology: One Mirror for the Future?

Among the technologies and industries of the twenty-first century, biotechnology offers one facet of the future mosaic. A consensus has been reached at the highest government levels in Japan that biotechnology is of substantial importance to the future of the Japanese economy.[117] Biotechnology is an element of a broader Japanese government strategy that emphasizes knowledge-intensive industries. Many in the Japanese government have stated their belief that the government, working through various agencies and policies, can and ought to affect the development of biotechnology in Japan.

Circumstances in Japan, however, now constrain the actions of government agencies and severely restrict their ability to achieve their desired goals. Deregulated capital markets reduce the government's ability to channel private funds to chosen firms and projects, while tight budgets restrict the scale of government largesse. International and domestic objections to protection eliminate the possibility of barring foreign competition until a domestic industry develops its capacity to challenge world markets. Moreover, an immature venture capital market and small number of doctorate-level biological scientists retard the creation of new firms; social and business norms create a reluctance by both new graduates and established scientists and engineers to move into new companies. Despite the targeting of biotechnology, it has been difficult for the Japanese government to make major overt steps to aid the industry. "The subtler and less financially onerous steps that the Japanese government has taken to guide biotechnology ... can be seen as limited compensation for the absence of a number of market processes and institutions, found in the United States, particularly beneficial to the development of high technology industries."[118]

As of 1984, the implementation of programs to back up the government's rhetoric of industrial targeting of biotechnology was woefully inadequate, especially in comparison with activities in the United States. The Japanese government allocated roughly $35 million to biotechnology in 1984, versus the U.S. government's 1982–83 commitment of $522 million (on an annual basis). U.S. federal funds were more than double the high estimates of biotechnology R&D from the combined governments of West Germany, Great Britain, France, and Japan.[119] Moreover, a large proportion of the Japanese funds went to fields at some distance from the biotechnology cutting edge: to energy research; to aid the structurally depressed chemical, pulp and paper, and textile industries; and to the traditionally strong area of fermentation. By 1990, the budget for all biological and health-related research totaled 73 billion yen or about $363 million at purchasing-power-parity conversion.[120] This figure included all of the disease and therapy research of the Ministry of Health and Welfare. A narrower definition places the 1990 biotechnology contribution at 31.5 billion yen, or about $158 million, still only about 30 percent of the U.S. expenditures in 1982–83.[121]

In addition to the U.S. government's direct R&D expenditures, in 1981 the Small Business Administration had already granted $7 million in subsidized loans to 22 new biotechnology firms.[122] As of late 1984, no Japanese firm had received any funding from comparable Japanese government agencies.

Between 1977 and 1983, 111 new American firms were formed with the explicit intention of exploiting biotechnology, and 108 established firms entered the field. Equity markets raised $1.5 billion for small U.S. firms (those with less than $5 million net worth). The market value of the equity of the largest biotechnology firms had reached $3.5 billion by 1984.[123]

Established firms had also invested $400 million through mid-1983 in new biotechnology companies, and four large established chemical and pharmaceutical companies had biotech R&D expenditures of over $300 million in the single year of 1982. The four largest firms active in biotechnology spent $468 million in R&D in 1985.[124]

The Japanese industrial scene was quite different. No new firms had entered the industry by 1985, the four largest established firms in the field spent less than $100 million, and total estimated private R&D was about $400 million, 15 percent less than the expenditures of just the top four U.S. firms. While the Japanese industry is being developed by established firms, the important role in the United States is played by new startups.

In 1982, more than 1,200 doctorate-level scientists and engineers were working in U.S. biogenetic engineering, while only 161 similarly trained personnel could be found in Japanese industrial laboratories.[125] A 1986 assessment noted that Japan was having difficulty training a sufficient number of biotechnology researchers, "and institutional barriers have so far made it difficult for Japanese firms to receive as much assistance from Japanese universities as their American counterparts. Indeed, nearly two-thirds of the Japanese biotechnology firms have indicated that they plan to send researchers abroad for training."[126]

By 1990, more than 500 new U.S. biotechnology companies had entered into business and 200 or so had gone public. These companies raised $1.2 billion in initial public offerings in 1986, but the figures dropped from this high point to $741 million and then $317 million in 1987 and 1988.[127] Many of these startups and their venture capital backers have been selling the new firms to larger companies after having demonstrated the product potential of their creations. Many of the buyers of these American companies are foreign, including Japanese. The combination of American scientific and entrepreneurial skills and Japanese capital is helping to speed the development of new technology and quicken the application of existing technology to an array of new products.[128]

Collaboration is not unwelcomed by either U.S. interests or Japanese participants. In fact, small U.S. biotechnology companies are frequent visitors to Japan, scouting out partners, licensees, and financial backers for their research.[129] U.S. universities are also benefiting from Japanese attention. The

University of California at Los Angeles has established a joint medical research program with Hitachi, and the Japanese cosmetics company Shiseido contributed more than $80 million to American medical schools and universities for biological research. Many Japanese companies are sending employees to U.S. graduate schools for the training they cannot find in Japan.

This biotechnology scenario may be one vision of the future: U.S. strengths in science, research, new products and concepts, graduate education, entrepreneurship, and venture capital combined with Japanese strengths in financial capital, production, and cost minimization. As the technology-constrained and productivity-disadvantaged Japanese industry of the postwar period compensated with innovations in production and R&D management, Japanese companies today are compensating for their scientific deficiencies by tapping U.S. capabilities in a variety of imaginative ways. But this vision is only one possible facet of the picture. The cash-rich Japanese capital market is unlikely to last out the century. American firms are struggling to understand and copy the Japanese production and product development processes. Moreover, fundamental questions persist abut the sources of innovation.

## Conclusions and Questions About Innovation

In large part, the innovation styles of Japan and the United States were unplanned results of postwar policies and circumstances. The restructuring of the Japanese economy led to an explosion of innovation in production, which carried over into R&D. Developments in the United States were more evolutionary, building on habitual strengths and on the technologies coming out of the war effort.

More recently, a partial convergence between the two countries is under way. High productivity methods are being diffused. U.S. scientific results are international public goods. The innovative, entrepreneurial activities in the United States are open to exploitation by a worldwide community through investment, acquisition, joint ventures, technology transfer agreements, licensing, and a score of other methods. Financial, product, and marketing arrangements are being integrated into global markets.

Yet differences remain among countries, and innovation will continue to be affected by national characteristics. Resource mobility differences between labor and capital, within and between countries, will affect the transferability of technology, science, and methods. Government involvement in science, education, and the promotion or restriction of cooperative and other business arrangements in R&D will influence the availability of trained personnel, the flow of scientific knowledge, and the ways in which the people and the science are used. Other government policies in such obvious areas as taxes will influence private decisions; but less obvious policies—such as those that affect housing markets, pensions, stock offerings, trade protection, antitrust, and deregulation—will influence labor and capital mobility and competition. Differences in all these areas are likely to persist into the next decade.

Finally, we are left with some puzzles related to capital and competition. Through the beginning of the 1980s, the evidence suggests that capital was cheaper in Japan than in the United States.[130] On an anecdotal level, a rich set of experiences indicates that many decisions on R&D investment and innovation were made in Japan, as if capital costs were of little concern. If true, capital cost differentials could account for much of the difference in results observed in the two countries—in particular, the fierce competition among companies entering into and expanding capacity in new areas.

Much of the evidence cited in this survey suggests that competitive forces played a crucial role in Japanese innovation behavior and in the differences between the United States and Japan. However, the relationship of competition to innovation raises questions having to do with industry structure. Why did Japanese companies compete so actively under the protection from foreign trade? U.S. experience is consistent with that from other countries: protection more often leads to complacency and higher prices than it does to competition and innovation. Why, for example, was the U.S. machine tool industry less productive than the Japanese? This was an industry with scores of mainline companies and thousands of parts and component suppliers;[131] also, barriers to entry were low. Yet the U.S. industry showed little of the dynamism revealed by the Japanese machine tool industry. Were there problems of access to capital for investment and R&D? Or does the competitive push for innovation depend on more than numbers of participants and the threat of market entry?

Any study on innovation would be amiss if it ended with tidy answers and solutions. The questions and genuine puzzles on the roles of capital, investment, and competition suggest that there is considerable research left to be done on this subject.

---

## NOTES

1. One important change following the oil-price shocks was a government deficit during the mid-1970s recession; the need to finance this deficit was instrumental in breaking down the close regulation of financial markets.

2. This list of circumstances is largely taken, with modification and amendment, from Yamamura (1986), pp. 169–171.

3. Yamamura (1986), p. 171.

4. Horioka (1990), pp. 71–76.

5. Cusumano (1985), pp. 15–23.

6. Total U.S. production in 1955 was 8 million vehicles, but Japan produced only 20,300. On a 365-day production basis, the U.S. average production rate was 22,000 vehicles per day.

7. Cusumano (1985), p. 23.

8. National Science Foundation (1988), Tables B–2, B–4.

9. Heaton (1988), p. 33. Cooperative research is discussed more fully in the following sections.

10. Some economists have questioned the broadly accepted view of subsidized interest rates. Sakakibara (1982); Horiuchi (1984).

11. More than 80 percent of Japan's 1,000 companies in the machine tool industry had fewer than 20 employees. The average size of such firms was only 1.6 people. Alexander (1990), p. 13; see also chapter 13 in this volume.

12. Friedman (1988), pp. 161–175, describes the financial support structure for small firms. This banking sector can be compared to the savings and loan industry in the United States, which is designed to support family home ownership and housing construction.

13. Graven (1989), p. 8.

14. *Japan Economic Journal,* May 6, 1989, p. 5.

15. Cusumano (1985), p. 319.

16. Mowery (1981), p. 51 (cited in Rosenberg, 1985, p. 21).

17. Rosenberg (1985), p. 24.

18. This assertion is based on an impressionistic review of military technology developments of the past 75 years.

19. Kupchan (1989), p. 449.

20. Chan (1985), p. 416.

21. Faini, Annez, and Taylor (1984).

22. Gold (1990), p. 3.

23. Browne (1988), p. 4.

24. Cited in Browne (1988), p. 4.

25. Ibid.

26. Alexander (1993).

27. Moving down a cost curve through increased volume was viewed as a more profitable strategy than focusing on production efficiency and driving the whole cost structure downward; the way to increase the quantity of goods sold (thereby

reducing costs) was to seize a temporary monopoly position by coming out with a new product before competitors could enter the market.

28. Mansfield (1988a), Table 4, p. 1771.
29. Ibid., Table 2, p. 1770.
30. Peck and Tamura (1976).
31. Mansfield (1988b), Table 2, p. 226.
32. Ibid., Table 3, p. 227.
33. NRC (1988).
34. Sixty questionnaires were distributed, and NRC received 26 responses; most were from the electronics industry, but universities and government laboratories responded as well. The report made no assessment of possible biases in the responses. However, since most of these experts were actively involved in company R&D, they were presumably aware of the capabilities of their competitors.
35. Ibid., Figure 3–1, p. 26. There were 11 critical technologies and six R&D functions, so the maximum number of cells was 66; however, since not every function is relevant to every technology, only 30 were technically relevant possibilities.
36. Clark et al. (1987).
37. Ibid., Table 1, p. 741.
38. Ibid., Table 2, p. 744.
39. Ibid., Table 3, p. 746–747.
40. Ibid.
41. Ibid., Table 9, p. 759.
42. Ibid., p. 760.
43. Imai et al. (1985); also published in a shorter version in Takeuchi and Nonaka (1986).
44. Mansfield (1988c), p. 1158.
45. Ibid., p. 1160.
46. Ibid., Tables 3 and 4, p. 1161.
47. Ibid., pp. 1163–1164.
48. Quoted by Heaton (1988), p. 35.
49. These figures are calculated from Yamamura (1986), Table 8.1, p. 194.
50. Heaton (1988), p. 37.
51. Wakasugi (1988), pp. 15–17.
52. Stowsky (1989), p. 252.
53. Ibid.
54. Yamamura (1986), Table 8.1, p. 194; Wakasugi (1988), Table 7, p. 16.
55. Finan and LaMond (1985), p. 171.
56. Ibid. The subsidy value of a soft loan should be calculated on the basis of the difference between the lower subsidized interest rate and the market rate of

comparably risky loans. Finan and LaMond seem to have simply added the face value of the loans rather than the value of the subsidy.

57. Yamamura (1986), p. 196.

58. Wakasugi (1988), p. 20.

59. This commonality of technology and the efficiency of transfer were difficult to achieve; initially, researchers from each firm pursued their own ideas in separate rooms within the common research facility. This situation persisted for more than a year before a MITI research director was able to persuade the participants to work together in greater collaboration. Yamamura (1986), p. 196.

60. Wakasugi (1988), p. 20.

61. Cusumano (1985), Table 46, p. 190. Vertical integration is defined as the ratio of value added (minus profits) to sales (minus profits).

62. Quoted by Cusumano (1985), p. 215.

63. Ibid., p. 217.

64. Krafcik (1988a), p. 13.

65. Ibid., pp. 55–56.

66. Ibid., p. 73. Since not all models were sold in the United States, only 24 plants appear in the quality sample.

67. Ibid., p. 107.

68. Krafcik (1988b), Figure 23, p. 95 (emphasis in original).

69. Cusumano (1988), pp. 34–35, provides a convenient historical treatment of the evolution of the JIT system at Toyota.

70. Ibid., p. 35.

71. Cusumano (1985), p. 285.

72. Parker and Slaughter (1988), p. 42.

73. Ibid.

74. In one copier plant I visited, each four-person team of assembly line workers was expected to make at least 100 suggestions per month on improving the product or the assembly process. Productivity in this plant had been increasing 30 percent per year for more than 20 years.

75. Krafcik (1988a), pp. 80–81.

76. Ibid., pp. 22–24.

77. Ibid., pp. 22–32.

78. Schmenner (1988b), p. 12.

79. The statistical results are reported in Schmenner (1988a).

80. Schmenner (1988b), p. 13.

81. Ibid.

82. Jones (1986), pp. 9–10 (emphasis added).

83. Jaikumar (1989), pp. 119–120.

84. Jaikumar (1986), p. 69.

85. Ibid., p. 72.
86. Ibid., p. 70.
87. Ibid., p. 72. All of the Japanese systems studied met the firms' return on invest-ment criterion of a three-year payback, which under reasonable assumptions implies a 26 percent rate of return.
88. Finan and LaMond (1985), p. 155.
89. Ibid., p. 157.
90. Klein (1977), p. 99.
91. Ibid., pp. 109–139.
92. *Japan Economic Journal,* August 12, 1989.
93. *Asian Wall Street Journal,* July 10, 1989.
94. *Japan Economic Journal,* August 12, 1989.
95. *Asian Wall Street Journal,* July 10, 1989.
96. *Asian Wall Street Journal,* February 13, 1989.
97. Ibid.
98. Jorgenson (1988), p. 218.
99. Dowrick and Nguyen (1989), pp. 1026–1027.
100. Vogel (1989), Table 15, p. 35.
101. *Japan Economic Institute Report,* February 2, 1990, p. 10.
102. National Science Foundation (1988), Table B–6, p. 53. International comparisons were made with purchasing power parities.
103. *Nihon Kezai Shimbun,* February 28, 1989, p. 13.
104. Japanese Science and Technology Agency (1989), Figure 5, p. 31.
105. *Japan Economic Journal,* March 11, 1989, p. 1.
106. Lynn (1986), p. 297.
107. Ibid., p. 298.
108. *Japan Economic Journal,* December 24, 1988, p. 4.
109. Dowrick and Nguyen (1989), p. 1021.
110. Nelson (1981), p. 1054.
111. Ibid.
112. N.R.C. (1988), Tables B–23, B–24, pp. 60–61.
113. Nelson (1981), p. 1054.
114. Balassa and Noland (1989), p. 183.
115. Ibid., p. 182.
116. Ibid., p. 185.
117. Saxonhouse (1986), p. 97.
118. Ibid.
119. Ibid., p. 107.
120. *Bio-Intelligence,* January 30, 1989.
121. *Japan Economic Institute,* February 9, 1990.

122. Saxonhouse (1986), p. 117.
123. Ibid., p. 120.
124. Ibid., p. 121.
125. Ibid., p. 126.
126. Lynn (1986), p. 300.
127. *Asian Wall Street Journal,* July 20, 1989.
128. *Asian Wall Street Journal,* November 1, 1989.
129. *Asian Wall Street Journal,* February 13, 1989.
130. Nachbar (1990). This review of studies on the comparative cost of capital in the United States and Japan shows that serious theoretical problems afflict most of the existing research. However, the weight of the evidence, though imperfect, suggests that, in an aggregate sense, capital was probably cheaper in Japan until the deregulation of domestic and international financial markets in the 1980s.
131. Alexander (1990).

### BIBLIOGRAPHY

Alexander, Arthur J. (1990). *Adaptation to Change in the U.S. Machine Tool Industry and the Effects of Government Policy.* RAND Corporation, N-3079-USJR/RC.

Alexander, Arthur J. (1993). "The Effects of Declining Defense R&D on the U.S. Economy." *JEI Report,* 15A, April 23.

*Asian Wall Street Journal* (1989). "Japan Boosts Stake in U.S. Biotechnology," November 1.

*Asian Wall Street Journal* (1989). "Japan Drug Firms Making a Push in U.S. in Struggle to Overcome a Research Lag," February 13.

*Asian Wall Street Journal* (1989). "Japan Is Employing Venture Capital Tactics to Promote Research by Private Consortiums," February 13.

*Asian Wall Street Journal* (1989). "New Biotech Firms Find Ready Buyers," July 20.

*Asian Wall Street Journal* (1989). "Venture Capitalist in Japan Goes Against Corporate Grain," July 10.

Balassa, Bela, and Marcus Noland (1989). "The Changing Comparative Advantage of Japan and the United States." *Journal of the Japanese and International Economies,* no. 3.

*Bio-Intelligence* (1989). "FY89 Biotechnology-Related Budget," January 30.

Browne, Lynn E. (1988). "Defense Spending and High Technology Development." *New England Economic Review,* September/October (reprinted in *Japan Economic Institute (JEI) Report,* January 20, 1989).

Chan, Steve (1985). "The Impact of Defense Spending on Economic Performance: A Survey of Evidence and Problems." *Orbis,* Summer.

Clark, Kim, Robert Hays, and Christopher Lorenz (eds.) (1985). *The Uneasy Alliance: Managing the Productivity-Technology Dilemma.* Cambridge, Mass.: Harvard Business School Press.

Clark, Kim, W. Bruce Chew, and Takahiro Fujimoto (1987). "Product Development in the World Auto Industry." *Brookings Papers on Economic Activities.*

Cusumano, Michael A. (1988). "Manufacturing Innovation: Lessons from the Japanese Auto Industry." *Sloan Management Review,* Fall.

Cusumano, Michael A. (1985). *The Japanese Automobile Industry: Technology and Management at Nissan and Toyota.* Council on East Asian Studies. Cambridge, Mass.: Harvard University Press.

Dowrick, Steve, and Duc Tho Nguyen (1989). "OECD Comparative Economic Growth (1950–1985): Catch-Up and Convergence." *American Economic Review,* December.

Faini, Riccardo, Patricia Annez, and Lance Taylor (1984). "Defense Spending, Economic Structure, and Growth: Evidence Among Countries and Over Time." *Economic Development and Cultural Change,* April.

Finan, William F. and Annette M. LaMond (1985). "Sustaining U.S. Competitiveness in Microelectronics: The Challenge of U.S. Policy," in Bruce R. Scott and George C. Lodge (eds.), *U.S. Competitiveness in the World Economy.* Cambridge, Mass.: Harvard Business School Press.

Friedman, David (1988). *The Misunderstood Miracle: Industrial Development and Political Change in Japan.* Ithaca, N.Y. : Cornell University Press.

Gold, David (1990). *The Impact of Defense Spending on Investment, Productivity, and Economic Growth.* Defense Budget Project, Washington, DC.

Graven, Katheryn (1989). "Fax Wars Highlight How Japan Firms Fight for Markets." *The Asian Wall Street Journal Weekly,* May 8, p. 8.

Heaton, George R., Jr. (1988). "The Truth About Japan's Cooperative R&D." *Issues in Science and Technology,* Fall.

Horioka, Charles Yuji (1990). "Why Is Japan's Saving Rate So High? A Literature Survey." *Journal of the Japanese and International Economies,* vol. 4.

Horiuchi, Akiyoshi (1984). "Economic Growth and Financial Allocation in Postwar Japan." Brookings Discussion Paper, no. 18.

Imai, Ken-ichi, Ikujiro Nonaka, and Hirotaka Takeuchi (1985). "Managing the New Product Development Process: How Japanese Companies Learn and Unlearn," in Kim Clark, Robert Hayes, and Christopher Lorenz (eds.), *The Uneasy Alliance: Managing the Productivity-Technology Dilemma.* Cambridge, Mass.:Harvard Business School Press.

Jaikumar, Ramchandran (1989). "Japanese Flexible Manufacturing Systems: Impact on the United States." *Japan and the World Economy,* no. 1.

Jaikumar, Ramchandran (1986). "Postindustrial Manufacturing." *Harvard Business Review,* November–December.

*Japan Economic Institute (JEI) Report* (1990). "Biotechology in Japan: 1990 Update," no. 6A, February 9.

*Japan Economic Institute (JEI) Report* (1990). "Japanese Research Spending Rises," February 2.

*Japan Economic Journal* (1988). "Firms Add Horsepower to High-Tech R&D Race," December 24.

*Japan Economic Journal* (1989). "Honda Has High Hopes from Low Output Plant," September 9.

*Japan Economic Journal* (1989). "Poll: U.S. Leads Japan in Research," March 11.

*Japan Economic Journal* (1989). "Semi-Majors Join Race to Produce 4M DRAMs," May 6.

*Japan Economic Journal* (1989). "Venture Firms Eye Japan's Deep Pockets," August 12.

Japanese Science and Technology Agency (1989). *White Paper on Science and Technology: Towards the Establishment of a New Creative Research Environment,* April.

Jones, Daniel T. (1986). *The Dynamics of the World Motor Vehicle Industry: Issues for Analysis.* Science Policy Research Unit, University of Sussex. Presented at the International Motor Vehicle Program meeting, Boston, Mass., September.

Jorgenson, Dale W. (1988). "Productivity and Economic Growth in Japan and the United States." *American Economic Association Papers and Proceedings,* May.

Klein, Burton H. (1977). *Dynamic Economics.* Cambridge, Mass.: Harvard University Press.

Krafcik, John F. (1988a). *Comparative Analysis of Performance Indicators at World Auto Assembly Plants.* M.S. dissertation, Sloan School of Management, January. Cambridge, Mass.: Massachusetts Institute of Technology.

Krafcik, John F. (1988b). "Triumph of the Lean Production System." *Sloan Management Review,* Fall.

Kupchan, Charles A. (1989). "Defense Spending and Economic Performance." *Survival,* September–October.

Lynn, Leonard (1986). "Japanese Research and Technology Policy." *Science,* July 18.

Mansfield, Edwin (1988a). "Industrial Innovations in Japan and the United States." *Science,* September 30.

Mansfield, Edwin (1988b). "Industrial R&D in Japan and the United States: A Comparative Study." *American Economic Association Papers and Proceedings,* May.

Mansfield, Edwin (1988c). "The Speed and Cost of Industrial Innovation in Japan and the United States: External vs. Internal Technology." *Management Science,* October.

Mowery, David (1981). "The Emergence and Growth of Industrial Research in America, 1899–45." Stanford University Doctoral Dissertation.

Nachbar, John (1990). *The Cost of Capital in the United States and Japan: A Survey of Some Recent Literature.* RAND Corporation, N-3088-CUSJR.

National Research Council, Manufacturing Studies Board (1988). *The Future of Electronics Assembly: Report of the Panel on Strategic Electronics Manufacturing Technologies.* Washington D.C.: National Academy Press.

National Science Foundation (1988). *The Science and Technology Resources of Japan: A Comparison with the United States.* NSF 88-318, Washington, DC.

Nelson, Richard R. (1981). "Research on Productivity Growth and Productivity Differences: Dead Ends and New Departures." *Journal of Economic Literature,* September.

*Nihon Kezai Shimbun* (1989). "Comments by Science Information Center Director Inose," February 28.

Parker, Mike, and Jane Slaughter (1988). "Management by Stress." *Technology Review,* October.

Peck, Merton, and Shuji Tamura (1976). "Technology," in Hugh Patrick and Henry Rosovsky, *Asia's New Giant.* Washington, D.C.: The Brookings Institute.

Rosenberg, Nathan (1985). "The Commercial Exploitation of Science by American Industry," in Kim Clark, Robert Hayes, and Christopher Lorenz (eds.), *The Uneasy Alliance: Managing the Productivity-Technology Dilemma.* Cambridge, Mass.: Harvard Business School Press.

Sakakibara, Eisuke (1982). *The Japanese Financial System in Comparative Perspective.* Joint Economic Committee, U.S. Congress, Washington, D.C.

Saxonhouse, Gary R. (1986). "Industrial Policy and Factor Markets: Biotechnology in Japan and the United States," in Hugh Patrick (ed.), *Japan's High Technology Industries.* Seattle: University of Washington Press.

Schmenner, Roger W. (1988a). "Behind Labor Productivity Gains in the Factory." *Journal of Manufacturing Operations Management,* no. 1.

Schmenner, Roger W. (1988b). "The Merit of Making Things Fast." *Sloan Management Review,* Fall.

Stowsky, Jay S. (1989). "Weak Links, Strong Bonds: U.S.-Japanese Competition in Semiconductor Production Equipment," in Chalmers Johnson, Laura D'Andrea Tyson, and John Zysman, *Politics and Productivity: The Real Story of Why Japan Works.* Berkeley Roundtable on the International Economy (BRIE), Cambridge, Mass.: Ballinger Publishing.

Takeuchi, Hirotaka, and Ikujiro Nonaka (1986). "The New Product Development Game." *Harvard Business Review,* February.

Vogel, Steven K. (1989). "Japanese High Technology, Politics, and Power." Research Paper #2, Berkeley Roundtable on the International Economy (BRIE), March.

Wakasugi, Ryuhei (1988). "Research and Development and Innovations in High Technology Industry: The Case of the Semiconductor Industry." *Japanese Economic Studies,* Fall.

Yamamura, Kozo (1986). "Caveat Emptor: The Industrial Policy of Japan," in Paul R. Krugman (ed.), *Strategic Trade Policy and the New International Economics.* Cambridge, Mass.: MIT Press.

# 12

# R&D and Innovation in Japan with Comparisons to the United States

Ryuhei Wakasugi

## INTRODUCTION

**R**esearch and development (R&D) expenditures in the private sector in the United States and Japan showed remarkably different patterns of growth in the 1980s. The resources allocated to R&D in Japan, expressed as the ratio of private R&D expenditures to gross national product (GNP), increased at a significant rate, but they were stagnant in the United States. As Figure 12.1 shows, in 1986 the ratio of manufacturing R&D expenditures to net sales in Japan rose to 3 percent—almost the same level as that in the United States (3.2 percent)—and in 1990 the former (3.3 percent) exceeded the latter (3.2 percent). Today, Japanese private R&D expenditures (as a percentage of GNP) surpass those in the United States.

Until the 1970s, the innovations of Japanese firms depended chiefly upon foreign technology, and their R&D expenditures were not large. Thereafter, the level of R&D funding rose rapidly. Part of this increase was due to rising private Japanese R&D expenditures in growing industries—such as electronics, data processing, and telecommunications. Firms belonging to the mature steel, nonferrous, and chemical industries have also now begun to match the R&D activities of those growing industries.

The technological efforts of Japanese firms are not merely imitative but are innovative as well. They are innovative enough to manufacture products of good quality and supply them to the market at a low price. They have heavily committed R&D resources in growth industries and have accelerated the commercialization of new products as well as the application of new production methods—even though they may not have conducted the basic research.

In contrast, U.S. firms have, in recent years, been losing international competitiveness in the commercialization of new products. In fact, their R&D expenditures have been static. The number of patent applications filed by U.S. firms has shown little increase, as compared to the sharply rising number of patent applications submitted by Japanese firms.

The purpose of this chapter is to explain the different patterns of R&D expenditures evidenced by U.S. and Japanese firms. I shall consider comparative modes of innovation and levels of competitiveness in the R&D efforts of both countries. First, I will describe the distinctive patterns of U.S. and Japanese corporate R&D expenditures and technology policies. Japanese technological efforts are distinctive in the market-oriented nature of R&D, initial dependence on imported technology, engineering-driven innovations, and job rotation of R&D personnel. Next I discuss a theoretical model to explain how corporate R&D expenditures can exceed the socially optimal level and result in a low fraction of basic research in total R&D outlays. Finally, I comment on the desirability of policies to accelerate private R&D expenditures on the commercialization of new products in the United States and to increase basic R&D funding by the private sector in Japan, and the implications of R&D expenditures for the industrial adjustment process.

**Figure 12.1**
**The ratio of R&D expenditures to net sales, 1970–1986:**
**Japan and the United States**

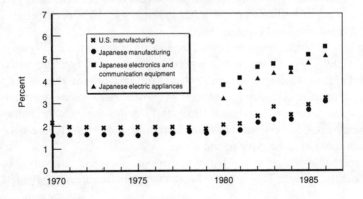

## SOME CHARACTERISTICS OF U.S. AND JAPANESE R&D

### Market-Oriented R&D

According to the 1988 *White Paper on Science and Technology in Japan,* the ratio of total R&D expenditures to national income stood at 3.49 percent in Japan—almost the same as the ratio in the United States, 3.16 percent. But as Figure 12.2 shows, recent rates of increase in total R&D funding in Japan are far higher than those in the United States. During the period 1980–85, total R&D increased by 50 percent in Japan and by 30 percent in the United States.

More than 70 percent of total Japanese R&D expenditures are made by private firms, a figure that distinguishes Japanese R&D activities from those of the United States. Table 12.1 shows the comparative composition of R&D funds by industry and government. In 1986, 76 percent of total R&D funds in Japan came from industry and only 19.4 percent from the government; in the United States, the industry portion was 51.3 percent and the government portion 46.6 percent. The large share of industry in R&D funds indicates that Japanese R&D activity is oriented toward profitability in the market.

Table 12.2 classifies industrial R&D expenditures according to the sources of the funds. In 1986, U.S. industries spent $83.6 billion on R&D; $54.6 billion of this amount came from industry itself (that is, 65.3 percent) and $29 billion from the government (34.7 percent). In the United States, then, a significant portion of government R&D funds is allocated to industry. In contrast, in Japan, $37.5 billion, or 97.9 percent of total industrial R&D, was funded by industry. The share funded by the government was only $689 million, about 1.8 percent of total industrial R&D. Thus, it appears that

**Table 12.1**
**Sources of R&D expenditures in the United States and Japan**
(Percent)

|  | United States | | | Japan | | |
|---|---|---|---|---|---|---|
| Source | 1970 | 1980 | 1986 | 1970 | 1980 | 1986 |
| Industry | 57.0 | 49.4 | 51.3 | 74.7 | 74.1 | 76.0 |
| Government | 40.0 | 47.1 | 46.6 | 25.2 | 25.8 | 19.4 |
| Universities | 1.8 | 2.1 | 2.1 | — | — | 4.6 |

*Sources:* Japan: Management and Coordination Agency, *Report on the Survey of Research and Development in Japan,* various years; United States: National Science Foundation, *National Patterns of Science and Technology Resources,* various years.

**Table 12.2**
**Sources of U.S. and Japanese funds devoted**
**to industrial R&D, 1986**
(Millions of U.S. dollars)

|  | United States | | Japan | |
|---|---|---|---|---|
| Total expenditures | 83,562 | | 38,312 | |
| Own funds | 54,574 | (65.3%) | 37,497 | (97.9%) |
| From government | 28,988 | (34.7%) | 689 | ( 1.8%) |
| From others | — | — | 126 | ( 0.3%) |

*Sources:* Japan: Management and Coordination Agency, *Report on the Survey of Research and Development in Japan, 1987*; United States: National Science Foundation, *National Patterns of Science and Technology Resources.*

Japanese industrial R&D is determined mainly by market profitability, while U.S. industrial R&D is strongly shaped by government policy.

The composition of government R&D expenditures in Japan differs markedly from that of the U.S. government. As Table 12.3 shows, U.S. government R&D is strongly biased toward defense-related projects, while Japanese government R&D is biased toward nondefense projects, such as education, general science, and technology advancement. In the United States, 62.4 percent of government R&D expenditure is earmarked for the Department of Defense, 7.3 percent for the National Aeronautics and Space Administration, 12.1 percent for the Department of Health and Human Services, 9.1 percent for the Department of Energy, and 2.8 percent for the National Science Foundation. In contrast, only 4.8 percent of Japanese government R&D expenditure is for defense purposes. Some 47.6 percent is for education, 25.3 percent for the advancement of general science and technology, and 13 percent for industrial technology. Thus, unlike the United States, government R&D expenditures in Japan have not been designed to accomplish specific technology goals, but to provide a productive atmosphere for R&D activities.

**Dependence on Imported Technology in Japan**

Postwar Japan's major forward push in technological innovation came from imported technology. Japanese firms have been very successful in borrowing and developing technologies created initially by foreign firms. Table 12.4 shows the ratio of payments for imported technology to industrial R&D expenditures in Japan for selected years. During the period 1960–65, an era of high economic growth, this ratio reached more than 15 percent. Japanese firms rushed to import advanced technologies in the steel, chemical, petrochemical, synthetic fiber,

**Figure 12.2**
**Increase in R&D expenditures, 1965–1985:**
**United States, Europe, and Japan (1980=100)**

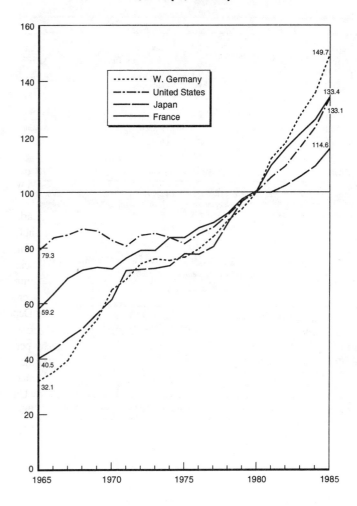

### Table 12.3
### Government R&D expenditures by department, 1988
(Percent)

| United States | | Japan | |
|---|---|---|---|
| Defense | 62.4 | Education | 47.6 |
| Health and Human Services | 12.1 | Science and Technology | 25.3 |
| Energy | 9.1 | Industry | 13.0 |
| National Aeronautics and Space Administration | 7.3 | Defense | 4.8 |
| National Science Foundation | 2.8 | Agriculture | 3.9 |
| Agriculture | 1.8 | Health | 2.6 |
| Commerce | 0.7 | Others | 2.8 |
| Others | 3.8 | | |
| Total | 100.0 | Total | 100.0 |

*Sources:* Japan: Science and Technology Agency, *White Paper on Science and Technology in Japan*, 1989; United States: National Science Foundation, *National Patterns of Science and Technology Resources,* various years.

### Table 12.4
### Imported technology and industrial R&D expenditures
### in Japan, selected years
(Billions of yen)

| Year | R&D Expenditure (a) | Payment for Imported Technology (b) | Percent (b) / (a) |
|---|---|---|---|
| 1971 | 895 | 135 | 15.08 |
| 1975 | 1,685 | 169 | 10.03 |
| 1980 | 3,142 | 240 | 7.64 |
| 1985 | 5,940 | 293 | 4.93 |

*Sources:* Japan: Science and Technology Agency, *White Paper of Science and Technology in Japan*; United States: National Science Foundation, *National Patterns of Science and Technology Resources.*

machinery, and electric machinery industries from U.S. and European firms. In doing so, they made incremental improvements to the foreign technologies to fit their production methods. Their R&D expenditures, then, were used to make incremental innovations upon a base of foreign technology.

Japanese firms imported this technology with a clear corporate strategy in mind. They wanted to shorten the time needed to catch up to the advanced technological level of U.S. and European firms and to compete with foreign rivals in the international market. To accomplish this, they examined thoroughly the content of foreign technologies before importing and adapting them to their own production system and capital-labor endowments.

However, it should be noted that Japan had established its own technological base before World War II. The use of imported technology accelerated the development of this technological base. The rapid decline in the proportion of imported technology in the 1970s and 1980s reflects a shift from heavy reliance on imported technology to the adoption of indigenous methods. In 1985, the use of imported technology fell below 5 percent of R&D expenditures. In the high-technology area, however, Japanese industries continued to import advanced knowledge from U.S. and European firms.

## Engineering Innovation

Technological development in Japanese firms is characterized by a close coordination of product design, manufacturing, marketing, and sales functions. A close connection between the R&D division, production, and marketing departments in Japanese firms has facilitated the small steps that are crucial to the technology development process. Like other divisions in the same company, the R&D division is more or less integrated into the overall corporate structure, which targets a single goal. As such, R&D divisions in Japanese firms seek not only to maximize divisional profits derived from fees on patent use and know-how, but also to maximize earnings and sales of the products of the firm as a whole by closely coordinating their activities with those of other corporate divisions. The R&D division is also expected to develop new technologies and products—not always independently, but frequently through exchanges of information with other divisions.

In contrast, firms in the United States are likely to compartmentalize the research and manufacturing functions. Many times, this has led to breakdowns in the development process, marked by finger pointing, where functionally specialized groups within the firm assign blame to each other or to external suppliers. Such breakdowns can leave competitors with easy opportunities to improve performance or reduce costs. Rosenberg and Steinmueller (1988) assert that although the United States pioneered both the scientific and the technological frontiers, Japanese firms have succeeded in applying technological improvements to the design of mass-produced goods. Products requiring a smooth coordination of different technologies (for example, electrical, electronic, and mechanical devices, such as plain-paper copiers, facsimile machines, floppy disk drives, and personal computer printers) are strongholds of Japanese commercial success. Thus, Japanese success in development has often more than matched America's innovative capabilities.

Japanese firms also make more systematic use of engineering skills and production worker experience throughout the development activities associated with introducing new products—including detailed aspects of the eventual manufacturing process. A study by Mansfield (1988) indicates that R&D specialists usually determine research themes in U.S. firms, whereas production and marketing divisions play this role in Japanese firms. Japanese firms base about one-third of their R&D projects on suggestions from their production personnel and from customers, U.S. firms only about one-sixth. The greater importance of production personnel as sources of R&D projects in Japan reflects a stronger emphasis on process technology. The larger R&D role of customers in Japan stems from the close relationship between firms and their customers. Production personnel and customers therefore tend to be both shapers and users of a Japanese firm's R&D results.

United States firms base a larger percentage of their R&D projects on suggestions from R&D personnel than do Japanese firms. One explanation for this is the greater proportion of U.S. R&D personnel that have advanced degrees in natural sciences rather than in engineering. Table 12.5 gives the number of bachelor, master, and Ph.D. degrees granted in the natural sciences and in engineering in the United States and Japan in selected years. In the United States, the number of researchers holding a Ph.D. in science is larger than that in engineering; in Japan the reverse is true. Furthermore, in Japan, a larger number of persons holding bachelor and master of science degrees in engineering enter firms than do persons with comparable degrees in science. As engineers, they play an important role in process innovation and quality improvement of products. These differences in technical orientation suggest that Japanese firms are better able to implement suggestions from users, while U.S. firms capitalize on opportunities arising from the research laboratory.

**Table 12.5**
**Research personnel in the United States and Japan**

|  | Year | Natural Sciences | | | Engineering | | |
|---|---|---|---|---|---|---|---|
|  |  | B.S. | M.S. | Ph.D. | B.S. | M.S. | Ph.D. |
| Japan | 1977 | 10,234 | 1,663 | 717 | 69,221 | 6,925 | 1,079 |
|  | 1984 | 12,698 | 2,006 | 774 | 71,396 | 8,290 | 1,290 |
| U.S. | 1975 | 88,990 | 17,560 | 8,040 | 53,520 | 18,400 | 3,130 |
|  | 1980 | 78,246 | 13,829 | 7,587 | 90,121 | 20,927 | 2,813 |

Sources: Japan: Ministry of Education, *International Comparison in Indices of Education*, various years; United States: National Science Foundation, *National Patterns of Science and Technology Resources*.

Finally, R&D personnel in Japan experience a wide range of job-rotation. They do not necessarily stay in the research laboratory throughout their careers, but enter production or marketing groups after a stint in the R&D division. This system of job-rotation further facilitates close relations between the research and production functions of Japanese firms.

## Allocation of R&D Funds

The composition of Japanese and American industrial R&D differ in several significant ways. Whereas American firms report that almost half of their R&D expenditures are going for projects aimed at entirely new products and processes, Japanese firms report that only about one-third of their R&D expenditures go for that purpose. Even more striking is the difference between Japanese and American firms in their allocation of R&D resources between projects aimed at improved product technology and projects aimed at improved process technology. United States firms put about two-thirds of their R&D expenditures into improved product technology and about one-third into improved process technology. Among Japanese firms, the proportions are reversed.

In Japanese firms, the strategic goals of the production and marketing divisions are strongly reflected in the allocation of research funds. According to Wakasugi (1990), in many Japanese firms, research funds are classified into three categories: (1) expenditures "for the R&D division," (2) "current expenses for development of products" for each manufacturing division, and (3) "research expenses for overall corporate product development based on long-term strategic policy." Research expenditures under the sole control of the R&D division are not very high, amounting to less than half of the aggregate R&D budget. Distribution of the rest of the research funds is strongly influenced by the objectives of the manufacturing divisions and headquarters management.

Under this kind of allocation system, the research division will attempt to maximize the funds assigned to it. Funds allocated to the research division in the future will be increased if it can prove that the R&D division contributes to the activities of other corporate divisions by generating efficient production methods or by creating products of higher quality that attract more buyers. In such an environment, more funds tend to be allocated for research and development with clear and substantive goals, such as applied research or product development. Funding for basic research, which is likely to produce results only over long periods of time, is given lower priority.

## Career Path of Researchers and Innovation

As noted above, a job-rotation scheme for R&D personnel exists in many Japanese firms. According to Wakasugi (1990), the first stage of the career path is an educational period, which begins after the recruit joins the firm and lasts until he reaches his late twenties. He provides support for R&D activities during this stage. In the next stage, in his early thirties, he becomes a full-fledged engineer. In the third stage, at the age of 35 to 40, he becomes a manager at the front line in the research division, perhaps a project leader or a section chief. Next, he leaves the forefront of R&D activities and joins general management. After completing the fourth stage, he is assigned to the division that manages R&D activities, but is often posted to sections that manage production, products, sales activities, or marketing. However, staying a long time in the research division does not necessarily mean promotion. To reward an excellent engineer, Japanese firms often assign him to the manufacturing, planning, or marketing division before promoting him to a higher post.

In U.S. and European firms, a researcher can choose from two career paths: one that leads to a lifetime engagement in R&D activities, or one that enables him to join the management or other divisions in mid-career. It is rare to see the first option in Japanese firms.

The Japanese version of the career path enables the R&D division to maintain close relationships with other business divisions of the firm. This has increased efficiency in the field of applied research and product development; also, it has led to active innovations in these fields. Japanese R&D personnel are channeled into a career path characterized by a spiral ladder. Such a system facilitates information exchange between the R&D division and the manufacturing and marketing divisions, strengthening cooperation among divisions and improving the ability to solve problems.

## EXCESSIVE R&D EXPENDITURES

On the basis of the model and the argument presented by Barzel (1968), I discuss here excessive spending on applied research and development in Japan. Let us assume that I is the cost of R&D required to complete an innovation. The duration of the R&D effort is determined by the rate of R&D spending. The faster the firm wants to finish the job, the earlier it spends. I also assume that the profit from R&D is acquired exclusively by the innovator, and that the size of the profit at time t ($S_t$) is proportional to the quantity of output supplied to the market. It is denoted by a percentage of total sales, $kQ_t$. The quantity of output ($Q_t$) increases over time at the rate p. These relationships are described by Eqs. (1) and (2):

$$Q_t = Q_0 e^{pt} \qquad (1)$$

$$S_t = k \cdot Q_t \qquad (2)$$

If an innovation is realized at time t, then the present value of net profit of the innovation, R, which is defined as total profit less the cost of R&D, evaluated at a constant discount rate r, is presented by Eq. (3):

$$R = \int_{t=0}^{t} S_t \cdot e^{-rt} \, dt - I \cdot e^{-rt} \qquad (3)$$

$$= \int_{t=0}^{t} S_0 \cdot e^{-(r-p)t} \, dt - I \cdot e^{-rt}$$

$$= [S_0 \cdot e^{-(r-p)t}]/(r-p) - I \cdot e^{-rt}, \text{ where } S_0 = k \cdot Q_0 \cdot e^{pt}$$

If the discount rate r is smaller than the rate of increase in market demand, the net profit of the innovator will become infinite. It will be restricted to the value R in Eq. (4) if the discount rate is larger than the rate of increase in demand:

$$R = [S_0 \cdot e^{-(r-p)t}]/(r-p) - I \cdot e^{-rt} \qquad (4)$$

As Figure 12.3 shows, the larger the present value of R&D expenditure, the earlier the innovation is completed.

The optimal time (tm) to accomplish the innovation satisfies dR/dt = 0, which is obtained by differentiating the net profit (R) with respect to time (t). Thus,

$$S_0 \cdot e^{-(r-p)t} = r \cdot I \cdot e^{-rt} \qquad (5)$$

$$t_m = (\ln I + \ln r - \ln S_0) / p \qquad (6)$$

The optimal timing is denoted as $t_m$ in Figure 12.3. From Eq. (5), the net profit (R) of the innovator is given by

$$[r / (r - p) - 1] \cdot I \cdot e^{-rt}$$

which is positive. Three propositions can be derived from this model, as follows.

*Proposition I.* The more competitive the R&D race among firms, the earlier the firm will spend R&D funds, if the profit from an innovation is acquired solely by the first innovator.

It is not guaranteed that the firm determines the timing of R&D expenditure so as to equate the marginal cost of innovation to the marginal profit of innovation. Firms will continue to enter the R&D race to acquire a monopolistic profit on innovation as long as a positive profit exists. As a result, R&D expenditures will exceed the socially optimal level because one firm will complete the innovation earlier than the other firms by spending R&D funds earlier than the others. Firms stop R&D expenditures if the profit of innovation completely disappears. That is, the timing of innovation is accelerated by R&D competition up to the point where net profit becomes zero. This timing $t_c$ satisfies Eq. (7):

$$[S_0 / (r - p)] \cdot e^{-(r-p)t} = I \cdot e^{-rt} \qquad (7)$$

Thus,

$$[r / (r - p)] \cdot S_0 \cdot e^{-(r-p)t} = r \cdot I \cdot e^{-rt} \qquad (7')$$

The timing $t_c$ is denoted by Eq. (8):

$$t_c = [\ln I + \ln (r - p) - \ln S_0] / p \qquad (8)$$

In this case, the profit of the innovator goes to zero. As Figure 12.3 indicates, $t_c$ occurs earlier than $t_m$. Firms tend to spend R&D funds earlier, thus reducing their profit.

The appropriability of innovation is high if it is protected by patent rights, or if it is firm-specific and difficult to imitate. Greater appropriability accelerates the R&D competition among firms because they can exclude their rivals from the profits of innovation. The characteristics of the innovation are important in determining the nature of the competition. Applied research and commercial development tend to encourage vigorous competition for profits, and thus, to cause R&D expenditures to exceed the socially desirable level.

*Proposition II.* The timing of R&D expenditures will be delayed, and the present value of such expenditures will be lower, if the innovative result obtained from R&D is less appropriable.

Let us assume that R&D expenditures result in a constant profit to the innovator, given by Eq. (2). The timing of expenditures—$t_m$ in Eq. (6), or $t_c$ in Eq. (8)—depends upon the value of k, which determines the profitability of the innovation. If the value of k becomes small, the profit $S_0$ is reduced to $S_0'$, shifting the curve

$$S_0 \cdot e^{-(r-p)t}$$

downward in Figure 12.3.

Generally, the results of basic research are less appropriable than those of applied research or development. The timing of expenditure on basic research tends to be delayed, compared with the timing of applied research and development.

*Proposition III.* Government support to applied research and development among private firms tends to speed up their R&D expenditures. The cost of R&D (I) will be reduced if the government subsidizes private firms. In Figure 12.3, the curve $r \cdot I \cdot e^{-rt}$ shifts downward to $r \cdot I' \cdot e^{-rt}$. In consequence, the timing of R&D expenditures—$t_m$ in Eq. (6) or $t_c$ in Eq. (8)—

**Figure 12.3**
**Timing of innovation and R&D expenditure**

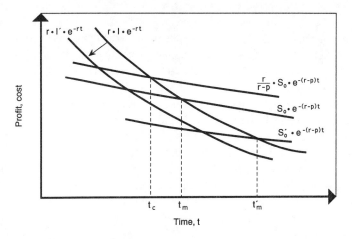

SOURCE: Bargel (1968).

will be accelerated. Government support to applied research or development among private firms shortens the delay in R&D spending; however, the delay may be excessively shortened if the result of the applied research or development is highly appropriable.

These three propositions suggest that the appropriability of innovation determines the level of private R&D expenditures. Above, I noted that a large part of defense-related U.S. government R&D funding has been given to private firms. Usually the results of defense-related R&D are not highly appropriable. Even the purely private R&D projects of U.S. firms are less appropriable than those of Japanese firms. The difference in appropriability of innovations in the two countries leads to the vigorous R&D expenditure of Japanese firms, on the one hand, and the static R&D expenditures of U.S. firms, on the other.

## POLICY PERSPECTIVE

The fact that the U.S. government provides private firms with significant amounts of R&D funds indicates that the government controls much of the allocation of R&D resources in the private sector. Private firms in the United States lose their independence in determining R&D strategies. They allocate a larger portion of R&D funds to basic research than Japanese firms do, for government funds are ordinarily allocated to basic research rather than to commercial R&D.

In contrast, the Japanese government provides private firms with only modest R&D funds. But Japanese firms have been able to maintain their independence in determining R&D strategies, which have been sensitive to profitability in the market. They have focused a large share of R&D resources on applied research and commercial development because the results are highly appropriable. Japanese R&D, in sum, is biased toward applied or commercial research.

Differences in the pattern of R&D expenditures between the two countries are due to both the distorted allocation of R&D funds stemming from vigorous competition and to government policy. This suggests that policy instruments in the United States should be directed toward encouraging applied research or development; to accomplish this policy goal, tax deductions on R&D expenditures would be desirable, rather than specific subsidies to, or a government contract with, private firms. In Japan, more government funds to basic R&D projects in the private sector, or more research contracts with private firms, are required if firms are to increase spending on basic research. In short, the direction of current technology policy in both countries should be reversed.

## CONCLUDING REMARKS

Japanese industrial R&D changed sharply after the second oil crisis. Japanese firms diversified their products and improved their production methods to respond quickly to the high-priced energy economy. They shifted their product composition from energy-intensive industries, such as steel and chemicals, to energy-saving industries. In the 1980s, Japanese firms increased their R&D expenditures in the electronics and communication equipment industries—now leading industries in the Japanese economy.

According to the *Report on the Survey of Research and Development in Japan* (1987), the industrial R&D expenditures in Japan have been concentrated in the electronics and telecommunication equipment industries since the 1980s. The rate of increase in the R&D expenditures of these industries was 23.3 percent from 1980 to 1985—10 percentage points higher than the average rate of increase in total industrial R&D expenditures. The R&D strategy of Japanese firms responded more sensitively to market signals than that of U.S. firms. From 1979 to 1984, the Japanese increased their R&D expenditures in the electronics industry by 135 percent, the United States by only 10 percent. More striking is the fact that not only the communication and electronics equipment industries but also the electric equipment, instrument, machinery, and related industries are devoting R&D funds to work on communication and electronics equipment.

A variety of industries are spending R&D funds in the high-technology area, leading to greater complexity in industrial R&D. Table 12.6 displays the sources and destinations of R&D funds for electronics and communication equipment from various industries in 1985. It shows that a large portion of R&D expenditures in the electronics and telecommunication fields derives from firms belonging to other industries. More than 40 percent of R&D expenditures in the electronics and telecommunication equipment industry comes from new entrants. The technological frontier in Japanese industry is thus becoming a fusion of complex technologies, and the goal of these industries is the diversification of their product ranges.

Corporate restructuring to enter new growth industries was accomplished more smoothly in Japan than in any other country, facilitated by the sensitive response of R&D to market signals. The vigorous R&D expenditure of Japanese firms was due to the severe competition in commercial R&D among firms. The rate of return of Japanese private R&D expenditures is not necessarily higher than that of the United States. According to estimates by Mansfield (1980), Goto and Wakasugi (1988), and others, there is no significant difference in the rate of return between the two countries. Japan-

### Table 12.6
### Diversification of R&D expenditures in Japan, 1985
(Billions of yen)

| Source Industry | Destination Industry | | | | | | | |
|---|---|---|---|---|---|---|---|---|
| | (A) | (B) | (C) | (D) | (E) | (F) | (G) | (H) |
| (A) | 302 | — | — | — | — | — | — | 21 |
| (B) | — | 158 | 22 | — | 6 | 2 | 1 | 51 |
| (C) | — | 2 | 222 | 9 | 30 | 17 | 19 | 34 |
| (D) | — | — | 32 | 196 | 272 | 64 | 12 | 14 |
| (E) | — | — | 52 | 420 | 794 | 1 | 9 | 9 |
| (F) | — | — | 14 | 2 | 1 | 728 | 1 | 39 |
| (G) | — | — | 23 | 17 | 25 | 4 | 96 | 15 |
| (H) | 84 | 5 | 132 | 43 | 245 | 37 | 16 | — |

(A): Drugs & medicines        (E): Communication & electronics equipment
(B): Iron & steel             (F): Motor vehicles
(C): Machinery                (G): Precision instruments
(D): Electric equipment       (H): Others

*Source*: Management and Coordination Agency, *Report on the Survey of Research and Development in Japan*, 1987.

ese firms have more actively appropriated the results of their R&D activities than U.S. firms. Japanese firms rushed early into R&D in growth areas—a major reason that Japanese private R&D expenditures are dynamically increasing and those of U.S. firms are currently static.

United States firms need to allocate more R&D resources to applied research and commercial development in order to recover international competitiveness in high-technology industries. Current U.S. technology policy is biased toward defense-related R&D, creating a distorting effect on the allocation of private R&D resources. The Japanese government, in contrast, should spend more R&D funds to remedy the distorted allocation of private R&D, which is biased to the commercial side, and to accelerate basic research.

### BIBLIOGRAPHY

Baily, M., and A. Chakrabarti (1988). *Innovation and the Productivity Crisis.* Washington D.C.: Brookings Institution.

Barzel, Y. (1968). "Optimal Timing of Innovations." *Review of Economics and Statistics,* 50, 3, 348–355.

Goto, A., and R. Wakasugi (1988). "Technology Policy," in R. Komiya, M. Okuno, and K. Suzumura (eds.), *Industrial Policy of Japan.* San Diego: Academic Press.

Mansfield, E. (1980). "Basic Research and Productivity Increase in Manufacturing." *American Economic Review,* 70, 5, 863–873.

——— (1988). "Industrial R&D in Japan and the United States: A Comparative Study." *American Economic Review,* 78, 2, pp. 223–228.

Rosenberg, N., and E. Steinmueller (1988). "Why Are Americans Such Poor Imitators?" *American Economic Review,* 78, 2, 229–234.

Spence, M. (1981). "The Learning Curve and Competition," *Bell Journal of Economics,* 12, 1, 49–70.

——— (1984). "Cost Reduction, Competition, and Industry Performance." *Econometrica,* 52, 1, 101–122.

Spencer, B., and J. Brander (1983). "International R&D Rivalry and Industrial Strategy." *Review of Economic Studies,* 50, 4, 707–722.

Wakasugi, R. (1990). "Why Are Japanese Firms So Innovative in Engineering Technology?" unpublished paper.

## V
—

**Case Studies of Troubled Industries**

# 13

## Adaptation to Change in the U.S. Machine Tool Industry

Arthur J. Alexander

### TRENDS IN THE U.S. MACHINE TOOL INDUSTRY

#### Long-Run Trends

The demand for machine tools, the quintessential investment good, is notably volatile. But for several decades following World War II, the customary cycle of boom and bust disguised a new feature of American industry: the slow, long-term decline of domestic demand. By the 1980s, the earlier gradual fall in U.S. machine tool production had accelerated toward an unprecedented and precipitous depression in orders, shipments, employment, and profits. Events in the 1980s had many of their origins in the preceding decades, but one new force arose to qualitatively change the nature of the industrial adjustment: the loss of export markets and the rapid growth of imports.

Not only are machine tools a primary input in the production process, but they are also used to produce other investment goods. As a consequence, they suffer a double effect of the classical accelerator principle. The swings in machine tool orders are magnified versions of the rises and falls of general economic demand and of industrial investment. Figure 13.1, which plots indexed values of industrial production, investment in producers' durables, and machine tool shipments, graphically depicts the volatility of the market.[1] The rate of return earned by machine tool companies as measured by the

**Figure 13.1**
**Indices of real U.S. industrial production, investment in plant and equipment, and machine tool shipments (1977 = 1.00)**

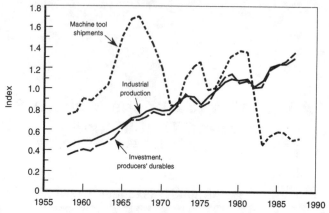

ratio of total net income before taxes of all companies to total assets of all companies averaged 10.3 percent over the 16-year period 1967–82; a measure of volatility of the average rate of return is the standard deviation of the time series, which was 6.6.[2] The machine tool industry's rate of return is highly correlated over time with a broader market portfolio; for example, the average return for all manufacturing was 10.2 percent, but its standard deviation was only 1.6.

Similarly, net income before taxes as a proportion of sales of the machine tool companies is quite like that of all manufacturing companies, but with a standard deviation about five times greater; for the period 1967 to 1982, the machine tool ratio of income to sales was 7.35 percent and 4.7 standard deviation versus 7.46 and 0.84 for all manufacturing.

The wide cyclical movements obscure longer-term trends in demand and production. As shown in Figure 13.2, U.S. machine tool consumption has fallen slowly when measured by the cycle-to-cycle peaks; the most recent cyclical high point, reached in 1980, is 8 percent lower than the 1967 peak demand, despite a 50 percent growth of industrial production.[3] As a share of total U.S. production and investment, the machine tool contribution is clearly falling. In the 1960s, machine tools were 15–20 percent of the value of total equipment expenditures; this ratio fell to 10–15 percent in the 1980s.[4] (See Figure 13.3.)

There are several explanations for the long-term decline in machine tool demand. First, machine tools are used to cut or form metal; in the past 40

## Figure 13.2
## Consumption, employment, and import share of consumption

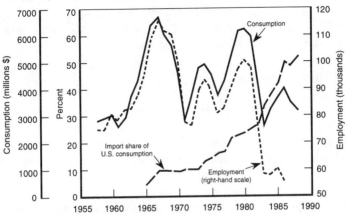

## Figure 13.3
## Ratios of consumption to manufacturing output and equipment investment

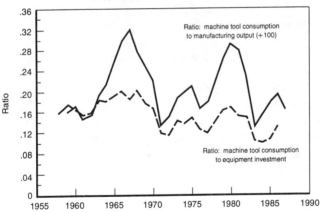

years, production processes and materials have gradually made more use of nonmetallic inputs. Second, other metal forming technologies have been developed; for example, chemical milling, electrical discharge machining, precision casting, and laser cutting now substitute for many of the production jobs formerly assigned to machine tools. Third, many products that had been heavy users of machined parts are either no longer produced in large volume or are designed with nonmetallic parts; for example, railroad equipment is in long-term decline, and electronics have replaced mechanical components in calculators and typewriters. Fourth, increased productivity of machine tools themselves has reduced the number of machines required by a user for a given level of output. Symbolic of this long-term decline is the 1988 name change of the industry association most closely linked to machine tools: the National Machine Tool Builders Association became known as NMTBA— The Association for Manufacturing Technology.

### Foreign Trade

In the past, cyclical downturns in U.S. machine tool demand were ameliorated by foreign demand, which was often out of phase with domestic market conditions. However, in the 1980s, the machine tool balance of trade turned sharply against U.S. producers. Historically, the United States had been a net exporter of machine tools. Since the 1860s, the names of U.S. companies were known worldwide for their innovative and efficient products. This export dominance began to fade in the 1970s and by 1978 had turned into a trade deficit. (The import share of U.S. consumption is shown in Figure 13.2.) Imports supplied about 10 percent of U.S. consumption from the late 1960s through the mid-1970s. This situation then changed rapidly as import penetration grew to 25 percent by 1981 and then accelerated to a 50 percent share of domestic consumption between 1981 and 1986. For lathes, drills, and machining centers, imports supplied more than two-thirds of domestic requirements.

In the mature technology sector of the market, developing industrial nations, such as Taiwan, Korea, and Spain, were able to compete effectively with low-cost production of standard machine types, often copying 1930s vintage U.S. designs. West Germany and Switzerland, together with the United States, had dominated export markets in the high-precision, advanced technology niches. In the mid-1970s, however, Japan rapidly increased its world export market share in both the high and low ends of the market and by 1984 had overtaken West Germany as the dominant machine tool exporter.

The recent Japanese penetration of the U.S. market was facilitated by several events. Two of these, an overvaluation of the U.S. dollar and the inability of the U.S. machine tool industry to meet peak demand in the 1979–81 period, were short-term occurrences that exacerbated a more serious decline in the ability of U.S. companies to meet the product competition of foreign suppliers. To buffer their production from the volatility of demand, U.S. producers typically allowed the backlog of unfilled orders to increase during boom times. As orders fell during recessions, this backlog would be worked off. During times of peak demand, customers would often have to wait two or three years for delivery of their machines. However, in the 1979–81 period, Japanese machine tool firms offered to provide immediate delivery to U.S. buyers. The availability of large stocks of machine tools enabled the Japanese producers to attract business away from U.S. suppliers. When demand subsequently turned down, the Japanese companies continued to produce machines, stocking the excess production in U.S. warehouses; this stock of product on the shelf allowed the Japanese companies again to provide immediate delivery when demand began to revive in 1984.

Both the U.S. and Japanese strategies are designed to even out production. In the U.S. approach, the customer pays for his volatile demand through delayed delivery. The Japanese strategy incurs the capital costs of stockpiled inventories (a portion of which will probably be passed on to buyers) as well as the risk of low demand for the stockpiled models.[5] The choice of this alternative strategy is influenced by the cost and availability of capital. A Japanese product strategy that emphasized standard models reduced the risk of low demand for out-of-date models in contrast to the U.S. marketing approach, which was oriented more toward tailored designs. A more severe challenge to the U.S. industry came from Japanese introduction of a new class of machine tools. Japanese companies introduced simplified, standardized, numerically controlled (NC) machines that did not aim at the high-performance NC niches favored by U.S. machine tool companies, but instead were directed toward the more numerous, low-tech machine shops. These NC lathes, milling machines, and machining centers[6] used standardized controls that were more reliable, less complex, easier to use, and less expensive than American products. By the mid-1980s, Japanese producers dominated the U.S. market in low-end NC machine tools. Since much of the growth in the United States was in this market segment—the rest of the market was stagnant or declining—Japanese sales appeared especially menacing to the beleaguered U.S. industry.

### Employment

As shipments of the domestic industry have fallen, employment has also declined from the peak postwar level of 125,000 reached in 1952 during the Korean War. In 1980, employment reached a high of 100,000 but then fell to a historic low of half that level only seven years later. However, an increasing share of components is being purchased from outside the machine tool industry—electronic controls being a prime example. The reported values, therefore, are an understatement of the total employment attributable directly to machine tools; this understatement appears to be growing over time. Nevertheless, in just the two years from 1981 to 1983, employment in the narrowly defined core industry fell by 40,000 people, a drop that led to political demands for action on imports.

Labor productivity has not demonstrated sustained growth over the years, a probable cause in itself for the declining competitiveness of the domestic industry. As shown in Figure 13.4, output of value added per labor-hour rose at a 2.8 percent annual rate from 1958 to 1969;[7] since then it has fallen, gradually at first and then at an accelerated pace, in the 1980s downturn in shipments. In 1986, labor productivity was below its 1958 value.

For comparison, productivity for all U.S. manufacturing is also shown in Figure 13.4. An eight-year slowdown in aggregate productivity began in 1973, but the general trend that resumed in the early 1980s was not reflected in machine tool industry figures.

Total factor productivity in machine tool production, adjusted for cyclical effects of capacity utilization, rose at a 2.39 percent annual rate from 1965 to 1973, but then fell by 0.53 percent per year from 1973 to 1979, and by an accelerated 2.26 percent rate through 1982.[8] Bailey and Chakrabarti (1988) link this productivity fall to reduced levels of innovation in the U.S. industry. From 1971 to 1977, the number of innovations in cutting machines fell to roughly half their level of the previous seven-year period. A rapid flow of innovations after 1978, however, was unable to affect productivity because of weak demand and an inability to capitalize on technological advances owing to low profitability and the intense competition of Japanese manufac-

**Figure 13.4**
**Labor productivity in the U.S. machine tool industry and in total manufacturing (1977 = 1.00)**

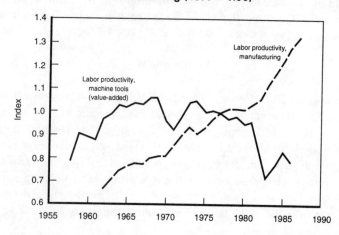

turers, whose innovation rate had been continuously higher than that in the U.S. industry.[9] Another possible reason for the decline in measured productivity is the trend toward outsourcing of key components. If these components require more skilled labor and more intensive capital inputs than the assembly and other operations retained in the final processing, then measured productivity levels will fall. However, as this process approaches long-run stability, the fall in productivity from this source should end.

## THE STRUCTURE OF THE MACHINE TOOL INDUSTRY

### Expectations from Economic Theory

The theoretical literature on declining industries is not large, but some insights flow from the few studies addressing the issue. In 1950 Joseph Schumpeter underlined the basic notion of change in a dynamic economy, in which "a process of mutation . . . incessantly revolutionizes the economic structure from within, incessantly destroying the old one, incessantly creating the new one."[10] Schumpeter noted that these changes embodied new methods of production and new forms of industrial organization, precisely the forces and processes at work in the machine tool industry today. The evolving new industry structure includes such elements as the disintegration and globalization of design, inputs, finance, and marketing; the increased role of specialized research and development as technological change from outside the industry impinges on traditional methods; the increased scale of some industrial processes such as R&D, finance, and marketing, while manufacturing itself appears to remain economic at fairly small levels of output.

Recent studies have analyzed the effects of long-run decline on industry structure.[11] One of the central conclusions of this work is that larger firms bear a disproportionate share of the burden of industry shrinkage in the absence of substantial economies of scale. Small firms and—even more— small establishments dominate the world's machine tool industry. The apparent absence of scale economies in manufacturing, therefore, leads us to expect that large firms will decline faster than small ones.[12]

A second point emerging from the analysis is that mergers of firms may be an effective method of increasing efficiency if the new firm can close some plants that are operating at low capacity and consolidate output in a smaller number of the most efficient plants. An individual firm with only a single plant cannot close it without going out of business and losing all of its past investment in product designs, marketing, technology, and human skills. The merged firm, however, can use many of these capabilities while producing more efficiently.

Recent theoretical efforts have attempted to relate observations about the changing nature of enterprise organization and management to a set of technological developments that have drastically altered the relative prices of production activities. Since many of these changes have affected the machine tool industry and its technology, this theory is especially applicable to an understanding of current developments.

Many advanced manufacturing firms have widened their product lines, shortened their product life cycles, placed greater emphasis on product quality, increased reliance on independent suppliers, and instituted a more flexible organization of work.[13] Milgrom and Roberts (1990) note that very often the shift to this new production paradigm involves "substantial and closely coordinated changes in a whole range of the firm's activities" rather than a sequence of small marginal adjustments.[14] They hypothesize that this paradigm shift is being caused by exogenous input price changes resulting from technological change, complementarities among elements of the firm's strategy, and nonconvexities arising from the indivisibilities and increasing returns associated with many of the changes and with their complementarities.

Lower relative prices are largely those arising in collecting, organizing, and communicating data, in designing and developing new products, and in managing and operating flexible manufacturing. These technological changes create multiple interactions that reinforce each other in complementary ways. The nonconvexities introduced by these changes help to explain why the successful adoption of modern manufacturing methods may not be a marginal decision.[15]

These observations are important to the story of the U.S. machine tool industry because the early diffusion of this new production paradigm largely took place in Japan, giving Japanese firms a competitive advantage in cost, quality, product development, and timely delivery over the slower moving U.S. industry.

## Industry Size

One of first things to strike one about the U.S. machine tool industry is its small size. U.S. machine tool consumption is only about two-tenths of 1 percent of manufacturing output. If the aggregate 1988 shipments of the entire industry ($2.4 billion) were attributed to a single company, its rank would be only 267 in the *Fortune* magazine list of the 500 largest U.S. companies, about the same size as Revlon. Even if we considered the 1981 peak industry sales of $5.1 billion, the industry would still only have been equal in sales to the eightieth largest company. The importance of machine tools, therefore, lies not in its absolute size but rather in its central position as a means of production and vehicle for productivity improvements for the rest of industry.

## Size of Machine Tool Establishments

The second important feature of the industry is the small size of individual firms. In 1982, more than two-thirds of all U.S. firms producing whole machine tools or components had fewer than 20 employees, and 90 percent had under 100 employees. Out of the almost 1,400 establishments, only eight had more than 1,000 employees. (See Table 13.1 for the size distribution of establishments in the United States and other countries.) These figures are not unique to either the 1982 census year or to the U.S. experience. Data on the number of establishments by size, for 30 years, indicate no tendency for a reduction in the number of small-scale establishments (see Figure 13.5). At the upper end of the size range, though, as predicted by theory, the number of large establishments of more than 1,000 employees fell after the late 1960s recession in investment goods, from a high of 25 in 1967 to a low of seven in 1986. Since 1967, this decline of the largest establishments spread to those larger than 250 employees, whereas the number of small establishments of fewer than 50 employees grew. (The intermediate range of 50 to 500 employees remained stable.) Data for other countries also show few large establishments; Germany had 20 large establishments of more than 1,000 employees, Great Britain had 5, and Japan 6.

Japan has an even larger percentage than the United States of the smaller size firms with more than 80 percent of all firms under 20 employees. In fact, in this category, the average size of the Japanese company is roughly 1.6

### Table 13.1
### Percentage distribution of establishments
### by employee-size categories

| Number of Employees | U.S. (1982) | Japan (1980) | Italy (1983) | W. Germany (1976) | U.K (1980) |
|---|---|---|---|---|---|
| 1–19 | 67.3 | 80.8 | 40.9 | — | — |
| 20–49 | 14.5 | 9.7 | 27.7 | — | — |
| 50–99 | 7.9 | 4.2 | 20.0[a] | — | — |
| 1–99 | 89.7 | 94.7 | 89.4[b] | 79 | — |
| 100–1,000 | 9.7 | 5.0 | 8.5[c] | 19 | — |
| > 1,000 | 1.8 | 0.3 | 2.1[d] | 2 | 1.7 |
| Number of establishments > 1,000 | 8 | 6 | 9[e] | 20 | 5 |

[a]Size range 50–150. [b]Size range 0–150. [c]Size range 150–500.
[d]Size range > 500. [e]More than 500 employees.
*Source:* USITC Publication 1428, 1983.

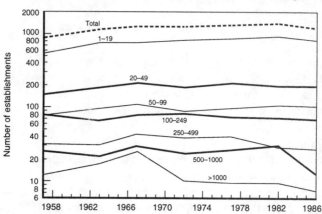

**Figure 13.5**
**Machine tool establishments by employee-size categories**

people—the prototypical Japanese machine tool company is an owner-operator of a numerical control machine tool and one helper supplying parts and components to a major machine tool company. In contrast, the average size of a U.S. firm in this smallest size category is six employees.

The largest establishments in the United States with more than 1,000 employees account for approximately 23 percent of the total industry work force. Comparable data on employment are lacking for Japan, but 37 percent of all shipments originate in the large companies.

### Economies of Scale

Because of the persistence and widespread nature of the small size of machine tool establishments, one can infer that economies of scale for organizations greater than 1,000 employees are absent. For example, a Japanese-owned machine tool plant in North Carolina was described as highly efficient and equipped with the latest production machinery from around the world but staffed with only 150 "easily managed" employees.[16] A British survey of machine tool firms concluded that the most successful of the surveyed companies regarded 500 employees as being "the maximum tolerable establishment size."[17] Another British study examined scale economies arising from several sources: (1) increased batch size of a given model of machine tool; (2) increased total annual production of a particular model; (3) increased firm size resulting from higher production of a fixed, narrow range of products; and (4) increased firm size from extending the range of products.[18] Pratten found scale effects that varied from a 22 percent reduction in costs for a doubling of output at small batch sizes and annual quantities (5 to 50 units) down to 8 percent at high volumes (100 to 800 units). Analysis of factory-wide cost reductions found modest scale effects that declined with increased output; costs fell by 9 percent as total quantity increased from 800 to 1,500 units, and by a further 6 percent and 5 percent for subsequent doublings of output to 300 and 600 units. Firm-wide effects from extending the range of products were harder to document; indeed, many of the surveyed firms identified disadvantages to broader scope. Several managers claimed that factories of 200–300 employees were the optimum size. Pratten concluded that "economies attributable to larger factories appear to be small in relation to other factors affecting performance."[19]

Despite this evidence, a British government policy in the 1960s encouraged mergers and the creation of larger units. To further this policy, the government supplied some £45 million to enable the Alfred Herbert Company to consolidate with several smaller companies; the Herbert group grew from 6,000 employees to a peak of 15,000 in the late 1960s, accounting for close to one-fifth of British machine tool output. Within a few years, however, the group was on the verge of liquidation and several subsidiaries had gone into receivership. A critical analysis of British government policy noted that no evidence had been put forth that *plants* of the size contemplated by government (and actually implemented by industry with official encouragement) were required for success in the industry. Moreover, no case was established for the advantage of large-scale *firms,* with benefits arising from consolidating several establishments under a single management umbrella.[20]

Diseconomies to an establishment of a particular size should show up in the gradual diminution of the number of firms in that size group or in a decline in their aggregate share of business or employment. As mentioned above, Figure 13.5, which plots the number of establishments in each size category over a period of 30 years, shows increases in the smallest categories and a sharp decline in the largest. If one considers the distribution of industry employment shown in Figure 13.6, a similar picture emerges. The share of employment of the establishments under 100 employees increases by about 5 percentage points, whereas the share of the largest establishments of more than 500 employees falls precipitously, by almost 30 percentage points from 1967 to 1986.[21]

### Mergers and Acquisitions

Consolidation through mergers, acquisitions, and the purchase of assets is a means for altering the structure of the industry. If scale economies were important, the incentive to engage in such activities would be especially powerful in industry downturns, when inefficiencies would be most harmful. Data on mergers, acquisitions, and purchases of assets were collected by the U.S. International Trade Commission for transactions involving machine tool builders. These data are reproduced in Table 13.2, together with the total number of mergers and acquisitions transactions for the United States as reported in *Mergers and Acquisitions* magazine.

Machine tool transactions were around ten per year, except for 1980, when 18 transactions occurred. The ratio of machine tool transactions to the total number varied within the range of .004 to .006, except for 1980, when it rose to .0115. The 1980 surge in acquisitions was probably related to profits, which were at a 20-year peak. Mergers and acquisitions at that time were undoubtedly motivated more by the attraction of the cash flow than by the possibility of improving operational economies. General merger activity throughout the economy increased by more than 50 percent in the next few years, but consolidations in the machine tool industry fell back to the earlier figures of about ten per year as industry profits sank with the level of sales.

My own attempt to gather acquisition data from the pages of *Mergers and Acquisitions* yielded similar results. Although the number of reported transactions among machine tool producers was small and spotty, there was no discernible trend; approximately three to seven transactions occurred each year with an apparently random dispersion over time.

From the late 1960s to the early 1980s, several large conglomerates acquired machine tool companies, including Litton, Ex-Cell-O Corporation, White Con-

**Figure 13.6**
**Percentage distribution of employment by**
**establishment size**

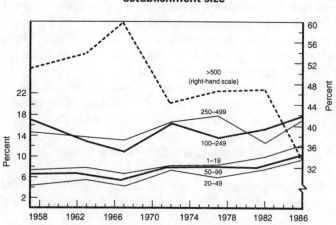

**Table 13.2**
**Mergers and acquisitions transactions in U.S.**
**industries and machine tool companies**

| Year | Total U.S. Transactions (All Industries)[a] | Machine Tool Transactions[b] | Ratio: Machine Tools in Total (%) |
|---|---|---|---|
| 1977 | 1,209 | 8 | 0.66 |
| 1978 | 1,452 | 7 | 0.48 |
| 1979 | 1,564 | 10 | 0.63 |
| 1980 | 1,565 | 18 | 1.15 |
| 1981 | 2,326 | 10 | 0.43 |
| 1982 | 2,296 | 11 | 0.48 |
| 1983 | 2,387 | 10 | 0.42 |

*Sources:*
[a]Annual totals, *Mergers and Acquisitions*, various issues, 1977–83.
[b]USITC, 1983, p. 19 (extracted from Federal Trade Commission data).

solidated Industries, Bendix, and Textron. Although their goals were mixed, there was a general belief that central engineering staffs, corporate level R&D, and centralized financing could overcome some of the perceived weaknesses faced by small companies in these nonmanufacturing functions. Within a few years, Ex-Cell-O was offering its machine tool subsidiary for sale; Textron sold its holdings of Bridgeport Machines, Jones & Lamson, and the Bryant Grinder Corp.; and Bendix sold its Warner and Swasey subsidiary just five years after having acquired it. Other conglomerates were also selling off their machine tool holdings; Litton Industries divested several of its operations, and Emhart Corp. sold 16 manufacturing units specializing in machine tools.[22]

Some of the conglomerate owners of machine tool companies have been accused of damaging the long-run viability of the industry and destroying particular companies, primarily through lack of reinvestment.[23] Textron, for example, was said to have channeled the steady stream of income from Bridgeport and Jones & Lamson to other activities in the firm rather than to new machine tool developments. Over a decade-long continuation of this policy, these two Textron divisions lacked new lines of competitive products, especially in numerical control.[24]

In the meantime, a new kind of conglomerate emerged—the machine tool holding company. An example of this is Stanwich Partners, a venture capitalist that has acquired several machine tool companies, including the holdings of White Consolidated Industries from the Swedish conglomerate Electrolux.[25] Stanwich management has stated that it could use mergers and cost-cutting measures to achieve efficiencies in an industry burdened with excess capacity. It is consolidating operations of several of its U.S. acquisitions into two plants in the United States; operations of two European acquisitions are being consolidated into a single English factory. By operating fewer plants closer to full capacity, the new owners are expecting to achieve better operating efficiency. With a larger sales base and hopes of further penetration in Europe and the Far East, the company is planning on spreading its increased R&D and engineering costs over a larger revenue base and realizing economies of scope in distribution of a broader product line.[26] So far, the new consolidated company appears to be profitable, but it remains to be seen whether rationalization within a holding company can achieve the desired effects that have so far eluded other business and government strategists.

### Disintegration of Production

Apart from the consolidation of machine tool companies, vertical disintegration is a growing phenomenon. Vertical disintegration was a dominant form of industrial organization in Japanese manufacturing; it is now increasing elsewhere.[27] Competitive alternatives to internal supply are emerging in the growth of specialized suppliers worldwide of standardized machine tool components. At first, these components used different technologies from the products of the machine tool companies; electric motors, for example, were bought from specialized companies from the first days of machine tool electrification at the turn of the century. More recently, specialist firms have supplied numerical controls, computers, and software, with these items accounting for one-third of the cost of a numerical-control machine.[28] Hydraulic control mechanisms, laser measuring devices, and electric servomotors have replaced lead screws, gear transmissions, and handwheels; the production techniques of the lead screws and other traditional components were products of the same mechanical technologies as the main structure of the machine tool, but the newer components require an expertise and production capability unlikely to be found in a machine tool company. Moreover, specialized companies in the United States even produce some of the traditional mechanical parts: for example, high precision leadways, tables, and gears.

Design changes in the machine tools that emphasize modularity have abetted specialization of component production. Through modularity and standardized families of components, machine tools virtually custom-designed for specific customers can be assembled from components available in a wide range of sizes and capabilities.

Many of the Japanese machine tool producers were among the first to grasp the nature of modularity. Their strength had earlier been in the production of standardized models, which allowed Japanese companies to gain the benefits of economies of scale; American companies tended to emphasize custom-built machines. The introduction of modular designs allowed Japanese companies to combine the advantages of scale economies and tailor-made products.[29] This disintegration and globalization process is illustrated by a Japanese machine tool company's U.S. plant installing controls on turning centers that were manufactured in a French joint venture, which uses a composite-based machine bed licensed from a Swiss concern.[30]

In interviews with U.S. companies acquired by Japanese owners, U.S. managers said that the major production change introduced by the new owners was the subcontracting of complex or specialized components. When questioned by their new owners as to why they continued to manufacture such components as gears, respondents said that their only reason was habit—they had done it that way for a hundred years.

This pattern of "outsourcing" is illustrated by the Bendix Corporation's strategic plan for its machine tool acquisitions. To meet worldwide competition, "the emphasis within the Group would be on design and assembly of superior products, with most of the technological development and manufacturing sourced from outside."[31]

Bendix's strategic view is echoed in an analysis of the implications of vertical disintegration. According to this analysis, producers of complete machine tools are likely to become more of an "R&D and assembly house," rather than a manufacturing concern.[32] With global competition, price will dominate the components business, and integrated manufacturing will probably suffer a cost disadvantage. Nevertheless, manufacturing will remain vitally important at the component level.

One measure of vertical disintegration is the ratio of value added to sales. If every firm in the industry were totally integrated, producing everything from raw materials to finished product, this ratio would be equal to one. As operations are contracted to other companies, the ratio falls; and as the sources are found in companies outside the machine tool industry, the ratio would fall even further. This ratio is plotted in Figure 13.7. From 1958 to the late 1970s, the ratio of value added to sales at the cyclical peaks was about 0.66, falling to 0.59 during industry recessions. Since the 1980s, however, both the peak and the trough values have declined, with an all-time low value of 0.52 reached in 1986—a year of partial recovery. Therefore, the data are consistent with the model of vertical disintegration within the machine tool industry.

Because vertical disintegration draws increasingly on sources outside the industry boundaries defined by the Standard Industrial Classification (SIC), a statistical view of the industry may become a distorted vision of what is actually happening. The number of reported employees, companies, establishments, and profits could easily undercount the totals and bias understanding of events, as companies in the electronics industries and other manufacturing industries become more important suppliers to machine tool producers. Beyond the machine tool industry, other types of metal forming and nonmetallic materials processing must also be taken into account for a fuller understanding of manufacturing processes.

### The Technology of Supply and Demand

Technological change was transforming the machine tool industry in the 1970s and 1980s. Numerical control (NC) and then the introduction of microprocessors in computer numerical control (CNC); computer-aided design and manufacturing (CAD-CAM); modularity in design and production; and specialization and disintegration all gradually evolved during this period. These technological changes were accompanied by the ability to produce machine tools in most of the developed and industrializing countries. The technological changes favoring flexibility in design, development, production, and marketing were reinforced by the emergence of worldwide competition; in concert, these changes led to shorter product cycles, faster and more responsive product developments, a technological capability as well as a market push for speedier order delivery, and an increased importance of R&D in nontraditional areas such as software and controls.

With these changes, standardized (but modular) NC machine tools were increasingly able to dominate market sectors that, at the low production end, were formally the realm of general-purpose machine tools and that, at the high-production end, were the home of special-purpose, high-volume manufacturing machines. The general introduction of NC and CNC brought flexibility and high rates of machine utilization, as well as a host of other benefits: for example, higher output quality, lower rejection rates, reduced inspection time, faster throughput, smaller inventories, fewer in-process parts, and less need for storage and in-plant conveyor capabilities.

To take full advantage of these changes, firms had to totally reorganize their methods of production, R&D, and management of customer orders. As more customers of the machine tool companies made these changes, their demand for flexible production machinery, fast delivery times, and high-quality inputs helped to fuel the process for change in the machine tool

**Figure 13.7**
**Ratio of value added to shipments**

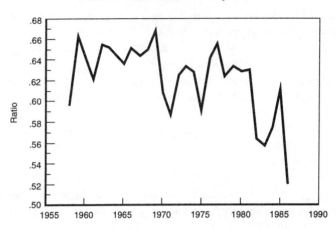

producers. Japanese companies and the Japanese machine tool industry adapted to these changing conditions a decade or more before U.S. industry.[33] Thus, by 1983, the number of NC/CNC machines was only 5 percent of the installed machine tool base in the United States, versus 30 percent in Japan. Most of these American machines were found in larger companies, with less than 20 percent in the shops of fewer than 20 employees; in Japan, over 25 percent of NC/CNC sales were to companies with under ten employees. By the 1980s, not only was the U.S. machine tool industry suffering from long-term secular decline and an overvalued dollar, but it was also caught short in product technology and management innovation.

## GOVERNMENT POLICIES AFFECTING MACHINE TOOLS

### Import-Export Policies

United States trade laws and regulations provide several avenues of relief to industries and companies suffering declines brought about by import competition. The arcane workings of the law in the foreign trade area permit relief to be sought on different grounds: Section 201 governs relief from serious injury caused by import competition; Section 301 responds to "unfair" foreign trade practices; and countervailing duties intended to deal with the dumping of goods at unfair prices may also be requested.

These laws and others are administered according to standardized procedures in open hearings where rebuttals and counterarguments are often pursued. The various statutory provisions for trade relief require a showing that the domestic industry has suffered injury caused by imports; some require that nations or foreign companies have engaged in unfair trade practices or market manipulation.

By contrast, relief under Section 232 (the National Security Clause) is mandated whenever it is shown that imports "threaten to impair the national security." It is not necessary to demonstrate unfair practices, or even that imports caused the conditions in the affected industry; the clause requires only showing that imports would impair national security, given the condition of the industry.

In addition to the above sections of the U.S. trade law, Section 103 of the Internal Revenue Code provides for suspension of the investment tax credit to buyers of articles produced in a foreign country that engages in discriminatory acts or cartel behavior.

In May 1982, Houdaille Industries, a leading machine tool producer, filed for relief under Section 103; and, in March 1983, the NMTBA submitted a petition under Section 232 on behalf of its members.

There was some speculation as to why Houdaille relied on Section 103, for, even if relief were granted, it would have affected the price of the imported products by only small amounts. One observer conjectured that Houdaille hoped to avoid the rigid standards established by the other regulatory procedures. Section 103 was an obscure clause in the tax law with little or no precedent for procedures and process; with this approach, it may have been possible to establish new precedents and standards.[34] Houdaille may also have been engaging in strategic behavior where it hoped that its petition, and perhaps others like it, would stimulate a Japanese government response to control exports through preemptive voluntary restraints.

The Office of the Special Trade Representative rejected the Houdaille petition in its entirety in April 1983. This rejection may have been due to an intervention by Japanese Prime Minister Nakasone, as asserted by the trade press at the time. Or it may have been that Houdaille could not support its case of cartel behavior, subsidies, and market manipulation. Scholarly examination of these issues has indicated that the allegations had little substance.[35]

The NMTBA Section 232 petition, however, was accepted in March 1986, only the second case to win approval under the National Security Clause. The Secretary of Commerce found that imports represented a threat to national security in 7 of the 18 product categories mentioned in the petition: machining centers, vertical and horizontal NC lathes, non-NC lathes, milling machines, and NC and non-NC punching and shearing machines. Rather than issuing unilateral presidential directives to control imports, the administration sought voluntary import restraints (Voluntary Restraint Agreements or VRAs) from the important export countries: Japan, Taiwan, Germany, and Switzerland. Japan and Taiwan formally signed VRAs to limit NC machines to their 1981 U.S. market share, and non-NC machines to their 1985 share. Germany and Switzerland refused to sign such agreements but were informed that their exports of a subset of the restricted machines must not exceed their market shares for the same years—1981 and 1985. Additionally, the VRAs specified that the product mix within categories would be maintained to prevent shifts into higher-valued product lines, a move often observed when quantitative restrictions were placed on other products.[36] These restrictions became effective on the first day of 1987.

To assess the effects of the VRAs on the American machine tool industry, Table 13.3 compares the change in U.S. import quantity, value, and price of the restricted items with imports of unrestricted items between 1986 and 1987. Apparently, the VRAs had a sharp effect as the import quantity of restricted products fell by almost 28 percent, compared with a 13 percent fall in all unrestricted goods. The same result is shown in value terms, where the restricted items fell by almost 16 percent, more than twice the decline of the unrestricted categories. An important side effect is the change in average price. For the products covered by the VRAs, prices rose an average 16.6 percent, whereas they rose only 6 percent for the unrestricted machines.[37]

For the individual product categories covered by the VRAs, both the number of imported units and the value of imports were measured in each category. Price increases tended to be highest in the NC items, and negative or low in the non-NC categories.

The VRAs had their intended effects, although perhaps at the cost of significant price increases in the restricted categories, unless importers were successful in shifting their product mix to higher-priced units, which was prohibited by the agreements.

If, in the absence of VRAs, the value of imports of restricted items had fallen at the same rate of decline of 7.3 percent as the unrestricted items, rather than the 15.8 percent decline actually observed, imports would have been roughly 8 percent higher than they actually were.[38] Domestic industry, therefore, benefited by roughly $80 million in additional shipments because

Table 13.3
Changes in imports, 1986–87, as influenced by
restrictions from voluntary trade agreements

|  | Percent Change | | |
| --- | --- | --- | --- |
| Category | Quantity | Price | Value |
| Restricted[a] | −27.8 | +16.6 | −15.8 |
| Unrestricted | −12.8 | + 6.3 | − 7.3 |

[a]Machine tools priced over $2,500.

of the VRAs, or about 3.5 percent of total shipments. This gain in sales could have generated an additional $6 million in profits, at the long-run ratio of profits to sales.[39]

The U.S. International Trade Commission (USITC) has also estimated the 1987 effects of the machine tool VRAs. According to the USITC analysis, elimination of the VRA quotas would have allowed the value of total imports to rise by $126 million, or 13.8 percent.[40] Price increases as a result of the VRA quotas were estimated at 4.4–4.9 percent. The USITC calculated the U.S. employment benefits of the quota at 658–671 workers. The major difference between the USITC estimate and my own is that they (apparently) did not take into account the decline in total imports; therefore, they would have overestimated the effects of the VRA quotas.

These falls in imports of the VRA categories could also have been caused by particularly weak demand for these particular products. However, the import *share* of U.S. consumption of the restricted categories also fell an average ten percentage points (ranging from a 1.5 percent fall for machining centers to 14.8 percent for punching and shearing machines). For all of U.S. machine tool consumption, though, imports barely changed their rate of penetration, falling a scant 0.7 percentage points from 49.4 to 48.7 percent. Therefore, the lower imports of VRA items represented a real loss of U.S. market share.

The reduced pressures from Japanese products could also have been caused by booming demand for machine tools in the domestic Japanese market. By mid-1989, home demand was said to be so great as to reduce the availability of units for export.[41] In three out of the six restricted VRA product categories, Japanese exporters filled only about 50 percent of their ceilings; all of the non-NC categories were underfilled.[42] This evidence is consistent with high Japanese demand, or over-zealous policing of quotas, or a shift to the more expensive NC machine tools.

Japan and Taiwan signed formal VRAs with the United States, whereas Germany and Switzerland were placed on notice that their imports into the United States would not be allowed to exceed certain specified limits. Import data for Japan and Germany allow us to test the effects of these two procedures. Table 13.4 shows U.S. imports from Japan for the metal-cutting sector of the market, which includes three of the restricted categories: lathes, milling machines, and machining centers (comparable data on punching and shearing machines are not provided in the NMTBA handbook). The number of units of the restricted categories shipped by Japanese producers to the United States dropped by more than 30 percent, more than twice the decline of unrestricted categories. In value terms, the decline relative to unrestricted items was even greater: a 26.5 percent fall for VRA items versus a 1.8 percent drop in other shipments. (U.S. government estimates had projected a 20.6 percent decline in value.)[43]

The German data, shown in Table 13.5, are mixed. German information is available only for lathes and punching and shearing machines. The shipment of lathes to the United States actually rose by 15.5 percent (rather than a U.S. projected increase of 13 percent), whereas punching and shearing machines fell by 7.6 percent (16 percent projected). The U.S. import value of all other German machine tools fell by about 8 percent. The evidence does not show unambiguously that the U.S. trade restriction policy affected German behavior in the absence of a formal VRA.

Despite the attempts in the VRA language to prevent exporters from working around the restrictions, experience with other kinds of ceilings and limits suggests that shifts and adaptations can be expected that will minimize the effects of the restrictions. The machine tool trade press has noted that Japanese companies have broadened their product offerings to include categories not covered by the VRA. Executives of U.S. operations of Japanese companies, for example, explicitly noted that the VRA was a main reason for their introduction of grinders and screw machines into the U.S. market.[44] Import statistics confirm that market penetration of imported grinders rose from 35 to 40 percent between 1986 and 1987. Out of 11 broad machine tool categories, the 4 restricted categories all lost U.S. market penetration share, whereas 4 of the unrestricted categories gained and the remaining 3 lost.

Another method of adapting to import restrictions has been for Japanese firms to increase production in their U.S. factories. Hitachi Seki, Mitsubishi Heavy Industries, and Yamazaki Mazak all expanded U.S. production. Total production by Japanese companies in the United States will be about 5,000 units in 1990, up about 40 percent over 1989.[45] These moves have led to a

### Table 13.4
### Percentage change of imports from Japan, 1986–1987, for categories covered by VRA

| Category | Quantity | Price | Value | Commerce Dept. Estimate of Effects on Value |
|---|---|---|---|---|
| Lathes | −28.2 | + 9.8 | −21.3 | −10.5 |
| Milling machines | −30.2 | +105.7 | +42.3 | +30.0 |
| Machining centers | −39.9 | + 9.9 | −34.0 | −28.4 |
| Restricted categories | −32.5 | + 9.0 | −26.5 | −20.6 |
| Unrestricted categories | −13.2 | + 13.6 | − 1.8 | — |

### Table 13.5
### Percentage change of imports from West Germany, 1986–1987, for categories covered by U.S. government declarations

| Category | Value | Commerce Dept. Estimate of Effects on Value |
|---|---|---|
| Lathes | +15.5 | +12.9 |
| Punching and shearing | − 7.6 | −16.4 |
| Restricted categories | + 7.1 | — |
| Unrestricted categories | − 8.1 | — |

quiet dispute between the U.S. and Japanese governments and industries as to what constitutes an import and what is "Made in the U.S.A." In early 1989, the U.S. government proposed that of the 21 major components in typical machine tools, more than 11 must be procured in the United States; the 11 components must include 10 "key" items, including numerical control and spindles.[46] The necessity for writing regulations of this specificity demonstrates the ability of companies to work around formal restrictions.

### Export Controls

United States machine tool exports were restricted by export administration regulations and foreign policy controls from about one-half of the world market outside the United States. The Soviet Union and Eastern Europe, as a bloc, imported approximately $1 billion per year since the mid-1970s, rising to $2 billion in the late 1980s. During the peak of the détente period with the USSR, the United States managed to gain 10 percent of this market. However, with the cooling of political and economic relationships, especially following the Soviet invasion of Afghanistan, U.S. sales fell to barely 1 percent of East bloc imports; in 1982, U.S. producers shipped only 12 machines, valued at $1.3 million, to the Soviet Union. During this same period in the early 1980s, Japan and Switzerland each shipped more than $100 million annually, West Germany supplied Eastern Europe and the Soviet Union with $350 million to $500 million in machine tools each year, and France's exports were three to five times the U.S. value, rising to over $100 million in selected years. The machine tool industry in the United States naturally complained of stringent controls that placed it at a competitive disadvantage, especially since the trade restrictions appeared to have little effect on the ability of the Soviet Union and its allies to import what they desired.[47]

Figure 13.8 shows the U.S. share of East bloc machine tool imports, the U.S. export share of world trade in machine tools, and the real (1982 dollars) value of shipments to the USSR and Eastern Europe. If the United States had been able to maintain the same share of East bloc trade as of global trade (around 5 percent in recent years), it could have exported over $100 million—$75 million to $80 million more than its current shipments. These lost sales represented roughly $5.5 million to $6.0 million in lost profits.[48]

## Trade Adjustment Assistance

The Trade Act of 1974 (as amended in 1981) authorized trade adjustment assistance (TAA) upon a finding and certification by the Secretary of Labor that increases in imports were a "substantial cause" of unemployment for many employees in a firm.[49] Assistance comprises cash payments as a supplement to unemployment insurance, training, job search and relocation allowances, and employment services. In 1981, benefit levels were set equal to unemployment insurance levels (roughly 50 percent of the average weekly wage); the combined duration of TAA and unemployment insurance was not to exceed 52 weeks, except for workers receiving training. From 1976 to 1980, the average annual benefits varied from $1,072 to $4,426, depending mainly on the average duration of unemployment.

In 1982, employment in the machine tool industry fell by 20,500 workers, 21 percent of the industry's total labor force. Petitions from 31 companies flowed into the Labor Department seeking assistance for 2,211 employees.[50] Of these 31 petitions, 7 were approved—covering 953 employees—8 were denied, and 2 terminated without decision. At the end of the year, 14 cases were still pending. If the pending cases were decided in the same proportions as those that actually went to decision, an additional 300 employees would have received assistance,

**Figure 13.8**
**East bloc machine tool trade—U.S. share, and share of world trade**

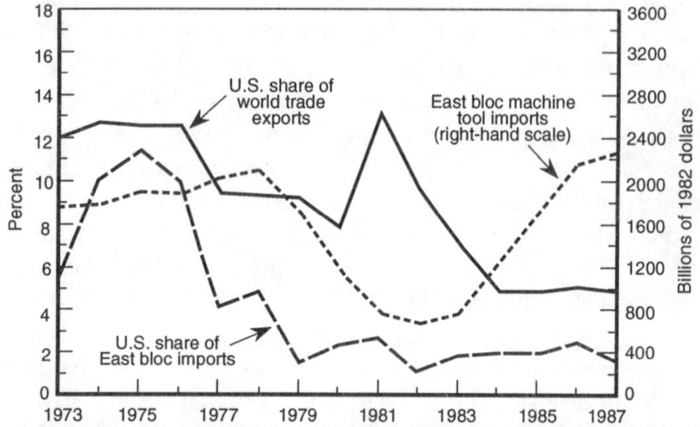

for a total of about 1,250, or about 6 percent of the total fall in machine tool employment. If each beneficiary received the highest average annual amount of assistance of the preceding five years ($4,426), then the total value of benefits would have been around $5.5 million; the actual level of benefits was most likely significantly less than $5 million.

According to these figures, TAA to machine tool employees did not substantially affect the overall welfare of unemployed machine tool workers. Although it certainly would have been welcomed by individual beneficiaries, its value seems to be more as a political bargaining chip than as a trade adjustment program.[51]

## NONTRADE-RELATED MACHINE TOOL PROGRAMS

### Department of Defense

The Department of Defense (DoD) has had a major influence on funding developments in manufacturing. Its Manufacturing Technology (ManTech) Program was responsible in the 1950s for the development and initial purchase of NC machine tools. It also promoted the development and dissemination of a standardized system of software for programming NC applications. From 1978 to 1982, annual ManTech funding levels increased from $100 million to $209 million, but then declined to $71 million in 1990.[52]

Total funding from 1978 to 1990 (unadjusted for inflation) was approximately $1.9 billion.

The U.S. Air Force has been the main actor in the ManTech Program, contributing more than 50 percent of the total funding. However, much of its effort has been aimed at areas other than the machine tool sector. In 1986, about 30 percent went to computer-integrated manufacturing, 20 percent to electronics integration and assembly, and 23 percent to improving the Air Force's own maintenance and repair activities.[53]

The effectiveness of the ManTech Program in promoting productivity has been questioned by many participants. An evaluation of the program noted that companies on the leading edge in process technology find themselves competing with government-sponsored programs supporting contractors that have chosen not to spend their own funds on production R&D. The question arises whether ManTech funds add incrementally to the field or substitute for R&D that industry would otherwise have paid for by itself.[54] Industry surveys also criticize the length of time it takes to get an idea funded, with a minimum two-year lag cited as the norm. Furthermore, industry participants suggest that the really good ideas are privately funded.

Although the ManTech Program is the largest U.S. government initiative in manufacturing processes, only a small portion of the funds go to the machine tool sector, the efficiency of the process may be low, and the funded projects themselves may not be in high-payoff areas. The major benefits noted by ManTech participants include a forum for the exchange of information free from antitrust constraints and management awareness of the importance of manufacturing investment and R&D.[55]

Other DoD programs include the Industrial Organization Incentives Program, which encourages defense contractors to invest in cost-saving technologies by sharing with contractors cost reductions brought about by innovations; the Integrated Computer Aided Manufacturing Program; the Air Force TechMod and Manufacturing Science programs; and the Navy's Precision Engineering and Industrial Modernization Incentives program. All of these DoD programs are intended to fund directly, or through various incentives to encourage, the development of more efficient, flexible, higher-capability, reliable, and less costly manufacturing processes.

A joint effort between private industry and the DoD created and financed the National Center for Manufacturing Sciences (NCMS). Organized in late 1987 as a cooperative venture of a hundred manufacturing companies (including machine tool builders, users, and suppliers), the NCMS is promoting as its first major project an effort to define and initiate development of a "next-generation controller." The DoD has committed $5 million per year for three years to the NCMS, and the Air Force is becoming involved in the controller project through its ManTech program.[56] Following great initial enthusiasm, considerable skepticism has developed in the industry over NCMS ability to achieve its goals.

The Defense Department operates two other major programs that affect the machine tool industry: the Defense Industrial Reserve and the Machine Tool Trigger Order Program. The industrial reserve is intended to cope with a mobilization of the type witnessed in the early stages of World War II and the Korean War. Many of the machine tools in the reserve were drawn largely from surplus machines produced for World War II and Korea. As a consequence, the 20,000 items in the reserve are obsolete equipment with an average age of more than 25 years. With such obsolescence occurring constantly, the rationale for maintaining such a stock has been seriously questioned.

Other mobilization investments include the system of government-owned plants, again a relic of World War II. Many of these plants no longer satisfy defense production requirements, and the government has been gradually eliminating them. Plant equipment packages are still another attempt to stock sets of necessary equipment to produce specific armaments and munitions. This program, too, is deficient in that the sets are out of date and incomplete, with an average age of more than 25 years.[57]

The Trigger Order Program allows the DoD to negotiate in advance the machine tool types and terms of sale that participating manufacturers would be expected to supply in the event of a declared national emergency. Trigger Orders, however, do not provide for the purchase of, or induce the production or improvement of, machine tools. Their main purpose is to save time negotiating contracts during a national emergency.[58]

These mobilization programs appear to have little effect on current machine tool activities and behavior. The other DoD programs that fund and encourage R&D do have lasting effects on machine tool and manufacturing technologies. In terms of adaptation to global competition, the "next-generation controller" project has the potential to greatly advance machine tool productivity throughout manufacturing, which in many applications is now limited by the speed, flexibility, and adaptability of the control systems.[59]

### National Bureau of Standards (NBS)

Since 1968, the NBS has operated a Center for Manufacturing under its National Engineering Laboratory. Much of their effort has been devoted to developing standardized interfaces permitting, for example, better communications among CAD-CAM systems. Other research on automation, control technology, and robotics evolved into the Automated Manufacturing Research Facility, a flexible manufacturing system intended to investigate precision machining and robotics and available to universities and private companies for nonproprietary research. Although this prototype computer-integrated manufacturing system was designed to support research on standards, it has been used by several companies for pioneering complex automated manufacturing systems. Cincinnati Milacron, for example, developed its hierarchical control concepts for its T-3 robot system on the NBS facility.[60]

From 1982 to 1984, NBS appropriated about $5.5 million annually on its manufacturing engineering program. Because of the unique contributions of much of its research work, the NBS funds are augmented by funds from other government agencies, including the three military services and NASA. In 1984, these additional funds added $5.3 million to the NBS appropriation.[61] This cooperation among NBS, the Navy, and equipment manufacturers led to an integrated, computerized work station at the U.S. Naval Shipyard at Mare Island, California. This operation represents the first attempt to transfer an entire system from NBS laboratories to a manufacturing environment.[62]

### National Science Foundation (NSF)

The primary manufacturing-related program of NSF is the Production Research Program. Its goals are to support research that may lead to substantially higher productivity, and to ensure a sufficient number of manufacturing engineers for universities and industry. The annual funding for the Production Research Program in the mid-1980s was about $4–5 million, which was allocated mainly for university research.[63]

### Government Laboratories

Many government laboratories, particularly in the Department of Energy (DoE), conduct research for their own agencies' use related to machine tools and manufacturing. Several laws in the 1980s attempted to make the results of research performed by government agencies more available to the public. Technology transfer programs were vigorously adopted by the Lawrence Livermore National Laboratory and other DoE laboratories. For example, Livermore has been instrumental in developing computing methods used in finite element analysis, an engineering method finding increased use in machine tool design. Although the total value of such research is unknown, it is likely at least to equal the sums spent by NBS and NSF.

## Summary

The machine tool industry has benefited from policies intended to ameliorate the declines in business related to imports, mainly VRAs and TAA. In other government programs, the DoD's ManTech is the most important and the largest of any government activity targeted explicitly at manufacturing and machine tools. The other military services also make sizable investments in manufacturing technology. The National Center for Manufacturing Sciences has declared that its controller project could cost up to $100 million over a three- to five-year period, although only initial, lower-funding levels have been authorized. Although the U.S. government contributes considerable amounts of resources to machine tools and the manufacturing sector, and is responsible for additional funds flowing to the industry through its trade policies, only a small proportion of these resources result from machine tools being defined as a declining or structurally adjusting industry. Many of the government's programs grow out of its own perceived needs as a buyer of the products ultimately produced by the products of the machine tool industry. Its other programs, those of the NSF and NBS, are intended to enhance the general productivity of the U.S. economy by funding programs with a potential for high social returns that few firms would wish to support on their own (for example, the establishment of industrial standards). However, some of the most important policies affecting the machine tool industry are not directly aimed at this target at all but act through general political and economic forces.

## NONSPECIFIC POLICIES AFFECTING THE MACHINE TOOL INDUSTRY

### Macroeconomic Policies

A rapid scan of the evidence on the cyclical nature of the machine tool business provides ample demonstration that government policies influencing macroeconomic behavior have a multiplier effect on machine tools. Similarly, the sharp decline in machine tool exports and the surge of imports in the 1980s followed from the same macroeconomic causes that created unprecedented trade deficits for the rest of the economy. The origins of most of the important government policies that affect machine tools have almost nothing to do with machine tools, or with secularly declining industries, or with the effects of trade on such industries, but with more general economic policies, political judgments, and world developments.

When I asked machine tool company officials to identify their most pressing problems, the typical responses were: "the high value of the dollar," "a weak U.S. economy," or "high interest rates." When pressed to suggest policies that would be most helpful, their common reply was to reduce the overwhelming problems facing them, rather than to initiate specific programs, such as trade adjustment assistance.

The chief economist of a nonprofit organization specializing in rescuing foundering machine tool companies placed government policies in three layers. At the top were those affecting the macroeconomic situation, such as unemployment levels and foreign trade conditions. These policies established the business climate in which the companies found themselves. At the middle level were policies specifically directed toward the industry; VRAs and TAA were examples. These were said to be helpful but ameliorative, at best. At the lowest level were the programs that a company, community, union, or management group could access directly. These programs usually involved financing: for inventory investment, employee or management buyout of a plant or company, equipment purchase to increase efficiency or to meet a potential order, or R&D to develop new models.

State governments in particular have been moving into the financial area with a variety of industrial financial boards, agencies, and public corporations. These entities were designed to fill a perceived gap in industrial financing. Massachusetts, for example, established an Economic Stabilization Trust that could make loans to troubled companies unable to secure financing from conventional sources. These state services are based on the explicit notion of a failure of financial markets to make profitable loans.

### Problems in Finance and Capital

In conversations, interviews, and reviews of the industry trade press and analytical studies, comments about insufficient financing appeared as a constant undercurrent. Adjustment to changing circumstances inevitably requires capital. High financing costs or barriers to financial sources will impede the ability of firms to adapt to competitive challenges. Understanding financial problems and their sources, therefore, is important in the responsiveness of the U.S. machine tool industry to shifting demands, new technology, and global markets. Although much of this is still conjectural, sufficient casual evidence exists to indicate the possibility of a major problem.

## Examples of Financing Problems

To demonstrate the variety of issues raised by perceptions of inadequate financing, I have drawn the following statements from a range of sources. Although these statements do not always explicitly deal with financial issues, problems of financial adequacy will be seen to lie behind them.

- When the demand for machine tools revives, it may be supplied in major part from enormous inventories of Japanese products in this country. . . . Unable to produce for inventory, U.S. manufacturers will lose increasingly more sales.[64]

*Problem: Compared with Japanese firms, U.S. firms are less able to finance inventories.*

- The industry's cycles have: (1) made a high debt-equity ratio imprudent, if not impossible, in light of the attitudes of lending institutions toward debt-service coverage during downturns in the business cycle; . . . and (3) restricted that industry's ability to expand its production rapidly in response to increases.[65]

*Problem: Cyclicality reduces financial backing.*

- The risks of investing in the machine tool business are reflected by the uncertainty of the industry's earning performance over the years. . . . Fluctuations are greater than those experienced by manufacturing industries generally. . . . Redeployment of capital within conglomerates may be prudent from the standpoint of the companies involved.[66]

*Problem: Fluctuating profits reduce financial attractiveness.*

- The Japanese may have manufactured machine tools for which there was no current demand simply to achieve production experience and the cost savings that it produces.[67]

*Problem: Japanese firms have sufficient capital to invest in cost-reducing production.*

- Historically, it has been difficult for the U.S. machine tool industry to generate capital. The cyclical nature of the industry . . . has made it difficult for machine tool producers to attract external equity or debt financing. . . . Since the majority of U.S. companies are small and privately held, few financial institutions are willing to assume the risk. Debt-to-equity ratios in the U.S. industry are typically below 50 percent.

... The ability to generate capital in foreign industries does not appear to be so burdensome. Japanese debt-to-equity ratios have been reported to range from 150 to 560 percent, ... and the risks associated with capital expansion are, in effect, assumed by the lending agency.[68]

*Problem: Small, cyclical, family-held firms in the United States cannot attract capital; this is not the case in Japan.*

- Some 80 percent of manufacturing in the U.S. is done by small shops of less than a few hundred people. They are really undercapitalized and not in any position to do any meaningful research.[69]

*Problem: Small firms cannot attract capital to perform R&D.*

- The severe swings in volume reduce the investment attractiveness of the industry and lead to undercapitalization. This, in turn, severely impedes the upgrading of facilities and introduction of new technology.... Small family-owned U.S. firms are poorly equipped to pursue international sales. Furthermore, Eximbank loan criteria focus on transactions that are much larger than typical machine tool sales.[70]

*Problem: Cyclical, small, family-owned firms are financially unattractive and cannot invest in equipment technology or foreign sales.*

- There will be more concentration in the industry because the cost of developing higher technology will be beyond the mom-and-pop operations—and the medium-size companies too.[71]

*Problem: Industry concentration (and monopolization) will increase because small firms cannot attract capital.*

- High-tech machines that Americans are capable of building have indeed been installed to a higher degree in Japan. Why? Japanese businesses can write off new investments in a short period of time with low-cost loans. Here, Gray said, we have the "the knowledge of the technique, but we don't have the wherewithal to buy it and put it in our plants."[72]

*Problem: U.S. tax rules impede investment.*

- Once in the U.S., Japanese companies expanded their presence, offering deep discounts below list prices and favorable financing terms.[73]

*Problem: Japanese firms can afford investments in low prices that will reduce profits in the short term, but gain market share at lower costs in the long term.*

- American industry is technology rich, but implementation poor. . . . One of the reasons is our costing strategy. Many companies have justification policies that require a capital investment to pay back in two years or less. . . . Justification windows should be at least five to seven years. Our foreign competition uses that time frame.[74]

  *Problem: U.S. firms require a rate of return that is very high.*

- It took little to convince LeBlond of the merger's benefits, since he had been searchi ig for some way to give family shareholders some stock liquidity. . . . In return, Japan's Makino Milling Machine Company would spend millions updating LeBlond's headquarters in Cincinnati, helping move the company into the latest technology while continuing to strengthen its lathe business.[75]

  *Problem: A family-owned firm could not raise capital.*

- In 1979 cash-rich Warner & Swasey faced an unfriendly takeover bid from AMCA International. But a white knight came to the rescue: Bendix Corporation was willing to pay $301 million, nearly twice book value. . . . And the business continued to boom. "We took out $100 million to $150 million of positive cash flow in the first 18 to 24 months after the acquisition," recalls William M. Agee, then Bendix's chairman. Smith says that this hurt Warner & Swasey's ability to respond to the market.[76]

  *Problem: A U.S. conglomerate had a short-time horizon, implying a high cost of capital.*

- U.S. firms have real difficulty in pricing competitively in overseas markets. This fact is a result of . . . the difficulty that the industry has in raising capital at a reasonable cost, and a host of other factors.[77]

  *Problem: High capital costs impede competitiveness.*

- When the Yamazaki Machinery Company in Japan installed an $18 million flexible manufacturing system, the results were truly startling: a reduction in machines from 68 to 18, in employees from 215 to 12, in production floor space from 103,000 square feet to 30,000 and in average processing time from 35 days to 1.5. However, the project's return [measured according to typical U.S. methods] was less than 10 percent per year. Since many U.S. companies use hurdle rates of 15 percent or higher and payback periods of five years or less, they would find it hard to justify this investment in new technology—despite its enormous savings in number of employees, floor space, inventory, and throughput times.[78]

*Problem: U.S. firms require high rates of return and may use inappropriate criteria.*

• When 67 Cleveland firms were asked whether they would be able to obtain finance for capital improvements, 51 percent said they would have a problem. . . . The highest percentage expecting problems represented the smallest firms. The difference among size classes was quite substantial: only 45 percent of those with more than 50 employees expected problems compared with 75 percent of small firms. Only two identified *availability* as a problem. The bulk identified the problem as excessively high payments.[79]

*Problem: The high cost of capital reduces capital improvements, especially for small firms.*

The purpose of this litany is to demonstrate the persistence and the diversity of effects that the capital and finance issue raises in the eyes of industry representatives and analysts. At this point, we cannot say whether these perceptions are accurate. These views could, on closer examination, turn out to be rationalizations for poor performance or well-rehearsed myths passed from one speaker to another.

### Hypotheses on Sources of Possible Financial Problems

Two reasons could explain the putative failure of financial markets to service the machine tool industry. The first reason is insufficient savings in the United States to channel into investments.[80] According to this argument, the cost of funds is "too high" relative to some unstated standard: a customary previous cost, the cost in other countries, the cost that would justify a desirable investment (desirable on other grounds than profitable rate of return), the cost that would prevail if some policy were changed. The second reason is that biases or imperfections exist in the capital market that affect some class of firms or investments and direct funds away from profitable investments; such biases could arise from regulatory or legal constraints on market structure or lending criteria, or from other failures in market behavior. These market failures or biases are implied to operate primarily against small firms.

According to the first hypothesis, aggregate savings rates are the culprit behind the presumed financial inadequacies. A great deal of evidence supports this view. For several decades, U.S. savings as a proportion of national income has fallen considerably below the levels of most other industrial countries, particularly those that are the most active competitors to U.S. industry. In the 1980s, the low rate of national savings was exacerbated by large and persistent government deficits and by household savings falling to unprecedentedly low levels. However, the 1980s also witnessed the rapid growth of international movements of capital, which tend to balance out the supply and demand for capital on a worldwide scale. Notwithstanding the massive transfers of capital across national boundaries, though, this market is still in the development stage and borders may still matter, especially for small firms. Although national savings insufficiency may be less of a problem in the future because of the internationalization of capital markets, past savings insufficiency may be a partial explanation for the perceptions of financial problems in the U.S. machine tool industry.

Despite the absence here of independent confirmation of capital market failures, one body of evidence is broadly consistent with the hypothesis that smaller companies in the United States suffer in comparison with large companies in financial markets. This evidence consists of the trend toward industrial concentration that has proceeded in the United States since the 1950s despite any compelling demonstration of scale economies in production. Mergers, takeovers, acquisitions, and buyouts appear to be driven largely by financial considerations, implying that a merged company is more profitable than unmerged firms. The structure of U.S. financial markets may be responsible for such a bias, especially when compared with the Japanese financial system.

### The Structure of Financial Markets

The U.S. financial system has been described as one based on capital markets that allocate resources by competitively established prices. This type of system places banks, firms, and governments in distinct and separate spheres, operating through arm's length relationships in which financial institutions will not routinely have influence inside business firms.[81]

A different kind of credit-based system has operated in Japan, although the Japanese financial system is now moving toward the U.S. model. In an abstracted model of such a system, market interrelationships are dominated by government-administered prices. Capital markets are not easily accessible to private borrowers. Firms must turn to lending institutions for the funds they need. The borderlines between government bureaucracy, finance, and borrowers blur, and banks operate in close collaboration with their borrowers. In this kind of system, bankers and firms form tight relationships with a great amount of detailed information passed to the banker for review and analysis. Debt-equity ratios that may appear forbidding to an arm's length lender could be more acceptable to a lender who participates almost as a company insider.

With the deregulation of the Japanese financial sector, however, one finds a major trend away from bank lending and toward market-oriented bond and equity financing. Although the regulated system of the past may have had many advantages, the removal of constraints has permitted firms to alter their previous behavior in a way that is apparently preferred to the old approach, and closer to the American approach to company finance.

The United States, then, has a highly developed capital market but one that many observers believe is designed to satisfy the needs of large and impersonal borrowers, about which considerable amounts of information are available to market participants. The country also has a solid venture-capital market designed to support start-up firms. But for a company of 50 employees seeking $20 million in financing to buy new production equipment or to invest in product development, the U.S. financial market may be inadequate.[82]

In Japan, the government and Diet structured capital markets to support small business through the creation of specialized banks, credit associations, and government lending agencies.[83] Because small business became the core of the postwar Liberal Democratic Party,

> successive legislative efforts created a vast array of private and government institutions committed to making loans for small-scale enterprises. In effect, the Japanese created an industrial equivalent of the American savings and loan system for the U.S. housing market. . . . This redirection of capital markets toward small firms nurtured the independent expansion of small companies.[84]

For example, mutual (*sogo*) banks and credit associations were tightly restricted to specific geographical areas. City banks were blocked from opening branches in many of these areas, leaving the small regional banks that served small local business in a favored competitive situation. The government also established several financial institutions to supply funds to the mutual banks and credit associations, and to small business directly. Thus, the Small and Medium Enterprise Finance Corporation was limited to lending to firms with fewer than three hundred employees. The Central Commercial and Industrial Bank was made the coordinating institution for credit unions and made 70 percent of its loans to small enterprises. The central government put up half its capital, and localities and other government institutions put up the rest.[85] However, as Japan ends a decade of deregulation and the internationalization of capital flows, these past advantages of small firms may be disappearing.

## Summary Issues

There are still many tantalizing analytical questions with an important bearing on policy. Is there a market failure in the United States in the capital market's behavior toward small firms? If so, does it arise from law or from other regulatory activity? Does Japanese political attention to small business correct deficiencies arising from market failure or is it a pure gift to important political backers? Does U.S. small business face inadequate financing, or does it only appear to by comparison with Japanese practice? What kind of government policies may be responsible for financial shortfalls, what may be done about them, and how would they affect the ability of U.S. machine tool producers to adapt to the contemporary situation? These questions would benefit from future research.

# FURTHER SPECULATIONS ON THE DECLINE OF THE U.S. MACHINE TOOL INDUSTRY

## The Clear and the Fuzzy Reasons for Decline

The decline of the American machine tool industry in the 1980s was undoubtedly the result of many forces well beyond the industry's control: a secular fall in the domestic demand for machine tools, an overvalued dollar, a sharp recession, and problems in capital availability. However, it must also be acknowledged that the worldwide demand for machine tools was growing; that hundreds of small companies in the United States (biotechnology firms, for example) were able to raise billions of dollars in new capital in that same, tight, high-interest decade; and that the machine tool industry had faced cyclical ups and downs for its entire 125-year history. Something else was clearly at work, and a good deal of that "something else" was Japanese.

One part of the U.S. machine tool industry's problem arose from the forces of the classic product life cycle. As products mature, they can often be produced more economically in countries with lower labor costs, even though the industrial capabilities of those countries are not equal to the capabilities of the more advanced economies. This pattern was seen in machine tools as South Korea, Taiwan, Spain, and Japan reproduced virtual copies of 1930s U.S. machine tool models and sold them cheaply around the world, competing at the lower technological end of the market.

## The Japanese Challenge

Product life cycle was only part of the story, as Japanese producers in the 1970s entered the market with cost-effective numerically controlled and computer numerically controlled machines; their earliest and most successful entry in this market was the CNC lathe. The key factor in the Japanese success was the design of lower-performance, smaller, simpler, less expensive models. The target market for these designs was primarily small and medium-sized machine shops and manufacturers, which demanded a somewhat different product from the larger firms. One measure of this difference is in the weight of the machine tool: In the 1970s, the average weight of Japanese CNC lathes was about 5 tons, whereas CNC lathes produced in West Germany were over 13 tons.[86]

The success of the Japanese companies in opening up and developing this market sector domestically, and then using this base to penetrate international markets, mirrors a broader pattern of Japanese behavior. The major force working on the Japanese machine tool companies was the fiercely competitive domestic market, which was characterized by thousands of medium and small enterprises that were simultaneously the potential customer base and the suppliers of parts and components of machine tool producers and other manufacturers. The machine tool builders concentrated on the requirements of these smaller firms, which were motivated to adopt the most productive equipment. To reduce costs, the machine tool producers emphasized standardized machines. The development of cheap, standardized control units by the Japanese electronics firms responded to the demands of the machine tool producers.[87]

The machine tool firms competed sharply among themselves because of rapid overexpansion of capacity and the entry of new companies into existing product lines. In 1975, for example, 25 companies fought for the CNC lathe market; this number expanded to 37 companies by 1983.

With the possibility of large unit sales to the small machine shops in mind, many of the machine tool firms invested in seemingly excessive plant capacity and priced their products with a view toward eventually achieving scale economies that would justify the low prices. Indeed, the five largest Japanese CNC lathe producers incurred losses from 1975 to 1978.[88] However, the production of these same five firms expanded from 275 units in 1978 to almost 2,200 by 1980, at which time the firms became quite profitable.[89]

This base of product design, production capacity, and reduced costs from both low-cost designs and high quantity of output placed the Japanese industry in a position to compete vigorously for the foreign market. In 1975, the Japanese share (by value) of the non-Japanese world market for CNC lathes was only 5.6 percent. Within five years, these companies had captured more than a third of the world market (35.7 percent). Penetration of the American market was even greater, reaching two-thirds of U.S. consumption by 1986.[90]

The reasons offered above for the success of the Japanese machine tool producers rest largely on the competitive nature of the producer and user industries, on the product designs, and on the risky expansion of capacity combined with pricing for quantity production and sales. Some other reasons have been suggested, but they often do not hold up to close inspection. The most commonly asserted explanations include Japanese government guidance and coordination, industry cartels, and government subsidies.

The Japanese Ministry of International Trade and Industry (MITI) did indeed have policies for the machine tool industry; in fact, it had had such policies since the 1930s. These policies emphasized the consolidation of firms into larger units, the allocation of machine types to established firms to gain scale economies, and the collaboration of firms within cartel-like associations to control capacity expansion. MITI also promulgated plans for exports, imports, and entry into NC markets. According to evidence on actual behavior gathered and analyzed by David Friedman, none of MITI's machinery policies was successful.

> In the period of planning and financial support, output objectives had no effect on industry performance, while government loans did not generate economic expansion. The cartelization phase did not reduce firm entry or market volatility, nor did it rationalize production. . . . NC development and export successes were not the result of government or private efforts to coordinate production and marketing abroad. Rather, they were generated by a domestic demand for new tools which producers in other countries apparently ignored. . . . In no single instance did MITI's policies lead to anticipated market outcomes. *This failure helped promote flexible manufacturing in Japan.*[91]

Government subsidies were granted mainly through loans from the Japan Development Bank (JDB), which accounted for 90 percent of all government support to the machinery industry. In the decade 1956–65—the years of most active government support—JDB loans averaged 11.5 percent of total capital investment in the machine tool industry.[92] In subsequent years, JDB loans were close to zero until 1983, when they rose to about 3–5 percent of industry investment. Interest rate savings on these loans averaged 0.8 percentage point under the prime rate.

Another alleged source of government subsidies was the "hidden" proceeds from gambling on bicycle and motorcycle racing. Estimates of the annual subsidies and grants from the source range from about $340,000[93] (mainly for the support of trade shows), to $112 million[94] (for the whole "machinery" industry), to $985 million.[95] Wolf's figure of $985 million would have amounted to about one-third of total industry sales in the early 1980s, a sum that would have been difficult to conceal. A smaller figure of $104 million, also cited by Wolf, is consistent with those of the other sources for the much broader machinery sector. Saxonhouse's figure of $340,000 is the machine tool share of the approximately $100 million going to the machinery sector. Certainly, a subsidy of close to a billion dollars would go a long way toward explaining the success of the Japanese machine tool industry. The better supported sum of $0.34 million, though, could not be a major contributor to industry performance.

## American Responsiveness

A central question regarding sources of Japanese success concerns the reasons for the American industry's failure to respond to the market opportunities of the small machine shop and to meet the Japanese challenge once that market was revealed. As in the Japanese case, numerous explanations have been offered, but these are usually little more than assertions and allegations with little research backing. Possible constraints could arise from the structure of capital markets and the cost of capital. March discusses in detail the litany of allegations explaining the collapse of the American industry, including: fragmentation and parochialism of small, family-owned firms and the insidious incentives on publicly held firms; industry cyclicality; lagging product innovation; weak user pull; competitive complacency among American manufacturers; low user sophistication; lagging producer investment; the effects of large user domination of NC developments; the failure of U.S. schools of engineering and management; short-term thinking and the structure of capital markets; and "the failure of American government policy leaders to develop a vision of, and political support for, the requirements for the long-term commercial viability of the United States, and the critical role of machine tools to that viability."[96]

These assertions, based on wide-ranging interviews, should be considered as hypotheses to be tested by the usual methods of empirical research. I suggest that some genuine puzzles confound our understanding of competitive markets, and that concepts of industry dynamism play an important, but poorly understood, role. The American machine tool industry ought to be competitive, according to the usual notions of numbers of actual or potential entrants. More than 40 firms produce milling machines; 37 companies produce products in machining centers; and 56 companies produce products in the turning machine business.[97] Each of these broad categories, however, is divided into specialized niches, the members of which may not compete against members of other niches; for example, the 56 turning machine companies are distributed in 12 separate categories. However, each of the categories has at least ten members, and the barriers impeding a company in one category from entering another are not large. Neither the required investment nor the additional learning for efficient production, design, and marketing is immense, as many of the major components of a machine tool are quite similar across different types.

The argument that small firms are not good at innovation is contradicted by almost every empirical study on the sources of innovation. For example, a study of 8,000 product and process innovations across 500 industries (standard industrial classification, four-digit industry classifications) found more than half of the innovations coming from firms with fewer than 500 employees. These smaller firms had about 50 percent more innovations per industry employee than larger firms.[98] Moreover, the smaller firms' innovations were as likely to be "significant" as those of the larger firms. However, the innovation rate per industry employee for industries with declining employment (which characterizes the machine tool industry) was only half as great as for those with growing employment, for both large and small companies.

A survey of nine studies sponsored by the Small Business Administration confirmed the generality of these results.[99] Some of the other studies also show that innovating smaller firms (in comparison with larger firms) conduct more basic and more applied research than development, bring an innovation to market more quickly, conduct more R&D per sales, and are as likely to export.[100] The export tendencies of small firms were demonstrated by the statistics that 41 percent of firms with 50–99 employees are exporters, 48 percent of firms with 100–499 employees, and only 27 percent for those over 500.[101] In the metalworking machinery sector, two-thirds of the companies with fewer than 100 employees are in the export markets.

What we are left with is a genuine puzzle. Why did not some American company introduce new ideas for products and production processes before the Japanese companies, and why has it been so difficult to respond to the competitive challenge? The answers to these puzzles will not be found in the recitation of opinions and the retelling of widely shared beliefs, but in real research.

The 1980s witnessed an unprecedented concatenation of circumstances affecting the U.S. machine tool industry. Recession; an overvalued dollar; the rise of the Japanese industry; the shift in technology toward electronics, software, and controls; the demands for flexibility and faster delivery; the vertical disintegration of production; the integration of single machines into larger systems; and the globalization of markets—all placed an unusually grave and complex set of problems before the machine tool industry, much of which was family owned and managed, dating back to the U.S. Civil War or earlier. Over the past century, many of these same companies met severe challenges posed by events as compelling as those faced today, although it is no exaggeration to say that the number and variety of challenges today meets, if not exceeds, anything seen in the past. How the U.S. machine tool industry adapts to shifting global forces will become apparent as we move through the 1990s.

---

### NOTES

1. Unless otherwise noted, figures cited in this chapter are taken from various issues of *The Economic Handbook of the Machine Tool Industry,* published by the NMTBA, The Association for Manufacturing Technology (formerly the National Machine Tool Builders Association).
2. The selection of these years as endpoints avoids the untypically severe downturn of 1983–86. If the calculation were extended over the full 21 years from 1967 to 1987, the mean percentage return (and standard deviation) would be 7.4 (8.1) for machine tools, and 9.6 (1.8) for all manufacturing.
3. "Consumption," as used here, measures the purchase of machine tools by U.S. industry; it is equal to domestic shipments plus imports minus exports. This definition is different from typical economic usage as applied to durable goods, which reflects the flow of services provided by a stock of capital.
4. Equipment expenditures are from the Bureau of the Census and cover all manufacturing establishments (*NMTBA Economic Handbook,* p. 17); its 1986 value was $34.5 billion.
5. In the late 1930s, to avert employee layoffs, IBM pursued a strategy similar to that of the Japanese machine tool producers. This gamble paid off when the new Social Security Administration chose IBM to supply punched-card calculating machines, partly because it was the only source of immediate delivery.
6. Machining centers are numerically controlled machine tools with automatic tool changers that can perform many of the functions that had been customarily assigned to separate machines, such as lathes and milling machines. Machining centers can often accomplish all of the metal-cutting operations on a complex part in a single setup, a task that formerly required several machines, plus the additional and costly setups, inspections, and parts transfers between machines.

7. Since a third to a half of the value of final shipments is purchased from outside the industry, a productivity measure defined as the ratio of value added to labor input is preferable to one based on gross shipments.

8. Bailey and Chakrabarti (1988), Table 4-2, p. 69.

9. Ibid., p. 77.

10. Schumpeter (1950), pp. 82–83.

11. See John McMillan, Ch. 2, this volume.

12. The reasoning behind this conclusion is that if the costs of maintaining plant capacity depend on the scale of capacity (it costs more to keep a large plant going than a small one), declining demand will impose a larger profit drain on a large plant than on a smaller one.

13. Milgrom and Roberts (1990), p. 513.

14. Ibid.

15. Ibid., pp. 514–515.

16. Winter (1990), p. 1.

17. Cited in Daly and Jones (1980), p. 55.

18. Pratten (1970–71), pp. 148–165.

19. Ibid., p. 161.

20. Daly and Jones (1980), p. 58.

21. The U.S. Census publishes combined employment figures only for establishments of more than 500 employees to prevent disclosures of individual establishment information.

22. *Metalworking News,* December 15, 1986, p. 6.

23. March (1989), p. 15.

24. Ibid., p. 78.

25. "Stanwich Sets Machine Tool Consolidation," *Metalworking News,* August 1, 1988, p. 1.

26. Moskal (1988), p. 28.

27. This point is made by Rendeiro (1985), p. 63. Friedman (1988), Ch. 4, also analyzes this issue.

28. "The Vise Tightens on Toolmakers," *Business Week,* December 6, 1982, p. 63.

29. March (1989), pp. 35, 40, 109. Japanese lathe producers, for example, were building 50–200 computer numerical control lathes monthly, whereas U.S. companies produced in the range of 15–40.

30. "Japanese Tool Builders Little Affected by VRAs," *Metalworking News,* June 19, 1989, p. 20.

31. Harvard Business School, *Case Study: Bendix Automation Group,* 9-684-035, 1983, p. 5.

32. Rendeiro (1985), p. 63.

33. For a more detailed discussion of this subject, see Alexander (1990); also Ch. 11, this volume.
34. These speculations are described in Saxonhouse (1986), p. 224.
35. Saxonhouse (1986), pp. 225–227; also see Friedman (1988), Ch. 3.
36. As part of a policy package associated with the VRAs, the government announced several other measures, including more favorable opportunities for the machine tool industry to obtain funding from the Defense Department's ManTech program and federal support of a new National Center for Manufacturing Sciences.
37. The aggregate figures do not allow the determination of whether the average price increase per unit arose from actual increases in prices of comparable machines or from the substitution of higher priced units in place of simpler, lower priced products.
38. The declining value of the dollar during this period was beginning to have a retarding effect on U.S. imports.
39. The Department of Commerce had projected a decline of value of $155 million from the VRAs in 1987, under the assumption that demand and imports would remain constant. The estimate in this paper takes into account the fact that imports of unrestricted items actually fell by more than 7 percent. See U.S. Department of Commerce (1986), p. 2.
40. Rousslang and Pollard (1989), Table 3-14, p. 3-16.
41. Jones (1989), p. 20.
42. Rousslang and Pollard (1989), Table 3-13, p. 3-15.
43. U.S. government projections were given in the "Data Fact Sheet" attached to the *Statement by the President,* Office of the Press Secretary, December 16, 1986.
44. "Japanese Broaden Range of Machine Tools Sent to U.S.: Led by non-VRA Grinders, Screw Machines," *Metalworking News,* September 19, 1988, p. 4.
45. "Help is on the Way for U.S. Toolmakers," *Japan Economic Journal,* May 26, 1990, p. 22.
46. "U.S. Seeks Higher Local Content in Machine Tools," *Japan Economic Journal,* April 1, 1989.
47. In particular, see Testimony of James Gray, *NMTBA Petition* (1983).
48. This estimate assumes a marginal profits-to-sales ratio of 7.4 percent.
49. The term "substantial cause" has been interpreted as a cause that is important, and not less important than any other cause of decreased sales and employment. Aho and Bayard (1984).
50. These figures come from *NMTBA Petition* (1983), pp. 117–118 and App. G.
51. Aho and Bayard (1984), p. 184, claim that the political gains of TAA "are enormous."
52. U.S. International Trade Commission, 1983, p. 38; "Air Force's ManTech Flying Despite Cuts," *Metalworking News,* November 27, 1989, p. 1.

53. Manufacturing Studies Board (1986), Table B-1, p. 41.
54. Ibid., pp. 31–32.
55. Ibid., p. 32.
56. "NCMS Joins Air Force on New Controller," *Metalworking News,* September 5, 1988, p. 1.
57. *NMTBA Petition* (1983), p. 180.
58. Ibid., pp. 184–185.
59. "Companies Team Up to Develop Better Tools," *The Wall Street Journal,* December 1, 1987.
60. "Tomorrow's Factories Today," *Manufacturing Technology,* September 1988, p. 50.
61. USITC (1983), p. 43.
62. "Tomorrow's Factories Today," p. 91.
63. USITC (1983), pp. 40–41 and App. G.
64. *NMTBA Petition* (1983), pp. 12–13. Various estimates placed the value of the Japanese stock of finished machines in the United States at $500 million, requiring at least $50 million per year in carrying charges (interest, warehousing costs, depreciation).
65. Ibid., p. 35.
66. Ibid., p. 128.
67. Ibid., p. 154.
68. USITC (1983), p. 99.
69. Statement by James Koontz, Chairman of the National Center for Manufacturing Sciences, quoted in "Companies Team Up to Develop Better Tools," *The Wall Street Journal,* December 1, 1987.
70. Hannay and Steele (1986), pp. 17–18.
71. Statement by Paine Webber's machine tool industry financial expert Eli Lustgarten, in "Will Machine Tools Survive This One?" *New England Business,* October 17, 1983, p. 15.
72. Statement by James Gray, NMTBA President, cited ibid., p. 17.
73. Statement by W. Paul Cooper, chairman of Acme-Cleveland Corp; cited ibid., p. 18.
74. "Machine Tool Technology: The March Presses On," *Modern Machine Shop,* February 1988, p. 93.
75. "LeBlond Gets All-American Management," *Cincinnati Inquirer,* August 3, 1987.
76. "Bendix: A Buy that Really Was Too Good to be True," *Business Week,* June 3, 1985, p. 93.
77. Testimony of James A. Gray, NMTBA president; *NMTBA Petition* (1983), App. K, p. 4.

78. Kaplan (1986), p. 87.
79. Reuter (1983), pp. 24–26.
80. Of course, this reason would apply to all industry, not just machine tools.
81. The arguments in these paragraphs flow from Zysman (1983).
82. A casual survey of knowledgeable individuals in the financial industry is strongly consistent with this statement, indicating that the small-business borrower suffers from grossly higher capital costs than large borrowers, mainly because of the structure of the financial market. This point needs additional investigation.
83. This argument follows Friedman (1988), pp. 161–175.
84. Ibid., p. 167.
85. Ibid., p. 170.
86. Jacobson (1986), Table 3.7, p. 48.
87. Ibid., p. 65.
88. Ibid., Table 3.10, p. 51.
89. Ibid., Table 3.9, p. 50.
90. This figure refers to vertical and horizontal NC turning machines. *NMTBA Statistical Report,* No. 57–89, May 3, 1989.
91. Friedman (1988), p. 72, emphasis added.
92. Ibid., p. 87.
93. Saxonhouse (1986), p. 226.
94. Okimoto (1986), p. 65.
95. Wolf (1983), p. 76.
96. March (1989), pp. 8–31.
97. These figures are the member companies of the NMTBA that are listed under the designated categories, *NMTBA Directory,* 1989.
98. Gordon and Edwards (1984).
99. Schrier (1989).
100. These additional findings are not found consistently across all the surveyed studies; sometimes the differences were statistically significant and other times not, but in no case was the opposite result found in the data.
101. Birch (1988), p. 42.

## BIBLIOGRAPHY

Aho, C. Michael, and Thomas O. Bayard (1984). "Costs and Benefits of Trade Adjustment Assistance," in Baldwin and Krueger (1984).

Alexander, Arthur J. (1990). *Approaches to Innovation in the United States and Japan.* RAND, R–3924–CUSJR.

Bailey, Martin Neil, and Alok K. Chakrabarti (1988). *Innovation and the Productivity Crisis.* Washington, D.C.: Brookings Institution.

Baldwin, Robert, and Anne Krueger (eds.) (1984). *The Structure and Evolution of Recent U.S. Trade Policy.* Chicago: University of Chicago Press.

Birch, David L. (1988). "Trading Places." *Inc.,* April.

Daly, Ann, and Daniel Jones (1980). "The Machine Tool Industry in Britain, Germany, and the United States." *National Institute Economic Review,* May.

*Economic Handbook of the Machine Tool Industry.* NMTBA, The Association for Manufacturing Technology, various issues.

Friedman, David (1988). *The Misunderstood Miracle: Industrial Development and Political Change in Japan.* Ithaca, N.Y.: Cornell University Press.

Gordon, Theodore J., and Keith L. Edwards (1984). *Characterization of Innovations Introduced on the U.S. Market in 1982.* Glastonbury, Conn.: The Futures Group, March.

Hannay, N. B., and Lowell W. Steele (1986). "Technology and Trade: A Study of U.S. Competitiveness in Seven Industries." *Research Management,* January–February.

Jacobson, Steffan (1986). "Growth and Market Structure in the International CNC Lathe Industry." *Electronics and Industrial Policy.* London: Allen & Unwin.

Jones, Sam L. (1989). "Japanese Tool Builders Little Affected by VRAs." *Metalworking News,* June 19.

Kaplan, Robert S. (1986). "Must CIM be Justified by Faith Alone?" *Harvard Business Review,* March–April.

Manufacturing Studies Board (1986). *The Role of the Department of Defense in Supporting Manufacturing Technology Development.* Washington, D.C.: National Academy Press.

March, Artemis (1989). "The U.S. Machine Tool Industry and its Foreign Competitors." *MIT Commission on Industrial Activity,* vol. 2. Cambridge, Mass.: MIT Press.

Milgrom, Paul, and John Roberts (1990). "The Economics of Modern Manufacturing; Technology, Strategy, and Organization." *The American Economic Review,* June.

Moskal, Brian (1988). "Twin Towers of Tools: Acquisitions Create a New Player." *Industry Week,* September 19.

NMTBA (1983). *Petition Under the National Security Clause, Section 232 of the Trade Expansion Act of 1962 for Adjustment of Imports of Machine Tools.*

Okimoto, Daniel (1986). "Regime Characteristics of Japanese Industrial Policy," in Patrick (1986).

Patrick, Hugh (ed.) (1986). *Japan's High Technology Industries.* Seattle: University of Washington Press.

Pratten, C. F. (1970–71). "Economies of Scale for Machine Tool Production." *The Journal of Industrial Economics,* vol. 19.

Rendeiro, Joao O. (1985). "How the Japanese Came to Dominate the Machine Tool Business." *Long Range Planning,* vol. 18, no. 3.

Reuter, Peter, (1983). *Cleveland Metal Stamping: A Case Study of an Industry in Transition.* RAND, N–1977–CF, April.

Rousslang, Donald J., and Walter A. Pollard (1989). *The Economic Effects of Significant U.S. Import Restraints, Phase 1: Manufacturing.* U.S. International Trade Commission, USITC 2222, October.

Saxonhouse, Gary R. (1986). "National Security Claims of the Trade Expansion Act," in Saxonhouse and Yamamura (1986).

Saxonhouse, Gary R., and Kozo Yamamura (eds.) (1986). *Law and Trade Issues of the Japanese Economy.* Seattle: University of Washington Press.

Schrier, William (1989). *Innovation, Small Business, and Government.* Small Business Administration, Washington, D.C.

Schumpeter, Joseph A. (1950). *Capitalism, Socialism, and Democracy,* 3d ed. New York: Harper & Row.

U.S. Department of Commerce, International Trade Administration (1986), *Fact Sheet, Machine Tools.* Washington D.C., December 16.

U.S. International Trade Commission (1983). *Competitive Assessment of the U.S. Metalworking Machine Tool Industry.* USITC 1428, September.

Winter, Ralph (1990). "Foreign Stake in Capital Goods Grows in U.S." *Asian Wall Street Journal,* January 23.

Wolf, Marvin J. (1983). *The Japanese Conspiracy.* New York: Empire Books.

Zysman, John (1983). *Governments, Markets, and Growth: Financial Systems and the Politics of International Change.* Ithaca, N.Y.: Cornell University Press.

# 14

## Structural Adjustment of the Japanese Cement Industry

### Hiromichi Mutoh

### INTRODUCTION

This chapter examines the structural adjustment process of Japan's cement industry under the *Law of Temporary Measures to Facilitate Structural Adjustment* (the Structural Adjustment Law) enacted in 1987. It analyzes the rationalization methods and patterns of capacity adjustment of the five largest cement manufacturers. It also draws tentative conclusions about the influence of adjustment on the competitiveness and efficiency of the industry.

This chapter is divided into three sections. The first section describes the changing circumstances that necessitated structural adjustment in the cement industry. The second section outlines the main features of the Structural Adjustment Law and its application to the cement industry. The final section examines the pattern of adjustment and arrives at a tentative assessment of the economic outcomes of capacity scrapping.

### BACKGROUND

In the early 1980s, the Japanese cement industry confronted, for the first time in its history, the necessity of structural adjustment. Figure 14.1 shows that cement production hit its peak of 87.4 million tons in 1980 and then fell into decline until 1986. This decline was brougnt about mainly by the reduction of domestic demand, although a sharp decrease in Japanese exports after 1983 further worsened conditions in the industry. Domestic demand fell as a result of several factors: (1) decreases in construction investment caused by stagnating fixed capital formation in both the private and public sectors; (2) decreases in the proportion of cement used in construction because of a shift of construction technology from the reinforced concrete method to the curtain-wall method; and (3) decreases in the proportion of cement used in ready-mixed concrete resulting from improvements in compound materials.

## Industry Responses

The cement industry's response to these adverse circumstances took two forms. First, the industry applied for approval to establish a recession cartel. It sought a cartel with several features: (1) a duration of six months (July 1 to December 31, 1983); (2) a cap on total domestic sales at 36.65 million tons; (3) freezing sales shares of each company at their average over the three most recent years; (4) having inventories of 2.5 million tons at the end of the period; and (5) setting the price at 15,500 yen per ton. The application was approved, but the outcome was not satisfactory for the industry; the price of bulk cement was set at 14,511 yen per ton in 1984, well below its target price.

Second, the industry applied for designation under the *Law on Temporary Measures for the Structural Improvement of Specified Industries* (the Structural Improvement Law) enacted in 1983.[1] The Ministry of International Trade and Industry (MITI) set up a cement industry subcommittee in the Industrial Structure Council to deliberate on how the industry might best carry out its structural improvements. The council outlined the following recommendations:

*A. Capacity scrapping:* Thirty million tons of production capacity should be scrapped, with priority placed on eliminating 25 million tons of obsolete production facilities. By doing so, the remaining capacity would be 99 million tons at the target year, with the forecasted demand for the year at 77–79 million tons.

*B. Establishing joint enterprises:* Five enterprises should be established to take charge of the joint-sales activities of groups of manufacturers in a proposed manufacturers association. Each group would have the following market shares and member firms:

- Onoda Group (share of sales, 19.3 percent): Onoda Cement, Nippon Steel Chemical, Toso Corporation, Hitachi Cement, Mitsui Mining.

- Nihon Group (21.4 percent): Nihon Cement, Osaka Cement, Daiichi Cement, Myojo Cement.
- Mitsubishi Group (16.7 percent): Mitsubishi Mining & Cement, Tokuyamasoda.
- Sumitomo Group (20.3 percent): Sumitomo Cement, Aso Cement, Denki Kagaku Kogyo, Nittetsu Cement, Hachinohe Cement, Toyo Cement, Kanda Cement.
- Ube Group (20.3 percent): Ube Industries, Chichibu Cement, Tsuruga Cement, Ryukyu Cement.

*C. Cooperative arrangements:* Member firms in each group should cooperate in: (1) intensifying production through specialization within each group; (2) sales exchanges and common utilization of distribution facilities; (3) cooperative sales through joint-sales enterprises; and (4) scrapping of excess capacity by mutual consent among member companies in each group.

The Cabinet approved designation of the cement industry under the Structural Improvement Law on April 27, 1984, and *The Basic Plan of Structural Improvement of the Cement Manufacturing Industry* was announced by MITI in August 1984. On this basis, the cement manufacturers association agreed in February 1985 to carry out capacity scrapping goals as shown in Table 14.1.

Capacity scrapping by the industry was completed on schedule. In total, 76 kilns (24.65 tons of capacity) were scrapped by the end of March 1985, and an additional 13 kilns (6.35 tons) were scrapped by the end of the following March. Recall, however, that the scrapped capacity included 25 million tons of obsolete capacity, so the reduction of real productive capacity was only 6 million tons.

Unification of sales outlets within each group was carried out more gradually. Nihon Cement group adopted a common brand name (Union) for cement-in-sacks in August 1985, followed by the other four groups in April 1986. This sales unification appears to have eased price competition among manufacturers. Prices rose slightly from 14,150 yen per ton in 1983 to 14,254 yen per ton in 1986. Profitability of cement manufacturers also improved, as shown in Figure 14.2. Although total sales of both the 17 cement-specialized manufacturers and the 6 non-specialized manufacturers were stagnant between 1983 and 1987, the ratio of their profits to sales improved considerably. It appears that restructuring under the Structural Improvement Law may have contributed, at least partly, to an improvement in the finances of cement manufacturers.

**Figure 14.1**
**Demand and supply of cement; construction investment**

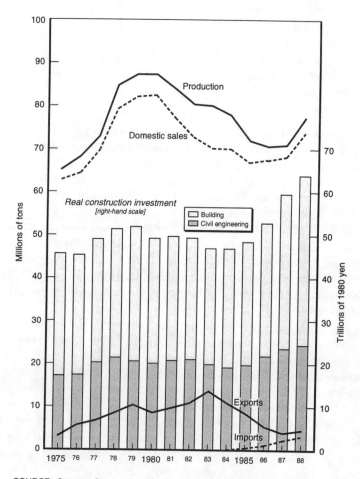

SOURCE: Semento Shimbunsha, *Semento Henkan*, (Cement Yearbook).

## Declining Competitiveness and Import Restrictions

Despite capacity reduction and improvement in profitability, excess capacity still existed in the industry. The ratio of cement production (on a clinker basis) to capacity was 65.5 percent in 1987, whereas it was 62.4 percent in

## Table 14.1
## Capacity scrapping by Japanese cement companies under the structural improvement law
(Capacity in tons)

| Company | Scrapped capacity | No. of kilns | Rate scrapping | Capacity remaining |
|---|---|---|---|---|
| Onoda Cement | 5,178 | (12) | 33.7 | 10,200 |
| Nippon Steel Chemical | 378 | ( 1) | 32.3 | 794 |
| Tosoh | 906 | ( 4) | 21.9 | 3,228 |
| Hitachi Cement | 671 | ( 3) | 43.5 | 872 |
| Mitsui Mining | 1,618 | ( 2) | 42.3 | 2,209 |
| Nihon Cement | 4,936 | (17) | 27.5 | 13,031 |
| Myojyo Cement | 699 | ( 2) | 22.2 | 2,451 |
| Daiichi Cement | 357 | ( 3) | 24.6 | 1,092 |
| Osaka Cement | 1,025 | ( 3) | 15.1 | 6,760 |
| Mitsubishi Mining & Cement | 1,321 | ( 2) | 9.4 | 12,799 |
| Tokuyama Soda | 1,780 | ( 5) | 25.8 | 5,106 |
| Sumitomo Cement | 2,345 | (10) | 18.7 | 10,213 |
| Hachinohe Cement | 0 | 0 | 0 | 1,310 |
| Toyo Cement | 593 | ( 2) | 100.0 | 0 |
| Aso Cement | 356 | ( 1) | 21.3 | 1,316 |
| Kanda Cement | 661 | ( 1) | 28.5 | 1,653 |
| Denki Kagaku Kogyo | 881 | ( 3) | 25.0 | 2,636 |
| Nittetsu Cement | 282 | ( 1) | 15.8 | 1,507 |
| Ube Industries | 363 | ( 1) | 3.3 | 10,524 |
| Ryuku Cement | 150 | ( 1) | 21.7 | 540 |
| Chichibu Cement | 5,020 | (12) | 46.5 | 5,777 |
| Tsuruga Cement | 248 | ( 1) | 13.1 | 1,645 |
| Tohoku Kaihatsu | 1,056 | ( 3) | 31.3 | 2,134 |
| Capacity totals | 31,004 | (89) | 24.0 | 97,981 |

*Source:* Semento Shimbunsha, *Semento Nenkan* (Cement Yearbook).

1984 and 71.7 percent in 1985. These figures still fell short of the target level of 80 percent.

One major reason why considerable excess capacity remained, although scrapping took place as scheduled, was the overestimation of future demand for cement. The Industrial Structure Council assumed that demand for cement (clinker basis) would decline from 81 million tons in 1983 to 77–79 million tons in 1987, while the actual figure fell to 64 million tons in that year.

Another major reason was the sharp increase in cement imports. As shown in Figure 14.1, cement exports decreased sharply beginning in 1983, from 13.7 million tons in that year to 4.8 million tons in 1987, while cement imports rose dramatically. At least two factors contributed to this change—

the rapid appreciation of the yen since 1985, and the growing competitiveness of Korean and Taiwanese cement manufacturers.

Figure 14.3 shows the movement of cement prices since 1980. The unit
domestic price moved between 10,000 yen and 12,000 yen per ton from 1980
to 1987, while the unit import price on a cargo-insurance-freight (CIF) basis
declined from about 10,000 yen per ton in 1985 to about 6,000 yen in 1987.
When transportation costs and distribution margins are taken into account,
the differential between the unit price of domestic cement and that of
imported cement was about 2,000 yen in 1987. In addition to price competitiveness, both Korean and Taiwanese manufacturers also increased their
capacity to supply cement in Japan. For example, Ssang Yong Cement of
Korea built six silos in Japan from 1986 to 1988, and other manufacturers,
such as Dong Yang Cement and Taiwan Cement, also increased their
distribution facilities in Japan.

In responding to the sharp increase in imported cement, Japan's cement
industry took direct steps to limit (at least temporarily) imports from Korea.
Through negotiations between the industry associations of the countries, the
following agreement was reached:

- Japan's cement imports from Korea were to be limited to 2.2 million
  tons, including 1 million tons of imports by Japanese manufacturers,
  for one year beginning in September 1986.
- Japanese manufacturers' imports would be channeled through Ssang
  Yong Japan, a subsidiary of the Ssang Yong Group of Korea.

Korean cement was imported by Japanese manufacturers, who mixed it with
domestically produced cement, both to stabilize domestic price and to
maintain cement quality. But the fact that domestic cement prices continued
a slight downward trend during this period seems to cast doubt on the
effectiveness of the agreed-upon import restrictions.[2]

## THE STRUCTURAL ADJUSTMENT LAW

As noted in the previous section, the capacity scrapping measures implemented under the Structural Improvement Law failed to diminish the
excess capacity problem in the Japanese cement industry. The problem was
exacerbated by import penetration by Korean and Taiwanese manufacturers.
Consequently, Japanese cement manufacturers decided to apply for designation under the Structural Adjustment Law enacted in April 1987.

**Figure 14.2**
**Sales and profit ratios of cement manufacturers**

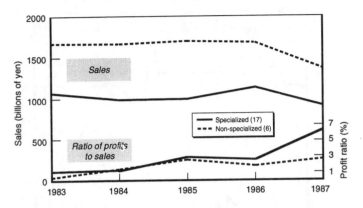

SOURCE: Semento Shimbunsha, *Semento Heckan*, (Cement Yearbook).

The purpose of this law was to facilitate structural adjustment by providing measures to help designated enterprises adapt to a new economic environment and, by providing measures to assist designated regions, to achieve economic stability and development. In contrast to the earlier Structural Improvement Law, which applied to specific industries suffering from adjustment problems, this law targeted equipment suffering from serious excess capacity due to a severe decline in demand that was caused by drastic changes in the economic environment and was projected to persist for a long time.

Once designated, enterprises may seek approval from the relevant minister for a structural adjustment plan (Article 6). Furthermore, as a group, they may propose and seek approval for cooperative production and joint-sales plans, mergers, and the like (Article 7). Advance examination by the relevant minister and the Japanese Fair Trade Commission would ensure that these cooperative arrangements do not violate the Antimonopoly Law.

### Kinds of Assistance

Several kinds of assistance are provided under the Structural Adjustment Law. In the structural adjustment plan, the law would facilitate (1) capacity scrapping by credit guarantees for borrowing, and extensions of the carrying-forward period for depreciation losses from scrapping; and (2) business switch-overs by financing through the Japan Development Bank, special

**Figure 14.3**
**Movement of cement prices since 1980**

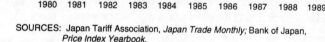

*Domestic wholesale price,*
*referenced to 1985 = 100*

*Unit price of portland*
*cement*

Domestic
producers'
price

Import price
from Korea

Import price
from Taiwan

Thousands of yen per ton

SOURCES: Japan Tariff Association, *Japan Trade Monthly;* Bank of Japan,
         *Price Index Yearbook.*

depreciation schemes, tax exemption from the land-property tax of the
designated region, and reduction of the enterprise tax of designated regions.
For the business tie-up plan, the law would provide special depreciation
schemes for equipment required for business tie-ups, reduction of the registration tax for mergers, and reduction of the real-estate acquisition tax for
business transfers.

## Application of the Law to Cement Manufacturers

MITI canceled its designation of the cement industry under the Structural Improvement Law in August 1987 before designating the industry under the Structural Adjustment Law. Kiln equipment was designated under the law in October 1987. However, the business tie-up plan proposed by the five joint enterprises was not approved until September 1988 and approval of the structural adjustment plan was further delayed.

These delays were the result of objections raised by the Japanese Fair Trade Commission (FTC).[3] The first point concerned plans to construct a cement-terminal company as a joint enterprise of five cement manufacturers: Nihon, Onoda, Mitsubishi, Ube, and Nittetsu. This terminal was intended to meet about 40 percent of the annual demand in the Ishikari region where it was to be constructed. This would, however, have exceeded the 25 percent market share that the FTC regarded as being large enough to control a market. The second point concerned the practice of cement manufacturers in limiting supply to ready-mixed concrete producers using imported cement. Some cement manufacturers reportedly did so because they felt they could not guarantee the quality of their cement once it was mixed with imported cement.

The FTC finally accepted establishment of the joint company once the majority of stock in the company was transferred to a public body. The business tie-up plan was approved by MITI in September 1988, and approval of the structural adjustment plan followed in December 1988.

## ONGOING STRUCTURAL ADJUSTMENTS

Thus far, I have provided a broad overview of structural adjustments in the cement industry beginning in the 1980s. These adjustments, or "restructurings," involve efforts by firms to regain competitiveness and to revitalize their business activities. They include: (1) rationalization involving material-cost saving, reduction of labor inputs, scrapping obsolete equipment, and exit or conversion; (2) cultivation of new businesses by strengthening research and development, by merger and acquisition, and by reorganizing subsidiaries or affiliated companies; and (3) globalization through foreign direct investment, acquisitions and business tie-ups, and establishment of overseas distribution networks. In this section, I review recent restructuring efforts by the five largest cement manufacturers—Onoda Cement, Nihon Cement, Sumitomo Cement, Mitsubishi Mining & Cement, and Ube Industries—the principal manufacturers in each of the five joint-sales enterprises.

## Material-Cost Saving

First, price competitiveness can be enhanced by savings in the use of intermediate inputs and fuel, which typically account for over half of the total costs of producing portland cement. The major materials used in portland cement are limestone and clay, to which a small quantity of calcium silicate and ferrous-oxide is added. In addition, gypsum is used to lengthen the setting time of cement.

Figure 14.4 shows recent trends in unit material inputs for cement production. Since 1985, per-unit limestone usage has been roughly stable, while unit inputs of clay have fallen sharply. The latter change can be partly explained by the increase in unit inputs of calcium silicate, which is added when the silica content is low. The slight increase in limestone unit use in 1987 seems to reflect the growing demand for high-strength, early-setting

**Figure 14.4**
**Material unit inputs (1985=100)**

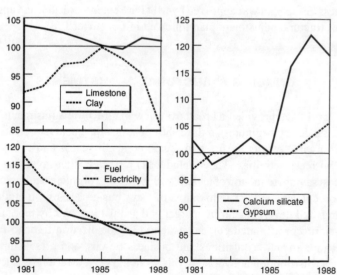

SOURCEs: Semento Shimbunsha, *Semento Nenkan* (Cement Yearbook)

cement. Moreover, unit inputs of gypsum have also increased since 1985, reflecting an increasing demand for different kinds of cement with a longer setting time. These changes suggest that the composition of demand for cement has changed over this period. Recent movements of unit material inputs, however, show no definitive trend toward further savings in material costs. On the other hand, energy unit inputs showed a remarkable decrease over this period—unit electricity usage fell from 108 kwh per ton in 1985 to 103 kwh per ton in 1988.

Table 14.2 shows that the proportion of materials and fuel to total costs has declined recently for the five largest manufacturers. For Onoda Cement, the sharp decline since 1985 was due to the separation of the Tawara and Kitakyushu factories. This was partly the result of these factories not having their own quarries and therefore having to buy limestone at market prices, and partly because the Tawara factory still relies on an outdated kiln that is more energy-using than NSP kilns with a new suspension preheater. A similar decline for Mitsubishi Mining & Cement reflects the scrapping of the Higashiya factory kiln. Material and fuel costs also benefited from declines in prices. Table 14.3 indicates that oil prices fell dramatically between October 1985 and March 1989. Of the different inputs, the largest price declines over this period were evidenced by heavy oil.

### Reduction and Reallocation of Labor

In terms of employment adjustment, the number of factory workers in the cement industry as a whole decreased from 8,800 in 1985 to 7,285 in 1988.

**Table 14.2**
**Proportion of material costs to total costs**
(Percent)

| Company | \multicolumn{6}{c}{Fiscal Year} | | | | | |
|---|---|---|---|---|---|---|
| | 1983 | 1984 | 1985 | 1986 | 1987 | 1988 |
| Onoda | 61.2 | 63.0 | 62.7 | 54.8 | 49.8 | 47.8 |
| Nihon | 48.3 | 48.2 | 46.6 | 46.0 | 45.0 | 45.3 |
| Sumitomo | 53.6 | 53.0 | 53.7 | 51.7 | 51.3 | 50.7 |
| Mitsubishi | 56.8 | 59.1 | 60.1 | 45.0 | 45.6 | 45.3 |
| Ube | 70.7 | 68.7 | 68.9 | 64.2 | 63.2 | 63.0 |

*Source:* Financial statements of each company.

## Table14.3
## Price of major materials and fuels

| Inputs | Unit of Measure | October 1985 | March 1989 |
|---|---|---|---|
| Heavy oil, C | 1,000 yen/kl | 49.4 | 17.3 |
| Chemical gypsum | 1,000 yen/ton | 5.1 | 3.8 |
| Powdering medium | 1,000 yen/ton | 122.5 | 117.0 |
| Sack | yen/unit | 43.9 | 41.9 |
| Electricity | yen/kwh | 14.48 | 10.57 |

*Source:* Nihon Cement Co. Ltd., financial statements

Looking at the employment figures for each company, however, one ob-
serves fairly large variations among the five largest companies. Table 14.4
shows that Onoda reduced its employment by about one-third from FY 1985
to FY 1988, while Sumitomo had a slight increase in the number of its
employees. Both Nihon and Ube reduced their work force by about 10
percent, while Mitsubishi kept the number of employees almost constant
over the same period. One feature common to these firms is that they reduced
the number of employees at their cement-producing factories.

These employment adjustments were the result of different adjustment
strategies adopted by each firm. The sharp decline of the Onoda workforce
was due to a series of corporate restructuring measures. These included: (1)
separating the sales department into a joint sales company, and (2) spinning
off the Tawara, Onoda, and Kitakyushu factories into new companies. The
increase in the number of main-office employees at Sumitomo was due to
the relocation of the central research laboratory, reflecting the firm's strategy
of intensifying its R&D activities. Ube announced a rationalization plan in
1986 to reduce its employees by 700 workers in 1986 and by 630 in 1987.
It offered an early retirement scheme for employees over fifty years old, and
a voluntary retirement scheme for those aged less than fifty to accomplish
its employment reduction targets.

Employee loaning was another important employment adjustment measure. The employee loaning system, which is widely used by companies
(usually large ones) with excess labor, involves the transfer of some
workers to other companies, primarily its affiliates and closely related
companies, with the sending company making up any wage differentials.
Between 1985 and 1988, the number of loaned employees rose from 1,804
to 2,349 workers for Onoda, from 432 to 512 for Nihon, and from 454 to

### Table 14.4
### Number of employees and distribution
### (Percent)

| Company | Fiscal Year | | | | | |
|---|---|---|---|---|---|---|
| | 1983 | 1984 | 1985 | 1986 | 1987 | 1988 |
| Onoda Cement[a] | 2559 | 2075 | 2028 | 1397 | 1460 | 1357 |
| Cement factory | 58.3 | 68.8 | 60.9 | 63.7 | 61.0 | 59.6 |
| Other factories | 0.8 | 0.5 | 6.3 | 5.5 | 0.2 | 0.2 |
| Main office | 21.5 | 25.5 | 27.2 | 28.8 | 36.3 | 37.9 |
| Others | 19.4 | 5.2 | 5.6 | 2.0 | 2.5 | 2.3 |
| | | | | | | |
| Nihon Cement[b] | 3114 | 3012 | 2432 | 2354 | 2204 | 2183 |
| Cement factory | 48.8 | 48.8 | 54.7 | 49.4 | 49.9 | 49.3 |
| Other factories | 10.1 | 9.9 | 10.2 | 13.2 | 13.1 | 11.7 |
| Main office | 24.7 | 24.6 | 23.7 | 25.6 | 24.5 | 26.4 |
| Others | 16.4 | 16.7 | 11.4 | 11.8 | 12.5 | 12.6 |
| | | | | | | |
| Sumitomo Cement[c] | 2001 | 1863 | 1860 | 1895 | 1908 | 1922 |
| Cement factory | 55.4 | 50.8 | 48.2 | 45.6 | 44.0 | 42.1 |
| Other factories | 0.9 | 1.0 | 1.0 | 1.0 | 1.2 | 1.3 |
| Main office | 26.2 | 30.3 | 32.9 | 35.9 | 37.4 | 39.4 |
| Others | 17.5 | 17.9 | 17.9 | 17.5 | 17.4 | 17.2 |
| | | | | | | |
| Mitsubishi Mining | 2087 | 1701 | 1787 | 1727 | 1745 | 1762 |
| Cement factory | 35.6 | 41.6 | 38.4 | 33.8 | 32.2 | 30.7 |
| Other factories | 7.7 | 11.5 | 11.4 | 12.5 | 14.1 | 13.4 |
| Main office | 21.3 | 23.6 | 23.1 | 27.7 | 28.0 | 27.4 |
| Others | 35.4 | 23.3 | 27.1 | 26.0 | 25.7 | 28.5 |
| | | | | | | |
| Ube Industries | 8694 | 8118 | 8122 | 7621 | 7309 | 7152 |
| Cement factory | 23.8 | 23.2 | 20.2 | 18.6 | 18.7 | 18.4 |
| Other factories | 42.4 | 44.0 | 43.0 | 41.1 | 42.2 | 41.8 |
| Main office | 16.4 | 16.4 | 18.8 | 20.3 | 18.9 | 20.0 |
| Others | 17.4 | 16.4 | 17.9 | 20.0 | 20.2 | 19.8 |

[a]Related business division separated in 1986. Tawara, Onada, and Kitakyushu plant separated in 1987.
[b]Includes loaned-out employees before 1985. Glass wool division separated in 1987.
[c]Includes loaned-out employees.
*Sources:* Financial statements of each company.

610 for Sumitomo; the number of loaned employees fell slightly (766 to 662) for Mitsubishi.

## Development of New Products

The recent downward trend in cement demand stimulated cement manufacturers to develop new products. Product development has taken two forms:

joint development for public construction projects, and new products for diversification purposes.

The first approach involved participation in the joint development of new cement products to meet the specifications required for public construction projects. The development of low-heat cement for mass concrete requested by the Honshu-Shikoku Public Corporation is a typical example of the joint development of new products. Eight manufacturers participated in this project.[4]

The second approach involved the development of new cement-related products by individual companies for future product diversification. The five largest firms have moved aggressively in this direction, but there are some differences among them over the approaches taken. For example, Sumitomo is emphasizing the development of new materials, such as a superminute particle and a coating fluid, while Mitsubishi is trying to improve construction materials, such as ceramic materials and ultralight concrete. The scope of Onoda's development efforts range from intelligent robots to new materials, while Nihon is developing not only new construction materials, but also construction machinery and a special material to harden wet ground. Ube has set up a chemical products division as large as its cement division, and is developing home-construction materials such as paneled concrete.

## Diversification Strategies

Since 1985, the five largest firms have developed medium-term plans that stress profitability in their cement businesses and sales in other product lines. These plans have been accompanied by organizational changes. Nihon Cement carried out its reforms in June 1986, establishing a cement division and a construction materials division. This corporate restructuring was based on a plan that set a goal of a 50–50 split of cement and noncement sales by 1992, up from the 70–30 shares that existed in 1988. Sumitomo started its three-year plan in April 1988 with the goal of raising the proportion of its new-business sales (primarily new materials and ceramic products) to 15 percent. Onoda set up a business development division and a real-estate division in May 1988 to realize its diversification strategy. It built suburban bookshops in 1987, ahead of other cement manufacturers, and moved into the so-called "green business," producing greeneries. Finally, Mitsubishi established a research laboratory in March 1988 for

**Figure 14.5**
**Share of cement sales to total sales**

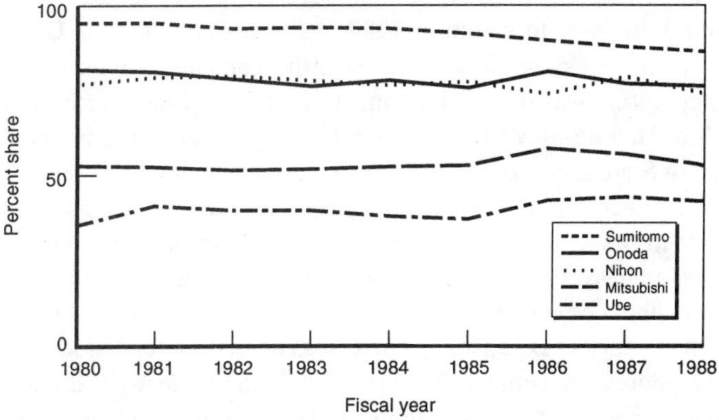

SOURCE: Financial statements of each company.

development of new products and today is expanding its real-estate sector through construction of rental buildings.

While it is clear that these five firms have made progress in diversification, their efforts have not yet had a dramatic impact on the proportion of cement to total sales. Figure 14.5 shows that while the cement sales ratio of Sumitomo experienced a downward trend, the ratios of the other four firms rose in either 1986 or 1987. Different factors are responsible for each firm's rise. For example, the 1986 spin-off of related-business divisions in Onoda increased its cement ratio in that year, as did the closure of Nihon's glass-wool division in May 1987. Diversification accompanied the elimination of unprofitable businesses in these two companies. Mitsubishi's sales of oil products fell sharply after 1986 because of yen appreciation and oil price declines. The combined effect of these two factors reduced the value of oil products shipments more (from 54.1 billion yen in 1985 to 31.6 billion yen in 1986) than the decline in cement sales (from 103 to 97 billion yen) over the same period. For Ube, similar dramatic changes in price occurred in the area of chemical products.

### Increasing Overseas Activity

Overseas activities of Japanese cement manufacturers have lagged behind those of companies in the automobile and electric machinery industries.

Since 1987, however, the five largest cement firms have intensified their push overseas.

Onoda Cement has been the most active in this regard. It granted technology licenses to China in 1987 and established Onoda-USA as its subsidiary in the same year. However, the company's most significant overseas venture was the establishment of the Lone Star–Northwest Company through a tie-up with Lone Star, the largest cement manufacturer in the United States. In this way, Onoda acquired cement silos, ready-mixed concrete factories, and aggregate material factories in Oregon, Washington, and Alaska. Lone Star had no cement plant in the above three states and, thus far, has only sold imported cement there. The tie-up was of mutual interest to both companies—the strengthening of downstream business for Lone Star, and the expansion of overseas activities for Onoda. Finally, Onoda acquired the cement division of the U.S. company Calmat in July 1988 and signed a joint venture agreement to construct a cement production facility in Talien, China, in November of the same year (construction began in March 1990).

Mitsubishi Mining & Cement has also been active overseas. It acquired a cement plant and silos from Kaiser in February 1988. Subsequently, it added a ready-mixed concrete factory and an aggregate factory so as to establish an integrated business network from production to distribution. Finally, in February 1989, it established a joint-venture with two ready-mixed concrete producers in California, and acquired yet another ready-mixed concrete factory in Nevada.

Nihon Cement is also expanding its overseas presence through investments in Nihon-Neelman of India and the establishment of a joint-venture in China.

### Improving Corporate Finances

Japanese cement companies have also sought to restructure their finances. Table 14.5 indicates the recent trends in income and expenditure of the five largest cement firms. Although the financial balance was negative for all manufacturers between 1984 and 1988, the magnitude of losses has decreased each year and has contributed to an increase in the current business surplus (the sum of the operating surplus and the balance of financial transactions).

The major reason why the balance of financial transactions has improved is the reduction of borrowings and the decline in interest rates. The

Table 14.5
Balance sheets of cement companies, 1984–1988 (Billions of yen)

| Company | Revenues | | | Expenditures | | | Current Profit |
|---|---|---|---|---|---|---|---|
| | Total | Interest Receipts | Sales Profit | Total | Interest Payments | Balance[a] | |
| Onoda | | | | | | | |
| 1984 | 4,899 | 2,569 | 1,030 | 13,265 | 13,265 | − 8,366 | 6,023 |
| 1985 | 6,129 | 2,435 | 2,289 | 11,947 | 10,708 | − 5,818 | 4,832 |
| 1986 | 4,005 | 1,895 | 980 | 9,405 | 8,406 | − 5,400 | 11,228 |
| 1987 | 2,544 | 1,311 | 124 | 6,986 | 6,341 | − 4,442 | 15,446 |
| 1988 | 3,146 | 727 | 1,186 | 6,343 | 5,831 | − 3,197 | 16,706 |
| Nihon | | | | | | | |
| 1984 | 5,018 | 2,659 | 936 | 13,621 | 13,324 | − 8,603 | 3,456 |
| 1985 | 5,339 | 2,798 | 1,105 | 13,359 | 12,690 | − 8,020 | 4,379 |
| 1986 | 3,642 | 2,219 | — | 11,133 | 10,003 | − 7,491 | 11,008 |
| 1987 | 3,569 | 1,780 | — | 8,544 | 7,338 | − 4,975 | 12,036 |
| 1988 | 4,158 | 2,079 | — | 8,171 | 6,683 | − 4,013 | 14,786 |
| Sumitomo | | | | | | | |
| 1984 | 4,204 | 3,138 | — | 12,891 | 12,504 | − 8,687 | 5,198 |
| 1985 | 4,217 | 3,341 | — | 11,361 | 11,361 | − 7,144 | 2,916 |
| 1986 | 3,209 | 2,455 | — | 8,817 | 8,817 | − 5,608 | 7,071 |
| 1987 | 3,130 | 2,336 | — | 7,439 | 7,439 | − 4,309 | 10,261 |
| 1988 | 2,380 | 1,542 | — | 5,759 | 5,759 | − 3,379 | 10,741 |

## Table 14.5—continued

| Company | Revenues | | | Expenditures | | | Current Profit |
|---|---|---|---|---|---|---|---|
| | Total | Interest Receipts | Sales Profit | Total | Interest Payments | Balance[a] | |
| **Mitsubishi** | | | | | | | |
| 1984 | 5,457 | 3,041 | 411 | 10,962 | 10,736 | − 5,469 | 7,016 |
| 1985 | 5,577 | 3,062 | 508 | 10,232 | 9,866 | − 4,655 | 6,808 |
| 1986 | 3,798 | 2,098 | 67 | 8,242 | 7,635 | − 4,444 | 8,406 |
| 1987 | 2,588 | 1,340 | — | 7,021 | 6,197 | − 4,433 | 10,754 |
| 1988 | 5,002 | 1,568 | 2,000 | 7,073 | 6,058 | − 2,071 | 14,623 |
| **Ube** | | | | | | | |
| 1984 | 18,969 | 5,841 | 8,636 | 37,693 | 33,861 | −18,724 | 6,484 |
| 1985 | 16,290 | 5,459 | 6,525 | 35,081 | 31,793 | −18,791 | 3,808 |
| 1986 | 12,073 | 4,248 | 3,948 | 29,358 | 26,553 | −17,285 | 6,193 |
| 1987 | 16,189 | 3,248 | 9,819 | 24,995 | 22,531 | − 8,806 | 20,360 |
| 1988 | 20,265 | 2,546 | 14,998 | 22,942 | 20,907 | − 2,677 | 31,926 |

[a] Total revenues minus total expenditures.
*Sources:* Financial statements of each company.

average interest rate charged by private banks fell from 6.7 percent in 1984 to 5 percent in 1988, enabling firms to reduce interest payments by as much as one-quarter, even though levels of debt remained unchanged. Interest payments of each company decreased even more sharply than the drop in interest rates, primarily because the five manufacturers reduced their long-term borrowing by between 40 and 80 percent from 1984 to 1988.[5]

## Industry's Adjustments Under the Structural Adjustment Law

I have described, above, a series of tax-reduction, accelerated-depreciation, special loans from the Japan Development Bank (JDB), and other measures available to companies designated under the Structural Adjustment Law. Here I examine the extent to which these measures were utilized by cement manufacturers, the effects on competition in the industry, and the capacity scrapping achieved by each firm. This assessment is tentative because of the limited availability of data at this moment.

*Use of policy measures:* Table 14.6 shows loans from the Japan Development Bank as a proportion of total long-term borrowing. Three of the five largest firms—Sumitomo, Mitsubishi, and Ube—increased the JDB

**Table 14.6**
**Japan Development Bank loans and its share**
**in long-term borrowing**
(Long-term borrowings from JDB in millions of yen;
percentage shares in parentheses)

| Company | Fiscal Year | | | | | |
|---|---|---|---|---|---|---|
| | 1983 | 1984 | 1985 | 1986 | 1987 | 1988 |
| Onoda | 15,028 | 12,944 | 11,097 | 8,814 | 6,837 | 5,184 |
| | (15.9) | (16.3) | (16.2) | (16.2) | (16.4) | (15.7) |
| Nihon | 11,126 | 9,622 | 9,057 | 7,865 | 6,372 | 5,267 |
| | (12.3) | (12.5) | (12.2) | (12.7) | (12.1) | (11.1) |
| Sumitomo | 16,335 | 16,106 | 14,258 | 12,738 | 10,661 | 9,785 |
| | (18.8) | (19.9) | (20.0) | (20.3) | (22.0) | (25.3) |
| Mitsubishi | 7,122 | 6,762 | 7,628 | 6,938 | 6,739 | 7,360 |
| | ( 9.2) | (10.2) | (12.8) | (13.7) | (16.3) | (17.8) |
| Ube | 24,316 | 25,952 | 26,239 | 25,593 | 24,032 | 24,000 |
| | ( 8.9) | ( 9.6) | (10.1) | (10.6) | (10.5) | (11.1) |

*Sources:* Financial statements of each company.

**Figure 14.6**
**Cement prices and share of imports**

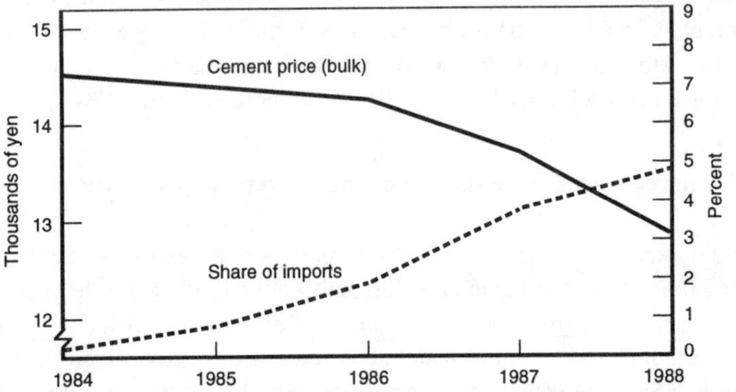

SOURCE: Semento Shimbunsha, *Semento Heckan*, (Cement Yearbook).

proportion of borrowing between 1987 and 1988 and all of them had designated equipment. In Nihon's case, the proportion of JDB borrowing fell in 1988 despite its scrapping of 17 kilns under the Structural Adjustment Law. These changes in the composition of long-term borrowing suggest that loan assistance from the JDB may have helped; however, it is difficult to draw a firm conclusion from these figures because the five manufacturers reduced their borrowings from the JDB in 1988. Similarly, the aggregate nature of company financial statements makes it difficult to identify the effects of tax reductions (since only aggregated tax payments are available) or to ascertain that depreciation rates increased as a result of accelerated depreciation provisions (the gross numbers did not show any change in reported depreciation rates).

*Effects on competitiveness:* Through business tie-ups, the five groups of cement manufacturers sought to reduce production costs by at least 1,000 yen per ton by rationalization within the group and by each individual manufacturer. A simple comparison of the unit price of domestic manufacturers with that of imported cement (CIF basis) shows a price gap of roughly 4,000 yen per ton. Taking into account profit margins and transportation costs, the real price gap between them is closer to about 2,000 yen per ton. In other words, domestic cement should be able to compete with imports if the price gap is narrowed to within a 1,000-yen-per-ton range, assuming quality differences between domestic and imported cement.

The unit price of portland cement sold by domestic manufacturers was 9,550 yen per ton during the January-March 1989 period. This price was lower than that prevailing during the same quarter of 1988 by 400 yen per ton, but higher by 70 yen than that of the previous quarter. This situation was brought about by the sharp increase in domestic demand for cement in both Korea and Taiwan, the two major suppliers to Japan. The tight demand in these countries constrained exports, thus reducing competitive pressures in the Japanese domestic market. The latter appears to be especially important in moderating prices in the Japanese market, as shown in Figure 14.6, where the price of bulk-cement fell over the period 1984 to 1988 as the proportion of imported cement to total sales increased.

Imports may have played a very important role in keeping the Japanese cement industry competitive and in inhibiting cartel actions to maintain the price of cement. In June 1990, the Japanese FTC began its investigations of major cement manufacturers suspected of violating Article 3 of the Anti-Monopoly Law, which prohibits illegal trade restrictions. Although still under investigation, successful prosecution of this case could undo efforts to regain competitiveness through the establishment of five joint-sales companies.

*Capacity scrapping and production efficiency:* Finally, I turn to patterns of capacity scrapping by cement manufacturers with different market shares. In their study of the strategic behavior of firms facing structural adjustment, Ghemawat and Nalebuff (1985) showed that inefficient outcomes might arise if firms with a larger market share exit first. However, by extending Ghemawat and Nalebuff's model, Whinston (1988) demonstrates that their conclusion is less definitive in the case of multiplant firms.

As panel A of Table 14.7 shows, the rate of capacity scrapping had little or no correlation with the company's market share under the earlier Structural Improvement Law (1984–86). In the more recent 1987–89 period (under the Structural Adjustment Law), there is a positive, but weak correlation between the two variables. Thus, results for both periods do not appear to strongly support Ghemawat and Nalebuff's hypothesis. The results are unchanged when we consider the correlation coefficients between the rate of scrapping and market share at the factory level, assuming each factory to be like a single-plant firm.

These correlations suggest a number of points. First, the predicted positive correlation is not empirically supported, possibly because several assumptions of the Ghemawat and Nalebuff model are violated—most cement manufacturers are multiplant firms (these yield ambiguous predictions, as Whinston notes); furthermore, capacity scrapping was carried out

### Table 14.7
### Correlations between the rate of capacity scrapping
### and related variables

| Period | Correlation Coefficient | |
| --- | --- | --- |
| | Company Basis | Factory Basis |
| A. *Rate of Scrapping and Market Share* | | |
| 1984–86 | – 0.0382 | 0.0266 |
| 1987–89 | 0.1829 | 0.1247 |
| B. *Rate of Scrapping and Excess Capacity Ratio* | | |
| 1984–86 | 0.5803 | 0.6499 |
| 1987–89 | 0.4947 | 0.5751 |
| 1984–89 | 0.8114 | 0.7308 |

cooperatively, which is not accounted for in Ghemawat and Nalebuff's model. Second, the rate of capacity scrapping is positively correlated with the ratio of excess capacity, as shown in panel B of Table 14.7. Because only seven manufacturers scrapped capacity under the Structural Adjustment Law, the correlation in the 1987–89 period, although positive, is relatively weak. When the two adjustment periods are combined, however, the positive correlation becomes stronger. Thus, capacity scrapping in the cement industry appears to be more sensitive to excess capacity than to market share. Finally, the two adjustment phases differ somewhat in the reduction of factor inputs. From 1984 to 1986, capacity (mostly number of kilns) was scrapped by 23 percent and the number of factory workers was reduced by 12.3 percent; the corresponding figures for the 1987–89 period were 8.9 percent and 9.1 percent, respectively. Thus, while adjustment under the Structural Improvement Law tended to scrap obsolete capacity, the burden of adjustment under the Structural Adjustment Law was shared equally by capital and labor.

## CONCLUDING REMARKS

Since the mid-1980s, the Japanese cement industry has been faced with excess capacity and import penetration. A review of structural adjustments in this industry leads to the following observations:

1. Cement manufacturers made massive efforts to respond to adverse conditions by restructuring. These include use of energy-saving tech-

nologies, scrapping of obsolete capacity, reduction and relocation of workers through early retirement schemes or employment loaning, and diversifying business into more promising lines of business.

2.  The industry sought designation under the Structural Improvement Law in 1984 and under the Structural Adjustment Law in 1987. Their application for designation under the Structural Adjustment Law was delayed by the Japanese Fair Trade Commission, which raised concerns about the potential monopoly resulting from establishment of a silo for joint use and about manufacturers' restrictive practices regarding supply to ready-mixed concrete producers using directly imported cement. These laws appear to have provided manufacturers with a venue for cooperative action and avoidance of cutthroat competition.

3.  At this stage, it is difficult to determine the extent to which each manufacturer utilized the measures provided by these laws. One problem is the paucity of data detailing their use. The relatively short time since implementation of the laws also makes it difficult to ascertain their impact from each company's financial statements. It should be noted, however, that manufacturers as a whole attained the target rate of capacity scrapping; in this sense, the government policy of promoting capacity scrapping was probably effective.

4.  Though not conclusive, government policies appear to have had a positive influence on increasing the industry's productive efficiency. Less efficient kilns tended to be scrapped in each of the two adjustment periods, although little support was found for the hypothesis that larger firms scrap more than smaller firms. More definitive conclusions must wait until better information becomes available on the extent to which the industry needed government intervention to scrap excess capacity and whether the same or more efficient outcomes might have been obtained without it.

From these observations, I draw two implications for adjustment policy toward industries facing excess capacity. First, these policies must balance trade-offs between cooperation among manufacturers, necessary to jointly reduce capacity and the risk of promoting collusion among manufacturers seeking monopolistic rents by raising prices. This suggests that policymakers should pay attention to potential competition-restricting behavior of producers. Closer surveillance, such as the June 1990 Fair Trade Commission investigation of alleged illegal cartel actions by the major cement manufacturers, is desirable. Second, in many cases it is difficult to know the extent to which different adjustment assistance measures were used, not only in the case of the Japanese cement industry, but in other troubled industries as well. To be effective, adjustment policies must be transparent, and improved data about their use are required to better evaluate the efficacy of these policies.

---

## NOTES

1. The cement manufacturers association established a study group on structural problems in October 1982 and applied for reorganization under the Structural Improvement Law in October 1983.

2. While imports were to be 1.2 million tons (excluding imports by manufacturers) under the voluntary restraint agreement by Korean manufacturers, actual total imports from Korea in 1987 totaled only 1.53 million tons. The shortfall arose because of the surge in domestic demand in Korea related to the construction boom of the Seoul Olympics. Imports from Taiwan, however, grew over this period.

3. *Nikkei Sangyo Shimbun* (Nikkei Industry Journal), May 31, 1988.

4. The eight manufacturers were Ube, Osaka, Onoda, Mitsubishi, Nippon Steel Chemical, Sumitomo, Tokuyama Soda, and Aso. Aso began its participation in 1988, the others in 1987.

5. Between FY 1984 and FY 1988, long-term borrowing of Onoda fell from 79.4 to 33.0 billion yen; of Nihon from 77.5 to 47.6 billion yen; of Sumitomo from 80.7 to 38.6 billion yen; of Mitsubishi from 66.6 to 41.3 billion yen; and of Ube from 271.0 to 215.5 billion yen.

## BIBLIOGRAPHY

Baden-Fuller, C. W. F. (1989). "Exit from Declining Industries and the Case of Steel Casting." *Economic Journal,* vol. 99, 949–961.

Ghemawat, P., and B. Nalebuff (1985). "Exit." *RAND Journal of Economics,* vol. 16, no. 2, 184–194.

Shaw, R. W., and S. A. Shaw (1983). "Excess Capacity and Rationalization in the West European Synthetic Fibres Industry." *Journal of Industrial Economics,* vol. 32, no. 2, 141–166.

Sumitomo Cement Co. (1987). *Sumitomo Semento Hachijunenshi* (80 Years History of Sumitomo Cement Co.). Tokyo, Japan.

Whinston, M. D. (1988). "Exit with Multiplant Firms." *RAND Journal of Economics,* vol. 19, no. 4, 568–588.

# 15

## Adjustment Responses of Troubled Industries in U.S. Manufacturing

### Hong W. Tan and Elizabeth Lewis

### INTRODUCTION

**H**ow do troubled industries adjust when faced with declining product demand and import competition? Earlier chapters described a variety of adjustment responses—firm exit, capacity reduction through plant closings, workforce retrenchment and wage cuts, ownership changes and mergers, investments in new plant and equipment, investments in research and development (R&D), product diversification or entry into new lines of business, as well as petitioning for import relief under U.S. trade statutes or through the political process. In this chapter, several of these adjustment responses—firm entry and exit, and petitioning for import relief—are pursued in greater detail using plant-level data for three troubled U.S. industries—machine tools, hydraulic cement, and industrial fasteners.

First, we pose the following questions: As demand declines, do all existing firms in the industry shrink their output uniformly, or are some firms more likely to be adversely affected than others? Is there entry of new firms into declining industries? Do competitive pressures, from both new domestic entrants and foreign competitors, force inefficient producers to shut down? These questions are of policy interest, not only for what they reveal about adjustment behavior of firms, but also for whether firm entry and exit is associated with the subsequent improvement in the efficiency and competitiveness of the troubled industry. Theoretical studies, such as those reviewed in Chapter 2, provide predictions about which firms are likely to exit first, but are generally silent on the issue of new firm entry. Several empirical studies have used plant-level data to document the patterns of firm entry and exit (e.g., Dunne, Roberts, and Samuelson, 1988; Lieberman, 1990; Deily, 1991), as well as their associated employment consequences (e.g., Dunne, Roberts, and Samuelson, 1989; Davis and Haltiwanger, 1990). However, with some exceptions (Liu, 1991), microevidence on the productivity consequences of firm entry and exit are scant.

Next, we ask questions about the firms that petition for import relief. What are the characteristics of petitioners? What factors shape the timing of when petitions are filed? Do petitioners tend to be more efficient or less efficient than other firms in the same industry? This issue is important since governments have to make decisions about dumping, injury, and import relief for a whole industry on the basis of information provided by firms that may turn out not to be typical of other firms in the industry. In Chapter 7, Tan and Lichtenburg provided some insights based on comparisons *across* petitioning and nonpetitioning industries at the four-digit SIC level. Here, we look at the relative efficiency of petitioning and nonpetitioning firms *within* a four-digit industry, hydraulic cement.

We address these issues using plant-level data from the Longitudinal Research Database (LRD) of the U.S. Census Bureau, and the RAND Petition Database (RANDPET). The longitudinal nature of the plant and firm-level data in the LRD confers a distinct advantage over more aggregated datasets; aggregate industry-level data can show only net flows (in the number of firms or in employment), but not the gross flows (entry and exit of firms and associated creation and loss of jobs) that are indispensable to the study of firm adjustment responses. Using the wealth of plant-level production information contained in the LRD, production functions can be estimated to compare the relative efficiency of firms that enter, survive, or exit the industry. Finally, linkage of the RANDPET data to the LRD allows petitioning firms to be identified, and their characteristics and levels of efficiency to be compared to that of other firms in the industry that do not petition.

The section that follows describes broad characteristics of the two datasets, variables of interest, and how they were linked. Next, information is presented on entries and exits in three four-digit industries—machine tools, hydraulic cement, and industrial fasteners—and their effects on the value of shipments and employment. Simple plant-level production functions are then estimated for each industry and used to derive a measure of "relative efficiency" for each plant, relative to the industry mean at each point in time. Plants are compared for insights into the relative efficiency levels of entries, incumbents, and exits in our same sample of troubled industries. Finally, findings are reported on firms petitioning for import relief, using the hydraulic cement industry as a case study. Characteristics of petitioners and nonpetitioners are compared, and an attempt is made to explain why some petitioned in some periods, but not in others.

## DATA SOURCES AND LINKED FILES

To study the adjustment responses of troubled U.S. firms, the authors created longitudinal analysis files on individual manufacturing plants in selected industries by linking together the LRD and the RANDPET databases. Together, they provide information on a variety of plant-level production variables (shipments, wages, capital stock, materials, energy, and employment); firm-level expenditures on R&D and sales; and petitioning activity (whether firms in fact petitioned, the timing of the petitions, the type of import relief petition, and their outcomes).

### The Longitudinal Research Database (LRD)

The LRD, a longitudinal database maintained at the center for economic studies in the U.S. Census Bureau, is an unbalanced panel of manufacturing establishments created by linking respondents in 5 Censuses of Manufacturing (CM) and 12 Annual Surveys of Manufacturing (ASM). The CM data are for the years 1963, 1967, 1972, 1977, and 1982; the ASM data for non-CM years between 1973 and 1986. By linking CM and ASM respondents across the years, the LRD provides a panel dataset on manufacturing plants spanning the census years between 1963 and 1972, and continuously (for most large plants) from 1973 to 1986, with sample sizes of between 300,000 and 350,000 manufacturing plants in CM years, about 70,000 plants in ASM years.

Respondents in CM and ASM years are linked by a plant identification number (PPN). A firm identification number (ID) permits establishments in multiplant firms to be associated with the firm, or when a plant's ID changes over time, to be identified as having undergone a ownership change (such as a sale or merger). Past Censuses of Manufacturing were not collected with the objective of following individual plants of firms over time. Substantial effort had to be devoted to matching individual respondents, a process that continues to this day (see Dunn, Roberts, and Samuelson, 1988). In addition to PPNs and

IDs, the LRD contains basic information on factors of production (the cost of such inputs as labor, materials, energy, physical plant, and equipment) and on output (primary products, value of shipments, and inventories).

For the analyses reported here, we selected three four-digit SIC industries for study, based on such criteria as petitioning activity, size of the market (value of shipments), number of establishments, and policy interest. The three industries are machine tools (SICs 3541 and 3542), hydraulic cement (SIC 3241), and nuts and bolts (SIC 3452). In selecting the samples, an establishment was included in the industry if it ever (even if only in one year) listed as its primary product any of the five-digit products contained in these four-digit industries. Primary product codes can (and do) change over time, usually within four-digit industry groups; however, a plants production of a specific four-digit product may continue and be listed as one of the plants secondary products. This sample-section criterion was intended to permit future study of product diversification as one (of many alternative) adjustment responses to declining product demand.

### The RAND Petition Database

The petition database was assembled by one of the authors from the U.S. International Trade Commission (ITC) and the International Trade Administration (ITA), Department of Commerce (see Chapter 7). Information was collected on three types of import relief petitions—escape clause petitions under section 201 of the 1974 Trade Law, and antidumping (sales at less than fair value) and countervailing-duty (foreign government subsidization of imports) petitions under the so-called Fair Trade Laws. Data on these petitions were assembled from docket logs, public use files, and other primary data sources at the ITC and ITA (including archival records on petitions filed at the U.S. Treasury Department prior to 1980). For each petition, information (incomplete in some years) was collected on the date of filing, the product and corresponding SIC code, the ITC and/or ITA determination, and the country (or countries) involved. Most important, for the analyses reported in this paper, the name(s) of the petitioner(s) was collected where available. These company names were used to link petitioner information to LRD.

### FIRM ENTRY AND EXIT

We begin by examining patterns of entry and exit, measured across census years, in three industries facing declining product demand and import competition, which responded by filing one or more import relief petitions. The three industries selected are machine tools (SICs 35411–35423), portland hydraulic cement (SIC 32410), and industrial fasteners, nuts, bolts, and screws (SICs 34524 and 34525). The three industries underwent very different experiences over the 1958–86 period—at one extreme, wide swings in output and employment in the machine tool industry, with a strong declining trend in after the late 1960s; at the other, moderate swings in both output and employment for the cement and industrial fasteners industries, with a gradual declining trend from the late 1970s on.

Descriptive information on rates of entry and exit of plants across census years, and on their contributions to total industry employment and value of shipments in each census year, is presented in Table 15.1. Entry and exits are defined as follows: in a given census year, a plant is defined as an entrant if it was not present in the past census (five years prior, except for the 1967 Census, when the interval was four years); similarly, an exit in a given census year is a plant not present in the following census. We shall define entry and exit "rates" in terms of the census year in which the pre- or post-census year comparison is made. Thus, an exit rate of 20 percent in the 1972–77 period means that 20 percent of plants in 1972 do not survive (exited) by 1977. An entry rate of 20 percent in 1972–77 implies that 20 percent of plants were not yet in operation by 1972.

The first two columns of Table 15.1 show the entry and exit rates of establishments over the four subperiods for each of the three industries. They reveal fairly high rates of *both* entry and exit in each industry, ranging between 10 and 20 percent. In most cases, these five-year rates suggest that between one-tenth and one-fifth of all plants operating in a given year either entered within the last five years or would leave within the next five years. In terms of total number of plants, the machine tools industry appears to have experienced a secular decline in the number of plants in operation beginning in 1972. In the first two subperiods (1960s and early 1970s), entry rates exceeded exit rates in the machine tool industry; moving into the 1970s and early 1980s, the trend is reversed and exit rates exceed entry rates. In other words, the number of machine tool plants increased up until 1972, after which it declined. Similar though less pronounced, time trends in the patterns of entry and exit are also observed in the case of industrial fasteners. In contrast, the hydraulic cement industry experienced both generally rising entry and exit rates over time. However, since entry rates always exceed exit rates, the number of cement plants in operation actually increased over time.

The third and fourth columns of Table 15.1 show the total value of industry shipments accounted for by entry and exit of plants from the

**Table 15.1**
**Entry and exit rates from selected troubled industries**
**in terms of plants, workers, and shipments**

| Industry<br>Time-Period | Plants<br>Entry<br>% | Plants<br>Exit<br>% | Shipments<br>Entry<br>% | Shipments<br>Exit<br>% | Workers<br>Entry<br>% | Workers<br>Exit<br>% |
|---|---|---|---|---|---|---|
| 1. Machine Tools | | | | | | |
| 1963–67 | 18.5 | 10.0 | 5.8 | 3.8 | 5.6 | 3.5 |
| 1967–72 | 17.5 | 16.5 | 8.5 | 10.9 | 8.8 | 10.9 |
| 1972–77 | 9.9 | 14.4 | 5.7 | 6.2 | 6.0 | 5.6 |
| 1977–82 | 9.3 | 17.7 | 4.7 | 7.1 | 4.2 | 7.5 |
| 2. Hydraulic Cement | | | | | | |
| 1963–67 | 13.6 | 9.1 | 5.0 | 5.1 | 5.2 | 5.8 |
| 1967–72 | 17.0 | 13.6 | 8.6 | 8.5 | 7.2 | 11.6 |
| 1972–77 | 16.6 | 14.4 | 4.7 | 6.3 | 4.4 | 6.9 |
| 1977–82 | 22.9 | 18.3 | 9.3 | 9.1 | 10.0 | 11.5 |
| 3. Screws & Fasteners | | | | | | |
| 1963–67 | 16.7 | 13.0 | 6.2 | 5.6 | 6.3 | 4.8 |
| 1967–72 | 17.6 | 18.4 | 11.8 | 12.9 | 9.7 | 12.1 |
| 1972–77 | 13.8 | 12.1 | 6.5 | 8.3 | 6.0 | 8.5 |
| 1977–82 | 10.9 | 16.7 | 8.1 | 8.8 | 7.1 | 9.4 |

*Note:* Entry in 1967–67 is defined as being in the 1967 Census but not in the 1963 Census. Exit in 1963–67 is defined in the 1963 Census but not in the 1967 Census. Figures for shipments and workers refer to the proportion of total industry sales and employment associated with new entrants and existing plants.

industry. Two points may be noted. First, plants that enter or exit the industry are generally smaller (in terms of the value of the shipments) than the plants that survive over the period. This follows from the fact that entry and exit rates are invariably higher than the share of shipments accounted for by either new entrants or existing plants, suggesting that surviving plants are larger. Second, the value of shipments in machine tools and industrial fasteners began to shrink in real terms (in inflation-adjusted millions of dollars) from the late 1960s on. To see this, note that beginning in the 1967–72 period, the share of shipments accounted for by exiting plants exceeded the share of shipments produced by new entrants. In the case of hydraulic cement, shipments appear to have remained roughly the same over this entire period since the value of shipments lost through exiting plants was roughly offset by new entrants.

The last two columns in Table 15.1 document the employment consequences of plant entry and exit. The main points raised above with respect to value of shipments are applicable here with respect to the smaller average size of the workforce in plants that enter and exit as compared to surviving plants.

In all three industries, total employment fell over the period since 1967, as exiting plants removed more jobs from the industry than the new jobs added by the opening of new plants. This may be seen in the generally higher shares of employment in plants that exit as compared to the employment shares of new entrants. Furthermore, consistent with the finding of other studies (e.g., Dunne, Roberts, and Samuelson, 1989; Davis and Haltiwanger, 1990), the data suggest that significantly more job turnover occurred in industrial restructuring than a simple comparison of employment levels in two years might indicate. Taking the case of industrial fasteners as an example, total industry employment declined from 63,970 to 52,215 workers between 1977 and 1982, or a *net job loss* of 11,755 jobs. In reality, the panel plant-level data suggest that jobs lost were much higher—6,013 jobs from plant closings and 9,399 jobs from workforce cutbacks by surviving plants, for a *gross job loss* of 15,412 positions. The difference between the gross and net figures is due to the addition of 3,707 jobs created by new plants.

To summarize, these data suggest several conclusions about the industrial adjustment process in troubled industries. First they suggest that aggregate industry measures conceal considerable entry and exit: many new plants enter the industry even when total demand for the industry's output is declining. Second, many exits tend to be concentrated among smaller plants (in terms of shipments), a finding that runs counter to the theories reviewed by McMillan in Chapter 2. Finally, the data suggest that net job loss estimates understate considerably the magnitude of job losses that arise as firms in troubled industries downsize or shut down plants.

## RELATIVE EFFICIENCY LEVELS OF ENTRY AND EXIT PLANTS

We seek to answer here the question of whether plants entering or exiting troubled industries are more or less efficient than incumbent or surviving plants. The issue is whether entry and exit of plants is associated with subsequent improvements in overall industry efficiency and competitiveness. One simple metric—labor productivity—was rejected in favor of a more comprehensive measure based on a simple four-factor production function. The data required for such estimation are readily available in the LRD. The production function, in double logarithmic form, had the following specification:

$$Q_{it} = a_o + a_t DT_{t=2,T} + b_1 K_{it} + b_2 L_{it} + b_3 E_{it} + b_4 M_{it} + e_{it} \qquad (1)$$

where Q is the value of shipments; DT represents year dummy variables for t=2 to T; K is the book value of capital stock (plant and equipment); L is total hours worked in production worker–equivalent units; E is the cost of purchased energy (electricity and fuel); M is the cost of materials; e is an error term, and the a's and b's are parameters to be estimated. All inputs and output were deflated to constant 1972 dollars using four-digit SIC input and output deflators. In this specification, the year dummy variables allow overall levels of productivity in the industry to shift over time (one measure of total factor productivity growth). The residual error term, $e_{it}$, thus provides a metric of how efficient plant i is relative to the industry average in each year t. By construction, the industry mean in each year has an expected value of zero.

For each industry, the production function was estimated on pooled cross-section time-series (CM and ASM years) data on all plants. The results are reported in Table 15.2. They suggest constant-returns-to-scale production in each of the three industries. Using these estimated parameters for each industry, we calculated a residual productivity variable for each plant-year, given the plant's endowments of (expenditures on) the four inputs in that year. We term this residual measure that plant's "relative efficiency."

Table 15.3 presents means of this relative efficiency measure for entrants, incumbents, and exits across the census years. First, averaging across census

**Table 15.2**
**Plant-level production function estimates**

| Industry (Observations) | Log (K) | Log (L) | Log (E) | Log (M) | R-squared |
|---|---|---|---|---|---|
| Machine Tools (5559) | .4211 (.0098) | .0956 (.0069) | .0820 (.0077) | .3701 (.0057) | .959 |
| Hydraulic Cement (2552) | .2982 (.0173) | .0826 (.0103) | .1544 (.0109) | .4425 (.0105) | .914 |
| Screws & Fasteners (4492) | .3891 (.0086) | .1331 (.0071) | .0507 (.0077) | .4225 (.0062) | .959 |

*Notes:*
1. Parameter estimates are based on a production function of shipments regressed on a constant, four inputs, and year dummy variables.
2. Standard errors in parentheses.
3. K = book value of building and equipment assets (1972 dollars).
   L = total hours worked in production-worker equivalent units.
   E = cost of purchased energy and fuel (1972 dollars).
   M = cost of materials (1972 dollars).

years, the efficiency levels of exiting plants are invariably negative (–0.48 percent in machine tools, –8.4 percent in cement, and –1.9 percent in industrial fasteners), meaning that their efficiency levels are lower than the industry average. In contrast, the efficiency levels of the incumbent or surviving plants are usually positive and close to the industry average. Thus, as one would hope, the less efficient plants exit and the more efficient plants remain. Second, "new" entrants likewise tend to be less efficient relative to the industry average than incumbent plants. This result, however, may be due to several factors. Some small new entrants may in time become relatively more efficient, moving up the experience or learning curve. Indeed, casual examination of the time path of each new entrant's relative efficiency (in ASM and CM years) reveals the presence of such learning-by-doing in some plants (for a more rigorous analysis of plant-level learning through experience, see Liu, 1991). Other entrants, however, may not improve efficiency levels and may exit before the next census. This interpretation appears to be consistent with models of industry evolution in which firms enter an industry and, over time, seek to ascertain their (initially unknown) levels of efficiency; those that have a comparative advantage grow, while those that do not, decline and exit (Jovanovic, 1982; Pakes and Ericson, 1990).

In short, these estimates suggest that troubles industries in the United States appear to restructure through higher rates of firm exit than entry, the departure of smaller and less efficient plants, and their replacement by (eventually) more efficient ones. To the extent that the firms that survive are relatively more efficient, the outcome is a smaller industry that is more productive and competitive.

## IMPORT RELIEF PETITIONS IN THE CEMENT INDUSTRY

Finally, we turn to a largely descriptive analysis of firms filing petitions for import tax relief, using the hydraulic cement industry as a case study. We are interested in several questions. First, can we learn anything from linking petition data to the LRD? In other words, does knowing whether, and when, a firm petitioned for import relief add to our ability to study its economic performance and behavior? Second, what are the characteristics of firms that petition, and are such firms very different from nonpetitioners? Third, what determines when a petition for import relief is filed? Finally, if all firms in the industry presumably experience similar demand declines or import competition at the same time, why do some firms participate in import relief petitions filed in some years but not in other petitions filed at another time?

**Table 15.3**
**Relative efficiency levels of plants**

| Industry/Time-Period | Entrants | Incumbents | Exits | Incumbents |
|---|---|---|---|---|
| 1. Machine Tools | −.0152 | .0039 | −.0048 | .0013 |
| 1963–67 | .0023 | −.0005 | −.0744 | .0173 |
| 1967–72 | −.0103 | .0008 | −.0032 | .0016 |
| 1972–77 | −.0157 | .0036 | .0086 | −.0032 |
| 1977–82 | −.0392 | .0080 | .0014 | .0018 |
| | | | | |
| 2. Hydraulic Cement | −.0359 | .0197 | −.0839 | .0196 |
| 1963–67 | −.0094 | .0012 | −.0789 | .0131 |
| 1967–72 | .0300 | .0027 | −.0641 | .0181 |
| 1972–77 | −.1273 | .0254 | −.1025 | .0193 |
| 1977–82 | −.0632 | .0436 | −.0963 | .0257 |
| | | | | |
| 3. Screws & Fasteners | .0130 | −.0035 | −.0192 | .0018 |
| 1963–67 | −.0145 | .0041 | −.0033 | −.0057 |
| 1967–72 | −.0064 | −.0004 | −.0251 | .0141 |
| 1972–77 | .0200 | −.0047 | −.0019 | −.0018 |
| 1977–82 | .0590 | −.0075 | −.0346 | .0047 |

*Note:* Relative productivity is estimated from a four-factor production function with building and machinery assets, labor, materials, and energy. See previous Table.

In the cement industry, antidumping petitions were filed in 1975, 1976, 1978, 1984, and 1984. All were unsuccessful in gaining import relief. For the analysis, it may be useful to group petitioning firms into three groups: (1) petitioners in the 1970s, (2) petitioners in the 1980s, and (3) petitioners in both periods. The first two groups of petitioners are mutually exclusive—the 1970s petitioners did not participate in the petitions filed in the 1980s, even though they were in the industry in that period; similarly, the 1980s petitioners did not join in any of the petitions in the 1970s. The most recent 1984 antidumping petition group was by far the largest, both in terms of the number of petitioning firms and in terms of the number of different countries cited.

Table 15.4 provides descriptive statistics on the cement plants in each of the three groups of petitioners and, for comparison, on firms that did not participate in any of these petitions (nonpetitioners). These figures are averages over the entire 1963–86 period. It is clear that petitioners tend to be larger firms than non-petitioners, both in terms of the number of plants operated and in terms of value of shipments. Moreover, petitioning firms appear to pay higher wage rates to their employees, with premiums in excess of 50 cents per hour (in 1972 dollars) over the mean wage rates paid by nonpetitioners. In addition, the mean value of the relative efficiency measure

Table 15.4
**Descriptive statistics on petitioners and non-petitioners**

| Variable Name | Petitioning Firms 1970s | 1980s | 1970 & 1980s | Non-Petitioners All Years |
|---|---|---|---|---|
| Plants in the firm | 7.411 (3.299) | 7.701 (4.296) | 7.757 (2.710) | 4.962 (4.940) |
| Distribution of plants 1–5 plants | .2719 (.4453) | .3714 (.4834) | .2038 (.4034) | .2696 (.4439) |
| 6–10 plants | .5223 (.4999) | .3739 (.4841) | .6584 (.4749) | .1768 (.3816) |
| 11 plus plants | .1807 (.3851) | .2337 (.4234) | .1349 (.3421) | .1720 (.3781) |
| Shipments (1972 $1,000s) | 9,748 (6,355) | 11,028 ( 8,126) | 9,420 (5,269) | 8,196 (6,507) |
| Hourly wage (1972 $) of production workers | 5.69 (.96) | 5.62 (.85) | 5.52 (.85) | 5.01 (1.44) |
| Relative efficiency (residual productivity) | −.0554 (.2931) | .0490 (.3606) | − .0681 (.2667) | −.020 (.384) |
| Do no R&D | .6733 (.4693) | .5448 (.4982) | .6473 (.4784) | .6650 (.4720) |
| R&D intensity (R&D as a fraction of sales) | .0018 (.0057) | .0072 (.0543) | .0024 (.007) | .0036 (.0374) |

*Note:* Standard deviations are shown in parentheses below the means.

is positive only for petitioners in the 1980s. Thus, this group of firms appears to have the most efficient plants in the industry. Finally, compared with other groups, these latter firms were also more likely to do research and development and to spend more on R&D as a proportion of sales. In contrast, firms petitioning in both periods had the lowest mean efficiency levels in the industry and about average levels of incidence and R&D intensity as 1970s petitioners and other nonpetitioners.

Table 15.5 reports the results of simple regressions (probit model) of indicator variables for each petitioner group on this set of plant/firm characteristics. (Future research will estimate multinomial logic models for the likelihood of being in each of the four groups.) This exercise allows us to ask how the attributes of each group differ from those of all other firms in the industry, holding other variables constant. These results confirm the basic differences across groups noted above from a simple comparison of variable means and will not be stated here. One point bears repeating: petitioners are heterogeneous. Some (the 1980s petitioners) have plants that are more

**Table 15.5**
**Characteristics of petitioners in the cement industry**
**probit [petitioner]$_{ijt}$ = G(X$_{it}$)j = 1970s, 1980s, 1970s & 1980s**

| | Petitioning Firms | | | | | |
| | 1970s | | 1980s | | 1970s & 1980s | |
| X Variables | coef. | t-stat. | coef. | t-stat. | coef. | t-stat. |
|---|---|---|---|---|---|---|
| Constant | −5.236 | (10.8) | −4.636 | (10.2) | −4.802 | ( 7.4) |
| Number of plants | | | | | | |
| 2–5 | 1.037 | ( 7.6) | 1.362 | (10.1) | 1.551 | ( 4.6) |
| 6–10 | 1.773 | (13.1) | 1.666 | (12.1) | 2.474 | ( 7.5) |
| 11 plus | .984 | ( 6.5) | 1.264 | ( 8.6) | 1.424 | ( 4.1) |
| Log (shipments) | .077 | ( 1.9) | .125 | ( 3.0) | .057 | ( 1.1) |
| Relative efficiency | − .505 | ( 4.9) | .288 | ( 3.2) | − .432 | ( 3.6) |
| Log (hourly wages) | 1.420 | ( 7.4) | 1.028 | ( 5.8) | .731 | ( 3.2) |
| Do no R&D | .357 | ( 4.7) | − .069 | ( 1.0) | .254 | ( 3.1) |
| R&D intensity | −7.497 | ( 1.3) | 1.143 | ( 1.8) | −1.298 | ( 0.6) |
| Sample size | 2,248 | | 2,248 | | 2,248 | |
| Log-likelihood | − 945 | | −1,161 | | − 690 | |

efficient than the industry average; others (the 1970s petitioners and firms petitioning in both decades) have mean efficiency levels lower than the industry average.

Thus far, we have compared the three groups of petitioners in terms of their average characteristics over the entire sample period (1963–86). Do these plant/firm characteristics evolve over time and with changes in economic conditions? If they change over time, do these changes explain the timing of petitions or why some firms petition in one period but not in others? To address these issues, we can compare the time paths of key economic variables for each group of petitioners, both before and after the year in which they file import relief petitions. At this point, we have completed comparisons of only the mean relative efficiency of each of the petitioner groups. We did this by estimating the following cross-sectional models, one for each year, in which the plant's relative efficiency level is regressed on indicator variables for each of the three groups of petitioners:

$$RE_{it} = a_t + b_t PET_{1it} + c_t PET_{2it} + d_t PET_{3it} + u_{it} \qquad (2)$$

where $RE_{it}$ is a measure of relative efficiency of plant i in year t; $PET_1$, $PET_2$, $PET_3$ are (0,1) indicator variables for petitioners in the 1970s, in the 1980s, and in both periods, respectively; and u is an error term. In each year, the estimated "a" coefficients provide a measure of the mean difference in efficiency levels between each group of petitioners and all other nonpetitioning firms.

Table 15.6 reports estimated coefficients for the years 1963, 1967, and 1972 to 1986. The time paths of these coefficients are presented graphically in Figure 15.1 for each of the three (mutually exclusive) groups of petitioners. The vertical axis measures efficiency levels as percentage deviations (both negative and positive) from the industry mean, which, by construction, equals zero in all years (the horizontal line). The horizontal axis depicts the year. For each petitioner group, vertical lines are drawn to the horizontal axis to highlight years in which firms participated in antidumping petitions.

Figure 15.1 illustrates two important points. First, it highlights striking differences in the time paths of relative efficiency among petitioner groups—about average (to moderately low) efficiency levels for 1970s petitioners; above average and rising efficiency levels for 1980s petitioners; and increasingly negative efficiency for the firms that petitioned in both periods. Second,

### Table 15.6
### Relative productivity differences between petitioners

| Model: $RE_{it} = a_t + b_t \cdot PET1970s_{it} + c_t \cdot PET1980s_{it} + d_t \cdot PET7080s_{it}$ | | | | | |
|---|---|---|---|---|---|
| | 1970s Petitions | | 1980s Petitions | | 1970/80s Petitions |
| Year | $b$-coef. | $t$-stat. | $c$-coef. | $t$-stat. | $d$-coef. | $t$-stat. |
| 1963 | −.0141 | (0.11) | −.0866 | (0.99) | .1470 | (0.87) |
| 1967 | −.0985 | (0.99) | .0285 | (0.46) | .0360 | (0.29) |
| 1972 | −.0588 | (0.67) | .2265** | (3.46) | .0060 | (0.04) |
| 1973 | −.0846 | (1.01) | .1573** | (2.41) | −.1434 | (1.20) |
| 1974 | −.0376 | (0.40) | .1595* | (2.19) | −.1595 | (1.20) |
| 1975 | −.1342 | (1.38) | .1235 | (1.62) | −.1774 | (1.28) |
| 1976 | .0615 | (0.67) | .1437* | (1.95) | −.3428** | (2.60) |
| 1977 | .2178* | (2.13) | .2363** | (2.96) | −.4162** | (2.81) |
| 1978 | −.0349 | (0.42) | .1953** | (2.30) | −.2096 | (1.75) |
| 1979 | −.0640 | (0.41) | .1506 | (1.37) | −.2642 | (1.22) |
| 1980 | −.0656 | (0.40) | .1768 | (1.51) | −.0421 | (0.18) |
| 1981 | .0690 | (0.25) | .2685 | (1.38) | −.3178 | (0.82) |
| 1982 | .0892 | (0.86) | .3398** | (5.03) | −.4816** | (3.49) |
| 1983 | −.1241 | (0.63) | .2454 | (1.66) | −.3625 | (1.28) |
| 1984 | −.0933 | (0.85) | .1183 | (1.55) | −.1988 | (1.33) |
| 1985 | −.0541 | (0.50) | .1470* | (1.96) | −.2241 | (1.51) |
| 1986 | .0754 | (0.68) | .1849** | (2.52) | −.3644** | (2.45) |

*Notes:* 1970s Petitions: Antidumping petitioners in 1975, 1976, 1978.
1980s Petitions: Antidumping petitioners in 1982, 1986.
1970/80s Petitions: Antidumping petitioners in both periods.
*Denotes statistical significance at the 5-percent level
**Denotes statistical significance at the 1-percent level

**Figure 15.1**
**Relative efficiency levels of cement petitioners**

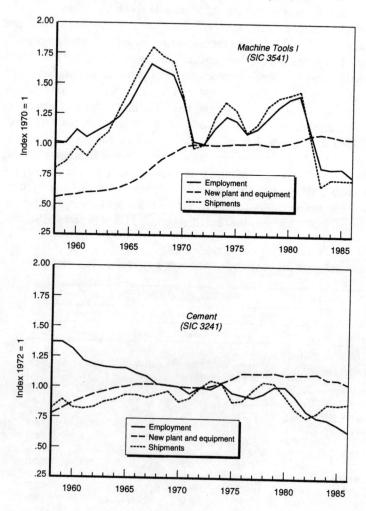

**Figure 15.1—continued**

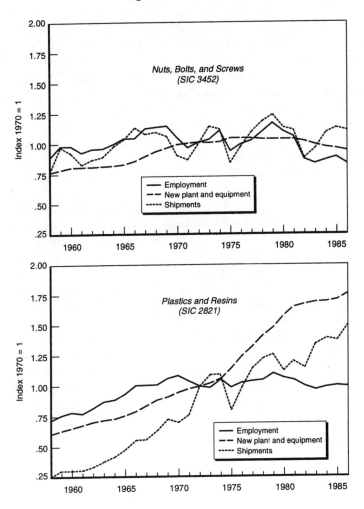

the timing of petition filings appears to coincide (with some exceptions) with large observed declines in relative efficiency levels, or with levels that are already substantially below the industry mean. This is most striking for petitions filed in 1978 by the 1970s petitioners, in 1984 by the 1980s petitioners, and in 1976 and 1982 by firms petitioning in both periods. The exceptions—the 1976 petition filed by the 1970s group and the 1982 petition filed by the 1980s group—are petitions filed when efficiency levels were rising above the industry mean.

Together, these two points suggest an explanation for why some firms petitioned in some years but not in others. Compared with 1970s petitioners, the 1980s petitioners had efficiency levels significantly above the industry average, even in 1975 and 1976 when several petitions were filed. Only in the early 1980s, when their own efficiency levels fell dramatically, did the 1980s firms participate in antidumping petitions. The response of firms that petitioned in both periods is certainly clear—their efficiency levels deteriorated through much of the 1970s and 1980s, so that by 1982 they were almost 50 percent below the industry average. Why the 1980s firms chose not to participate in the 1970s petitions, or the 1970s firms in the 1980s petitions, is less clear. Possibly, both groups of firms were able (at different times) to "free ride" on the third group's investments in lobbying for import protection (Pincus, 1975).

In conclusion, we note that at least for the one industry that we studied—hydraulic cement—firms that filed antidumping petitions tended to be less technically efficient compared to other firms in the industry. The issue for policymakers is whether experiences of petitioners should be interpreted as somehow being "representative" of the industry as a whole in making judgments about import relief. Our findings suggest that petitioners are not typical of the industry as a whole.

## BIBLIOGRAPHY

Baldwin, Robert (1985). *The Political Economy of U.S. Import Policy.* Cambridge, Mass: MIT Press.

Baldwin, Robert, and Richard Green (1988). "The Effects of Protection on Domestic Output," in Robert Baldwin (ed.), *Trade Policy Issues and Empirical Analysis.* Chicago: University of Chicago Press.

Davis, Steve, and John Haltiwanger (1990). "Growth, Job Creation, and Destruction: Microeconomic Evidence and Macroeconomic Implications." U.S. Census Bureau, CES Working Paper 90–10, September.

Deily, Mary E. (1991). "Exit Strategies and Plant-Closing Decisions: The Case of Steel," *RAND Journal of Economics,* vol. 22, 2, 250–263.

Dunne, Timothy, Mark Roberts, and Larry Samuelson (1988). "Patterns of Firm Entry and Exit in U.S. Manufacturing Industries." *RAND Journal of Economics,* vol. 19, no. 4, Winter, 495–515.

——— (1989). "Plant Turnover and Gross Employment Flows in the U.S. Manufacturing Sector." *Journal of Labor Economics*, vol. 7, no. 1, 48–71.

Evans, D. S. (1987). "Tests of Alternative Theories of Firm Growth." *Journal of Political Economy,* vol. 95

Huffbauer, Gary, Diane Berliner, and Kimberly Elliot (1986). "Trade Protection in the United States: 31 Case Studies." Institute for International Economics, Washington, D.C.

Jovanovic, Boyan (1982). " Selection and Evolution of Industry." *Econometrica,* vol. 50, no. 3, May, 649–670.

Lichtenburg, Frank, and Donald Seigel (1987). "Productivity and Changes in Ownership of Manufacturing Plants," *Brookings Papers on Economic Activity,* vol. 3, Brookings Institution, Washington D.C.

Lieberman, Marvin (1990). "Exit from Declining Industries: 'Shakeout' or 'Stakeout'?" *RAND Journal of Economics,* vol. 21, no. 4, 538–554.

Liu, Lili (1991). "Entry, Exit, Learning and Productivity Change: Evidence from Chile." The World Bank, PRE Working Paper, September.

Pakes, Ariel, and Richard Ericson (1990). "Empirical Implications of Alternative Models of Firm Dynamics." Unpublished paper, February.

Pincus, Jonathan (1975). "Pressure Groups and the Pattern of Tariffs." *Journal of Political Economy.* vol. 83, no. 4, August, 757–778.

Tan, Hong W. (1994). "Policies Toward Troubled Industries in the United States: An Overview," Ch. 5 in this volume.

Tan, Hong W., and Frank Lichtenburg (1994). "An Industry-Level Analysis of Import Relief Petitions Filed by U.S. Manufacturers, 1958–85," Ch. 7 in this volume.

# INDEX